GOVERNMENT SERIES

# Statutory Construction and Interpretation



## General Principles and Recent Trends; Statutory Structure and Legislative Drafting Conventions; Drafting Federal Grants Statutes; and Tracking Current Federal Legislation and Regulations

Compiled by TheCapitol.Net
Authors: Larry M. Eig, Yule Kim, M. Douglass Bellis, Tobias Dorsey, Malcolm S. Mason, Pamela A. Hairston, and Judy Schneider

TheCapitol.Net

For over 30 years, TheCapitol.Net and its predecessor, Congressional Quarterly Executive Conferences, have been training professionals from government, military, business, and NGOs on the dynamics and operations of the legislative and executive branches and how to work with them.

Our training and publications include congressional operations, legislative and budget process, communication and advocacy, media and public relations, research, business etiquette, and more.

TheCapitol.Net is a non-partisan firm.

Our publications and courses, written and taught by *current* Washington insiders who are all independent subject matter experts, show how Washington works.™ Our products and services can be found on our web site at <*www.TheCapitol.Net*>.

Additional copies of *Statutory Construction and Interpretation* can be ordered online: <*www.GovernmentSeries.com*>.

Design and production by Zaccarine Design, Inc., Evanston, IL; 847-864-3994.

♾ The paper used in this publication exceeds the requirements of the American National Standard for Information Sciences—Permanence of Paper for Printed Library Materials, ANSI Z39.48-1992.


PO Box 25706
Alexandria, VA 22313-5706
703-739-3790 Toll free: 1-877-228-5086
<*www.TheCapitol.Net*>


Printed in the United States of America.

v 1

*Statutory Construction and Interpretation*, softbound:
ISBN: 158733-192-6
ISBN 13: 978-1-58733-192-3

# Summary Table of Contents



 

# Table of Contents



 

C. Some examples confirm that view

D. The Supreme Court repeatedly finds grant statutes not clear

E. Ambiguity is sometimes deliberate and sometimes justified but should be held to a reasonable minimum

F. Who should be interested in grant statute drafting problems?

II. Planning an assistance program

A. Choice of instrument

1. Is the program to be a grant program as opposed to a direct federal operation
2. Use a grant when two conditions are present
   a. There is an important federal purpose to be served
   b. There are also local concerns that should share in shaping the remedy for the problem perceived, and should be encouraged to supply drive, imagination, creativity, modification to local circumstances
3. Should the program instrument be a grant or a contract?
4. Why should it matter whether one instrument or the other is used?
5. If the program is to be assistance, is the instrument to be a grant or cooperative agreement?

B. Types of grants

C. Various programs in addition to grants have assistance elements

D. Grants in context

1. A grant program need not and generally does not stand alone
2. Good grant statute drafting calls for at least consideration of setting the proposed grant statute in a context of such other activities, and adjusting the various elements to each other

E. The constitutional basis for grants

F. Grants are a congressional monopoly

G. The administering office

1. If a program is to be a grant program, who should administer it?
2. It is recommended that absent clear reasons to the contrary, grant authority should normally be conferred on agency heads with express or implied power of delegation rather than on specified subordinates

H. How much discretion should be left to the executive?

I. What should be the funding mechanics of the program?

J. What is the intended class of recipients?

K. Should there be a requirement for local sharing in the costs?

L. Should there be a requirement for maintenance of local effort?

M. Should there be a requirement that federal funds not be used to supplant local efforts?

III. Planning a grant statute

How should a grant statute be structured

A. Outline of a typical grant statute

Sec. 1. Short title

Sec. 2. Table of contents

Sec. 3. Findings and purposes

— State your sources of power explicitly

— State your purposes explicitly

 

# Introduction

## Statutory Construction and Interpretation

### General Principles and Recent Trends; Statutory Structure and Legislative Drafting Conventions; Drafting Federal Grants Statutes; and Tracking Current Federal Legislation and Regulations

The exercise of the judicial power of the United States often requires that courts construe statutes in applying them in particular cases and controversies. Judicial interpretation of the meaning of a statute is authoritative in the matter before the court. Beyond this, the methodologies and approaches taken by the courts in discerning meaning can help guide legislative drafters, legislators, implementing agencies, and private parties.

This book reviews the primary rules courts apply to discern a statute's meaning. However, each matter of interpretation before a court presents its own challenges, and there is no unified, systematic approach used in all cases. While schools of statutory interpretation may vary on what factors should be considered, all approaches start (if not necessarily end) with the language and structure of the statute itself. In analyzing a statute's text, courts are guided by the basic principle that a statute should be read as a harmonious whole, with its separate parts being interpreted within their broader statutory context.

Still, the meaning of statutory language is not always evident. To help clarify uncertainty, judges have developed various interpretive tools in the form of canons of construction.

When drafting federal law, the most important audience is the federal courts—and, in particular, the Supreme Court of the United States. Fortunately, it is not difficult to get inside the mind of the Court and understand how it thinks. The Court makes this process public in its published opinions; collectively, the process is known as statutory interpretation. (It is also known as statutory construction; the differences between the two terms are not great.)

There are other audiences, of course. The draft will be read and interpreted by legislators, lobbyists, public officials, private individuals, industry leaders, journalists, and scholars, to name a few. In some ways these audiences are very different, but in two ways they are all alike: Each wants to know the effect of the draft, and each recognizes that the effect is ultimately determined by the courts, through judicial methods of statutory interpretation. The courts always have the last word, and the Supreme Court has the very last word.

It is true that many principles of statutory interpretation are simply general principles about how best to read English prose. But many are not. Some are obvious, some are subtle, some are counterintuitive, some are traps for the unwary.

Also included is a chapter on drafting federal grants statutes. Several rules of drafting have special relevance to statutes in the field of federal assistance (grants), and those are set forth with a discussion of the special problems facing drafters of grants laws.

 

Legislation can be drafted without paying attention to statutory interpretation. But rules of interpretation are like rules of the road: Drive on the right; stop on red; signal before turning; pedestrians have the right of way. If you don't know all the rules, sooner or later you will park in front of a fire hydrant or go the wrong way down a one-way street.

Links to Internet resources are available on the book's web site at <*TCNSI.com*>.

 

Congressional Research Service

# Statutory Interpretation: General Principles and Recent Trends

**Larry M. Eig**
Specialist in American Public Law

**Yule Kim**
Legislative Attorney

October 14, 2009

**Congressional Research Service**
7-5700
www.crs.gov
97-589

CRS Report for Congress
*Prepared for Members and Committees of Congress*

 

# Summary

The exercise of the judicial power of the United States often requires that courts construe statutes in applying them in particular cases and controversies. Judicial interpretation of the meaning of a statute is authoritative in the matter before the court. Beyond this, the methodologies and approaches taken by the courts in discerning meaning can help guide legislative drafters, legislators, implementing agencies, and private parties.

The Supreme Court has expressed an interest "that Congress be able to legislate against a background of clear interpretive rules, so that it may know the effect of the language it adopts." To this end, this report reviews the primary rules the Court applies to discern a statute's meaning. However, each matter of interpretation before the Court presents its own challenges, and there is no unified, systematic approach used in all cases.

While schools of statutory interpretation may vary on what factors should be considered, all approaches start (if not necessarily end) with the language and structure of the statute itself. In analyzing a statute's text, the Court is guided by the basic principle that a statute should be read as a harmonious whole, with its separate parts being interpreted within their broader statutory context.

Still, the meaning of statutory language is not always evident. To help clarify uncertainty, judges have developed various interpretive tools in the form of canons of construction. Canons broadly fall into two types. "Language," or "linguistic," canons are interpretive "rules of thumb" for drawing inferences based on customary usage, grammar, and the like. For example, in considering the meaning of particular words and phrases, language canons call for determining the sense in which terms are being used, that is, whether words or phrases are meant as terms of art with specialized meanings or are meant in the ordinary, "dictionary" sense. Other language canons direct that all words of a statute be given effect if possible, that a term used more than once in a statute ordinarily be given the same meaning throughout, and that specific statutory language ordinarily trumps conflicting general language. "Ordinarily" is a necessary caveat, since any of these "canons" gives way if context reveals a contrary meaning.

Not infrequently the Court stacks the deck, and subordinates the general, linguistic canons of statutory construction, as well as other interpretive principles, to overarching presumptions that favor particular substantive results. When one of these "substantive" canons applies, the Court frequently requires a "clear statement" of congressional intent to negate it. A commonly invoked "substantive" canon is that Congress does not intend to change judge-made law. Other substantive canons disfavor preemption of state law and abrogation of state immunity from suit in federal court. As another example, Congress must strongly signal an intent to the courts if it wishes to apply a statute retroactively or override existing law. The Court also tries to avoid an interpretation that would raise serious doubts about a statute's constitutionality.

Interpretive methods that emphasize the primacy of text and staying within the boundaries of statutes themselves to discern meaning are "textualist." Other approaches, including "intentionalism," are more open to taking extrinsic considerations into account. Most particularly, some Justices may be willing to look to legislative history to clarify ambiguous text. This report briefly reviews what constitutes "legislative history," including, possibly, presidential signing statements, and the factors that might lead the Court to consider it.



 

# Contents





 

## Contacts





 

# Introduction

Article I, section 1 of the Constitution vests all federal legislative power in Congress, while Article I, section 7 sets forth the process for effectuating this power through passage of legislation by both Houses and either presidential approval or veto override. The exercise of the judicial power of the United States often requires that courts construe statutes so enacted in applying them in particular cases and controversies. Judicial interpretation of the meaning of a statute is authoritative in the matter before the court. Beyond this, the methodologies and approaches taken by the courts in interpreting meaning can help guide legislative drafters, legislators, implementing agencies, and private parties on how a statute may ultimately be construed.[1]

This report provides an overview of the Supreme Court's approach to statutory interpretation, with particular emphasis on rules and conventions that focus on the text itself.[2] That is, to inform Congress on how the Court might go about analyzing the meaning of particular legislative language, this report emphasizes "textualist"-based means of interpretation. "Textualism" considers the "law" to be embodied in the language of the statute, as expressed in its "plain meaning," which can be discerned through the aid, as necessary, of various judicially developed rules of interpretation.[3] This report also briefly discusses "intentionalist"-based means of interpretation and the Court's approach toward relying on legislative history and other extrinsic considerations. This report is not intended as an examination of all schools of judicial decision-making, nor as an analysis of the merits or limits of the many methodologies used by courts in applying statutes in specific cases.[4] In this regard, even though textualism may be the primary approach toward interpreting statutes, individual Supreme Court opinions often continue to

---

[1] Though different actors in the political and legal processes share an interest in "what a statute means," they can come to the issue in different contexts and with different concerns. Often, the question may not be one of what is the "best" interpretation of particular legislative language. For example, as legislation is deliberated and compromises are struck, legislators may be concerned with what substantive and regulatory "gaps" are being created, who likely will fill them (e.g., executive agencies or the courts) and in accordance with what standards, and the prospects that the legislature will revisit an issue because of how a statute is implemented or interpreted. Similarly, an implementing agency may look for silence or ambiguity in a statute as an implicit delegation of broad regulatory powers. Private parties may be primarily concerned with assessing what options they have to act. The pertinent query in many instances might be whether a particular interpretation is "reasonable," not whether it is the "best." For one leading commentator's view on compromise as part of the legislative process and why courts should be cautious in "filling in the blanks" left open by a legislature, see Frank H. Easterbrook, *Statutes' Domains*, 50 U. CHI. L. REV. 533, 540-42 (1983).

[2] In places, the report also refers to opinions of United States courts of appeals and scholarly discussion of statutory interpretation generally.

[3] It is sometimes disputed whether the rules characterized as "substantive" canons of construction in this report, and also variously as "overarching presumptions" or "normative canons," properly fit within "textualism," which most often is associated with the linguistic, or "language," canons.

[4] There is an extensive body of legal literature on statutory interpretation by the courts. A small sampling includes: James J. Brudney & Corey Ditslear, *The Warp and Woof of Statutory Interpretation: Comparing Supreme Court Approaches in Tax Law and Workplace Law*, 58 DUKE L.J. 1231 (2009); Alexander Volokh, *Choosing Interpretive Methods: A Positive Theory of Judges and Everyone Else*, 83 N.Y.U. L. REV. 769 (2008); David L. Shapiro, *Continuity and Change in Statutory Interpretation*, 67 N.Y.U. L. REV. 921 (1992); Cass R. Sunstein, *Interpreting Statutes in the Regulatory* State, 103 HARV. L. REV. 405 (1989); William N. Eskridge, Jr., *Dynamic Statutory Interpretation*, 135 U. PA. L. REV. 1479 (1987). *See also* Symposium, *A Reevaluation of the Canons of Statutory Interpretation*, 45 VAND. L. REV. 529 (1992). Methods of interpretation other than textualism and intentionalism, such as "pragmatism," "purposivism," and "practical reasoning," generally are more open to considering the functional effects of a particular decision, changed circumstances since a statute's enactment and how the current Congress might view an issue, and the broad aims of Congress in passing a specific law.



 

employ multiple types of statutory analysis to support their conclusions and critique majority/dissenting opinions with which they do not agree.[5]

In reading statutory text, the Supreme Court uses content-neutral canons developed by the judiciary that focus on word usage, grammar, syntax and the like. Sometimes, the Court also brings to bear various presumptions that reflect broader judicial concerns and can more directly favor particular substantive results. Other conventions assist the Court in determining whether to go beyond the corners of a statute and judicial-based rules of interpretation to also consider the congressional deliberations that led to a statute's passage. Although there is some overlap and inconsistency among these rules and conventions, and although the Court's pathway through the mix is often not clearly foreseeable, an understanding of interpretational possibilities may nonetheless aid Congress in choosing among various drafting options. To this end, the Court has expressed an interest "that Congress be able to legislate against a background of clear interpretive rules, so that it may know the effect of the language it adopts."[6]

Of course, Congress can always amend a statute to supersede the reading given it by the Court. In interpreting statutes, the Court recognizes that legislative power resides in Congress, and that Congress can legislate away interpretations with which it disagrees.[7] Congress has revisited statutory issues fairly frequently to override or counter the Court's interpretations.[8] Corrective amendment can be a lengthy and uncertain process, however.[9]

---

[5] *See, e.g.*, Frank B. Cross, *The Significance of Statutory Interpretive Methodologies*, 82 NOTRE DAME L. REV. 1971 (2007).

[6] Finley v. United States, 490 U.S. 545, 556 (1989). As is evident from this report, many of the interpretive challenges faced by the Court arise from lack of completeness and specificity. In this regard, Executive Order 12988, which in part provides guidance to agencies in drafting proposed legislation for possible congressional consideration, directs agencies to "make every reasonable effort to ensure" that proposed legislation, "as appropriate ... specifies in clear language"—(A) whether causes of action arising under the law are subject to statutes of limitations; (B) the preemptive effect; (C) the effect on existing Federal law; (D) a clear legal standard for affected conduct; (E) whether arbitration and other forms of dispute resolution are appropriate; (F) whether the provisions of the law are severable if one or more is held unconstitutional; (G) the retroactive effect, if any; (H) the applicable burdens of proof; (I) whether private parties are granted a right to sue, and, if so, what relief is available and whether attorney's fees are available; (J) whether state courts have jurisdiction; (K) whether administrative remedies must be pursued prior to initiating court actions; (L) standards governing personal jurisdiction; (M) definitions of key statutory terms; (N) applicability to the Federal Government; (O) applicability to states, territories, the District of Columbia, and the Commonwealths of Puerto Rico and the Northern Mariana Islands; and (P) what remedies are available, "such as money damages, civil penalties, injunctive relief, and attorney's fees." 61 Fed. Reg. 4729 (February 5, 1996), *reprinted in* 28 U.S.C. § 519. Many items in this list are addressed in this report because statutes have lacked clear guidance on them.

However, it would be a mistake to conclude that all "lapses" of completeness and specificity result from oversights. As observed by Frank H. Easterbrook, now Chief Judge of the United States Court of Appeals for the Seventh Circuit, in an article written in 1983: "Almost all statutes are compromises, and the cornerstone of many a compromise is the decision, usually unexpressed, to leave certain issues unresolved.... What matters to the compromisers is reducing the chance that their work will be invoked subsequently to achieve more, or less, than they intended, thereby upsetting the balance of the package." Frank H. Easterbrook, *Statutes' Domains*, 50 U. CHI. L. REV. 533, 540 (1983).

[7] It is because "Congress is free to change this Court's interpretation of its legislation," that the Court adheres more strictly to the doctrine of *stare decisis*, or adherence to judicial precedents, in the area of statutory construction than in the area of constitutional interpretation, where amendment is much more difficult. Neal v. United States, 516 U.S. 284, 295 (1996) (quoting Illinois Brick Co. v. Illinois, 431 U.S. 720, 736 (1977)); Shepard v. United States, 544 U.S. 13, 23 (2005). "*Stare decisis* is usually the wise policy [for statutes], because in most matters it is more important that the applicable rule of law be settled than that it be settled right." Burnet v. Coronado Oil & Gas Co., 285 U.S. 393, 406 (1932) (Justice Brandeis, dissenting).

[8] One scholar identified 187 override statutes from 1967 to 1990. William N. Eskridge, *Overriding Supreme Court Statutory Interpretation Decisions*, 101 YALE L.J. 331 (1991). *See also* Deborah A. Widiss, *Shadow Precedents and the Separation of Powers*, 84 NOTRE DAME L. REV. 511 (2009). One prominent override addressed the Supreme Court (continued...)



 

# Statutory Text

## In General—Statutory Context and Purpose

The starting point in construing a statute is the language of the statute itself. The Supreme Court often recites the "plain meaning rule," that, if the language of the statute is plain and unambiguous, it must be applied according to its terms. There is no single test to assay the clarity of statutory language. A narrow focus on the meaning of particular words and phrases is the frequent starting point. This view is commonly supplemented by perspectives provided from elsewhere within the statute. How has Congress used or distinguished the same terms in other places in the statute? How does the section in which language at issue appears fit within the statute's structure? What do the structure and language of a statute reveal about the statute's overall purposes?

The primacy of text in statutory analysis would appear to marginalize whatever insight legislative history or other extrinsic aids might provide. The strictures of a text-based "plain meaning rule" were once thought honored more in the breach than in the observance. However, this perception has changed: More often than before, statutory text is thought to be the ending point as well as the starting point for interpretation.[10]

Under text-based analysis, the cardinal rule of construction is that the whole statute should be drawn upon as necessary, with its various parts being interpreted within their broader statutory context in a manner that furthers statutory purposes. Justice Scalia, who has been in the vanguard of efforts to redirect statutory construction toward statutory text and away from legislative history, has aptly characterized this general approach. "Statutory construction ... is a holistic endeavor. A provision that may seem ambiguous in isolation is often clarified by the remainder of the statutory scheme—because the same terminology is used elsewhere in a context that makes its meaning clear, or because only one of the permissible meanings produces a substantive effect that is compatible with the rest of the law."[11] In 1850 Chief Justice Taney described the same process: "In expounding a statute, we must not be guided by a single sentence or member of a sentence, but look to the provisions of the whole law, and to its object and policy."[12] Thus, the meaning of a

(...continued)

decision in *Ledbetter v. Goodyear Tire & Rubber Co., Inc.* (550 U.S. 618 (2007)), which held that a plaintiff had failed to file a timely suit for past sex discrimination that was prohibited under Title VII of the Civil Rights Act. Congress superseded the decision in the Lilly Ledbetter Fair Pay Act of 2009, which amended Title VII to clarify the time limit to sue employers in a way that did not foreclose a suit of the type Ms. Ledbetter brought. Lilly Ledbetter Fair Pay Act of 2009, P.L. 111-2, 123 Stat. 5 (2009).

[9] The extent and intended effect of overrides vary, and courts may not always give an override the breadth of application Congress desired. Deborah A. Widiss, *Shadow Precedents and the Separation of Powers*, 84 NOTRE DAME L. REV. 511 (2008).

[10] For an example of an empirical study finding decreased reliance on legislative history by the Supreme Court from 1969 to 2008, see James J. Brudney & Corey Ditslear, *The Warp and Woof of Statutory Interpretation: Comparing Supreme Court Approaches in Tax Law and Workplace Law*, 58 DUKE L.J. 1231, 1258 (2009).

[11] United Savings Ass'n v. Timbers of Inwood Forest Associates, 484 U.S. 365, 371 (1988) (citations omitted).

[12] United States v. Boisdoré's Heirs, 49 U.S. (8 How.) 113, 122 (1850) (opinion of Court). For a modern example of examining statutory language "in place," see Brotherhood of Locomotive Engineers v. Atchison, T. & S.F.R.R., 516 U.S. 152, 157 (1996) (purpose of Hours of Service Act to promote safety by ensuring that fatigued employees do not operate trains guides the determination of whether employees' time is "on duty").



 

specific statutory directive may be shaped, for example, by that statute's definitions of terms, by the statute's statement of findings and purposes, by the directive's relationship to other specific directives, by purposes inferred from those directives or from the statute as a whole, and by the statute's overall structure. Beyond this, courts also may look to the broader body of law into which the enactment fits.[13]

The Supreme Court often cites general rules, or canons, of construction in resolving statutory meaning. The Court, moreover, presumes "that Congress legislates with knowledge of our basic rules of statutory construction."[14] It is well to keep in mind, however, that the overriding objective of statutory construction has been to effectuate statutory purpose as expressed in a law's text. As Justice Jackson put it more than 65 years ago, "[h]owever well these rules may serve at times to decipher legislative intent, they long have been subordinated to the doctrine that courts will construe the details of an act in conformity with its dominating general purpose, will read text in the light of context and will interpret the text so far as the meaning of the words fairly permits so as to carry out in particular cases the generally expressed legislative policy."[15]

# "Language" Canons of Construction

## In General

The "language" canons of construction are neutral, analytical guides for discerning the meaning of particular text that might otherwise appear unclear.[16] That is to say, these canons are based on general linguistic principles, many of them of the common-sense variety, for drawing inferences about the meaning of language. The meaning of a word or phrase can be shaped by its ordinary or specialized meaning, its context in the statute, the usage of similar terms in the statute, the statute's structure, and other factors. The language canons are "axioms of experience," but none "preclude[s] consideration of persuasive [contrary] evidence if it exists."[17] Each canon provides its own perspective, and different takes from different views can give different insights into the meaning of what is being observed. Considering and weighing the value of various views would appear to be a sound process for ensuring well-reasoned interpretations. However, the language

---

[13] Green v. Bock Laundry Machine Co., 490 U.S. 504, 528 (1990).

[14] McNary v. Haitian Refugee Center, 498 U.S. 479, 496 (1991) (referring to presumption favoring judicial review of administrative action). *See also* United States v. Fausto, 484 U.S. 439, 463 n.9 (1988) (Justice Stevens, dissenting) (Court presumes that "Congress is aware of this longstanding presumption [disfavoring repeals by implication] and that Congress relies on it in drafting legislation").

[15] SEC v. Joiner, 320 U.S. 344, 350-51 (1943). Justice Jackson explained that some of the canons derived "from sources that were hostile toward the legislative process itself," and that viewed legislation as "'interference'" with the common law "'process of intelligent judicial administration.'" 320 U.S. at 350 & n.7 (quoting the first edition of SUTHERLAND, STATUTES AND STATUTORY CONSTRUCTION). A more recent instance of congressional purpose and statutory context trumping a "canon" occurred in General Dynamics Land Systems, Inc. v. Cline, 540 U.S. 581, 594-599 (2004), the Court determining that the word "age" is used in different senses in different parts of the Age Discrimination in Employment Act, and that consequently the presumption of uniform usage throughout a statute should not be followed.

[16] This report separately addresses "substantive" canons of construction, which often are referred to as "normative" canons or "overarching presumptions." Unlike the linguistic rules that are the "language" canons, the substantive canons derive from broader judicial notions of constitutionalism, federalism, effective judicial administration, and other overarching policy concerns of the courts. Unless they are rebutted, these presumptions can favor particular outcomes.

[17] Boston Sand & Gravel Co. v. United States, 278 U.S. 41, 48 (1928) (Justice Holmes for Court).



 

canons are intrinsic aids only, not "rules of law." Discerning what Congress probably meant by particular language for the purpose of applying it to a particular set of facts can be a difficult judicial exercise that is not amenable to formulaic resolution.

The sheer number and variety of canons have been cited to emphasize their limited utility as a stand-alone method of statutory construction. Still influential, for example, is a 1950 article by Professor Karl Llewellyn that lists many canons (both language canons and substantive canons) juxtaposed to equally "correct" but opposing canons.[18] Professor Llewellyn's main point was to argue that judges should take current circumstances into account in applying a statute in a case—he was critical of the impression that "formalism" gave of there being "only one single correct answer possible" in reading text. Nevertheless, many have broadened his message into a charge that canons are useless because judges may pick and choose among them to achieve whatever result they desire.

However, accepting that there may be more than one "correct" answer in resolving the meaning of a statutory provision—a premise that seems unremarkable in many cases at the Supreme Court level[19]—does not necessarily mean that a Court majority begins with a preferred policy outcome and then marshals only those canons that support it. Given an array of established templates to guide interpretation, one may be a particularly apt fit in a given case, and the case's outcome will in large measure be driven by the rationale of the canon applied. This might particularly be so when a substantive canon of interpretation (*e.g.*, avoidance of constitutional issues) is in play. (These canons are discussed below.)

In any event, one possible suggestion of the indeterminacy of canons is that statutory construction should be a narrow pursuit, not a broader one: "[C]anons of construction are no more than rules of thumb that help courts determine the meaning of legislation, and in interpreting a statute a court should always turn first to one, cardinal canon before all others.... [C]ourts must presume that a legislature says in a statute what it means and means in a statute what it says there. When the words of a statute are unambiguous, then, this first canon is also the last: 'judicial inquiry is complete.'"[20]

## Ordinary and Specialized Meaning

Determining how a statute is to be applied often comes down to considering what a particular word or phrase means *as used in the statute*. In this exercise, a threshold inquiry is whether language is being used in the "ordinary," "general dictionary" sense or in a narrower, specialized sense or as a term of art.[21] Also, the appropriate reference is what a term meant to Members when Congress passed the statute, not its meaning at the time the statute is being adjudicated.[22]

---

[18] Karl Llewellyn, *Remarks on the Theory of Appellate Decision and the Rules or Canons About How Statutes Are To Be Construed*, 3 VAND. L. REV. 395 (1950).

[19] "As is true with most of the statutory interpretation questions that come before this Court, the question in this case is not like a jigsaw puzzle. There is simply no perfect solution to the problem before us." Corley v. United States, No. 07-10441, slip op. at 4 (Scalia, J., dissenting).

[20] Connecticut Nat'l Bank v. Germain, 503 U.S. 249, 253-54 (1992) (citations omitted). The Court takes much the same approach when it chooses congressional intent rather than statutory text as its touchstone: a canon of construction should not be followed "when application would be tantamount to a formalistic disregard of congressional intent." Rice v. Rehner, 463 U.S. 713, 732 (1983).

[21] On occasion, disagreement within a sharply divided Court plays out over whether a term is being used in a (continued...)



 

## Terms of Art

If the word or phrase is defined in the statute (federal statutes frequently collect definitions in a "definitions" section), or elsewhere in the *United States Code*,[23] then that definition governs if applicable in the context used.[24] Even if the word or phrase is not defined by statute, it may have an accepted meaning in the area of law addressed by the statute,[25] it may have been borrowed from another statute under which it had an accepted meaning,[26] or it may have had an accepted and specialized meaning at common law.[27] In each of these situations the accepted meaning

(...continued)

specialized sense or in accordance with ordinary meaning. *See, e.g.,* Sullivan v. Stroop, 496 U.S. 478 (1990) (5-Justice majority holding that "child support" in the AFDC statute is restricted to that term's specialized use in the Child Support program under the Social Security Act, while 4-Justice minority argue that "child support" in the AFDC statute has a broader, common use meaning).

[22] Saint Francis College v. Khazraji, 481 U.S. 604 (1987). The Court there held that a citizen of Arab ancestry could bring an action under 42 U.S.C. § 1981, which gives to all persons certain rights to the extent they are enjoyed by "white citizens": "Plainly, all those who might be deemed Caucasian today were not thought to be of the same race at the time § 1981 became law [in the 19th century]." Id. at 610. *See also, e.g.,* Cuomo v. Clearing House Assn., L.L.C., No. 08-453, slip op. (U.S. Jun. 29, 2009), where the ability of a State to take certain enforcement actions against national banks depended on the meaning of "visitorial powers" when the National Bank Act was enacted in 1864.

[23] The Dictionary Act, ch. 388, 61 Stat. 633 (1947), as amended, 1 U.S.C. §§ 1-6, has definitions of a few common terms used in federal statutes (*e.g.*, "person," "vessel," and "vehicle"). These definitions govern in all federal statutes "unless the context indicates otherwise." *See also* Stewart v. Dutra Constr. Co., 543 U.S. 481, 489 (2005) (relying on Dictionary Act's definition of "vessel").

[24] Colautti v. Franklin, 439 U.S. 379, 392 (1979). If the context indicates otherwise, *i.e.*, if a mechanical application of a statutory definition throughout a statute would create an "obvious incongruity" or frustrate an evident statutory purpose for a particular provision, then it is permissible to depart from the definition. Lawson v. Suwannee S.S. Co., 336 U.S. 198, 201 (1949); Rowland v. California Men's Colony, 506 U.S. 194 (1993) (context indicates otherwise; the term "person" as used in 28 U.S.C. § 1915(a) refers only to individuals and does not carry its Dictionary Act definition, which includes associations and artificial entities). But, as noted below, a term appearing in several places in a statute is ordinarily interpreted as having the same meaning each time it appears.

[25] *See, e.g.*, Sullivan v. Stroop, 496 U.S. 478, 483 (1990) (5-Justice majority holding that "child support" in the AFDC statute is restricted to that term's specialized use in the Child Support program under the Social Security Act). Note also that "where a phrase in a statute appears to have become a term of art ..., any attempt to break down the term into its constituent words is not apt to illuminate its meaning." *Id.*

[26] In appropriate circumstances, courts will assume that "adoption of the wording of a statute from another legislative jurisdiction carries with it the previous judicial interpretations of the wording." Carolene Products Co. v. United States, 323 U.S. 18, 26 (1944) (finding, however, that circumstances were inappropriate for reliance on the principle). For the presumption to operate, the previous judicial interpretations must have been "known and settled." Capital Traction Co. v. Hof, 174 U.S. 1, 36 (1899). *See also* Yates v. United States, 354 U.S. 298, 310 (1957) (in the absence of legislative history indicating that decisions of lower state courts were called to Congress' attention, Court "should not assume that Congress was aware of them"). Variations in statutory wording may also refute the suggestion that Congress borrowed an interpretation. Shannon v. United States, 512 U.S. 573, 581 (1994) (Congress did not borrow the terms of the Insanity Defense Reform Act of 1984 from the District of Columbia Code).

[27] *See, e.g.*, Community for Creative Non-Violence v. Reid, 490 U.S. 730, 739-40 (1989) (relying on traditional common law agency principles for meaning of term "employee"). *See also* Nationwide Mut. Ins. Co. v. Darden, 503 U.S. 318, 323 (1992) (following the same course after finding ERISA's "circular" definition of "employee" to be useless); Clackamas Gastroenterology Assocs., P.C. v. Wells, 538 U.S. 440, 444 (2003) (same construction of similarly "circular" definition of "employee" in ADA).



 

governs[28] and the word or phrase is considered a technical term or "term of art." Justice Jackson explained why this reliance is appropriate:[29]

> [W]here Congress borrows terms of art in which are accumulated the legal tradition and meaning of centuries of practice, it presumably knows and adopts the cluster of ideas that were attached to each borrowed word in the body of learning from which it was taken and the meaning its use will convey to the judicial mind unless otherwise instructed. In such a case, absence of contrary direction may be taken as satisfaction with widely accepted definitions, not as departure from them.

## Ordinary Meaning and Dictionary Definitions

Words that are not terms of art and that are not statutorily defined are customarily given their ordinary meanings, often derived from the dictionary.[30] Thus, the Court has relied on regular dictionary definitions to interpret the word "marketing" as used in the Plant Variety Protection Act,[31] and the word "principal" as used to modify a taxpayer's place of business for purposes of an income tax deduction,[32] and relied on Black's Law Dictionary for the meaning of the word "cognizable" as used in the Federal Tort Claims Act to identify certain causes of action.[33]

Of course application of dictionary definitions is not always a clear course; many words have several alternative meanings, and context must guide choice among them, where possible.[34] However, "[a]mbiguity is a creature not of definitional possibilities but of statutory context."[35] Consider two cases in which context did not clearly point to whether a term was to be given its broadest dictionary meaning or was to be construed narrowly according to "common understanding." In one case, the Supreme Court concluded that "use of a firearm" in commission of a drug offense or crime of violence included trading a gun for drugs, that is "use of a firearm" was not confined to its use as a weapon.[36] This conclusion may be compared to a finding that

---

[28] "[W]here a common law principle is well established, ... the courts may take it as a given that Congress has legislated with an expectation that the principle will apply except 'when a statutory purpose to the contrary is evident.'" Astoria Federal Savings & Loan Ass'n v. Solimino, 501 U.S. 104, 108 (1991) (quoting Isbrandtsen Co. v. Johnson, 343 U.S. 779, 783 (1952)).

[29] Morissette v. United States, 342 U.S. 246, 263 (1952).

[30] In the absence of a statutory definition, "we construe a statutory term in accordance with its ordinary or natural meaning." FDIC v. Meyer, 510 U.S. 471, 476 (1994).

[31] Asgrow Seed Co. v. Winterboer, 513 U.S. 179, 187 (1995).

[32] Commissioner v. Soliman, 506 U.S. 168, 174 (1993).

[33] FDIC v. Meyer, 510 U.S. 471, 476 (1994).

[34] *See, e.g.*, MCI Tel. Corp. v. American Tel. & Tel. Co., 512 U.S. 218, 226-28 (1994) (FCC's authority to "modify" requirements does not include the authority to make tariff filing optional; aberrant dictionary meaning "to make a basic or important change" is antithetical to the principal meaning of incremental change and is more than the statute can bear); and Nixon v. Missouri Municipal League, 541 U.S. 125 (2004) (preemption of state laws that prohibit "any entity" from providing telecommunications service means, in context, "any private entity," and does not preempt a state law prohibiting local governments from providing such services). If the court views the issue as one of deference to an administrative interpretation, then the agency's choice of one alternative dictionary definition over another may indicate sufficient "reasonableness." Smiley v. Citibank (South Dakota), 517 U.S. 735, 744-47 (1996).

[35] Brown v. Gardner, 513 U.S. 115, 118 (1994).

[36] Smith v. United States, 508 U.S. 223 (1993). Dissenting Justice Scalia argued for a narrower reading: "[to] use an instrumentality normally means to use it for its intended purpose. When someone asks 'Do you use a cane?' he is not inquiring whether you have your grandfather's silver-handled walking-stick on display in the hall; he wants to know whether you walk with a cane. Similarly, to speak of 'using a firearm' is to speak of using it for its distinctive purpose, *i.e.*, as a weapon." *Id.* at 242. The Court had less difficulty with the provision in 1995, overruling a lower court's (continued...)



 

purchasing drugs over a cell phone did not constitute the felony of "facilitating" drug trafficking through a communication device: "[S]tatutes are not read as a collection of isolated phrases ... 'A word in a statute may or may not extend to the outer limits of its definitional possibilities.' We think the word here does not."[37] In close cases such as these, the Court may go beyond the words of a statute for guidance and look to the statute's broader purpose or its fit with other laws.[38] As Judge Learned Hand observed, "it is one of the surest indexes of a mature and developed jurisprudence not to make a fortress out of the dictionary; but to remember that statutes always have some purpose or object to accomplish, whose sympathetic and imaginative discovery is the surest guide to their meaning."[39]

## And/Or

Ordinarily, as in everyday English, use of the conjunctive "and" in a list means that all of the listed requirements must be satisfied,[40] while use of the disjunctive "or" means that only one of the listed requirements need be satisfied.[41] Courts do not apply these meanings "inexorably," however; if a "strict grammatical construction" will frustrate evident legislative intent, a court may read "and" as "or," or "or" as "and."[42] Moreover, statutory context can render the distinction secondary.[43]

---

(...continued)

holding that proximity and accessibility of a firearm are alone sufficient to establish "use." Bailey v. United States, 516 U.S. 137 (1995) (driving car with gun located in bag in car's trunk does not constitute "use" of gun; person who sold drugs after retrieving them from room in which gun was found in a locked trunk in a closet did not "use" that gun in sale). The *Bailey* Court, however, defined "use" in such a way ("active employment") as to leave the *Smith* holding intact. *See also* Muscarello v. United States, 524 U.S. 125 (1998) (the companion phrase "carries a firearm," found in the same statutory provision, is a broader category that includes transporting drugs with a handgun locked in the glove compartment of a vehicle).

[37] Abuelhawa v. United States, No. 08-192, slip op. at 3 (U.S. May 26, 2009) (quoting Dolan v. Postal Service, 546 U.S. 481, 486 (2006)).

[38] The majority in *Smith*, which construed "use of a firearm" broadly, stated there was a general understanding that drugs and firearms are a dangerous combination and saw no reason why Congress would want to distinguish use of a firearm as a weapon in a drug crime from use of a firearm in barter in a drug crime; according to the majority, both circumstances involved a grave possibility of violence and death. 508 U.S. at 240. The unanimous Court in *Abuelhawa*, which construed "facilitate" narrowly, stated that a broad reading (which would have led to higher criminal penalties) could be inconsistent with the gradation of similar and more serious offenses. Slip op. at 5-8.

[39] Cabell v. Markham, 148 F.2d 737, 739 (2d Cir. 1945). Justice Stevens has expressed a preference for established interpretation over dictionary definitions. "In a contest between the dictionary and the doctrine of *stare decisis*, the latter clearly wins." Hibbs v. Winn, 542 U.S. 88, 113 (2004) (J. Stevens, concurring).

[40] *See, e.g.*, Pueblo of Santa Ana v. Kelly, 932 F. Supp. 1284, 1292 (D. N. Mex. 1996).

[41] *See, e.g.*, Zorich v. Long Beach Fire and Ambulance Serv., 118 F.3d 682, 684 (9th Cir. 1997); United States v. O'Driscoll, 761 F.2d 589, 597-98 (10th Cir. 1985). A corollary is that use of the disjunctive "or" creates "mutually exclusive" conditions that can rule out mixing and matching. United States v. Williams, 326 F.3d 535, 541 (4th Cir. 2003) ("a crime may qualify as a serious drug offense by meeting all the requirements of (i) or all the requirements of (ii), but not some of the requirements of (i) and some of (ii)").

[42] *See, e.g.*, United States v. Moore, 613 F.2d 1029 (D.C. Cir. 1979); De Sylva v. Ballentine, 351 U.S. 570, 573 (1956) ("the word 'or' is often used as a careless substitute for the word 'and'"). Both "and" and "or" are context-dependent, and each word "is itself semantically ambiguous, and can be used in two quite different senses." LAWRENCE E. FILSON, THE LEGISLATIVE DRAFTER'S DESK REFERENCE, § 21.10 (1992).

[43] *See, e.g.*, United States v. 141st St. Corp., 911 F.2d 870 (2d Cir. 1990) (holding that an affirmative defense to forfeiture of real property used in a drug offense, applicable if the offense was committed "without the knowledge or consent" of the property owner, applies if the property owner had knowledge of the crime, did not consent, and took all reasonable steps to prevent illicit use of his property).



 

## Definite/Indefinite Article

As in common usage, a drafter's choice between the definite and indefinite article can affect meaning. "The definite article 'the' particularizes the subject which it precedes. It is a word of limitation as opposed to the indefinite or generalizing force of 'a' or 'an.'"[44]

## Shall/May

Use of "shall" and "may" in statutes also mirrors common usage; ordinarily "shall" is mandatory and "may" is permissive.[45] These words must be read in their broader statutory context, however, the issue often being whether the statutory directive itself is mandatory or permissive.[46] Use of both words in the same provision can underscore their different meanings,[47] and often the context will confirm that the ordinary meaning of one or the other was intended.[48] Occasionally, however, context will trump ordinary meaning.[49]

## Singular/Plural

An elementary rule of statutory construction is that the singular includes the plural, and vice-versa.[50] Thus, a statutory directive that the Secretary of Transportation require automakers to install a warning system in new cars to alert drivers "when *a* tire is significantly under-inflated" is

[44] American Bus Ass'n v. Slater, 231 F.3d 1, 4-5 (D.C. Cir. 2000). *See also* Reid v. Angelone, 369 F.3d 363, 367 (4th Cir. 2004) ("because Congress used the definite article 'the,' we conclude that ... there is only one order subject to the requirements"); Warner-Lambert Corp. v. Apotex Corp., 316 F.3d 1348, 1356 (Fed. Cir. 2003) (reference to "the" use of a drug is a reference to an FDA-approved use, not to "a" use or "any" use); Freytag v. Commissioner, 501 U.S. 868, 902 (1991) (concurring opinion of Justice Scalia) (contending that use of the definite article in the Constitution's conferral of appointment authority on "*the* Courts of Law" "obviously narrows the class of eligible 'Courts of Law' to those courts of law envisioned by the Constitution"). *But cf.* Sprietsma v. Mercury Marine, 537 U.S. 51, 63 (2002) (reference in a preemption clause to "a law or regulation" "implies a discreteness—which is embodied in statutes and regulations—that is not present in the common law").

[45] "The mandatory 'shall' ... normally creates an obligation impervious to judicial discretion." Lexecon, Inc. v. Milberg Weiss Bershad Hynes & Lerach, 523 U.S. 26, 35 (1998). "The use of a permissive verb—'may review' instead of 'shall review'—suggests a discretionary rather than mandatory review process." Rastelli v. Warden, Metro. Correctional Center, 782 F.2d 17, 23 (2d Cir. 1986). "Should" sometimes is substituted for "may" as a permissive word. Union Elec. Co. v. Consolidation Coal Co., 188 F.3d 998, 1001 (8th Cir. 1999). "Will" and "must" can be additional mandatory words. Bankers Ins. Co. v. Florida Res. Prop. & Cas. Jt. Underwriting Ass'n, 137 F.3d 1293, 1298 (11th Cir. 1998).

[46] See IA SUTHERLAND, STATUTES AND STATUTORY CONSTRUCTION § 25:4 (Norman J. Singer ed., 6th ed. 2002 rev.).

[47] *See, e.g.*, Lopez v. Davis, 531 U.S. 230, 241 (2001) ("Congress' use of the permissive 'may' ... contrasts with the legislators' use of a mandatory 'shall' in the very same section"); and United States ex rel. Siegel v. Thoman, 156 U.S. 353, 359-60 (1895) ("in the law to be construed here it is evident that the word 'may' is used in special contradistinction to the word 'shall'").

[48] *See, e.g.*, Escoe v. Zerbst, 295 U.S. 490, 493 (1935) ("doubt ... is dispelled when we pass from the words alone to a view of [the statute's] ends and aims").

[49] *See, e.g.*, Moore v. Illinois Cent R.R., 312 U.S. 630, 635 (1941) (substitution of "may" for "shall" "was not, we think, an indication of a change in policy, but was instead a clarification of the [Railway Labor Act's] original purpose [of establishing] a system for peaceful adjustment and mediation voluntary in its nature"). *See also* discussion in Gutierrez de Martinez v. Lamagno, 515 U.S. 417, 432 n.9 (1995) ("shall" sometimes means "may").

[50] The Dictionary Act provides that "unless the context indicates otherwise," "words importing the singular include and apply to several persons, parties, or things; words importing the plural include the singular." 1 U.S.C. § 1.



 

not satisfied by a system that fails to warn when two tires on the same side, or all four tires, are significantly under-inflated.[51]

## General, Specific, and Associated Words

Ordinarily, the specific terms of a statute override the general terms. "However inclusive may be the general language of a statute, it will not be held to apply to a matter specifically dealt with in another part of the same enactment."[52] As with other canons, context can dictate a contrary result.[53]

Another interpretational guide used from time to time is the principle *noscitur a sociis*, that "words grouped in a list should be given related meaning."[54] Thus, a tax provision that advantaged "income resulting from exploration, discovery, or prospecting" was held not to apply to income derived from patented cameras and pharmaceuticals that the taxpayers had "discovered." "Discovery," as used in conjunction with "exploration" and "prospecting," limited the scope of "discovery" to activities associated with the oil and gas and mining industries.[55]

A corollary, *ejusdem generis*, instructs that, "where general words follow an enumeration of specific items, the general words are read as applying only to other items akin to those specifically enumerated."[56] Thus, an exemption from arbitration for "contracts of employment of seamen, railroad employees, or any other class of workers engaged in ... commerce" did not apply to the case of a salesperson at a consumer electronics store: only contracts for the employment of individuals who transported goods and materials were to be exempted.[57]

The Court has explained that these canons (like many others) are only vehicles for ascertaining the correct meaning of words when there is uncertainty.[58] A less charitable assessment is that the

[51] Public Citizen, Inc. v. Mineta, 340 F.3d 39, 54 (2d Cir. 2003).

[52] Fourco Glass Co. v. Transmirra Products Corp., 353 U.S. 222, 228 (1957) (citations omitted). The same principle is used to resolve conflict between two statutes. *See, e.g.*, United States v. Estate of Romani, 523 U.S. 517, 532 (1998) (later, more specific statute governs). *See also* Morton v. Mancari, 417 U.S. 535, 550-51 (1974) (a general statute will not be held to have repealed by implication a more specific one unless there is "clear intention otherwise").

[53] *See, e.g.*, Adams v. Woods, 6 U.S. (2 Cranch) 336, 341 (1805).

[54] Dole v. United Steelworkers of America, 494 U.S. 26, 36 (1990); Gustafson v. Alloyd Co., 513 U.S. 561, 575 (1995) (reading a statutory definition as limited by the first of several grouped words).

[55] Jarecki v. G.D. Searle & Co., 367 U.S. 303, 307 (1961). "The maxim *noscitur a sociis*, that a word is known by the company it keeps, while not an inescapable rule, is often wisely applied where a word is capable of many meanings in order to avoid the giving of unintended breadth to Acts of Congress." *Id.*

[56] Harrison v. PPG Industries, Inc., 446 U.S. 578, 588 (1980); Washington Dep't of Social Servs. v. Keffeler, 537 U.S. 371, 384 (2003) (relying on both *noscitur a sociis* and *ejusdem generis*). The principle cannot be applied if the enumerated categories are too "disparate." Arcadia v. Ohio Power Co., 498 U.S. 73, 78 (1990). And, of course, context may reveal that application is inappropriate. Norfolk & Western Ry. v. Train Dispatchers, 499 U.S. 117, 129 (1991) (exemption of carriers from "the antitrust laws and all other law, including State and municipal law," is "clear, broad and unqualified," and obviously applies outside of antitrust and similar laws).

[57] Circuit City Stores, Inc. v. Adams, 532 U.S. 105, 114-15 (2001). "Canons of construction need not be conclusive and are often countered, of course, by some maxim pointing in a different direction. The application of the rule of *ejusdem generis* in this case, however, is in full accord with other sound considerations bearing upon proper interpretation of the clause." *Id.* at 115.

[58] *See* Norfolk & Western Ry. v. Train Dispatchers, 499 U.S. 117, 129 (1991) ("the canon does not control ... when the whole context dictates a different conclusion"); United States v. Turkette, 452 U.S. 576, 580-82 (1981) (appeals court erred in finding that a second category was merely a more general description of the first; context and language instead (continued...)



 

maxims do not aid in ascertaining meaning or deciding cases, but rather serve only to "classify and label results reached by other means."[59]

## Grammatical Rules, Punctuation

The old rule, borrowed from English law, was that "[p]unctuation is no part of the statute," and that "[c]ourts will ... disregard the punctuation, or repunctuate, if need be, to render the true meaning of the statute."[60] The modern Court recognizes that grammar and punctuation often clarify meaning, and that skilled drafters can be expected to apply good grammar.[61] The Court has also found plain meaning resulting from verb tense.[62]

The Court remains reluctant, however, to place primary importance on punctuation. "A statute's plain meaning must be enforced ..., and the meaning of a statute will typically heed the commands of its punctuation."[63] So said the Court—not, however, in applying a plain meaning consistent with punctuation, but instead while justifying a departure from that meaning. The Court went on to explain that "a purported plain meaning analysis based only on punctuation is necessarily incomplete and runs the risk of distorting a statute's true meaning."[64] "Overwhelming evidence from the structure, language, and subject matter" of the law led the Court to conclude that "in this unusual case" the punctuation at issue was the result of "a simple scrivener's error."[65] While the Court has relied on comma placement to find that a plain meaning was "mandated by the grammatical structure of the statute," the Court in that case also found other support for its reading.[66] In another case in which punctuation was a factor, the Court cited periods after each item in a list of alternatives as strongly suggesting that a modifying phrase in the last item did not apply to previous items.[67]

The reference to the use of periods in a list in the above case was part of a broader argument favoring application of the rule of the last antecedent: Because a limiting clause or phrase should ordinarily be read as modifying only the noun or phrase that it immediately follows, a condition

(...continued)
reveal two contrasting categories).

[59] Reed Dickerson, The Interpretation and Application of Statutes, 234 (1975).

[60] Hammock v. Loan and Trust Co., 105 U.S. (15 Otto) 77, 84-85 (1881) (disregarding a comma). *See also* United States v. Shreveport Grain & Elevator Co., 287 U.S. 77, 82-83 (1932) (also disregarding a comma).

[61] *See, e.g.*, Arcadia v. Ohio Power Co., 498 U.S. 73, 79 (1990) ("In casual conversation, perhaps, such absent-minded duplication and omission are possible, but Congress is not presumed to draft its laws that way.")

[62] Ingalls Shipbuilding v. Director, OWCP, 519 U.S. 248, 255 (1997) (present tense of verb is an element of plain meaning); Dole Food Co. v. Patrickson, 538 U.S. 468, 478 (2003) (interpretation required by "plain text" derived from present tense).

[63] United States Nat'l Bank of Oregon v. Independent Ins. Agents, 508 U.S. 439, 454 (1993).

[64] *Id. See also* Costanzo v. Tillinghast, 287 U.S. 341, 344 (1932) ("It has often been said that punctuation is not decisive of the construction of a statute.... Upon like principle we should not apply the rules of syntax to defeat the evident legislative intent.").

[65] *Independent Ins. Agents*, 508 U.S. at 462. This "unusual case" held that Congress did not in 1918 repeal a statutory provision enacted in 1916 allowing national banks located in small communities to sell insurance. The "scrivener's error" had erroneously credited the 1916 enactment with having amended a provision that was repealed by the 1918 enactment.

[66] United States v. Ron Pair Enterprises, 489 U.S. 235, 241 (1989).

[67] Jama v. Immigration & Customs Enforcement, 543 U.S. 335, 344 (2005).



 

requiring a receiving country's permission prior to an alien being deported that was contained in the last item of a list of possible destinations did not require the receiving country's approval before removing a alien to other, alternative destinations.[68] But, again, though the rule of the last antecedent may guide an initial reading, it is rarely determinative. Not untypical was the Court's refusal to apply the last antecedent rule, even though it could easily have concluded on the basis of the statutory language that application of the last antecedent rule was "mandated by the [statute's] grammatical structure." The rule "is quite sensible as a matter of grammar," the Court explained, but it "is not compelled."[69] So too, in another case the Court shied away from "the most natural grammatical reading" of a statute to avoid an interpretation that would have raised a serious issue of constitutionality.[70]

Refusal to be bound by the rules of punctuation and grammar, it seems, gives the Court some flexibility in construing statutes. This is not to say, however, that grammatical rules should be disregarded in statutory drafting, since such rules are ordinarily strong guides to meaning. There are cases decided largely on the basis of what constitutes the most "natural reading" of a statute according to common rules of grammar, without extended reference to particular canons or other interpretational aids.[71]

## Statutory Language Not to be Construed as "Mere Surplusage"

A basic principle of statutory interpretation is that courts should "give effect, if possible, to every clause and word of a statute, avoiding, if it may be, any construction which implies that the legislature was ignorant of the meaning of the language it employed."[72] The modern variant is that statutes should be construed "so as to avoid rendering superfluous" any statutory language: "A statute should be construed so that effect is given to all its provisions, so that no part will be inoperative or superfluous, void or insignificant.... "[73] A related principle applies to statutory amendments: there is a "general presumption" that, "when Congress alters the words of a statute, it must intend to change the statute's meaning."[74] Resistance to treating statutory words as mere

[68] *Id.* at 343.

[69] Nobelman v. American Savings Bank, 508 U.S. 324, 330-31 (1993). *See also* Lamie v. United States Trustee, 540 U.S. 526, 534 (2004) ("The statute is awkward, and even ungrammatical; but that does not make it ambiguous.").

[70] United States v. X-Citement Video, Inc., 513 U.S. 64, 68 (1994). Justice Scalia, dissenting, insisted that the language was perfectly clear, and that the rejected interpretation was "the only grammatical reading." *Id.* at 81.

[71] *E.g.,* Flores-Figueroa v. United States, No. 08-108, slip op. (U.S. May 4, 2009).

[72] Montclair v. Ramsdell, 107 U.S. 147, 152 (1883).

[73] Hibbs v. Winn, 542 U.S. 88, 101 (2004) (quoted in Corley v. United States, No. 07-10441, slip op. at 9 (U.S. Apr. 6, 2009)); Astoria Federal Savings & Loan Ass'n v. Solimino, 501 U.S. 104, 112 (1991); Sprietsma v. Mercury Marine, 537 U.S. 51, 63 (2003) (interpreting word "law" broadly could render word "regulation" superfluous in preemption clause applicable to a state "law or regulation"). *See also* Bailey v. United States, 516 U.S. 137, 146 (1995) ("we assume that Congress used two terms because it intended each term to have a particular, nonsuperfluous meaning") (rejecting interpretation that would have made "uses" and "carries" redundant in statute penalizing using or carrying a firearm in commission of offense). The presumption also guides interpretation of "redundancies across statutes." Two overlapping statutes may be given effect so long as there is no "positive repugnance" between them. Connecticut Nat'l Bank v. Germain, 503 U.S. 249, 253 (1992) (finding that, in spite of considerable overlap between two provisions, each addressed matters that the other did not).

[74] United States v. Wilson, 503 U.S. 333, 336 (1992) (nonetheless attributing no significance to deletion of a reference to the Attorney General; the reference "was simply lost in the shuffle" of a comprehensive statutory revision that had various unrelated purposes); Stone v. INS, 514 U.S. 386, 397 (1995) ("When Congress acts to amend a statute, we presume it intends its amendment to have real and substantial effect."). There is an exception for minor, unexplained changes in phraseology made during recodification—changes that courts generally assume are "not intended to alter the (continued...)



 

surplusage "should be heightened when the words describe an element of a criminal offense."[75] There can be differences of opinion, of course, as to when it is "possible" to give effect to all statutory language and when the general rule should give way in the face of evident contrary meaning.[76]

A converse of the rule that courts should not read statutory language as surplusage is that, as discussed below, courts should not add language that Congress has not included.

## Same Phrasing in Same or Related Statutes

"A term appearing in several places in a statutory text is generally read the same way each time it appears."[77] This presumption is "at its most vigorous when a term is repeated within a given sentence."[78] It also has been applied to the appearance of a term in inter-related programs.[79] Additionally, the Court in at least one instance referred to a broader "established canon" that similar language contained with the same section of a statute be accorded a consistent meaning.[80]

The general presumption is not rigid, however, and "readily yields when there is such variation in the connection in which the words are used as reasonably to warrant the conclusion that they were employed in different parts of the act with different intent."[81] In other words, context can override the presumption.

(...continued)

statute's scope." Walters v. National Ass'n of Radiation Survivors, 473 U.S. 305, 318 (1985).

[75] Ratzlaf v. United States, 510 U.S. 135, 140-41 (1994).

[76] *See, e.g.*, Moskal v. United States, 498 U.S. 103 (1990). Dissenting Justice Scalia objected to the Court's straining to avoid holding that "falsely made" is redundant in the federal forgery statute, which prohibits receipt of "falsely made, forged, altered, or counterfeited securities." "The principle [against mere surplusage] is sound, but its limitation ('if possible') should be observed. It should not be used to distort ordinary meaning. Nor should it be applied to obvious instances of iteration to which lawyers, alas, are particularly addicted." *Id.* at 120.

[77] Ratzlaf v. United States, 510 U.S. 135, 143 (1994). *See also* Gustafson v. Alloyd Co., 513 U.S. 561, 570 (1995); and Wisconsin Dep't of Revenue v. William Wrigley, Jr. Co., 505 U.S. 214, 225 (1992).

[78] Brown v. Gardner, 513 U.S. 115, 118 (1994); Reno v. Bossier Parish Sch. Bd., 528 U.S. 320, 329-30 (2000).

[79] Sullivan v. Stroop, 496 U.S. 478, 484 (1990) ("child support" as used in the Child Support program under the Social Security Act points toward the same use of "child support" in the closely related AFDC program, and thus "child support" as used in the AFDC program does not include OASDI payments under title II of the Social Security Act.).

[80] National Credit Union Admin. v. First Nat'l Bank & Trust Co., 522 U.S. 479, 501(1998).

[81] Atlantic Cleaners & Dyers, Inc. v. United States, 286 U.S. 427, 433 (1933). *See also* Robinson v. Shell Oil Co., 519 U.S. 337, 342-43 (1997) (term "employees" means current employees only in some sections of Title VII of Civil Rights Act, but in other sections includes former employees); United States v. Cleveland Indians Baseball Co., 532 U.S. 200 (2001) (different statutory contexts of worker eligibility for Social Security benefits and "administrability" of tax rules justify different interpretations); General Dynamics Land Systems, Inc. v. Cline, 540 U.S. 581, 594-595 (2004) (word "age" means "old age" when included in the term "age discrimination" in the Age Discrimination in Employment Act even though it is used in its primary sense elsewhere in the act). For disagreement about the appropriateness of applying this limitation, contrast the Court's opinion in *Gustafson v. Alloyd Co.*, 513 U.S. at 573, with the dissenting opinion of Justice Thomas in the same case, *id.* at 590 (interpreting a definition that, by its terms, was applicable "unless the context otherwise requires").



 

## Different Phrasings in Same Statute

The other side of the coin is that "where Congress includes particular language in one section of a statute but omits it in another ..., it is generally presumed that Congress acts intentionally and purposely in the disparate inclusion or exclusion."[82] The Court cited this maxim when Congress had restricted certain access by Guantanamo detainees to the courts immediately but did not expressly restrict access in pending cases through petitions for writs of habeas corpus: "A familiar principle of statutory construction ... is that a negative inference may be drawn from the exclusion of language from one statutory provision that is included in other provisions of the same statute."[83] In another case on the availability of habeas review, the Court referred to the history of the provision that treated habeas relief and other access to the courts differently: "[N]egative implications raised by disparate provisions are strongest when the portions of a statute treated differently had already been joined together and were being considered simultaneously when the language raising the implication was inserted."[84] This maxim has been applied by the Court—or at least cited as a justification—in distinguishing among different categories of veterans benefits[85] and among different categories of drug offenses.[86] A court can only go so far with the maxim, of course; establishing that language does *not* mean one thing does not necessarily establish what the language *does* mean.[87]

## "Congress Knows How to Say ..."

Occasionally the Court draws a contrast between the language at issue and other statutory language that clearly and directly requires the interpretation being pressed by one of the parties. There are some instances—e.g., failure to employ terms of art or other language normally used for such purposes—in which this can be a fairly persuasive argument. For example, the Court reasoned that, although "Congress knew how to impose aiding and abetting liability when it chose to do so," it did not use the words "aid" and "abet" in the statute, and hence did not impose aiding and abetting liability.[88] To say that Congress did not use the most precise language,

---

[82] Keene Corp. v. United States, 508 U.S. 200, 208 (1993) (quoting Russello v. United States, 464 U.S. 16, 23 (1983)). *See also* Bailey v. United States. 516 U.S. 137, 146 (1995) (distinction in one provision between "used" and "intended to be used" creates implication that related provision's reliance on "use" alone refers to actual and not intended use); and Bates v. United States, 522 U.S. 23, 29 (1997) (inclusion of "intent to defraud" language in one provision and exclusion in a parallel provision).

[83] Hamdan v. Rumsfeld, 548 U.S. 557, 578 (2006).

[84] Lindh v. Murphy, 521 U.S. 320, 330 (1997) (statute was explicit in making one section applicable to habeas cases pending on date of enactment, but was silent as to parallel provision).

[85] King v. St. Vincent's Hospital, 502 U.S. 215, 220-21 (1991) ("given the examples of affirmative limitations on reemployment benefits conferred by neighboring provisions, we infer that the simplicity of subsection (d) was deliberate, consistent with a plain meaning to provide its benefit without conditions on length of service").

[86] Chapman v. United States, 500 U.S. 453, 459 (1991) (fact that, with respect to some drugs, Congress distinguished between a "mixture or substance" containing the drug and a "pure" drug refutes the argument that Congress' failure to so distinguish with respect to LSD was inadvertent).

[87] *See* Field v. Mans, 516 U.S. 59, 67 (1995) ("without more, the ['negative pregnant'] inference might be a helpful one," but other interpretive guides prove more useful).

[88] Central Bank of Denver v. First Interstate Bank, 511 U.S. 164, 176-77 (1994). *See also* Franklin Nat'l Bank v. New York, 347 U.S. 373, 378 (1954) (finding "no indication that Congress intended to make this phase of national banking subject to local restrictions, as it has done by express language in several other instances"); Meghrig v. KFC Western, Inc., 516 U.S. 479, 485 (1996) ("Congress ... demonstrated in CERCLA that it knew how to provide for the recovery of cleanup costs, and ... the language used to define the remedies under RCRA does not provide that remedy."); FCC v. NextWave Personal Communications, Inc., 537 U.S. 293, 302 (2003) (when Congress has intended to create exceptions (continued...)



 

however, does not necessarily aid the court in determining what the less precise language means in its statutory context.[89] Some statutes may not be well drafted,[90] but others represent conscious choices, born of political compromise, that may or may not signal that a different result is intended or that Congress is leaving final interpretation to agencies, courts, or future legislatures.[91] It may be inappropriate question begging to assume, therefore, that "[i]f Congress had intended such an irrational result, surely it would have expressed it in straightforward English."[92]

## Statutory Silence

Nothing compels Congress to act comprehensively when it legislates on a subject. It is not safe to assume that Congress intends to address all ancillary issues directly whenever it acts. "As one court has aptly put it, '[n]ot every silence is pregnant.' In some cases, Congress intends silence to rule out a particular statutory application, while in others Congress' silence signifies merely an expectation that nothing more need be said in order to effectuate the relevant legislative objective. In still other instances, silence may reflect the fact that Congress has not considered an issue at all. An inference drawn from congressional silence certainly cannot be credited when it is contrary to all other textual and contextual evidence of congressional intent."[93] Occasionally, however, the Court identifies a pregnant statutory silence, as, for example, when that silence contrasts with a consistent pattern in federal statutes under which departures from a general rule had been expressly authorized.[94]

---

(...continued)

to bankruptcy law requirements, "it has done so clearly and expressly"); Dole Food Co. v. Patrickson, 538 U.S. 468, 476 (2003) (Congress knows how to refer to an "owner" "in other than the formal sense," and did not do so in the Foreign Sovereign Immunities Act's definition of foreign state "instrumentality"); Whitfield v. United States, 543 U.S. 209, 216 (2005) ("Congress has included an express overt-act requirement in at least 22 other current conspiracy statutes, clearly demonstrating that it knows how to impose such a requirement when it wishes to do so.").

[89] *See, e.g.*, Jackson v. Birmingham Bd. of Educ., 544 U.S. 167 (2005) (Title IX's prohibition on sex discrimination encompasses retaliation despite absence of an explicit prohibition on retaliation such as those contained in Title VII, the ADA, and the Age Discrimination in Employment Act).

[90] *See, e.g.*, the provisions of the Plant Variety Protection Act at issue in Asgrow Seed Co. v. Winterboer, 513 U.S. 179 (1995). Justice Scalia in his opinion for the Court in *Asgrow* called 7 U.S.C. § 2543 a "verbal maze," and conceded that "it is quite impossible to make complete sense of the provision." *Id.* at 185-86. In another case, the Court found statutory language "incoherent" due to use of three different and conflicting standards identifying an evidentiary burden. Concrete Pipe & Products v. Construction Laborers Pension Trust, 508 U.S. 602, 627 (1993). The Court resolved the issue by treating the "incoherence" as ambiguity, and by applying the one possible construction that did not raise constitutional issues. *Id.* at 628-30.

[91] *See, e.g.*, Landgraf v. USI Film Products, 511 U.S. 244, 263 (1994) ("The history of the 1991 [Civil Rights] Act conveys the impression that the legislators agreed to disagree about whether and to what extent the Act would apply to preenactment conduct.").

[92] FMC Corp. v. Holliday, 498 U.S. 52, 66 (1990) (Justice Stevens, dissenting, objecting to Court's interpretation of convoluted preemption language in ERISA).

[93] Burns v. United States, 501 U.S. 129, 136 (1991) (quoting Illinois Dep't of Public Aid v. Schweiker, 707 F.2d 273, 277 (7th Cir. 1983)).

[94] Director, OWCP v. Newport News Shipbuilding Co., 514 U.S. 122 (1995) (agency in its governmental capacity is not a "person adversely affected or aggrieved" for purposes of judicial review). *See also* United States v. Bestfoods, 524 U.S. 51, 62 (1998) ("against this venerable common-law backdrop, the congressional silence is audible"); Elkins v. Moreno, 435 U.S. 647, 666 (1978) (absence of reference to an immigrant's intent to remain citizen of foreign country is "pregnant" when contrasted with other provisions of "comprehensive and complete" immigration code); Meyer v. Holley, 537 U.S. 280 (2003) (ordinary rules of vicarious liability apply to tort actions under the Fair Housing Act; statutory silence as to vicarious liability contrasts with explicit departures in other laws).



 

While Congress may not anticipate and address *all* issues that may arise, the Court sometimes assumes that when Congress does wish to address major issues, it does so directly. In other words, a finding of intentional silence can be a preferred outcome. "Congress ... does not alter the fundamental details of a regulatory scheme in vague terms or ancillary provisions—it does not ... hide elephants in mouseholes."[95] This premise underlays the Court's reasoning in concluding that the FDA lacked authority to regulate tobacco. "Congress could not have intended to delegate a decision of such economic and political significance to an agency in so cryptic a fashion."[96]

A variation on the statutory silence theme is the negative inference: *expressio unius est exclusio alterius* (the inclusion of one is the exclusion of others). Thus, in a situation where Congress subjected specific categories of ticket sales to taxation but failed to cover another category, either by specific or by general language, the Court refused to extend the coverage. To do so, given the "particularization and detail" with which Congress had set out the categories, would amount to "enlargement" of the statute rather than "construction" of it.[97] Relatedly, "[w]here Congress explicitly enumerates certain exceptions to a general prohibition, additional exceptions are not to be implied, in the absence of a contrary legislative intent."[98] The Court applied the principle, albeit without express recognition, in holding that a statute requiring payment of an attendance fee to "a witness" applies to an incarcerated state prisoner who testifies at a federal trial. Because Congress had expressly excepted another category (detained aliens) from eligibility for these fees, and had expressly excepted any "incarcerated" witness from eligibility for a different category of fees, "the conclusion is virtually inescapable ... that the general language 'witness in attendance' ... includes prisoners ..."[99] But here again, context may render the principle inapplicable. A statutory listing may be "exemplary, not exclusive," the Court once concluded.[100]

---

[95] Whitman v. American Trucking Ass'ns, Inc., 531 U.S. 457, 468 (2001). *See also* MCI Telecommunications Corp. v. AT&T, 512 U.S. 218, 231 (1994) (conferral of authority to "modify" rates was not a cryptic conferral of authority to make filing of rates voluntary); Director of Revenue of Mo. v. CoBank, ACB, 531 U.S. 316, 323 (2001) ("it would be surprising, indeed," if Congress had effected a "radical" change in the law "*sub silentio*" via "technical and conforming amendments").

[96] FDA v. Brown & Williamson Tobacco Corp., 529 U.S. 120, 160 (2000). Ordinarily the Court does not require reference to specific applications of general authority, but in this instance ("hardly an ordinary case") the Court majority attached importance to the FDA's longstanding disavowal of regulatory authority, and to subsequently enacted tobacco-specific legislation that stopped short of conferring authority to ban sale of the product.

[97] Iselin v. United States, 270 U.S. 245, 250 (1926). *See also* Lamie v. United States Trustee, 540 U.S. 526, 537 (2004) (courts should not add an "absent word" to a statute; "there is a basic difference between filling a gap left by Congress' silence and rewriting rules that Congress has affirmatively and specifically enacted"). Obviously, the line between the permissible filling in of statutory gaps and the impermissible adding of statutory content may be indistinct in some instances, and statutory context, congressional purpose, and overriding presumptions may tip the scales. For example, the Court made no mention of the "absent word" rule in holding that a reference to "any entity" actually meant "any *private* entity" in the context of preemption. Nixon v. Missouri Municipal League, 541 U.S. 125 (2004) (preemption of state laws that prohibit "any entity" from providing telecommunications service does not preempt a state law prohibiting local governments from providing such service).

[98] Andrus v. Glover Const. Co., 446 U.S. 608, 616-17 (1980) (citing Continental Casualty Co. v. United States, 314 U.S. 527, 533 (1942)).

[99] Demarest v. Manspeaker, 498 U.S. 184, 188 (1991). Congress quickly acted to override this result and prohibit payment of witness fees to prisoners, P.L. 102-417, 106 Stat. 2138 (1992), the House Judiciary Committee expressing the belief that "Congress never intended" that prisoners be paid witness fees. H.Rept. 102-194, 102d Cong., 1st Sess. 2 (1991).

[100] NationsBank v. Variable Annuity Life Ins. Co., 513 U.S. 251, 257 (1995) (endorsing Comptroller of the Currency's interpretation).



 

## De Minimis Principle

"The venerable maxim *de minimis non curat lex* ('the law cares not for trifles') is part of the established background of legal principles against which all enactments are adopted, and which all enactments (absent contrary indication) are deemed to accept.... Whether a particular activity is a *de minimis* deviation from a prescribed standard must ... be determined with reference to the purpose of the standard."[101]

# "Substantive" Canons of Construction

There are a number of instances in which the Court subordinates the general, linguistic canons of statutory construction, as well as other interpretive principles, to overarching presumptions that, unless rebutted, favor particular substantive results. Some of the "weighty and constant values" protected by these "substantive" canons of construction are derived from the Constitution, others from notions of federalism, and yet others from interests in judicial administration and ordered governance.[102] Application of a substantive canon often, but not always,[103] results in some form of "clear statement" rule, requiring that Congress, if it wishes to achieve a particular result inconsistent with the Court's view of legal traditions, must state such an intent with unmistakable clarity.[104]

## Departure from Common Law or Established Interpretation

Congress is presumed to legislate with knowledge of existing common law. When it adopts a statute, related judge-made law (common law) is presumed to remain in force and work in conjunction with the new statute absent a clear indication otherwise. Thus, when Congress adopted the common law on abandonment of property as part of the Bankruptcy Code, it was deemed to have also implicitly adopted all the judge-made corollaries and exceptions that attended the abandonment law: "The normal rule of statutory construction is that if Congress intends for legislation to change the interpretation of a judicially created concept, it makes that

[101] *See* Abbott Laboratories v. Portland Retail Druggists, 425 U.S. 1, 18 (1976) (occasional emergency dispensation of drugs to walk-in patients is *de minimis* deviation from Robinson-Patman Act's exemption for hospitals' purchase of supplies "for their own use"); Industrial Ass'n v. United States, 268 U.S. 64, 68 (1925) (3 or 4 "sporadic and doubtful instances" of interference with interstate commerce in what was in essence an intrastate matter were insufficient to establish a violation of the Sherman Act).

[102] For an extensive listing of substantive canons, by type, used in Supreme Court decisions from 1986-2006, along with accompanying case citations, see WILLIAM N. ESKRIDGE, JR., PHILLIP P. FRICKEY & ELIZABETH GARRETT, CASES & MATERIALS ON LEGISLATION: STATUTES & THE CREATION OF PUBLIC Policy at Appendix B 29-41 (4th ed. 2007).

[103] For example, in *Astoria Federal Savings & Loan Assn. v. Solimino* (501 U.S. 104 (1991)), the Court addressed whether a federal cause of action under the Age Act was bound by unreviewed findings of a state administrative board, as might be the case if the common law doctrine of collateral estoppel applied. In this instance, Justice Souter characterized the maxim that judge-made law implicitly continues to apply as an analytical starting point only, one that would give way as statutory context or purpose indicates. The opinion eschewed any formulaic application that would make the maxim dispositive absent a "clear statement" in the statute to the contrary. 501 U.S. at 508-10

[104] Judge Wald described one such presumption as requiring that Congress "signal[ ] its intention in neon lights." Patricia M. Wald, *Some Observations on the Use of Legislative History in the 1981 Supreme Court Term,* 68 IOWA L. REV. 195, 208 (1983). *See generally* pp. 206-14 of the article. *See also* William N. Eskridge, Jr. and Philip P. Frickey, *Quasi-Constitutional Law: Clear Statement Rules as Constitutional Lawmaking*, 45 VAND. L. REV. 593 (1992).



 

intent specific."[105] In another bankruptcy case the Court declared that "[w]e will not read the Bankruptcy Code to erode past ... practice absent a clear indication that Congress intended such a departure."[106] The notion that common-law rights and causes of action survive absent clear intent to the contrary continues to arise in a variety of contexts.[107] In some instances, the presumption that common law principles continue to apply has been overcome by general reference to a statute's purpose, even absent a "clear statement."[108]

## Displacing State Law, Impinging on State Operations

The Supremacy Clause of the Constitution, Article VI, cl. 2, provides that federal law supersedes inconsistent state law. Whether a particular statute does so is a matter of congressional intent. A substantive canon positions the starting point of analysis "with the assumption that the historic police powers of the States were not to be superseded by [a federal law] unless that was the clear and manifest purpose of Congress."[109] Many federal regulatory statutes contain a statement of preemptive scope, either preempting state law or disclaiming intent to do so. Nevertheless, both preemption and savings statements have presented the Court with difficult interpretive analyses, based on a statute's structure and purpose, of precisely which state-based causes of action and regulations have been foreclosed or preserved[110] When a statute is silent on preemption, the Court has asked three questions in determining whether state law has been preempted implicitly: Is there a direct conflict between federal and state law—can they be implemented simultaneously? Would implementation of state law "frustrate congressional purpose"? Has federal law has

---

[105] Midlantic Nat'l Bank v. New Jersey Dep't of Envt'l Protection, 474 U.S. 494, 501 (1986) (quoting Edmonds v. Compagnie Generale Transatlantique, 443 U.S. 256, 266-67 (1979)).

[106] Pennsylvania Pub. Welfare Dep't v. Davenport, 495 U.S. 552, 563 (1990) (nonetheless finding that the statutory language plainly evidenced an intent to depart from past practice).

[107] *E.g.,* Atlantic Sounding Co., Inc. v. Townsend, No. 08-214, slip op. (U.S. June 25, 2009) (availability of punitive damages in maritime cases under common law not superseded by Jones Act); Norfolk Southern Railway v. Sorrell, No. 05-746, slip op. (U.S. Jan. 10, 2007) (common-law negligence principles continued to apply in action under the Federal Employers' Liability Act); United States v. Dixon, 548 U.S. 1 (2006) (common-law burden on defendant to prove affirmative defense of duress applied in prosecution for firearms-related offenses); Bates v. Dow Agrosciences LLC, 544 U.S. 431 (2005) (continued availability of certain state common law tort remedies after Federal Insecticide, Fungicide, and Rodenticide Act).

[108] See Astoria Federal Savings & Loan Assn. v. Solimino, 501 U.S. 104 (1991).

[109] Rice v. Santa Fe Elevator Corp., 331 U.S. 218, 230 (1947); Wisconsin Public Intervenor v. Mortier, 501 U.S. 597, 605 (1991). *See also* Medtronic Inc. v. Lohr, 518 U.S. 470, 485 (1996) ([B]ecause the States are independent sovereigns in our federal system, we have long presumed that Congress does not cavalierly pre-empt state-law causes of action.").

[110] *E.g.,* Bates v. Dow Agrosciences LLC, 544 U.S. 431 (2005) (continued availability of certain state common law tort remedies after Federal Insecticide, Fungicide, and Rodenticide Act); Rush Prudential HMO v. Moran, 536 U.S. 355 (2002) (5-4 decision finding that Illinois regulation fell within ERISA's preservation of state insurance laws); Cipollone v. Liggett Group, Inc., 505 U.S. 504 (1992) (preemptive reach of Federal Cigarette Labeling and Advertising Act).

A statement asserting preemption or disclaiming intent to preempt must be clear not only as to preemptive intent, but also as to scope. In International Paper Co. v. Ouellette, 479 U.S. 481 (1987), for example, the Court ruled that some aspects of state law were preempted in spite of a savings clause in the citizens suit provision of the Clean Water Act declaring that "nothing in this section" should be read as affecting an injured party's right to seek relief under any statute or common law. Other parts of the act outside of the citizens suit section were read as implying preemption. "Because we do not believe Congress intended to undermine this carefully drawn statute [leaving a source state responsible for control of point-source discharges within its boundaries] through a general savings clause, we conclude that the CWA precludes a court from applying the law of an affected state against an out-of-state source." *Id.* at 484.



 

"occupied the field" of regulation? These latter two categories lack precision, and, almost always, the surer course of legislative drafting is to spell out intended preemptive effect.

Also in deference to the states, the Court will not lightly infer that Congress has enacted legislation that restricts how states may constitute their own governments. In ruling that state judges are not "employees" for purposes of the Age Discrimination in Employment Act, the Court required a plain statement rule applicable to laws limiting the authority of the States to determine the qualifications of their most important government officials—an authority protected by the Tenth Amendment and by the Guarantee Clause.[111] "This plain statement rule is nothing more than an acknowledgment that the States retain substantial sovereign powers under our constitutional scheme, powers with which Congress does not readily interfere."[112]

## Abrogation of States' Eleventh Amendment Immunity

Also protective of state sovereignty is the rule that, in order to abrogate the states' Eleventh Amendment immunity from suit in federal court, "Congress must make its intention 'unmistakably clear in the language of the statute.'"[113] Congress has limited authority to abrogate states' Eleventh Amendment immunity, to begin with; the Court held in *Seminole Tribe of Florida v. Florida*, that Congress's general legislative powers under Article I may not be used to "circumvent the constitutional limitations placed upon federal jurisdiction [by the Eleventh Amendment]."[114] This leaves Section 5 of the Fourteenth Amendment (specific power to enforce the Amendment's guarantees) as the principal source of power to abrogate state immunity. Despite these restrictions, Congress has been found to have abrogated immunity when it made its intent "unmistakably clear" in the language of the statute and acted under a valid exercise of its Fourteenth Amendment powers.[115]

## Nationwide Application of Federal Law

Congress may, if it chooses, incorporate state law as federal law.[116] Federal law usually applies uniformly nationwide,[117] however, and there is a presumption that, "when Congress enacts a statute ... it does not intend to make its application dependent on state law."[118]

---

[111] Gregory v. Ashcroft, 501 U.S. 452 (1991).

[112] *Id.* at 461. *See also* Nixon v. Missouri Municipal League, 541 U.S. 125 (2004) (indicating that the plain statement rule is also appropriate for laws "interposing federal authority between a State and its municipal subdivisions").

[113] Hoffman v. Connecticut Income Maint. Dep't, 492 U.S. 96, 101 (1989) (quoting Atascadero State Hosp. v. Scanlon, 473 U.S. 234, 242 (1985)).

[114] 517 U.S. 44, 73 (1996).

[115] Nevada Dept. of Human Resources v. Hibbs 538 U.S. 721 (2003) (Family and Medical Leave Act).

[116] *See, e.g.*, the Assimilative Crimes Statute, 18 U.S.C. § 13, governing crimes within the special maritime and territorial jurisdiction of the United States.

[117] Jerome v. United States, 318 U.S. 101, 104 (1943). Arguably, the *Jerome* Court actually overstated the case, citing United States v. Pelzer, 312 U.S. 399, 402 (1941), for the proposition that "the application of federal legislation is nationwide." *Pelzer* was far less sweeping, holding only that "in light of their general purpose to establish a nationwide scheme of taxation uniform in its application," provisions of the *revenue laws* "should not be taken as subject to state control or limitation unless the language or necessary implication of the section involved makes its application dependent on state law." 312 U.S. at 402-03.

[118] Dickerson v. New Banner Inst., 460 U.S. 103, 119 (1983) (quoting NLRB v. Randolph Elec. Membership Corp., 343 F.2d 60, 62-63 ($4^{th}$ Cir. 1965)).



 

## Waiver of Sovereign Immunity

"[T]he Government's consent to be sued 'must be construed strictly in favor of the sovereign.'"[119] Waiver of sovereign immunity must be effected by unequivocal expression in the statutory text itself; legislative history "has no bearing" on the issue.[120] As a consequence, "statutes which in general terms divest pre-existing rights or privileges will not be applied to the sovereign without express words to that effect."[121]

A separate issue from whether Congress has clearly and unequivocally waived immunity is the availability of money damages when immunity has been waived. Here, the Court reads the statute under a "fair interpretation" standard that is "demonstrably" less exacting than the "clear and unequivocal" test to determine whether immunity has been waived in the first place.[122]

## Non-retroactivity / Effective Date

"[A]bsent a clear direction by Congress to the contrary, a law takes effect on the date of its enactment."[123] There is a general rule, based on the unfairness of attaching new legal consequences to already-completed events, disfavoring retroactive application of civil statutes. Statutory provisions do not apply to events antedating enactment unless there is clear congressional intent that they so apply. "Requiring clear intent assures that Congress itself has affirmatively considered the potential unfairness of retroactive application and determined that it is an acceptable price to pay for the countervailing benefits."[124] The prohibitions on *ex post facto* laws, of course, impose a constitutional bar to retroactive application of penal laws.[125]

---

[119] United States v. Nordic Village, Inc., 503 U.S. 30, 34 (1992); Ardestani v. INS, 502 U.S. 129, 137 (1991) (partial waiver).

[120] *United States v. Nordic Village*, 503 U.S. at 37. For criticism of the rule, see John Copeland Nagle, *Waiving Sovereign Immunity in an Age of Clear Statement Rules*, 1995 WISC. L. REV. 771, 836.

[121] UMW v. United States, 330 U.S. 258, 272 (1947) (United States is not an "employer" for purposes of the Norris-LaGuardia Act); Vermont Agency of Nat. Resources v. United States ex rel. Stevens, 529 U.S. 765, 780-81 (2000) (state is not a "person" for purposes of *qui tam* liability under the False Claims Act).

[122] United States v. White Mt. Apache Tribe, 537 U.S. 465, 472-73 (2003).

[123] Gozlon-Peretz v. United States, 498 U.S. 395, 404 (1991). Ordinarily, and in the absence of special circumstances, the law does not recognize fractions of the day, so a law becomes effective "from the first moment" of the effective date. Lapeyre v. United States, 17 Wall. 191, 198 ( 1872). However, "whenever it becomes important to the ends of justice ... the law will look into fractions of a day." Louisville v. Savings Bank, 104 U.S. 469, 474 (1881). *See* Burgess v. Salmon, 97 U.S. 381 (1878) (a law signed in the afternoon could not be applied to fine a person for actions he had completed on the morning of the same day); United States v. Will, 449 U.S. 200, 225 n.29 (1980) (a judicial salary increase had taken effect at the beginning of the day, and was already in effect when the President later in the day signed legislation reducing cost-of-living increases).

[124] Landgraf v. USI Film Products, 511 U.S. 244, 272-73 (1994) (finding no such clearly expressed congressional intent with respect to the civil rights law's new compensatory and punitive damages remedies and the associated right to a jury trial). *See also* Fernandez-Vargas v. Gonzales, 548 U.S. 30 (2006).

[125] Art. I, § 9, cl. 3 prohibits Congress from enacting *ex post facto* laws; Art. I, § 10 applies the prohibition to the states. *See* Lynce v. Mathis, 519 U.S. 433, 439 (1997); and Johnson v. United States, 529 U.S. 694, 701 (2000), for general discussion.



 

## Avoidance of Constitutional Issues

The doctrine of "constitutional doubt" requires courts to construe statutes, "if fairly possible, so as to avoid not only the conclusion that it is unconstitutional but also grave doubts upon that score."[126] "[W]here an otherwise acceptable construction of a statute would raise serious constitutional problems, the Court will construe the statute to avoid such problems unless such construction is plainly contrary to the intent of Congress ... 'The elementary rule is that every reasonable construction must be resorted to, in order to save a statute from unconstitutionality.' This approach not only reflects the prudential concern that constitutional issues not be needlessly confronted, but also recognizes that Congress, like this Court, is bound by and swears an oath to uphold the Constitution."[127] As with other issues, of course, it is the view of the majority that prevails: "Grave doubt" as to constitutionality does not arise simply because a Court minority—even a minority of four Justices—believes a statute may be constitutionally suspect.[128]

## Extraterritorial Application Disfavored

"It is a longstanding principle of American law 'that legislation of Congress, unless a contrary intent appears, is meant to apply only within the territorial jurisdiction of the United States.' This 'canon of construction' ... serves to protect against unintended clashes between our laws and those of other nations which could result in international discord."[129]

## Judicial Review of Administrative Action

There is a strong presumption that Congress intends judicial review of administrative action: "[A] survey of our cases shows that judicial review of a final agency action by an aggrieved person will not be cut off unless there is persuasive reason to believe that such was the purpose of Congress."[130] The Court requires that a statute contain "clear and convincing evidence" of an

[126] United States v. Jin Fuey Moy, 241 U.S. 394, 401 (1916); Almendarez-Torres v. United States, 523 U.S. 224, 237-38 (1998); Jones v. United States, 529 U.S. 848, 857 (2000). *See also* Ashwander v. Tennessee Valley Authority, 297 U.S. 288, 347 (1936) (J. Brandeis, concurring) ("The Court will not pass upon a constitutional question, although properly presented by the record, if there is also present some other ground upon which the case may be disposed of. [ ... ] Thus, if a case can be decided upon two grounds, one involving a constitutional question, the other a question of statutory construction or general law, the Court will decide only the latter.").

[127] DeBartolo Corp. v. Florida Gulf Coast Trades Council, 485 U.S. 568, 575 (1988) (quoting Hooper v. California, 155 U.S. 648, 657 (1895)). *Accord*, Burns v. United States, 501 U.S. 129, 138 (1991); Gollust v. Mendell, 501 U.S. 115, 126 (1991).

[128] Almendarez-Torres v. United States, 523 U.S. 224, 239 (1998) (citing Rust v. Sullivan, 500 U.S. 173, 191 (1991), in which the Court concluded, over the dissent of four Justices, that abortion counseling regulations "do not raise the sort of 'grave and doubtful constitutional questions,' ... that would lead us to assume Congress did not intend to authorize their issuance").

[129] EEOC v. Arabian American Oil Co., 499 U.S. 244, 248 (1991) (quoting Foley Bros, Inc. v. Filardo, 336 U.S. 281, 285 (1949)). *See also* Microsoft Corp. v. AT&T, 550 U.S. 437, 454-55 ( 2007) ("The presumption that United States law governs domestically but does not rule the world applies with particular force in patent law."); Smith v. United States, 507 U.S. 197, 203-04 (1993) (interpretation of Federal Tort Claims Act as inapplicable in Antarctica is reinforced by presumption against extraterritorial application). *Cf.* Hartford Fire Ins. Co. v. California, 509 U.S. 764, 796 (1993) (Sherman Act applies to foreign conduct producing, and intended to produce, substantial effects in United States).

[130] Abbott Laboratories v. Gardner, 387 U.S. 136, 140 (1967).



 

intent to preclude judicial review of decisions made under it.[131] Also, the Court tends to construe preclusions narrowly. Thus, even where a statute has barred judicial review of the merits of individual cases, the Court nevertheless has found that the regulations and practices for determining cases may be reviewed.[132]

While the presumption of reviewability predated the enactment of the Administrative Procedure Act in 1946, the APA embodied the presumption in statute. Under the APA, final agency actions for which there is no other adequate remedy in a court are subject to judicial review,[133] "except to the extent that ... statutes preclude judicial review; or ... agency action is committed to agency discretion by law."[134] As to the first exception, the presumption of reviewability may be overcome by specific statutory language, but it also "may be overcome by inferences of intent drawn from the statutory scheme as a whole."[135] The second exception applies "in those rare instances where 'statutes are drawn in such broad terms that in a given case there is no law to apply.'"[136]

An aspect of the second exception is that "review is not to be had if the statute is drawn so that a court would have no meaningful standard against which to judge the agency's exercise of discretion."[137] Thus, the Court in *Webster v. Doe* looked at the structure of the National Security Act and language allowing the Director of Central Intelligence to terminate an employee as the Director deemed necessary or advisable, and concluded that a court could not, as a general matter, review the necessity or advisability of terminating an employee based on sexual orientation.[138] But, as in many other judicial review cases, the *Webster* Court was very precise as to what review a statute foreclosed. Though the Court found decisions on whether a dismissal was necessary or advisable resided with the Director alone, this discretion did not go so far as to preclude court consideration of colorable constitutional claims arising from the actions of the Director. In the

---

[131] *E.g.,* Bowen v. Michigan Academy of Family Physicians, 476 U.S. 667, 671 ("This ['clear and convincing evidence'] standard has been invoked time and again.... ").

[132]Bowen v. Michigan Academy of Family Physicians, 476 U.S. 667 (1986) (finding that the method for determining the amount of benefits that are payable under Medicare Part B is reviewable even though the individual determinations themselves are not). *See also* McNary v. Haitian Refugee Center, 498 U.S. 479, 496 (1991) ("it is most unlikely that Congress intended to foreclose all forms of meaningful judicial review," given the presumption "that Congress legislates with knowledge of our basic rules of statutory construction").

*See also* Lindahl v. OPM, 470 U.S. 768, 778 (1985) (provision in Civil Service Retirement Act stating that OPM's "decisions ... concerning these matters are final and conclusive and are not subject to review" interpreted as precluding review only of OPM's factual determinations, but as not precluding review of legal interpretations). The *Lindahl* Court contrasted other statutory language said to be "far more unambiguous and comprehensive" in precluding review. *Id.* at 779-80 & n.13 (citing 5 U.S.C. § 8128(b)) ("action of the Secretary ... is final and conclusive for all purposes and with respect to all questions of law and fact"); and 38 U.S.C. § 211(a) ("decisions of the Administrator on any question of law or fact ... shall be final and conclusive and no other official or any court of the United States shall have power or jurisdiction to review any such decision").

[133] 5 U.S.C. § 704.

[134] 5 U.S.C. § 701(a).

[135] Block v. Community Nutrition Inst., 467 U.S. 340, 349 (1984) (judicial review of milk marketing orders not available to consumers). *Accord,* United States v. Fausto, 484 U.S. 439, 452 (1988) (congressional intent to preclude judicial review is clear from the purposes of the Civil Service Reform Act, from the entirety of its text, and from the structure of the statutory scheme).

[136] Citizens to Preserve Overton Park, Inc. v. Volpe, 401 U.S. 402, 410 (1971) (citing S.Rep. 79-752 (1945).

[137] Heckler v. Chaney, 470 U.S. 821, 830 (1985).

[138] 486 U.S. 592 (1988).



 

Court's view, a clearer statement from Congress is necessary before courts should refrain from reviewing constitutional claims of administrative error.[139]

## Deference to Administrative Interpretation

Interpreting statutes is not solely a matter for the courts. Executive agencies charged with implementing regulatory statutes adopt policies and processes to put statutes into action.[140] Agency decisions might set operational rules of general application or might arise during agency adjudications; they might be the result of more or less formal processes; they might purport to be more or less binding. But they all involve interpreting the law to some degree, and courts considering challenges to agency decisionmaking face the issue of how much to defer to an agency reading of the law or to proceed to interpret the law on their own.

Under current precedent, when a court reviews an agency's formal interpretation of a statute that the agency administers, and when the statute has not removed agency discretion by compelling a particular disposition of the matter at issue, courts defer to any reasonable agency interpretation. This is the *Chevron* rule announced in 1984.[141] In two decisions, one in 2000[142] and one in 2001,[143] the Court clarified and narrowed *Chevron's* application, ruling that *Chevron* deference applies only if an agency's interpretation is the product of a formal agency process, such as adjudication or notice-and-comment rulemaking, through which Congress has authorized the agency "to speak with the force of law."[144] Other agency interpretations that are made without the protections of a formal and public process often are reviewed under pre-*Chevron* principles set forth in *Skidmore v. Swift & Co.*[145] Additional variations of deference analysis also may come into play in individual cases, depending on subject matter and other factors.[146]

As in other matters of interpretation, it is congressional intent that counts. Under *Chevron*, the first question is "whether Congress has directly spoken to the precise question at issue."[147] If the court, "employing the traditional tools of statutory construction," determines that Congress has addressed the precise issue, then that is the end of the matter, because the "law must be given effect."[148] But if the statute does not directly address the issue, "the court does not simply impose its own construction of the statute," but rather determines "whether the agency's answer is based on a permissible construction of the statute."[149]

---

[139] 486 U.S. at 601-605. *See also* Johnson v. Robison, 415 U.S. 361 (1974).

[140] Clearly, the courts and administrative agencies have different interests and different types of expertise, and their respective processes differ in their openness to policy considerations, both in initially interpreting a statute and amending an interpretation over time.

[141] Chevron U.S.A. v. Natural Resources Defense Council, 467 U.S. 837 (1984).

[142] Christensen v. Harris County, 529 U.S. 576 (2000).

[143] United States v. Mead Corp., 533 U.S. 218 (2001).

[144] *Mead Corp.*, 533 U.S. at 229.

[145] 323 U.S. 134 (1944).

[146] William N. Eskridge, Jr. & Lauren E. Baer, *The Continuum of Deference: Supreme Court Treatment of Agency Statutory Interpretation from* Chevron *to* Hamdan, 96 GEO. L.J. 1083 (2008).

[147] *Chevron*, 467 U.S. at 842.

[148] 467 U.S. at 843 n.9.

[149] *Id.* at 843. Many scholars and courts opine that the "permissible construction," or "reasonable" interpretation, inquiry under this second step of *Chevron* analysis is essentially the same as determining whether an agency action is (continued...)



 

On its face, the *Chevron* rule is quite deferential, and was perceived as a significant break from the multi-factored approach that preceded it.[150] One would expect that a court's conclusion as to whether Congress has "directly spoken" to the issue would be decisive in most cases, that most of the myriad of issues that can arise in the administrative setting would not be directly addressed by statute, and that, consequently, courts would most often defer to what are found to be "reasonable" agency interpretations.[151] However, *Chevron* did not usher in a sea change of increased deference by the Supreme Court.[152] The Court has frequently determined that in fact Congress *has* settled the matter, and that consequently there is no need to proceed to the second, more deferential step of the inquiry.[153] The Court has also found that, even though Congress has left the matter for agency resolution, the agency's interpretation is unreasonable.[154]

In determining whether Congress has "directly spoken," there is much territory between an express delegation to an agency to address a particular issue and express legislative language resolving the issue statutorily. Imprecision on an issue may reflect an oversight by Congress, a failure to anticipate what might arise, a political compromise, an implicit assumption that the gap would be filled in by the agency with technical expertise, or other considerations. With this in mind, the Court has recognized circumstances in which it is less likely that Congress intended to leave resolution of statutory uncertainty to the administering agency, especially when it appears that the agency may be citing vague terms to justify jurisdiction over controversial matters with major policy implications traditionally resolved by Congress or another agency.[155] Thus, in holding that the Food and Drug Administration lacked authority to regulate tobacco products as "drugs" and "devices" under the Food, Drug, and Cosmetic Act, the Court concluded that "Congress could not have intended to delegate a decision of such economic and political significance to an agency in so cryptic a fashion."[156] The Court ruled that Congress had "directly

(...continued)

"arbitrary, capricious, and an abuse of discretion" for purposes of judicial review under the Administrative Procedure Act, though some question whether the *Chevron* and APA standards are, or should be, wholly congruent in all cases. *See, e.g.,* Kenneth A. Bamberger & Peter L. Strauss, Chevron's *Two Steps*, 95 VA. L. REV. 611 (2009) and authorities cited therein.

[150] *See, e.g.,* Kenneth W. Starr, *Judicial Review in the Post-*Chevron *Era*, 3 YALE J. ON REG. 283 (1986).

[151] *See, e.g.,* Sullivan v. Everhart, 494 U.S. 83 (1990) (regulations are a reasonable interpretation of Social Security Act); Smiley v. Citibank (South Dakota), 517 U.S. 735 (1996) (upholding Comptroller of the Currency's interpretation of 1864 Bank Act); and Lopez v. Davis, 531 U.S. 230, 240 (2001) (Bureau of Prisons regulation denying early release is reasonable interpretation of discretionary authority).

[152] An extensive study of more than 1000 Supreme Court case decided between the issuance of *Chevron* in 1984 and the end of the Court's 2005 Term concluded that *Chevron* analysis is but one of a broad array of deference regimes that continue to be applied by Court. William N. Eskridge, Jr. & Lauren E. Baer, *The Continuum of Deference: Supreme Court Treatment of Agency Statutory Interpretation from* Chevron *to* Hamdan, 96 GEO. L.J. 1083 (2008).

[153] *See, e.g.,* Sullivan v. Zebley, 493 U.S. 521 (1990) (regulations "are simply inconsistent with the statutory standard"); and Dole v. Steelworkers, 494 U.S. 26 (1990) (deference to OMB interpretation of Paperwork Reduction Act is foreclosed by Court's finding of clear congressional intent to contrary).

[154] Whitman v. American Trucking Ass'ns, Inc., 531 U.S. 457 (2001).

[155] *See, e.g.,* MCI Telecommunications Corp. v. AT&T Co., 512 U.S. 218, 231 (1994) ("it is highly unlikely that Congress would leave the determination of whether an industry will be entirely, or even substantially, rate-regulated to agency discretion").

As to an agency assertion of jurisdiction delegated elsewhere, the Court stated the following in overturning a rule by the Attorney General declaring that use of a controlled substance for physician-assisted suicide is not a legitimate medical practice for purposes of the Controlled Substances Act: "*Chevron* deference ... is not accorded merely because the statute is ambiguous and an administrative official is involved. To begin with, the rule must be promulgated pursuant to authority Congress has delegated to the official." Gonzales v. Oregon, 546 U.S. 243, 258 (2006).

[156] FDA v. Brown & Williamson Tobacco Corp., 529 U.S. 120, 160 (2000).



 

spoken" to the regulatory issue—not through the FDCA itself, but rather through subsequently enacted tobacco-specific legislation and through rejection of legislative proposals to confer jurisdiction on the FDA.[157] In another case, the Court found deference to be inappropriate where the agency interpretation "invokes the outer limits of Congress' power," and there is no "clear indication" that Congress intended that result.[158]

A logical consequence of applying *Chevron* is to render irrelevant whether an agency interpretation was "contemporaneous" with a statute's enactment, or whether an agency's position has been consistent over the years. "Neither antiquity nor contemporaneity with the statute is a condition of validity."[159] The fact that an agency has changed its position over the years "is not fatal," because "the whole point of *Chevron* is to leave the discretion provided by the ambiguities of a statute with the implementing agency."[160]

Agency interpretations that take place in the many less formal contexts where *Chevron* deference is inapplicable (*e.g.*, opinion letters, policy statements, agency manuals, and enforcement guidelines, "all of which lack the force of law"[161]) can still be "entitled to respect,"[162] "but only to the extent that [they] have the power to persuade."[163] As the Court put it in *Skidmore v. Swift & Co.*, agency interpretations "constitute a body of experience and informed judgment to which courts and litigants may properly resort.... The weight of such a judgment in a particular case will depend upon the thoroughness evident in its consideration, the validity of its reasoning, its consistency with earlier and later pronouncements, and all those factors which give it power to persuade, if lacking power to control."[164] These factors may include whether an interpretation

---

[157] The subsequent legislation created "a distinct regulatory scheme for tobacco products." 529 U.S. at 159. As Justice Breyer's dissent pointed out, tobacco products clearly fell within the generally worded jurisdictional definitions of the Food, Drug, and Cosmetic Act, and it was also clear that Congress had not spoken directly to the issue anywhere else in that act. 529 U.S. at 162. The Court's different resolution of a similar issue concerning patent protection for plant breeding illustrates that a subsequently enacted "distinct regulatory scheme" does not always trump general authority. The Court ruled in 1980 and again in 2001 that neither the Plant Patent Act of 1930 nor the Plant Variety Protection Act—both premised on the understanding that the Patent and Trademark Office lacked authority to issue plant patents under its general utility patent authority—deprived the Office of authority to issue plant patents pursuant to that general authority. Diamond v. Chakrabarty, 447 U.S. 318 (1980); J.E.M. Ag Supply, Inc. v. Farm Advantage, Inc., 534 U.S. 124 (2001).

[158] Solid Waste Agency v. Army Corps of Engineers, 531 U.S. 159, 172 (2001). In *Rapanos v. United States*, the plurality opinion took issue with the breadth of the Corps of Engineers' claim to jurisdiction through its interpretation of the term "the waters of the United States": "The extensive federal jurisdiction urged by the Government would authorize the Corps to function as a *de facto* regulator of immense stretches of intrastate land ... We ordinarily expect a 'clear and manifest' statement from Congress to authorize an unprecedented intrusion into traditional state authority.... Likewise ... the Corps' interpretation stretches the outer limits of Congress' commerce power.... Even if the term 'the waters of the United States' were ambiguous as applied to channels that sometimes host ephemeral flows of water ... we would expect a clearer statement from Congress to authorize an agency theory of jurisdiction that presses the envelope of constitutional validity." 547 U.S. 715, 738 (2006).

[159] Smiley v. Citibank (South Dakota), 517 U.S. 735, 740 (1996) (upholding regulation issued more than 100 years after statute's enactment).

[160] *Id.* at 742. In other words, the Court presumes "that Congress, when it left ambiguity in a statute meant for implementation by an agency, understood that the ambiguity would be resolved, first and foremost, by the agency.... " *Id.* at 740-41.

[161] Christensen v. Harris County, 529 U.S. 576, 587 (2000).

[162] Skidmore v. Swift & Co., 323 U.S. 134 (1944).

[163] Christensen v. Harris County, 529 U.S. at 587.

[164] *Skidmore v. Swift & Co.*, 323 U.S. at 140.



 

applied technical expertise on a complex matter with agency jurisdiction,[165] whether an agency's decision was well-reasoned,[166] and whether the agency's interpretation was longstanding or consistent.[167] It should be emphasized that, far from being superseded by *Chevron*, the Court continues to consider agency interpretations under *Skidmore*-like analyses with some frequency.[168]

## Repeals by Implication

If Congress intends one statute to repeal an earlier statute or section of a statute *in toto*, it usually says so directly in the repealing act. There are other occasions when Congress intends one statute to supersede an earlier statute to the extent of conflict, but intends the earlier statute to remain in effect for other purposes. This too is often spelled out, usually in a section captioned "effect on existing law," "construction with other laws," or the like. "[It] can be strongly presumed that Congress will specifically address language on the statute books that it wishes to change."[169]

Not infrequently, however, conflicts arise between the operation of two federal statutes that are silent as to their relationship. In such a case, courts will try to harmonize the two so that both can be given effect. A court "must read [two allegedly conflicting] statutes to give effect to each if [it] can do so while preserving their sense and purpose."[170] Only if provisions of two different federal statutes are "irreconcilably conflicting,"[171] or "if the later act covers the whole subject of the earlier one and is clearly intended as a substitute,"[172] will courts apply the rule that the later of the two prevails. "[R]epeals by implication are not favored, ... and will not be found unless an intent to repeal is clear and manifest."[173] And in fact, the Court rarely finds repeal by implication.[174] As

[165] *See, e.g.*, Aluminum Co. v. Central Lincoln Util. Dist., 467 U.S. 380, 390 (1984).

[166] *See, e.g.*, Investment Co. Inst. v. Camp, 401 U.S. 617, 626-27 (1971).

[167] *See, e.g.*, General Electric Co. v. Gilbert, 429 U.S. 125, 142-43 (1976).

[168] WILLIAM N. ESKRIDGE, JR., PHILLIP P. FRICKEY & ELIZABETH GARRETT, CASES & MATERIALS ON LEGISLATION: STATUTES & THE CREATION OF PUBLIC Policy at 1225 (4th ed. 2007).

[169] United States v. Fausto, 484 U.S. 439, 453 (1988).

[170] Watt v. Alaska, 451 U.S. 259, 267 (1981). *See also* Lewis v. Lewis & Clark Marine, Inc., 531 U.S. 438 (2001) (reconciling "tension" between the saving to suitors clause and the Limitation of Liability Act); Ruckelshaus v. Monsanto Co., 467 U.S. 986, 1017-18 (1984) (rejecting a contention that the Federal Insecticide, Fungicide, and Rodenticide Act repealed by implication a Tucker Act remedy for governmental taking of property without just compensation, and reconciling the two statutes by implying a requirement that remedies under FIFRA must be exhausted before relief under the Tucker Act could be obtained). *But see* Stewart v. Smith, 673 F.2d 485, 492 (D.C. Cir. 1982) (interpreting a statute authorizing agency heads to set maximum age limits for law enforcement officers as an exception to the Age Discrimination in Employment Act). Even though the laws might have been harmonized through a "strained reading," the court concluded that doing so would thwart the maximum age law's sense and purpose. The *Stewart* court relied on legislative history to find a "clear" congressional intent "to employ maximum entry ages as a means towards securing a 'young and vigorous' work force of law enforcement officers," and concluded that furtherance of this policy required "consideration of factors not ordinarily accounted for" under ADEA procedures.

[171] *Watt v. Alaska*, at 266. For an example of securities law being held to preclude enforcement of antitrust law, see *Credit Suisse Securities (USA) LLC v. Billing*. No. 05-1157, slip op. (U.S. Jun. 18, 2007).

[172] Posadas v. National City Bank, 296 U.S. 497, 503 (1936).

[173] Rodriguez v. United States, 480 U.S. 522, 524 (1987) (citations omitted). *See also* Morton v. Mancari, 417 U.S. 535, 550-51 (1974).

[174] For an instance in which the Court arguably found repeal by implication, see Argentine Republic v. Amerada Hess Shipping Corp., 488 U.S. 428, 438 (1989) (concluding that Congress had intended to "deal comprehensively with the subject of foreign sovereign immunity in the [Foreign Sovereign Immunities Act of 1976]," and that consequently suit against the Argentine Republic could not be brought under the Alien Tort Statute). *But see* Branch v. Smith, 538 U.S. (continued...)



 

Judge Posner has pointed out, this canon is "a mixed bag. It protects some old statutes from ... inadvertent destruction, but it threatens to impale new statutes on the concealed stakes planted by old ones."[175]

### Laws of the Same Session

The presumption against implied repeals "is all the stronger" if both laws were passed by the same session of Congress.[176] But, in the case of an irreconcilable conflict between two laws of the same session, the later enactment will be deemed to have repealed the earlier one to the extent of the conflict.[177] Because the focus here is on legislative intent (or presumed legislative intent), time of legislative consideration, rather than effective dates of the statutes, is the key to determining which enactment was the "later" one.[178]

### Appropriations Laws

The doctrine disfavoring repeals by implication also "applies with even *greater* force when the claimed repeal rests solely on an Appropriations Act," since it is presumed that appropriations laws do not normally change substantive law.[179] Nevertheless, Congress can repeal substantive law through appropriations measures if intent to do so is clearly expressed.[180]

## Rule of Lenity

The "rule of lenity" requires that "before a man can be punished as a criminal ... his case must be plainly and unmistakably within the provisions of some statute."[181] Lenity principles "demand resolution of ambiguities in criminal statutes in favor of the defendant."[182] The reasons for the

(...continued)

254, 293 (2003), in which Justice O'Connor asserted that the Court last found a repeal by implication in 1975, in Gordon v. New York Stock Exchange, 422 U.S. 659 (antitrust laws impliedly repealed (in part) by Securities Exchange Act). Other cases refusing to find a repeal by implication include *Hamdan v. Rumsfeld* (548 U.S. 557, 593-94 (2006)) and *Granholm v. Heald* (544 U.S. 460, 483 (2005)).

[175] Friedrich v. City of Chicago, 888 F.2d 511, 516 (7th Cir. 1989). Judge Posner describes the assumption on which the canon rests—that Congress surveys and envisions the whole body of law before legislating—as "unrealistic": how could Congress do so, he has questioned, "given the vast expanse of legislation that has never been repealed and the even vaster expanse of judicial and administrative rulings glossing that legislation." In re Doctors' Hospital of Hyde Park, 337 F.3d 951, 960 (7th Cir. 2003). On the plus side, the rule serves the "superior values of harmonizing different statutes and constraining judicial discretion in the interpretation of the laws." Astoria Federal Savings & Loan Ass'n v. Solimino, 501 U.S. 104, 109 (1991).

[176] Pullen v. Morgenthau, 73 F.2d 281 (2d Cir. 1934).

[177] SUTHERLAND, STATUTES AND STATUTORY CONSTRUCTION § 23:18 (Norman J. Singer ed., 6th ed. 2002 rev.).

[178] *Id.*

[179] TVA v. Hill, 437 U.S. 153, 190 (1978) (emphasis added).

[180] United States v. Will, 449 U.S. 200, 222 (1980).

[181] United States v. Gradwell, 243 U.S. 476, 485 (1917).

[182] Hughey v. United States, 495 U.S. 411, 422 (1990). *See also* United States v. Granderson, 511 U.S. 39, 54 (1994) ("In these circumstances—where text, structure, and [legislative] history fail to establish that the Government's position is unambiguously correct—we apply the rule of lenity and resolve the ambiguity in [the defendant's] favor"); Cleveland v. United States, 531 U.S. 12, 25 (2000) (before choosing a "harsher alternative" interpretation of the mail fraud statute, "it is appropriate ... to require that Congress should have spoken in language that is clear and definite").



 

rule are that "'fair warning should be given to the world in language that the common world will understand, of what the law intends to do if a certain line is passed'" and that "'legislatures and not courts should define criminal activity.'"[183] Consequently, the rule "places the weight of inertia upon the party that can best induce Congress to speak more clearly and keeps courts from making criminal law in Congress's stead."[184] If statutory language is unambiguous,[185] the rule of lenity is inapplicable.[186]

## Scienter

Intent is generally a required element of a criminal offense, and consequently there is a presumption in favor of a scienter or *mens rea* requirement in a criminal statute. The presumption applies "to each of the statutory elements which criminalize otherwise innocent conduct."[187] The Court may read an express scienter requirement more broadly than syntax would require or normally permit,[188] and may read into a criminal prohibition a scienter requirement that is not expressed.[189] The Court recognizes some "strict liability" exceptions, especially for "public welfare" statutes regulating conduct that is inherently harmful or injurious and that is therefore unlikely to be perceived as lawful and innocent.[190] Determining whether such an exception

[183] Ratzlaf v. United States, 510 U.S. 135, 148-49 (1994) (quoting Boyle v. United States, 283 U.S. 25, 27 (1931) (Justice Holmes for Court)).

[184] United States v. Santos, No. 06-1005, slip op. at 6 (June 2, 2008) (Scalia, J., plurality opinion).

[185] The judicial quest to discern whether a penal statute is sufficiently clear can at times appear abstruse in itself. *Compare, e.g.,* the 4-Justice plurality opinion and the 4-Justice dissent in *United States v. Santos*. No. 06-1005, slip ops. (June 2, 2008).

[186] Beecham v. United States, 511 U.S. 368, 374 (1994) (quoting Chapman v. United States, 500 U.S. 453, 463-64 (1991)). *Accord*, National Org. for Women v. Scheidler, 510 U.S. 249, 262 (1994). *See also* United States v. Hayes, No. 07-608, slip op. at 12-13 (U.S. Feb. 24, 2009).

In *Muscarello v. United States*, a 5-Justice majority eschewed application of the rule of lenity and found that a mandatory sentence for carrying a weapon during a drug crime included having a firearm in a locked glove box or in the trunk of a car while transporting drugs for sale: "The simple existence of some statutory ambiguity ... is not sufficient to warrant application of [the rule of lenity], for most statutes are ambiguous to some degree.... To invoke the rule, we must conclude that there is a 'grievous ambiguity or uncertainty'.... [T]his Court has never held that the rule of lenity automatically permits a defendant to win." 524 U.S. 125, 138-39 (1998). Consider as well the 4-Justice dissent in *United States v. Santos*: "[T]he rule of lenity does not require us to put aside the usual tools of statutory interpretation or to adopt the narrowest possible dictionary definition of the terms in a criminal statute." No. 06-1005, slip op. at 19 (June 2, 2008) (Alito, J., dissenting).

[187] United States v. X-Citement Video, Inc., 513 U.S. 64, 72 (1994). *See also* Flores-Figueroa v. United States, No. 08-108, slip op. (U.S. May 4, 2009).

[188] "Our reluctance to simply follow the most grammatical reading of the statute is heightened by our cases interpreting criminal statutes to include broadly applicable scienter requirements, even where the statute by its terms does not contain them." *X-Citement Video*, 513 U.S. at 70. *See also* Staples v. United States, 511 U.S. 600 (1994) (National Firearms Act interpreted to require that defendant knew that the weapon he possessed was a "firearm" subject to the act's registration requirements); and Liparota v. United States, 471 U.S. 419 (1985) ("knowingly" read as modifying not only operative verbs "uses ... or possesses," but also "in a manner not authorized").

[189] Posters 'N' Things, Ltd. v. United States, 511 U.S. 513 (1994) (interpreting drug paraphernalia law as requiring that merchant knew that customers in general are likely to use the merchandise with drugs). On reading a *mens* rea requirement into a statute, Justice Scalia has stated that "[i]t is one thing to infer the common-law tradition of a *mens rea* requirement where Congress has not addressed the mental element of a crime. It is something else to expand a *mens rea* requirement that the statutory text has carefully limited." Flores-Figueroa v. United States, No. 08-108, slip op. at 2 (U.S. May 4, 2009) (Scalia, J., concurring) (internal citations omitted).

[190] *See, e.g.*, United States v. Dotterweich, 320 U.S. 277 (1943) (upholding punishment of corporate officer whose company shipped misbranded and adulterated drugs in violation of Food and Drug laws); United States v. Freed, 401 U.S. 601 (1971) (upholding conviction under National Firearms Act for possession of unregistered hand grenades; Act (continued...)



 

applies can be difficult.[191] However, if the statute does not preclude a holding that scienter is required, and if the public welfare exception is deemed inapplicable, "far more than the simple omission of the appropriate phrase from the statutory definition is necessary to justify dispensing with an intent requirement."[192] On the other hand, while "it is fair to begin with a general presumption that the specified *mens rea* applies to all elements of an offense, ... it must be recognized that there are instances in which context may well rebut that presumption."[193]

## Remedial Statutes

One can search in vain for recent Supreme Court reliance on the canon that "remedial statutes" should be "liberally" or "broadly" construed.[194] This is probably due to a variety of factors, including recognition that the principle is difficult to apply and almost hopelessly general.[195] This is because many statutes are arguably "remedial," and consequently courts have wide discretion in determining scope of application. There may also be uncertainty over what "liberal" or "broad" construction means.[196] But if the principle is reformulated as merely requiring that ambiguities in a remedial statute be resolved in favor of persons for whose benefit the statute was enacted,[197] the principle should be no more difficult to apply (once a "remedial" statute has been identified) than the rule of lenity, which counsels resolution of ambiguities in penal statutes in favor of defendants.[198] Absence of this principle from the current Court's lexicon, therefore, may reflect substantive preferences of the Justices as well as recognition of its limitations. Then too, the

(...continued)

does not and need not require proof of knowledge that weapons were not registered).

[191] *Compare* United States v. Freed, 401 U.S. 601 (1971) (knowledge of unregistered status of hand grenades not required for conviction under National Firearms Act) *with* Staples v. United States, 511 U.S. 600 (1994) (conviction under the Firearms Act must be predicated on defendant's knowledge of the particular characteristics making a semi-automatic rifle convertible to a machine gun and hence subject to registration requirement). The *Staples* Court distinguished *Freed*, partly on the basis that, given the "long tradition of widespread lawful gun ownership by private individuals in this country," possession of a semi-automatic rifle should not be equated with possession of hand grenades. *See* 511 U.S. at 610-12.

[192] United States v. United States Gypsum Co., 438 U.S. 422, 438 (1978) (applying principle to Sherman Act violation).

[193] Flores-Figueroa v. United States, No. 08-108, slip op. at 2 (U.S. May 4, 2009) (Alito, J., concurring).

[194] For not-so-recent reliance on the canon, see Peyton v. Rowe, 391 U.S. 54, 65 (1968) (petitioner is "in custody" in violation of Constitution for purposes of federal habeas corpus statute if any of consecutive sentences he is scheduled to serve was imposed as a result of deprivation of his rights); Tcherepnin v. Knight, 389 U.S. 332, 336 (1967) (term "security" should be construed broadly, in part because "Securities Exchange Act quite clearly falls into the category of remedial legislation"); and Chisholm v. Georgia, 2 U.S. (2 Dall.) 419, 475 (1793) (opinion of Chief Justice Jay) (Constitution's extension of judicial power over controversies between a state and citizens of another state is "remedial, [and] therefore, to be construed liberally").

[195] The Court once referred to a variant of the canon (a statute should be liberally construed to achieve its purposes) as "that last redoubt of losing causes," explaining that "[e]very statute proposes, not only to achieve certain ends, but also to achieve them by particular means—and there is often a considerable legislative battle over what those means ought to be." Director, OWCP v. Newport News Shipbuilding, 514 U.S. 122, 135-36 (1995).

[196] Justice Scalia has inveighed against the maxim in a lecture reprinted as a law review article, calling it a "prime example[ ] of lego-babble." The rule, Justice Scalia concluded, "is both of indeterminate coverage (since no one knows what a 'remedial statute' is) and of indeterminate effect (since no one knows how liberal is a liberal construction)." Antonin Scalia, *Assorted Canards of Legal Analysis*, 40 CASE W. RES. L. REV. 581, 586 (1989-90).

[197] *See, e.g.*, Smith v. Heckler, 820 F.2d 1093, 1095 (9th Cir. 1987) (Social Security Act "is remedial, to be construed liberally ... and not so as to withhold benefits in marginal cases").

[198] This is not to say, however, that the same fairness considerations that underlie the rule of lenity justify application of the "remedial statute" rule.



 

Court may employ more specific or limited presumptions in circumstances in which earlier Courts might have cited the liberal-remedial maxim,[199] or may instead prefer in such circumstances to analyze a statute without reliance on canonical crutches. Categorizing a statute as "remedial," or even as a "civil rights statute," is often employed as a springboard to more refined analysis of the purposes of the particular statute at issue.[200]

### Statutes Benefitting Indian Tribes

Another subcategory of the "remedial" statutes canon is the proposition that "statutes passed for the benefit of dependent Indian tribes ... are to be liberally construed to favor Indians."[201] Most cases resolving issues relating to tribal matters implicate some variation of this proposition,[202] but frequently there are also statute-specific considerations that amplify[203] or outweigh[204] any such generalities. One recent statutory construction case did not mention an interpretive canon to favor Indians in disallowing a protective measure taken by the Secretary of the Interior to benefit a tribe.[205]

## Miscellany

### Titles of Acts or Sections

Although "it has long been established that the title of an Act 'cannot enlarge or confer powers,'"[206] the title of a statute or section "can aid in resolving an ambiguity in the legislation's

[199] *See, e.g.*, King v. St. Vincent's Hosp., 502 U.S. 215, 220 n.9 (1991) ("provisions for benefits to members of the Armed Services are to be construed in the beneficiaries' favor"); FDIC v. Meyer, 510 U.S. 471, 480 (1994) ("sue-and-be-sued" waivers of sovereign immunity should be liberally construed).

[200] *See, e.g.*, Felder v. Casey, 487 U.S. 131, 149 (1988) ("the Congress which enacted [42 U.S.C.] § 1983 over 100 years ago would have rejected [a requirement of exhaustion of state remedies] as inconsistent with the remedial purposes of its broad statute"); Sullivan v. Little Hunting Park, 396 U.S. 229, 237 (1969) ("A narrow construction of § 1982 would be inconsistent with the broad and sweeping nature of the protection meant to be afforded by § 1 of the Civil Rights Act of 1866"); Northeast Marine Terminal v. Caputo, 432 U.S. 249, 268 (1977) ("The language of the 1972 Amendments [to the LHWCA] is broad and suggests that we should take an expansive view of the extended coverage. Indeed such a construction is appropriate for this remedial legislation.").

[201] Bryan v. Itasca County, 426 U.S. 373, 392 (1976) (quoting Alaska Pacific Fisheries v. United States, 248 U.S. 78, 89 (1918)). An even less restrictive statement is the following: "statutes are to be construed liberally in favor of the Indians, with ambiguous provisions interpreted to their benefit." Montana v. Blackfeet Tribe, 471 U.S. 759, 766 (1985).

[202] *See, e.g.*, Washington v. Confederated Tribes, 447 U.S. 134, 154 (1980) (tribal sovereignty is subordinate only to the federal government, not to the states); Bryan v. Itasca County, 426 U.S. 373, 393 (1976) (states may tax reservation Indians only if Congress has indicated its consent); Hagen v. Utah, 510 U.S. 399, 411-12 (1994) (mild presumption against statutory diminishment of reservation land).

[203] *See, e.g.*, California v. Cabazon Band of Mission Indians, 480 U.S. 202, 214-22 (1987) (federal policy promoting tribal self-government and self-sufficiency, reflected in numerous statutes, is frustrated by state and county restrictions on operation of bingo and card games, profits from which were Tribes' sole source of income).

[204] *See, e.g.*, Negonsott v. Samuels, 507 U.S. 99, 110 (1993) (fact that Kansas Act unambiguously confers jurisdiction on Kansas courts over crimes on reservations makes resort to canon inappropriate).

[205] Carcieri v. Salazar, No. 07-526, slip op. (U.S. Feb. 24, 2009). Justice Stevens observes the failure of the Court to take this remedial canon into account in his dissent. Carcieri v. Salazar, No. 07-526, slip op. at 13-14 (U.S. Feb. 24, 2009) (Stevens, J., dissenting).

[206] Pennhurst State Sch. & Hosp. v. Halderman, 451 U.S. 1, 19 n.14 (1981) (quoting United States v. Oregon & California R.R., 164 U.S. 526, 541 (1896) and Cornell v. Coyne, 192 U.S. 418, 430 (1904), and citing United States v. (continued...)



 

text."[207] As Chief Justice Marshall explained, "[w]here the mind labours to discover the design of the legislature, it seizes everything from which aid can be derived."[208] A title or heading, however, being only "a short-hand reference to the general subject matter involved" and "not meant to take the place of the detailed provisions of the text,"[209] can provide only limited interpretive aid. Thus, a heading may shed light on the section's basic thrust,[210] or on ambiguous language in the text, but it "cannot limit the plain meaning of the text,"[211] and "has no power to give what the text of the statute takes away."[212]

## Preambles ("Whereas Clauses")

Preambles, or "whereas clauses," precede the enacted language, have no "operative effect,"[213] "are not part of the act," and consequently "cannot enlarge or confer powers, nor control the words of the act, unless they are doubtful or ambiguous."[214] Nonetheless, "whereas clauses" sometimes serve the same purpose as findings and purposes sections, and can provide useful insight into congressional concerns and objectives.[215] Preambles can sometimes help resolve ambiguity in enacted language.[216]

## Findings and Purposes Sections

To apply the principle that statutory language be interpreted consistent with congressional intent, courts may consult the stated purposes of legislation to resolve ambiguities in the more specific language of operative sections. For example, the Court relied in part on the stated purpose of the Racketeer Influenced and Corrupt Organizations (RICO) statute to seek "the eradication of organized crime in the United States," to conclude that the term "enterprise" as used in the act includes criminal conspiracies organized for illegitimate purposes, and is not limited to legitimate

(...continued)

Fisher, 2 Cranch 358, 386 (1805) and Yazoo & Mississippi Valley R.R. v. Thomas, 132 U.S. 174, 188 (1889)).

207 INS v. National Center for Immigrants' Rights, 502 U.S. 183, 189-90 (1991) (citing Mead Corp. v. Tilley, 490 U.S. 714, 723 (1989); and FTC v. Mandel Bros., Inc., 359 U.S. 385, 388-89 (1959)).

208 United States v. Fisher, 6 U.S. (2 Cranch) 358, 386 (1805).

209 Trainmen v. Baltimore & Ohio R.R., 331 U.S. 519, 528 (1947).

210 *See, e.g.*, Almendarez-Torres v. United States, 523 U.S. 224, 234 (1998) (words "criminal penalties" in section heading relied on as one indication that the section does not define a separate crime, but instead sets out penalties for recidivists); INS v. National Center for Immigrants' Rights, 502 U.S. 183, 189 (1991) ("text's generic reference to 'employment' should be read as a reference to the 'unauthorized employment' identified in the paragraph's title").

211 Trainmen v. Baltimore & Ohio R.R., 331 U.S. 519, 529 (1947); Intel Corp. v. Advanced Micro Devices, Inc., 542 U.S. 241, 256 (2004) (quoting *Trainmen*).

212 Demore v. Kim, 538 U.S. 510, 535 (2003) (O'Connor, J., concurring) (citing INS v. St. Cyr, 533 U.S. 289, 308-09 (2001)).

213 Hawaii v. Office of Hawaiian Affairs, No. 07-1372, slip op. at 10 (U.S. Mar. 31, 2009) (quoting District of Columbia v. Heller, No. 07-290, slip op. at 4 n.3 (U.S. Jun. 26, 2008)).

214 Yazoo and Mississippi Valley R.R. v. Thomas, 132 U.S. 174, 188 (1889).

215 *See, e.g.*, Donovan v. Dewey, 452 U.S. 594, 602 n.7 (1981) (citing the preamble to the Mine Safety and Health Act as evidence of congressional awareness of the hazardous nature of the mining industry); Gray v. Powell, 314 U.S. 402, 418 (Justice Roberts, dissenting) (citing the preamble of the Bituminous Coal Act as evidence of congressional purpose).

216 "[T]he preamble may be referred to in order to assist in ascertaining the intent and meaning of a statute fairly susceptible of different constructions." Price v. Forrest, 173 U.S. 410, 427 (1899).



 

businesses that are infiltrated by organized crime.[217] The Court also cited legislative findings in the Americans with Disabilities Act in determining the scope of the act's coverage: By finding that "some 43 million Americans" suffered from one or more physical or mental disabilities, Congress indicated that the ADA was not meant to cover all individuals with uncorrected, but correctable, infirmities (*e.g.*, severe myopia).[218]

It is easy, however, to place too much reliance on general statutory purposes in resolving narrow issues of statutory interpretation. Legislation seldom if ever authorizes each and every means that can be said to further a general purpose,[219] and there is also the possibility that stated or inferred purposes may in some instances conflict with one another.[220]

## "Sense of Congress" Provisions

"Sense of Congress" language is appropriate if Congress wishes to make a statement without making enforceable law. Ordinarily, a statement that it is the "sense of Congress" that something "should" be done is merely precatory, and creates no legal rights.[221] In the appropriate context "sense of Congress" language can have the same effect as statements of congressional purpose—that of resolving ambiguities in more specific language of operative sections of a law—but if that is the intent the more straightforward approach is to declare a "purpose" rather than a "sense."[222]

## Savings Clauses

Savings (or "saving") clauses are designed to preserve remedies under existing law. "The purpose of a savings clause is merely to nix an inference that the statute in which it appears is intended to

[217] United States v. Turkette, 452 U.S. 576, 588-90 (1981) (relying on RICO statement of findings and purpose, 18 U.S.C. § 1961 nt.). *See also* Knebel v. Hein, 429 U.S. 288, 292 n.9 (1977) (rejecting, in view of Secretary of Agriculture's broad discretion to administer the Food Stamp Program, and in view of broad purpose of Act to "increase [households'] food purchasing power" (7 U.S.C. § 2011), a holding that the Secretary lacked authority to determine that receipt of commuting expenses to attend a training program should be counted as household "income" determining eligibility for food stamps).

[218] Sutton v. United Airlines, Inc., 527 U.S. 471, 484-86 (1999) (holding that sisters denied jobs as pilots because of poor, but correctable, eyesight did not suffer from a "disability" under the ADA).

[219] "[N]o legislation pursues its purposes at all costs. Deciding what competing values will or will not be sacrificed to the achievement of a particular objective is the very essence of legislative choice—and it frustrates rather than effectuates legislative intent simplistically to assume that *whatever* furthers the statute's primary objective must be the law." Rodriguez v. United States, 480 U.S. 522, 525-26 (1987) (*per curiam*) (emphasis in original).

[220] *Compare* Justice Brennan's opinion of the Court in Mississippi Band of Choctaw Indians v. Holyfield, 490 U.S. 30, 50-51 (1989) (Congress used undefined term "domicile" so as to protect tribal jurisdiction in child custody cases), *with* Justice Stevens' dissent, *id.* at 54 (Congress intended to protect the parents as well as the tribe).

[221] Monahan v. Dorchester Counseling Ctr., Inc., 961 F.2d 987, 994-95 (1st Cir. 1992) ("sense of Congress" that each state "should" review and revise its laws to ensure services for mental health patients); Yang v. California Dep't of Social Services, 183 F.3d 953, 958-61 (9th Cir. 1999) ("sense of Congress" that Hmong and other Lao refugees who fought in Vietnam war "should" be considered veterans for purposes of receiving certain welfare benefits).

[222] *See* Accardi v. Pennsylvania R.R., 383 U.S. 225, 229 (1966) ("sense of Congress" that reemployed veterans should not lose seniority as a result of military service evidenced "continuing purpose" already established by existing law); State Highway Comm'n v. Volpe, 479 F.2d 1099, 1116 (8th Cir. 1973) ("sense of Congress" language "can be useful in resolving ambiguities in statutory construction," and in reinforcing the meaning of earlier law).



 

be the exclusive remedy for harms caused by the violation of the statute."[223] A corollary is that a savings clause typically does not create a cause of action.[224]

Inclusion of a savings clause, however, does not make all pre-existing remedies compatible with the newly enacted law. If there is a conflict, the savings clause gives way.[225] Courts will attempt to give the savings language some effect, but may have to narrow that effect to avoid eviscerating the new law. A reference to specific remedies to be preserved can ease interpretation.[226] In some cases, the legislative history of the savings provision can reveal its purpose.[227] In other cases courts must reason from the scope and purpose of the new statute. For example, when the Carmack Amendment to the Interstate Commerce Act imposed comprehensive federal regulation governing the liability of interstate carriers, the Court held that savings language preserving "any remedy or right of action ... under existing law" applied only to federal, not state remedies. To allow resort to state law remedies that were inconsistent with the federal regulation would negate the Amendment's effect. "[T]he act cannot be said to destroy itself," the Court concluded.[228] Even very clear savings language will not be allowed to thwart what the Court views as the objective of the federal enactment.[229]

## "Notwithstanding Any Other Provision of Law"

Congress sometimes seeks to underscore the primacy of a statutory directive by stating that it is to apply "notwithstanding" the provisions of another, specified statute or class of statutes. Courts

---

[223] PMC, Inc. v. Sherwin-Williams Co., 151 F.3d 610, 618 (7th Cir. 1998).

[224] The "sole function" of a saving clause in CERCLA, the Superfund law, is to clarify that the provision authorizing a limited right of contribution "does nothing to 'diminish' any cause(s) of action for contribution that may exist independently.... " Cooper Industries v. Aviall Servs., 543 U.S. 157, 165-68 (2004).

[225] Even if there is no conflict, courts may construe a savings clause narrowly. *See, e.g.*, City of Rancho Palos Verdes v. Abrams, 544 U.S. 113, 125 (2005) (relief is not available under 42 U.S.C. § 1983 as an alternative to a new statutory cause of action to enforce a new statutory right; a savings clause providing that the amendments do not "impair" existing law has "no effect" on the availability of section 1983 actions because no such relief was available prior to creation of the new right).

[226] *See, e.g.*, 30 U.S.C. § 189, which provides that nothing in the Mineral Leasing Act shall be construed to affect the rights of state and local governments to levy and collect taxes on improvements and "output of mines." The Supreme Court relied on this language in holding that states may impose severance taxes on coal extracted from federal lands. Commonwealth Edison Co. v. Montana, 453 U.S. 609, 631-33 (1981).

[227] *See, e.g.*, Merrill, Lynch, Pierce, Fenner, & Smith v. Curran, 456 U.S. 353, 386-87 (1982) ("saving clause" stating that an amendment to the Commodity Exchange Act was not intended to "supersede or limit the jurisdiction" of state or federal courts, placed in the bill to alleviate fears that the new remedies would be deemed exclusive, was an indication of congressional intent not to eliminate an implied private right of action under the act).

[228] Adams Express Co. v. Croninger, 226 U.S. 491, 507 (1913). *Accord*, AT&T v. Central Office Tel., Inc., 524 U.S. 214, 227 (1998). In City of Milwaukee v. Illinois, 451 U.S. 304, 328-29 (1981), the Court held that the Federal Water Pollution Control Act of 1972 created a comprehensive regulatory program that eliminated previously available federal common law remedies. Savings language in the citizen suit section providing that "nothing in this section shall restrict any right which any person ... may have under ... common law" was irrelevant, since it was the act's standards-setting and permitting provisions, not the citizen suit section, that ousted federal common law.

[229] *See, e.g.*, Geier v. American Honda Motor Co., 529 U.S. 861 (2000) (state common law negligence action against auto manufacturer is preempted by a federal motor vehicle safety standard in spite of statute's savings clause providing that "compliance with" a safety standard "does not exempt any person from any liability under common law"). *But see* Sprietsma v. Mercury Marine, 537 U.S. 51, 63 (2003) (finding no such conflict preemption, and concluding that the Federal Boat Safety Act's savings clause, providing that compliance with federal standards "does not relieve a person from liability at common law," "buttresses" the conclusion that the act's preemption language does not encompass common-law claims).



 

take into account this expressed intent to override the provisions specified in a "notwithstanding" clause,[230] but when the clause purports to override "any other provision of law," its preclusive scope often is unclear. One court, for example, ruled that a directive to proceed with timber sale contracts "notwithstanding any other provision of law" meant only "notwithstanding any provision of *environmental* law," and did not relieve the Forest Service from complying with federal contracting law requirements governing such matters as non-discrimination, small business set-asides, and export restrictions.[231] "We have repeatedly held that the phrase 'notwithstanding any other law' is not always construed literally ... and does not require the agency to disregard all otherwise applicable laws."[232] Still, there are cases that have given full measure to "any other provision of law."[233] As a rule, though, it might be more effective to spell out which other laws are to be disregarded,[234] and it must be kept in mind, of course, that no "notwithstanding" clause can foreclose subsequent legislation that supersedes it expressly or implicitly.

---

[230] For example, several cases have given effect to the provision of the Mandatory Victims Restitution Act that states a restitution order can be enforced against any property of the person fined under the order, "[n]otwithstanding any other Federal law." *E.g.*, United States v. Hyde, 497 F.3d 103 (1st Cir. 2007) (superseding bankruptcy law); United States v. Novak, 476 F.3d 1041 (2007) (superseding ERISA).

[231] Oregon Natural Resources Council v. Thomas, 92 F.3d 792 (9th Cir. 1996). The court harmonized the "notwithstanding" phrase with other provisions of the act that pointed to the limiting construction.

[232] *Id.* at 796. The Three-Sisters Bridge saga offers another example. After a court decision had ordered a halt to construction of the bridge pending compliance with various requirements in D.C. law for public hearings, etc., the project was abandoned. Congress then directed that construction proceed on the bridge project and related highway projects "notwithstanding any other provision of law, or any court decision or administrative action to the contrary." The same section, however, directed that "such construction ... shall be carried out in accordance with all applicable provisions of title 23 of the United States Code." The federal appeals court held that, notwithstanding the "notwithstanding" language, compliance with federal highway law in title 23 (including requirements for an evidentiary hearing, and for a finding of no feasible and prudent alternative to use of parkland) was still mandated. D.C. Fed'n of Civic Ass'ns v. Volpe, 434 F.2d 436 (D.C. Cir. 1970). Then, following remand, the same court ruled that compliance with 16 U.S.C. § 470f, which requires consultation and consideration of effects of such federally funded projects on historic sites, was also still mandated. 459 F. 2d 1231, 1265 (1972).

[233] *See, e.g.*, Schneider v. United States, 27 F.3d 1327, 1331 (8th Cir. 1994). The court there rejected an argument that language in the Military Claims Act ("[n]otwithstanding any other provision of law, the settlement of a claim under section 2733 ... of this title is final and conclusive") does not preclude judicial review, but merely cuts off other administrative remedies. Noting different possible interpretations of "final," "final and conclusive," and the provision's actual language, the court concluded that "[t]o interpret the section as precluding only further administrative review would be to render meaningless the phrase 'notwithstanding any other provision of law.'"

[234] To be sure, not every potential roadblock can be anticipated and averted by narrowly tailored language, and broad language may be necessary to ensure that statutory purposes are not frustrated. But, in spite of the interpretation in *Schneider*, the "notwithstanding" phrase is a blunt instrument. The Trans-Alaska Pipeline Authorization Act may be a better model for such situations. That act directed that the Pipeline "be constructed promptly without further administrative or judicial delay or impediment," specified that construction was to proceed generally in accordance with plans set forth in the already-prepared Final Environmental Impact Statement, declared that no further action was to be required under the National Environmental Policy Act, specified which subsections of the law governing rights-of-way across federal land (a law that had been relied upon in earlier litigation to enjoin the project) were to apply, and severely limited judicial review. *See* 43 U.S.C. § 1652. For a less complete identification of laws to be disregarded, and some concomitant interpretational problems, see Norfolk & Western Ry. v. Train Dispatchers, 499 U.S. 117, 138-39 (1991) (two dissenting Justices disputed the Court's conclusion that the exemption of a carrier in a rail consolidation from "the antitrust laws and all other law, including State and municipal law," comprehended an exemption from the terms of a collective bargaining agreement).



 

## Implied Private Right of Action

From time to time courts have held that a federal statute that does not explicitly create a private cause of action nonetheless *implicitly* creates one.[235] This notion traces to the old view that every right must have a remedy.[236] As the Supreme Court put it in an early implication case, where "disregard of the command of a statute ... results in damage to one of the class for whose especial benefit the statute was enacted, the right to recover damages from the party in default is implied."[237]

The Court has gradually retreated from that position,[238] and now is willing to find an implied private right of action only if it concludes that Congress intended to create one. This raises an obvious question: if Congress intended to create a cause of action, why did it not do so explicitly?[239] While the Court has attempted to explain that it does not mean *actual* intent,[240] the test now seems weighted against finding an implied private cause of action.[241] The Court appears particularly reluctant to find that a violation of a condition placed on funding (*e.g.*, barring education funds to schools that do not require consent for release of student records) gives rise to a private remedy.[242]

---

[235] What is usually at issue in these cases is whether a federal statute creates a right in a private individual to sue another private entity. Persons alleging that federal statutory rights have been violated by state or local governmental action may be able to sue state officials under 42 U.S.C. § 1983.

[236] Marbury v. Madison, 5 U.S. (1 Cranch) 163 (1803) (citing Blackstone's Commentaries).

[237] Texas & Pacific Ry. v. Rigsby, 241 U.S. 39-40 (1916).

[238] *See, e.g.*, Cort v. Ash, 422 U.S. 66 (1975) (creating a four-part test to determine whether a private right of action was implied, one part of which was congressional intent); and Touche Ross & Co. v. Redington, 442 U.S. 560, 575 (1979) (calling congressional intent the "central inquiry").

[239] There may be plausible answers for some older statutes. Congress may have enacted the law at a time when the old rule held sway favoring remedies for statutory rights, or Congress may have patterned the language after language in another law that had been interpreted as creating a private right of action. *See, e.g.*, Cannon v. University of Chicago, 441 U.S. 677, 710-11 (1979) (Congress patterned Title IX of the Civil Rights Act after Title VI, and believed that Title VI was enforceable by private action).

[240] "Our focus on congressional intent does not mean that we require evidence that Members of Congress, in enacting the statute, actually had in mind the creation of a private right of action. The implied cause of action doctrine would be a virtual dead letter were it limited to correcting drafting error when Congress simply forgot to codify its evident intention.... " This "intention," the Court went on, "can be inferred from the language of the statute, the statutory structure, or some other source." Thompson v. Thompson, 484 U.S. 174, 179 (1988). Concurring in the same case, Justice Scalia found himself "at a loss to imagine what congressional intent to create a private right of action might mean, if it does not mean that Congress had in mind the creation of a private right of action." *Id.* at 188. Justice Scalia instead advocated "[a] flat rule that private rights of action will not be implied in statutes hereafter enacted," explaining that "[a] legislative act so significant, and so separable from the remainder of the statute, as the creation of a private right of action seems to me so implausibly left to implication that the risk should not be endured." *Id.* at 192.

[241] *See, e.g.*, Alexander v. Sandoval, 532 U.S. 275, 285 (2001) (there is no private right of action to enforce disparate-impact regulations issued under the general regulation-issuing authority of section 602 of Title VI of the Civil Rights Act; even though a private right of action does exist to enforce the anti-discrimination prohibition of section 601, the disparate-impact regulations "do not simply apply § 601," but go beyond it). For analysis of the whole topic, including the changing approach by the Court, see Susan J. Stabile, *The Role of Congressional Intent in Determining the Existence of Implied Private Rights of Action*, 71 NOTRE DAME L. REV.. 861 (1996).

[242] *E.g.*, Gonzaga Univ. v. Doe, 536 U.S. 273 (2002) (federal funding provisions provide no right for private recourse under § 1983 absent clear, unambiguous intent to the contrary).



 

## Incorporation by Reference

Interpretational difficulties may also arise if one statute incorporates by reference provisions of an existing statute. A leading treatise declares that incorporations by "general reference" normally include subsequent amendments, but that incorporations by "specific reference" normally do not.[243] A general reference "refers to the law on the subject generally," while a specific reference "refers specifically to a particular statute by its title or section number."[244]

## Severability

When one section of a law is held unconstitutional, courts are faced with determining whether the remainder of the statute remains valid, or whether the whole statute is nullified. "Unless it is evident that the Legislature would not have enacted those provisions which are within its power, independently of that which is not, the invalid part may be dropped if what is left is fully operative as a law."[245] Congress frequently includes a *pro forma* severability clause in a statute,[246] and this may reinforce a "presumption" of severability by removing much of the doubt about congressional intent.[247] A severability clause does not guarantee, however, that what remains of a statute after a portion has been invalidated is "fully operative"; courts sometimes find that valid portions of a statute cannot stand on their own even though Congress has included a severability clause.[248] Far less frequently, Congress includes non-severability language providing that remaining sections of a law shall be null and void if a part (sometimes a specified part) is held unconstitutional.[249] Case law is sparse,[250] but there is no apparent reason why courts should refuse to honor a clearly expressed non-severability directive.[251]

---

[243] 2B SUTHERLAND, STATUTES AND STATUTORY INTERPRETATION, § 51.07 (Norman J. Singer ed., 6th ed. 2000 revision).

[244] *Id.* A clear example of a general incorporation was afforded by § 20 of the Jones Act, providing that in an action for wrongful death of a seaman, "all statutes of the United States conferring or regulating the right of action for death in the case of railway employees shall be applicable." As the Court explained in Panama R.R. Co. v. Johnson, 264 U.S. 375, 391-92 (1924), this "generic reference" was "readily understood" as a reference to the Federal Employer Liability Act and its amendments.

[245] Alaska Airlines, Inc. v. Brock, 480 U.S. 678, 684 (1987) (quoting Buckley v. Valeo, 424 U.S. 1, 108 (1976)).

[246] *See, e.g.*, 2 U.S.C. § 1438 (§ 509 of the Congressional Accountability Act of 1995): "If any provision of this Act or the application of such provision to any person or circumstance is held to be invalid, the remainder of this Act and the application of the provisions of the remainder to any person or circumstance shall not be affected thereby." These provisions are also sometimes called "separability" clauses. *See, e.g.*, 29 U.S.C. § 114.

[247] Alaska Airlines, 480 U.S. at 486. Absence of a severability clause does not raise a presumption *against* severability. New York v. United States, 505 U.S. 144, 186 (1992).

One observer stated the following on the Court and severability: "Despite the unambiguous command of severability and inseverability clauses, the Court has repeatedly held that they create only a rebuttable presumption that guides—but does not control—a reviewing court's severability determination.... [T]he Court has chosen instead to focus on extrinsic evidence of legislative intent and on the potential functionality of the post-severance statutory scheme.... " Michael Shumsky, *Severability, Inseverability, and the Rule of Law*, 41 HARV. J. ON LEGIS. 227, 230 (2004).

[248] "A severability clause requires textual provisions that can be severed." Reno v. ACLU, 521 U.S. 844, 882 (1997). *See also* Hill v. Wallace, 259 U.S. 44 (1922); and Carter v. Carter Coal Co., 298 U.S. 238, 312-16 (1936).

[249] *See, e.g.*, 25 U.S.C. § 941m(a) (§ 15(a) of the Catawba Indian Tribe of South Carolina Land Claims Settlement Act of 1993): "If any provision of section 941b(a), 941c, or 941d of this title is rendered invalid by the final action of a court, then all of this subchapter is invalid."

[250] *But see, e.g.*, Zobel v. Williams, 457 U.S. 55, 65 (1982) (observing in dictum that, due to inclusion of non-severability language in an Alaska law, "we need not speculate as to the intent of the Alaska Legislature").

[251] *See* Israel E. Friedman, Comment, *Inseverability Clauses in Statutes*, 64 U. CHI. L. REV. 903 (1997). Friedman (continued...)



 

## Deadlines for Administrative Action

"If a statute does not specify a consequence for noncompliance with statutory timing provisions, the federal courts will not in the ordinary course impose their own coercive sanction."[252] Absent specified consequences, such deadlines "are at best precatory rather than mandatory,"[253] and are read "as a spur to prompt action, not as a bar to tardy completion."[254] "A statute directing official action needs more than a mandatory 'shall' before the grant of power can sensibly be read to expire when the job is supposed to be done."[255] Thus, agency actions taken after a deadline are ordinarily upheld as valid.[256] Although courts are loath to impose "coercive" sanctions that would defeat the purpose of the underlying agency duty, courts sometimes will lend their authority, backed by the possibility of contempt for recalcitrant agency officials, by ordering compliance with statutory directives after a missed deadline.[257]

# Legislative History

## Plain Meaning Rule

Different schools of statutory interpretation regard text differently. Textualists regard the words embodied in the text of a statute as the "law": "Congress' intent is found in the words it has chosen to use."[258] Intentionalism and related methods are less sanguine about whether statutory language alone can fully and adequately embody the "law" for purposes of applying statutes in individual cases.[259] Yet textualists on occasion recognize the value of extrinsic perspectives, and intentionalists regard statutory language as the analytical starting point and at least strong evidence of what a law intends.

---

(...continued)

contends that "inseverability clauses are fundamentally different from severability clauses and should be shown greater deference." Id. at 904. Inseverability clauses, he points out, "are anything but boilerplate," usually are included only after extensive debate, and are often designed to preserve a legislative compromise. Id. at 911-13.

[252] United States v. James Daniel Good Real Property, 510 U.S. 43, 63 (1993) (failure of customs agent to "report immediately" a customs seizure should not result in dismissal of a forfeiture action).

[253] Liesegang v. Secretary of Veterans Affairs, 312 F.3d 1328, 1377 (Fed. Cir. 2002).

[254] Barnhart v. Peabody Coal Co., 537 U.S. 149, 172 (2003).

[255] Barnhart v. Peabody Coal Co., 537 U.S. at 161.

[256] In *Peabody Coal*, the Court held that a deadline in the Coal Industry Retiree Health Benefit Act for assignment of retired beneficiaries to coal companies did not prevent assignment after the deadline. *See also* United States v. Montalvo-Murillo, 495 U.S. 711 (1990) (failure to comply with the Bail Reform Act's requirement of an "immediate" hearing does not mandate release pending trial); Brock v. Pierce County, 476 U.S. 253 (1986) (Secretary of Labor's failure to comply with the statutory deadline for beginning an investigation about misuse of federal funds does not divest the Secretary of authority to launch a tardy investigation).

[257] *See, e.g.*, NRDC v. Train, 510 F.2d 692 (D.C. Cir. 1975) (setting general guidelines, based on equitable principles, for courts to follow in mandating agency compliance following missed deadlines); Sierra Club v. Thomas, 658 F. Supp. 165 (N.D. Cal. 1987) (using the length of time initially set by Congress as the measure of how much additional time to allow EPA after the agency missed a deadline for promulgating regulations).

[258] Harbison v. Bell, No. 07-8521, slip op. at 3 (U.S. Apr. 1, 2009) (Thomas, J., concurring).

[259] *See, e.g.*, Stephen Breyer, *On the Uses of Legislative History in Interpreting Statutes*, 65 S. CAL. L. REV. 845, 848 (1992) ("Using legislative history to help interpret unclear statutory language seems natural. Legislative history helps a court understand the context and purpose of a statute.").



 

The primacy of text in discerning meaning is expressed in the "plain meaning rule." That rule holds that where the language of a statute is plain, the sole role of the courts is to enforce it according to its terms. In practice, the cases vary in characterizing the rule as mandatory or prudential, and those differences often play out indirectly through arguments about whether particular language is sufficiently clear and unambiguous to preclude further inquiry.

There seems to be general consensus that the plain meaning rule aptly characterizes interpretational priorities (statutory language is primary, other considerations of intent and purpose secondary).[260] However, agreement on the basic meaning of the plain meaning rule—if it occurs—does not guarantee agreement in the rule's application. There have been cases in which Justices of the Supreme Court have agreed that the statutory provision at issue is plain, but have split 5-4 over what that plain meaning is.[261] There are other cases in which strict application is simply ignored; courts, after concluding that the statutory language is plain, nonetheless look to legislative history, either to confirm that plain meaning,[262] or to refute arguments that a contrary interpretation was "intended."[263] The one generally recognized exception to the rule is that a plain meaning is rejected if it would produce an "absurd result."[264] Nevertheless, even in cases of "absurd results" Justices can disagree over whether it is appropriate to consult legislative materials for interpretational insight.[265]

---

[260] Different views on the strictures posed by statutory text are not new. The classic extremes are represented by Caminetti v. United States, 242 U.S. 470 (1917), and Church of the Holy Trinity v. United States, 143 U.S. 457 (1892). In *Caminetti*, the Court applied the plain meaning rule to hold that the Mann Act, or "White Slave Traffic Act," which prohibits transportation of women across state lines for purposes of "prostitution, debauchery, or any other immoral purpose," clearly applies to noncommercial immorality, in spite of legislative history showing that the purpose was to prohibit the commercial "white slave trade." In *Holy Trinity*, the Court held that a church's contract with a foreigner to come to this country to serve as its minister was not covered by a statutory prohibition on inducements for importation of aliens "to perform labor or service of any kind." The Court brushed aside the fact that the statute made no exception for ministers, although it did so for professional actors, artists, lecturers, singers, and domestic servants, and declared the law's purpose to be to prevent importation of cheap *manual* labor. "A thing may be within the letter of the statute and yet not within the statute, because not within its spirit, nor within the intention of its makers," the Court explained. 143 U.S. at 459.

[261] *See, e.g.*, Sedima, S.P.R.L. v. Imrex Co., 473 U.S. 479 (1985) (disagreement over the scope of civil RICO). *See also* Corley v. United States, No. 97-10441, slip op. (U.S. Apr. 6, 2009).

[262] Thunder Basin Coal Co. v. Reich, 510 U.S. 200, 209 (1994) ("The legislative history of the Mine Act confirms this interpretation").

[263] *See* Darby v. Cisneros, 509 U.S. 137, 147 (1993) ("Recourse to the legislative history of § 10(c) is unnecessary in light of the plain meaning of the statutory text. Nevertheless, we consider that history briefly because both sides have spent much of their time arguing about its implications."); Toibb v. Radloff, 501 U.S. 157, 162 (1991) ("even were we to consider the sundry legislative comments urged [upon us] ..., the scant legislative history does not suggest a 'clearly expressed legislative intent [to the] contrary'"); Arcadia v. Ohio Power Co., 498 U.S. 73, 84 n.2 (1990) (rejecting reliance on legislative history said to be "overborne" by the statutory text). The Court has declared that it will not allow a literal reading of the statute to produce a result "demonstrably at odds with the intentions of its drafters," but in the same breath has indicated that it is only "the exceptional case" in which that can occur. Griffin v. Oceanic Contractors, Inc., 458 U.S. 564, 571 (1982).

[264] *See, e.g.*, United States v. Granderson, 511 U.S. 39, 47 n.5 (1994) (dismissing an interpretation said to lead to an absurd result); Dewsnup v. Timm, 502 U.S. 410, 427 (1992) (Justice Scalia, dissenting) ("[i]f possible, we should avoid construing the statute in a way that produces such absurd results"); Public Citizen v. Department of Justice, 491 U.S. 440, 454 (1989) ("[w]here the literal reading of a statutory term would compel 'an odd result,' ... we must search for other evidence of congressional intent to lend the term its proper scope").

[265] Concurring in *Green v. Bock Laundry Machine Co.*, Justice Scalia agreed on the appropriateness of consulting legislative history for the limited purpose of determining whether what appeared to be an absurd meaning of a key statutory term was indeed considered and intended. Beyond this, however, "[t]he meaning of terms on the statute books ought to be determined, not on the basis of which meaning can be shown to have been understood by a larger handful of the Members of Congress; but rather on the basis of which meaning is (1) most in accord with context and ordinary (continued...)



 

The commonest bridge from text to legislative history is a finding that the statutory language is not plain, but instead is unclear or "ambiguous."[266] Significant differences arise, however, in the willingness of courts to label particular statutory language as "ambiguous" and thereby resort to legislative history. Some judges are more confident than others in their ability to interpret statutory text, and some are more convinced than others of the propriety of attempting to do so without resort to the "extrinsic" aid of legislative history.[267] Correspondingly, there are basic differences in approach, from narrow focus on the clarity or ambiguity of the particular statutory phrase at issue, to recognition that phrases that may seem ambiguous in isolation may be clarified by statutory context.[268] And, inevitably, there are real differences in the clarity of statutory language.[269]

## Uses of Legislative History

Over time, the Court has by turns been relatively more receptive or skeptical toward mining the legislative process for insight into a statute's meaning.[270] Statute-making is a collective exercise. Drafters seek to capture a sponsor's intent in words, however imperfectly. Language introduced as legislation is subjected to examination, criticism and revision in diverse congressional fora—large and small, formal and informal—as it moves toward approval—again, by diverse groups with varying degrees of expertise and interest—and eventual enactment into law. Particularly

(...continued)

usage, and thus most likely to have been understood by the *whole* Congress which voted on the words of the statute (not to mention the citizens subject to it, and (2) most compatible with the surrounding body of law into which the provision must be integrated ... I would not permit any of the historical and legislative material discussed by the Court, or all of it combined, to lead me to a different result from the one that these factors suggest." 490 U.S. 504 at 527, 528 (1989) Scalia, J., concurring).

[266] "In aid of the process of construction we are at liberty, if the meaning be uncertain, to have recourse to the legislative history of the measure and the statements by those in charge of it during its consideration by the Congress." United States v. Great Northern Ry., 287 U.S. 144 (1932). On the other hand, "we do not resort to legislative history to cloud a statutory text that is clear." Ratzlaf v. United States, 510 U.S. 135, 147-48 (1994).

[267] "When aid to the construction of the meaning of words, as used in the statute, is available, there certainly can be no 'rule of law' which forbids its use, however clear the words may appear on 'superficial examination.'" United States v. American Trucking Ass'ns, 310 U.S. 534, 543-44 (1940). Justice Frankfurter, dissenting in United States v. Monia, 317 U.S. 424 (1943), made much the same point: "[t]he notion that because the words of a statute are plain, its meaning is also plain, is merely pernicious oversimplification." Justice Scalia explains why he opposes ready resort to legislative history: "Judges interpret laws rather than reconstruct legislators' intentions. Where the language of those laws is clear, we are not free to replace it with an unenacted legislative intent." INS v. Cardoza-Fonseca, 480 U.S. 421, 452-53 (1987) (concurring).

[268] United Savings Ass'n v. Timbers of Inwood Forest Associates, 484 U.S. 365, 371 (1988) ("only one of the permissible meanings [of an ambiguous phrase] produces a substantive effect that is compatible with the rest of the law").

[269] *Compare* United States v. Locke, 471 U.S. 84, 92 (1985) (a requirement that a filing be made "*prior* to December 31" could not be stretched to permit a filing *on* December 31) *with* Davis v. United States, 495 U.S. 472, 479 (1990) (phrase "for the use of"—a phrase which "on its face ... could support any number of different meanings," is narrowed by reference to legislative history). In *Locke* the Court explained that "the plain language of the statute simply cannot sustain the gloss appellees would put on it.... [W]ith respect to filing deadlines a literal reading of Congress' words is generally the only proper reading of those words. To attempt to decide whether some date other than the one set out in the statute is the date actually 'intended' by Congress is to set sail on an aimless journey." 471 U.S. at 93. Despite the evident clarity of this language, three Justices dissented.

[270] *See generally* William N. Eskridge, Jr., Phillip P. Frickey & Elizabeth Garrett, Cases & Materials on Legislation: Statutes & the Creation of Public Policy at 689-798 (4th ed. 2007) (historical survey, with example cases, of theories of interpretation applied by the federal courts and the role of legislative history in them). .



 

since the 1980s, some Court opinions have characterized modern congressional processes as too fractured to admit any statement or explanation made in any step along the way as an authoritative declaration by Congress as a whole (assuming Congress had a discernible "collective understanding" on the matter at issue before the Court in the first place[271]).[272] Adding to this reluctance is the perception of some that the published history may be skewed by the partisanship of committee staff or subject to interest group manipulation.[273]

More recently, some commentators and jurists who look at congressional processes have had a different take. They, too, see complexity and fragmentation in Congress, but argue that one can ascribe an "institutional purpose" to legislation even though the motives of individual legislators may be unknown or unknowable. Under this "busy Congress" model, for example, congressional committees, as specialists in their field, are regarded as reporting accurate accounts of information and insight to their respective chambers so that Members may better consider legislation they have limited knowledge of.[274]

The stuff of legislative history itself potentially comprises a wide variety of materials. On the one hand, a current statute may be compared to its predecessors and differences among their language and structure analyzed. This use is limited to examining language passed by Congress, which, unlike materials attending congressional deliberations, is often thought to best reflect the intent of Congress as a whole. Considering past statutes and their evolution is not a particularly controversial exercise.[275] On the other hand are the committee reports, hearings, floor debates, and other records of deliberations and correspondence on legislation as it moves through the legislative process. One aspect of examining this material can be to compare different versions of a provision as it progresses, a use somewhat like the comparing of statutes to their predecessors, but without each version having been approved by Congress as a whole.

Courts may read contemporaneous congressional materials for many reasons: background information and context, explanations of specific legislative language, or expectations of how a provision will be applied to the particular fact situation before them. Reliance on these materials varies among courts, with the circumstances of a statute's passage and its clarity or complexity being factors. Courts also may be more willing to consult committee reports and the like for insight into the particular problem Congress sought to address than they are to consult language that purports to direct certain interpretations or outcomes. The nature of the issue before a court is another variable that may bear on what materials the court uses and why.[276]

---

[271] *See, e.g.,* Frank H. Easterbrook, *Statutes' Domains*, 50 U. Chi. L. Rev. 533, 547 (1983) ("Because legislatures comprise many members, they do not have "intents" or "designs," hidden yet discoverable. Each member may or may not have a design. The body as a whole, however, has only outcomes.").

[272] *E.g.,* Antonin Scalia, Matter of Interpretation: Federal Courts and the Law 31-34 (1997).

[273] *See, e.g.,* Blanchard v. Bergeron, 489 U.S. 87, 98-99 (1989) (Scalia, J., concurring). The complexity and volume of legislative materials also has been said to make use of legislative history malleable and susceptible of supporting any number of outcomes. As an oft-quoted passage in an article by Judge Patricia Wald stated: "It sometimes seems that citing legislative history is still ... akin to 'looking over a crowd and picking out your friends.'" Patricia Wald, *Observations on the Use of Legislative History in the 1981 Supreme Court Term*, 68 Iowa L. Rev. 195, 214 (1983) (quoting Judge Harold Leventhal).

[274] *See* Stephen Breyer, *On the Uses of Legislative History in Interpreting Statutes*, 65 S. Cal. L. Rev. 845 (1992); *see also* Charles Tiefer, *The Reconceptualization of Legislative History in the Supreme Court*, 2000 Wisc. L. Rev. 205 (2000) (discussing the "Breyer-Stevens" concept of "institutional" legislative history).

[275] *See, e.g.,*Powerex Corp. v. Reliant Energy Services Inc., No. 05-85, slip op. at 6-7 (U.S. June 18, 2007).

[276] James J. Brudney & Corey Ditslear, *The Warp and Woof of Statutory Interpretation: Comparing Supreme Court* (continued...)



 

Among published history, some sources may be considered relatively more authoritative. As a rule, committee report explanations, and especially those of conference committees, are considered more persuasive and reliable than statements made during floor debates or hearings. Within floor debates, statements of sponsors and explanations by floor managers are usually accorded the most weight, and statements by other committee members of the reporting committee[s] next. Floor statements by Members not associated with sponsorship or committee consideration of a bill have little weight, and statements by bill opponents less weight still. Hearings may be useful in providing background, less so as to illuminating the meaning of particular language.

This hierarchy generally characterizes where a court might go to seek to clarify an unclear statute, but several factors might tip the scales in favor of one bit of history or another of a particular bill. Final language might have arisen from a floor amendment, in which case earlier reports and debates may be of interest only as a point of contrast. Similarly, final language might have been added by the second chamber to consider a bill, in which case the history developed in it would be most pertinent, especially absent conference consideration. Also, a court's willingness to delve into the more remote reaches of legislative history can vary with the issue at hand and the point sought to be clarified.

Again, courts may consult explanatory documents to gain a better feel for context or to shed light on particular language. Reference to legislative history for background is commonplace. A "proper construction frequently requires consideration of [a statute's] wording against the background of its legislative history and in the light of the general objectives Congress sought to achieve."[277] Looking to published history to help explain the meaning of statutory terms[278] may be more controversial, either because contrary indications may be present in other passages of legislative history,[279] or because the degree of direction or detail may be an unwarranted narrowing of a more general statutory text.[280] The concern in the latter instances is whether the legislative history is a plausible explanation of language actually contained in the statutory text, or whether instead explanatory language (e.g., report language containing committee directives or "understandings") outpaces that text. As the Court observed in rejecting reliance on "excerpts" said to reflect congressional intent to preempt state law, "we have never [looked for]

(...continued)

*Approaches in Tax Law and Workplace Law*, 58 DUKE L.J. 1231 (2009).

277 Wirtz v. Bottle Blowers Ass'n, 389 U.S. 463, 468 (1968). For examples of reliance on legislative history for guidance on broad congressional purposes, see Shell Oil Co. v. Iowa Dep't of Revenue, 488 U.S. 19, 26 (1988) (purposes of OCSLA, as evidenced in legislative history, confirm a textual reading of the statute and refute the oil company's reading); Wilder v. Virginia Hosp. Ass'n, 496 U.S. 498, 515 (1990) (reference to Senate report for evidence of "the primary objective" of the Boren amendment to the Medicaid law).

278 *See, e.g.*, Reves v. Ernst & Young, 507 U.S. 170, 179-83 (1993) (RICO section proscribing "conduct" of racketeering activity is limited to persons who participate in the operation or management of the enterprise); Gustafson v. Alloyd Co., 513 U.S. 561, 581-82 (1995) (legislative history supports reading of "prospectus" in Securities Act as being limited to initial public offerings); Babbitt v. Sweet Home Chapter, 515 U.S. 687, 704-06 (1995) (relying on committee explanations of word "take" in Endangered Species Act).

279 The dissent in *Babbitt v. Sweet Home* found legislative history that suggested a narrower use of the word "take," reflecting a consistent distinction between habitat conservation measures and restrictions on "taking" of endangered species. 515 U.S. at 726-30 (Justice Scalia).

280 "The language of a statute—particularly language expressly granting an agency broad authority—is not to be regarded as modified by examples set forth in the legislative history." Pension Benefit Guaranty Corp. v. LTV Corp., 496 U.S. 633, 649 (1990).



 

congressional intent in a vacuum, unrelated to the giving of meaning to an enacted statutory text ... [U]nenacted approvals, beliefs, and desires are not laws."[281]

A distinct but related inquiry focuses not on the explanations that accompanied committee or floor consideration, but rather on the sequence of changes in bill language. Consideration of the "specific history of the legislative process that culminated in the [statute at issue] affords ... solid ground for giving it appropriate meaning" and for resolving ambiguity present in statutory text.[282] Selection of one House's version over that of the other House may be significant.[283] In some circumstances rejection of an amendment or earlier version can be important,[284] but there is no general "rejected proposal rule."[285] While courts are naturally reluctant to attribute significance to the failure of Congress to act,[286] that reluctance may be overcome if it can be shown that Congress considered and rejected bill language that would have adopted the very position being urged upon the court.[287]

---

[281] Puerto Rico Dep't of Consumer Affairs v. Isla Petroleum Corp., 485 U.S. 495, 501 (1988). The Court explained further that, "without a text that can, in light of those [legislative history] statements, plausibly be interpreted as prescribing federal pre-emption it is impossible to find that a free market was mandated by federal law." *See also* Secretary of the Interior v. California, 464 U.S. 312, 323 n.9 (1984) (a committee report directive purporting to require coordination with state planning is dismissed as purely "precatory" when the accompanying bill plainly exempted federal activities from such coordination); Shannon v. United States, 512 U.S. 573, 583 (1994) (Court will not give "authoritative weight to a single passage of legislative history that is in no way anchored in the text of the statute"); and Roeder v. Islamic Republic of Iran, 333 F.3d 228, 237-38 (D.C. Cir. 2003) (explanatory statement accompanying conference report purported to explain a previous enactment rather than the current one, and could not operate to abrogate an executive agreement). For what is arguably a departure from the general principle, *see* Wisconsin Project on Nuclear Arms Control v. United States Dep't of Commerce, 317 F.3d 275 (D.C. Cir. 2003) (relying on "congressional intent" relating to a lapsed statute). As dissenting Judge Randolph characterized the majority's approach, "the statute has expired but its legislative history is good law." *Id.* at 285.

[282] United States v. Universal C.I.T. Credit Corp., 344 U.S. 218, 222 (1952). "Statutory history" as well as bill history can also be important. *See, e.g.*, United States v. Wells, 519 U.S. 482, 492-93 (1997) (consolidation of a number of separate provisions supports the "natural reading" of the current law); Booth v. Churner, 532 U.S. 731, 740 (2001) (elimination of "the very term" relied on by the Court in an earlier case suggests that Congress desired to preclude that result in future cases).

[283] *See, e.g.*, United States v. Riverside Bayview Homes, 474 U.S. 121, 136-37 (1985) (attaching significance to the conference committee's choice of the Senate version, retaining the broad definition of "navigable waters" then in current law, over a House version that would have narrowed the definition).

[284] In *Hamdan v. Rumsfeld*, the Court examined three provisions of the Detainee Treatment Act. In two of the provisions, Congress had immediately restricted access to the courts by individuals in certain pending military proceedings, but the third provision did not expressly limit access to the courts by individuals in pending proceedings through petitions for writs of habeas corpus. The Court recounted that Congress had adopted its final language only after having rejected versions that would have immediately curtailed habeas relief in pending cases: "Congress' rejection of the very language that would have achieved the result the Government urges here weighs heavily against the Government's interpretation." 548 U.S. 557, 579-80 (2006).

[285] Compare Justice Scalia's plurality opinion in *Rapanos v. United States*, which saw no significance in Congress's rejection of an amendment to overcome wetlands regulations, to Justice Stevens dissent, which saw such rejection as evidence of acquiescence. 547 U.S. 715, 749-52, 797 (2006). For a leading example of reading acquiesce into an extended history of congressional rejection of regulatory legislation, see FDA v. Brown & Williamson Tobacco Corp., 529 U.S. 120 (2000).

[286] "This Court generally is reluctant to draw inferences from Congress' failure to act. Indeed, those members of Congress who did not support these bills may have been as convinced by testimony that the NGA already provided 'broad and complete ... jurisdiction and control over the issuance of securities' as by arguments that the matter was best left to the States." Schneidewind v. ANR Pipeline Co., 485 U.S. 293, 306 (1988).

[287] Pacific Gas & Elec. Co. v. Energy Resources Conserv. & Dev. Comm'n, 461 U.S. 190, 220 (1983) (noting that language had been deleted to insure that there be no preemption); INS v. Cardoza-Fonseca, 480 U.S. 421, 441-42 (1987) (rejection of Senate language limiting the Attorney General's discretion in granting asylum in favor of House language authorizing grant of asylum to any refugee); Doe v. Chao, 540 U.S. 614, 622 (2004) ("drafting history (continued...)



 

Even more than in the case of legislative language, discussed above, silence in the published legislative history of a bill is seldom significant.[288] There is no requirement that "every permissible application of a statute be expressly referred to in its legislative history."[289] The Court does, however, occasionally attach import to the absence of any indication in a statute or its legislative history of an intent to effect a "major change" in well-established law.[290] And sometimes the Justices disagree over the significance of congressional silence.[291]

## Inferences Based on "Subsequent" Legislative History

Once a statute is enacted, later Congresses may comment on it or choose to revisit it (or not) as circumstances change. Views expressed in the documents or deliberations of a subsequent Congress generally are eschewed.[292] It has been stated in this context that "[t]he legislative history of a statute is the history of its consideration and enactment. 'Subsequent legislative history'—which presumably means the *post*-enactment history of a statute's consideration and enactment—is a contradiction in terms."[293]

(...continued)

show[s] that Congress cut the very language in the bill that would have authorized any presumed damages").

[288] "[A] statute is not to be confined to the 'particular application[s] ... contemplated by the legislators.'" Diamond v. Chakrabarty, 447 U.S. 303, 315 (1980) (ruling that inventions not contemplated when Congress enacted the patent law are still patentable if they fall within the law's general language) (quoting Barr v. United States, 324 U.S. 83, 90 (1945)).

[289] Moskal v. United States, 498 U.S. 103, 111 (1990). *Accord*, Pittston Coal Group v. Sebben, 488 U.S. 105, 115 (1988) ("it is not the law that a statute can have no effects which are not mentioned in its legislative history"); PBGC v. LTV Corp., 496 U.S. 633, 649 (1990) ("the language of a statute—particularly language expressly granting an agency broad authority—is not to be regarded as modified by examples set forth in the legislative history"). *See also* Oncale v. Sundowner Offshore Servs., 523 U.S. 75, 79 (1998) (male-on-male sexual harassment is covered by Title VII although it "was assuredly not the principal evil Congress was concerned with"); and Cook County v. United States ex rel. Chandler, 538 U.S. 119, 128-29 (2003) (local governments are subject to *qui tam* actions under the expansive language of the False Claims Act even though the enacting Congress was primarily concerned with fraud by Civil War contractors).

[290] Edmonds v. Compagnie Generale Transatlantique, 443 U.S. 256, 266-27 (1979) (silence of legislative history "is most eloquent, for such reticence while contemplating an important and controversial change in existing law is unlikely"); United Savings Ass'n v. Timbers of Inwood Forest Assocs., 484 U.S. 365, 380 (1988) (major change "would not likely have been made without specific provision in the text of the statute," and it is "most improbable that it would have been made without even any mention in the legislative history"); Dewsnup v. Timm, 502 U.S. 410, 419 (1992) (Court reluctant to interpret the Bankruptcy Code as effecting "a major change in pre-Code practice that is not the subject of at least some discussion in the legislative history").

[291] *Compare* Justice Stevens' opinion for the Court in Chisom v. Roemer, 501 U.S. 380, 396 n.23 (1991) ("Congress' silence in this regard can be likened to the dog that did not bark") *with* Justice Scalia's dissenting rejoinder, *id.* at 406 ("apart from the questionable wisdom of assuming that dogs will bark when something important is happening, we have forcefully and explicitly rejected the Conan Doyle approach to statutory construction in the past").

[292] Sullivan v. Finkelstein, 496 U.S. 617, 628 n.8 (1990). An extensive, long-running record of hearings and statements across subsequent Congresses may, in combination with other factors, weigh in favor of interpreting a statute narrowly. *See* FDA v. Brown & Williamson Tobacco Corp., 529 U.S. 120, 147-55(2000).

[293] *Id.* at 631 (Justice Scalia, concurring in part).



 

The Court also is wary about reading significance into the actions of a subsequent Congress, having warned that they are "a hazardous basis for inferring the intent of an earlier one.'"[294] To the degree congressional action is considered (as opposed to the statutory language), it is the enacting Congress that is key, and interpretation is ordinarily not affected by the several different kinds of congressional actions and inactions frequently characterized as "post-enactment history." However, depending on context, including intervening developments, what a subsequent Congress does may have interpretational value.

## Subsequent Legislation

If the views of a later Congress are expressed in a duly enacted statute, then the views embodied in that statute must be interpreted and applied. Occasionally a later enactment declares congressional intent about interpretation of an earlier enactment rather than directly amending or clarifying the earlier law. Such action can be given prospective effect because, "however inartistic, it ... stands on its own feet as a valid enactment."[295] "Subsequent legislation declaring the intent of an earlier statute is entitled to great weight in statutory construction."[296] Other statutes may be expressly premised on a particular interpretation of an earlier statute; this interpretation may be given effect, especially if a contrary interpretation would render the amendments pointless or ineffectual.[297]

The Court closely adheres to judicial precedents in interpreting statutes, on the grounds that Congress is free to supersede the Court's interpretation of a particular statute through subsequent legislation. But it may not always be evident exactly how far Congress went in subsequent legislation to sweep aside an earlier construction. For example, when Congress acts narrowly against a result in a Court decision, is it also discrediting the Court's reasoning that led to the result? A female employee who is adversely affected by a discriminatory seniority system is barred from relief under a Supreme Court decision that holds Title VII's statute of limitation clock is intended to tick solely from the time of the discriminatory act, not from the time harm is realized.[298] Congress adopts a provision that specifies time of harm as restarting the statute of limitations clock for those discriminated against under a seniority system. Later, a female brings suit alleging that she had been discriminated against in raise decisions over time and that consequently her pay continued to be lower than that of men in similar positions. Is the Court's

[294] Mackey v. Lanier Collection Agency & Serv., 486 U.S. 825, 840 (1988) (quoting United States v. Price, 361 U.S. 304, 313 (1960)).

[295] REED DICKERSON, THE INTERPRETATION AND APPLICATION OF STATUTES 179 (1975).

[296] Red Lion Broadcasting Co. v. FCC, 395 U.S. 367, 380-81 (1969). By contrast, a "mere statement in a conference report ... as to what the Committee believes an earlier statute meant is obviously less weighty" because Congress has not "proceeded formally through the legislative process." South Carolina v. Regan, 465 U.S. 367, 379 n.17 (1984).

[297] Mount Sinai Hosp. v. Weinberger, 517 F.2d 329, 343 (5th Cir. 1975), quoted with approval in Bell v. New Jersey, 461 U.S. 773, 785 n.12 (1983). *See also* Merrill Lynch, Pierce, Fenner & Smith v. Curran, 456 U.S. 343, 382-87 (1982), relying on congressional intent to preserve an implied private right of action as the reason for a "savings clause" on court jurisdiction. In FDA v. Brown & Williamson Tobacco Corp., 529 U.S. 120, 156 (2000), the Court ruled that, because legislation restricting the advertising and labeling of tobacco products had been premised on an understanding that the FDA lacked jurisdiction over tobacco, Congress had "effectively ratified" that interpretation of FDA authority. Additionally, the labeling statutes were "incompatible" with FDA jurisdiction in one "important respect"—although supervision of product labeling is a "substantial component" of the FDA's regulatory authority, the tobacco labeling laws "explicitly prohibit any federal agency from imposing any health-related labeling requirements on ... tobacco products."

[298] Lorance v. AT&T Technologies, Inc., 490 U.S. 900 (1989).



 

more general "time of the act" interpretation in the seniority case still to be accorded weight in the later raise discrimination case, even though the interpretation no longer pertains in a seniority system context? In *Ledbetter v. Goodyear Tire & Rubber Co., Inc.*, five Justices substantially relied on the earlier interpretation to hold that the raise discrimination was barred by the statute of limitations, over the objection of a four-Justice dissent.[299]

## Reenactment

If Congress reenacts a statute and leaves unchanged a provision that had received a definitive administrative or judicial interpretation, the Court sometimes holds that Congress has ratified that interpretation.[300] The stated rationale is that "Congress is presumed to be aware of an administrative or judicial interpretation of a statute and to adopt that interpretation when it re-enacts a statute without change."[301] Similarly, if Congress in enacting a new statute incorporates sections of an earlier one, "Congress normally can be presumed to have had knowledge of the interpretation given to the incorporated law, at least insofar as it affects the new statute."[302] However, congressional ratification of a judicial interpretation will not be inferred from reenactment unless "the supposed judicial consensus [is] so broad and unquestioned that Congress knew of and endorsed it."[303] Also, the reenactment presumption is usually indulged only if the history of enactment shows that Congress conducted a comprehensive review of the reenacted or incorporated statute, and changed those aspects deemed undesirable.[304] Though the presumption can come into play in the absence of evidence that Congress directly considered the issue at hand, the Court may require other indicia of congressional awareness of the issue before reading significance into reenactment. Congress may have simply overlooked the matter, or may have intended to leave it "for authoritative resolution in the courts."[305]

[299] 550 U.S. 618 (2007). On January 29, 2009, the Lilly Ledbetter Fair Pay Act of 2009 was enacted as P.L. 111-2. Criticizing the Supreme Court in its finding, the act restarts the statute of limitation clock on compensation claims each time harm is realized from past unlawful discrimination (including each paycheck). Also, the act explicitly extends beyond Title VII to claims under other specified civil rights laws. For an extended discussion of the persistence of more general interpretations beyond narrow congressional overrides, see Deborah A. Widiss, *Shadow Precedents and the Separation of Powers*, 84 NOTRE DAME L. REV. 511 (2009).

[300] Pierce v. Underwood, 487 U.S. 552, 567 (1988) (reenactment of "a statute that had in fact been given a consistent judicial interpretation ... generally includes the settled judicial interpretation"). *See also* Farragher v. City of Boca Raton, 524 U.S. 775, 792 (1998) ("[T]he force of precedent here is enhanced by Congress's amendment to the liability provisions of Title VII since the *Meritor* decision, without providing any modification of our holding."). In *Pierce*, however, a committee report's approving reference to a minority viewpoint was dismissed as not representing a "settled judicial interpretation," since 12 of the 13 appellate circuits had ruled to the contrary. *See also* Metropolitan Stevedore Co. v. Rambo, 515 U.S. 291, 299 (1995) (reenactment carried with it no endorsement of appellate court decisions that were not uniform and some of which misread precedent).

[301] Merrill Lynch, Pierce, Fenner & Smith v. Curran, 456 U.S. 343, 382 n.66 (1982), quoting Lorillard v. Pons, 434 U.S. 575, 580 (1978).

[302] Lorillard v. Pons, 434 U.S. 575, 581 (1978).

[303] Jama v. Immigration and Customs Enforcement, 543 U.S. 335, 349-52 (2005).

[304] Lorillard, 434 U.S. at 582. The Court "bluntly" rejects ratification arguments if Congress "has not comprehensively revised a statutory scheme but has made only isolated amendments." Alexander v. Sandoval, 532 U.S. 275, 292 (2001) (also expressing more general misgivings about the ratification doctrine's reliance on congressional inaction).

[305] Zenith Radio Corp. v. Hazeltine Research, Inc., 401 U.S. 321, 336 n.7 (1971). "[C]ongressional inaction is perhaps the weakest of all tools for ascertaining legislative intent, and courts are loath to presume congressional endorsement unless the issue plainly has been the subject of congressional attention. Extensive hearings, repeated efforts at legislative correction, and public controversy may be indicia of Congress's attention to the subject." Butterbaugh v. Department of Justice, 336 F.3d 1332, 1342 (Fed. Cir. 2003) (citations omitted).



 

## Acquiescence

Congressional inaction is sometimes construed as approving or "acquiescing" in an administrative or judicial interpretation.[306] There is no general presumption that congressional inaction in the face of interpretation bespeaks acquiescence, and there is no consistent pattern of application by the Court. When the Court does infer acquiescence, the most important factor seems to be congressional awareness that an interpretation has generated widespread attention and controversy.[307] As with reenactment, however, there are other inferences that can be drawn from congressional silence.[308]

## "Isolated Statements"

Although congressional inaction or silence is sometimes accorded importance in interpreting an earlier enactment, post-enactment explanations or expressions of opinion by committees or members are often dismissed as "isolated statements" or "subsequent legislative history" not entitled to much if any weight. As the Court has noted, statements as to what a committee believes an earlier enactment meant are "obviously entitled to less weight" than is subsequent legislation declaring such intent, because in the case of the committee statement Congress had not "proceeded formally through the legislation process."[309] The Court has also explained that "isolated statements by individual Members of Congress or its committees, all made after enactment of the statute under consideration, cannot substitute for a clear expression of legislative intent at the time of enactment."[310] "It is the function of the courts and not the Legislature, much less a Committee of one House of the Legislature, to say what an enacted statute means."[311] The

[306] Although acquiescence and reenactment are similar in that each involves an inference that Congress has chosen to leave an interpretation unchanged, there is a fundamental difference: reenactment purports to involve interpretation of duly enacted legislation, while acquiescence attributes significance to Congress' failure to act. *Cf.* INS v. Chadha, 462 U.S. 919 (1983) (Congress may legislate only in conformity with the bicameralism and presentment requirements of Art. I, § 7). At times, acquiescence and reenactment have been used in tandem. *See* Zuni Pub. Sch. Dist. No. 89 v. Department of Educ., 550 U.S. 81, 90-91 (2007).

[307] In Bob Jones Univ. v. United States, 461 U.S. 574, 601 (1983), for example, the Court, in finding congressional acquiescence in a revenue ruling that denied tax-exempt status to educational institutions with racially discriminatory policies, pointed to inaction on a number of bills introduced to overturn the ruling as evidencing Congress' "prolonged and acute awareness of so important an issue." *See also* United States v. Rutherford, 442 U.S. 544 (1979) (finding acquiescence, and pointing to congressional hearings as evidencing congressional awareness of FDA policy). On the other hand, failure to include in an amendment language addressing an interpretation described as then-prevailing in a memo placed in the *Congressional Record* is "too slender a reed" on which to base an inference of congressional acquiescence. McLaughlin v. Richland Shoe Co., 486 U.S. 128, 132 n.8 (1988).

[308] "The 'complicated check on legislation' ... erected by our Constitution creates an inertia that makes it impossible to assert with any degree of assurance that congressional failure to act represents (1) approval of the status quo, as opposed to (2) inability to agree upon how to alter the status quo, (3) unawareness of the status quo, (4) indifference to the status quo, or even (5) political cowardice." Johnson v. Transportation Agency, 480 U.S. 616, 672 (1987) (Justice Scalia, dissenting).

[309] Consumer Product Safety Comm'n v. GTE Sylvania, 447 U.S. 102, 118 n.13 (1980) (dismissing as not "entitled to much weight here" a statement at hearings made by the bill's sponsor four years after enactment, and language in a conference report on amendments, also four years after enactment).

[310] Southeastern Community College v. Davis, 442 U.S. 397, 411 n.11 (1979) (dismissing 1974 committee report language and 1978 floor statements purporting to explain 1973 enactment). *See also* Los Angeles Dep't of Water & Power v. Manhart, 435 U.S. 702, 714 (1978) (one member's "isolated comment on the Senate floor" a year after enactment "cannot change the effect of the plain language of the statute itself").

[311] NLRB v. Health Care & Retirement Corp., 511 U.S. 571, 582 (1994) ("isolated statement" in 1974 committee report accompanying amendments to other sections of act is not "authoritative interpretation" of language enacted in 1947).

disfavor in which post-enactment explanations are held is sometimes expressed more strongly when the views are those of a single member. The Court has declared that "*post hoc* observations by a single member carry little if any weight."[312]

## Presidential Signing Statements

Under the Constitution, the President's formal role in enacting statutes is one of "take it or leave it." Article I, section 7, clause 2 provides that, after Congress passes a bill and presents it to the President, "if he approves he shall sign it, but if not he shall return it, with his Objections to that House in which it shall have originated, who shall enter the Objections at large on their Journal, and proceed to reconsider it." Thus, the recording of a President's views as part of the constitutional lawmaking process is limited to objections attending a veto. Also, the President may not amend the language of a presented bill before acting on it. Nor may the President pick and choose which provisions of a presented bill to sign into law, while vetoing others. The President's options are "thumbs up" or "thumbs down" on a bill in its entirety.[313] The President may have an integral role in the enactment of statutes into law, but "[a]ll legislative Powers" reside in Congress,[314] and it is exclusively up to the Houses of Congress, at least formally, to come to common agreement on statutory language.

Nevertheless, recent Presidents have frequently used the occasion of signing a bill into law to issue statements that contend that portions of the bill are unconstitutional, that claim a law is of limited application, or that otherwise signal that a law will be implemented strictly in accord with the President's views of the office's prerogatives and authorities.[315] Assertions in signing statements vary in specificity and purported scope; the statements would not appear to have any immediate, direct legal effect in and of themselves; and they may best be understood in the context of the enduring tension between the political branches over accountability, control of executive agencies, and similar institutional concerns.[316] At the same time, Administrations since the 1980s have asserted that signing statements have weight as legislative history and should be taken into account by courts.[317] There is no legal impediment to a President commenting on a

[312] Bread Political Action Comm. v. FEC, 455 U.S. 577, 582 n.3 (1982) (1977 litigation affidavit of a Senator and his aide as to intent in drafting a 1974 floor amendment cannot be given "probative weight" because such statements, made after enactment, represent only the "personal views" of the legislator). *But see* North Haven Bd. of Educ. v. Bell, 456 U.S. 512, 530-31 (1982), citing a bill summary placed in the *Congressional Record* by the bill's sponsor after passage, and explanatory remarks made two years later by the same sponsor; and Pacific Gas & Elec. Co. v. Energy Resources Conserv. & Dev. Comm'n, 461 U.S. 190, 220 n.23 (1983) (relying on a 1965 explanation by "an important figure in the drafting of the 1954 [Atomic Energy] Act").

[313] Clinton v. City of New York, 524 U.S. 417 (1998).

[314] U.S. CONST., art. I, § 1.

[315] Signing statements have a long history, but their frequency and intent changed beginning with the Reagan Administration. WILLIAM N. ESKRIDGE, JR., PHILLIP P. FRICKEY & ELIZABETH GARRETT, CASES & MATERIALS ON LEGISLATION: STATUTES & THE CREATION OF PUBLIC Policy at 1043-44 (4th ed. 2007).

[316] *See* CRS Report RL33667, *Presidential Signing Statements: Constitutional and Institutional Implications*, by T. J. Halstead.

[317] In a 1986, Samuel A. Alito Jr., then a Deputy Assistant Attorney General in DOJ's Office of Legal Counsel, drafted a memorandum to a Litigation Strategy Working Group on how "to ensure that Presidential signing statements assume their rightful place in the interpretation of legislation.... [I]n interpreting statutes, both the courts and litigants (including lawyers in the Executive branch) invariably speak of "legislative" or "congressional" intent. Rarely if ever do courts or litigants inquire into the President's intent. Why is this so?" He proceeded to review potential obstacles to wider acceptance and proposed a course of action for overcoming them.



 

statute's meaning in a signing statement,[318] and the political reality is that an Administration is not a passive spectator during congressional deliberations.[319] Often, the Administration forwards draft legislation for introduction, and liaisons from the executive branch regularly communicate its views on bills as they proceed. If the President or his Administration worked closely with Congress in developing the legislation, and if the approved version incorporated the President's recommendations, reference to a signing statement may help complete the picture of a bill's purpose, especially in the absence of published congressional documents on a bill.[320] The same might also be said with respect to bills whose final content arose from compromise negotiations between the Administration and Congress.[321]

Citation of signing statements may be more controversial when statutory language appears clear or the meaning attributed in a signing statement conflicts with congressional history. Congress has no opportunity during the legislative process to respond as an institution to a characterization in a signing statement.[322] Giving the President "the last word" on the meaning of a bill he approves, it may be pointed out, stands in contrast to the procedure for congressional consideration of the President's objections in the case of a vetoed bill.

---

[318] A report by a task force of the American Bar Association that was critical of the types of constitutional and institutional assertions being made in presidential signing statements apparently had no objection to the President using signing statements to voice views on the meaning, purpose, or significance of bills. American Bar Association, Report of the Task Force on Presidential Signing Statements and the Separation of Powers Doctrine at 5 (2006).

[319] *See, e.g.*, Frank B. Cross, *The Constitutional Legitimacy and Significance of Presidential "Signing Statements,"* 40 ADMIN. L. REV. 209 (1988).

[320] "It may ... be appropriate for the President, when signing legislation, to explain what his (and Congress's) intention was in making the legislation law, particularly if the Administration has played a significant part in moving the legislation through Congress." Department of Justice, Office of Legal Counsel, "The Legal Significance of Presidential Signing Statements," 17 U.S. Op. Off. Legal Counsel 131, 136 (1993).

[321] "[T]hough in some circumstances there is room for doubt as to the weight to be accorded a presidential signing statement in illuminating congressional intent ..., President Reagan's views are significant here because the Executive Branch participated in the negotiation of the compromise legislation." United States v. Story, 891 F.2d 988, 994 (2d Cir. 1989).

[322] *See* Marc N. Garber & Kurt A. Wimmer, *Presidential Signing Statements as Interpretations of Legislative Intent: An Executive Aggrandizement of Power*, 24 HARV. J ON LEGIS. 363, 367 (1987) ("The danger inherent in [an 'executive history' statement] is that its author will graft ambiguities and exceptions onto an act that was not so encumbered during the legislative process.... "). *Compare* Curtis A. Bradley & Eric A. Posner, *Presidential Signing Statements and Executive Power,* 23 CONST. COMMENTARY 307, 344-47 (2006).



 

There is no consensus as to whether courts should rely at all on signing statements: there has been no definitive ruling by the Supreme Court, and even lower courts have seldom had to resolve cases that require a choice between conflicting presidential and congressional interpretations.[323] Presidents' routine use of signing statements to try to influence statutory interpretation by courts is a relatively recent development,[324] Courts cite signing statements from time to time, but usually in situations where the interpretation is not critical to case outcome.[325]

Judicial reluctance to consider signing statements would not appear to be contrary to judicial deference to agency action. Deference is premised on the conclusion that Congress has, by statute, authorized the agency to "speak with the force of law" through a rulemaking or other formal process. Congress has not authorized the President (or, indirectly, an agency) to speak with the force of law through signing statements. So, although signing statements may influence or even control agency implementation of statutes, it is the implementation, and not the signing statement itself, that would be measured against the statute's requirements.[326] At most, signing statements might be considered analogous to informal agency actions, entitled to respect only to the extent that they have the power to persuade.[327]

---

[323] *See, e.g.*, William D. Popkin, *Judicial Use of Presidential Legislative History: A Critique*, 66 IND. L.J. 699 (1991); Brad Waites, *Let Me Tell You What You Mean: An Analysis of Presidential Signing Statements*, 21 GA. L. REV. 755 (1987); Marc N. Garber and Kurt A. Wimmer, *Presidential Signing Statements as Interpretations of Legislative Intent: An Executive Aggrandizement of Power*, 24 HARV. J. ON LEGIS. 363 (1987); Frank B. Cross, *The Constitutional Legitimacy and Significance of Presidential "Signing Statements,"* 40 ADMIN. L. REV. 209 (1988); Kristy L. Carroll, Comment, *Whose Statute Is It Anyway?: Why and How Courts Should Use Presidential Signing Statements When Interpreting Federal Statutes*, 46 CATH U. L. REV. 475 (1997); Department of Justice, Office of Legal Counsel, "The Legal Significance of Presidential Signing Statements," 17 U.S. Op. Off. Legal Counsel 131 (1993).

[324] President Andrew Jackson used a signing statement in 1830, and in 1842 an ad hoc congressional committee strongly condemned President Tyler for having filed a statement of his reasons for signing a bill (See 4 Hinds' Precedents § 3492), but routine use of signing statements began during the Reagan Administration, when Attorney General Meese persuaded West Publishing Company to include the President's signing statements with legislative histories published in *United States Code Congressional and Administrative News*. The Attorney General explained this as facilitating availability of signing statements to courts "for future construction of what the statute actually means." Address by Attorney General Edwin Meese, III, National Press Club (February 25, 1986). Presidents since Reagan have continued this practice.

[325] *See, e.g.*, United States v. Perlaza, 439 F.3d 1149, 1163 (9th Cir. 2006) (citing President Clinton's signing statement to reinforce statement of purpose in the conference report); Berry v. Department of Justice, 733 F.2d 1343, 1349 (9th Cir. 1984) (citing signing statement as well as congressional committee reports as affirming one of the broad goals of the Freedom of Information Act); Clifton D. Mayhew, Inc. v. Wirtz, 413 F.2d 658, 661-62 (4th Cir. 1969) (cited as elaborating on floor manager's explanation of good-faith defense in Portal-to-Portal Act); United States v. Yacoubian, 24 F.3d 1, 8 (9th Cir. 1994) (cited along with conference report to establish rational purpose of statute); Taylor v. Heckler, 835 F.2d 1037, 1044 n.17 (3d Cir. 1987) (refusing to consider a signing statement that was "largely inconsistent" with legislative history on which the court had previously relied); Caruth v. United States, 688 F. Supp. 1129, 1146 n.11(N.D. Tex. 1987) (relying extensively on legislative history but refusing to give "any weight" to signing statements).

[326] If Congress has directed that the President rather than an agency implement a statute, then, by analogy, it can be argued that Congress has implicitly delegated to the President whatever policymaking authority is necessary to fill in gaps and implement the statutory rule. But here again, the signing statement would not usually constitute an act of implementation.

[327] The Constitution's vesting in the President of the executive power and of the duty to "take care that the laws be faithfully executed" implies authority to interpret the law in order to determine how to execute it, but this implicit authority would not appear to require change to the *Chevron/Skidmore* deference approaches.



 

## Author Contact Information

Larry M. Eig
Specialist in American Public Law
leig@crs.loc.gov, 7-7896

Yule Kim
Legislative Attorney
ykim@crs.loc.gov, 7-9138

## Acknowledgments

This report was originally prepared by George Costello. It has now been updated by Larry M. Eig and Yule Kim, who are available to answer questions on these issues.



 

# Statutory Structure and Legislative Drafting Conventions: A Primer for Judges

M. Douglass Bellis

*Deputy Legislative Counsel*
*United States House of Representatives*

Federal Judicial Center 2008

This Federal Judicial Center publication was undertaken in furtherance of the Center's statutory mission to develop and conduct education programs for the judicial branch. The views expressed are those of the author and not necessarily those of the Federal Judicial Center.

 

# Contents



iii

 

## Introduction

The circumstances under which statutes are drafted in Congress are often incompatible with long reflection or careful revision. The political moment comes briefly, and the statutory iron must then be struck, or left to cool unfashioned. As a result, judges often have to puzzle over the solidified remains of a messy political process. It is sometimes difficult to discern any underlying intent through the blurred surface of the legislative language.

Nevertheless, there are a variety of sometimes little-known conventions that will ease the way of a federal judge through the sometimes opaque world of legislation. Some of these conventions have statutory or case-law origins. Others have evolved from the experience of drafters over the years, especially drafters in the separate Offices of the Legislative Counsel for the House and the Senate. By the third quarter of the twentieth century, one or both of those offices participated in the drafting of practically every piece of legislation that passed through Congress. Attorneys in the offices often spend their entire careers there, and the two offices retain a relationship that stems from their common origin in a demonstration project conducted early in the twentieth century by Columbia University Law School's Legislative Drafting Research Fund. Consequently, the attorneys influence each other and try to develop a consensus over time on how drafting should be done. New attorneys are taught to draft by drafting under the guidance of more experienced attorneys. Thus essentially oral traditions are passed down and become conventions. Collectively, the attorneys in the two offices influence outside drafters, further reinforcing conventions over time. Even such matters as how the subdivisions of Acts of Congress are named have largely been a product of this process.

This guide describes the statutory framework of federal law and examines some legislative drafting conventions, the knowledge of which may help judges with statutory interpretation.[1]

Caution should be exercised, however, in automatically applying any given convention precisely because the drafting of legislation is not the careful academic exercise we might hope for. Not only do various political imperatives bring in legislative language written by persons unfamiliar with the usual conventions, but the conventions themselves change over time to reflect changes in public thinking and legal trends. Luckily, the careful observer can usually

1. For a more detailed examination of federal drafting conventions and techniques in general, one can consult either *The Legislative Drafter's Desk Reference*, Lawrence E. Filson & Sandra L. Strokoff (2007), or *Legislative Drafter's Deskbook: A Practical Guide*, Tobias A. Dorsey (2006).



 

articulate a reason for a departure from the conventions in use at the time a particular piece of legislation was drafted. Thus, starting with the conventions can greatly help in the task of interpreting a statute, even if the task cannot be a simple mechanical one. Before we turn to a few of the drafting conventions currently in use, let's examine a preliminary problem for judges trying to interpret statutes. How do we establish a reliable text of a statute?

## Part I. Sources of Statutory Law

### *A. What is the authoritative text of federal legislation?*

What constitutes the authoritative text of federal legislation has deeply affected drafting conventions and approaches, especially how amendments are drafted and reflected in widely used editions of the law. In order to understand how congressional enactments address statutes, we need to understand the structure of our hybrid system of statutory law.

Even though virtually all of federal law is statutory in derivation, we are still in fact a "common-law" country in the sense that our statutes are not formally arranged in a code that is officially promulgated according to civil-law standards. (See 1 U.S.C. § 106a for what we call "promulgation"—actually just putting the official copy as passed by each House into the U.S. National Archives.) In fact, as we will see, the U.S. Code itself is not a fully authoritative edition of all, or even most—maybe not of any—laws of the United States.

Technically, the only authentic version of a law of the United States is the actual physical document that was passed by Congress, authenticated by signatures of the appropriate Congressional officers according to the customs of Congress, and either signed by the President or allowed to become law through the President's inaction or over the President's veto. These documents are, as we mentioned, kept in the National Archives. In rare cases judges might have to examine them, if there is any reason to doubt the accuracy of some purported copy of them presented to the court as being the law of the United States. As we will see, some copies or versions of law based on these documents are "prima facie" evidence, and some are "legal" evidence. None is conclusive. In effect, judges are expected to take judicial notice of statutes to which they have no regular direct access. This in general seems to work just fine, perhaps because a number of enterprises earn their living by providing reliable copies of laws.



 

### *B. The problem of later amendments to earlier statutes in the "common-law" tradition*

There is one area where this system is a little creaky: where there are amendments by later Congresses to laws passed by earlier ones. How can these amendments be integrated into the original statute so that the lawyers and judges can know what the law as amended looks like? The only form in which the amendments are found in the statute books is as a set of instructions for changing the earlier, original statute's text, which continues to exist in the books in its original form. Usually, these amendments are in a form called "cut and bite" amendments, striking parts of existing legislation and adding or substituting others.[2] This form of amendment often results in there being no fully authoritative text of the original law as later amended by another statute. Indeed, sometimes through inadvertence the amendments made by a later law cannot actually be literally executed to the earlier law. What then?

This problem of how to show changes is even more significant in federal law than it would be in a purer "judge-made" common-law system where statutes are not the only, and perhaps not the most important, source of rules of decision.

The attempts of Congress to deal with this problem have created a rather confused cross between a civil-law code system and a common-law statute system for federal law. Many of the conventions of federal drafting owe something to this fact.[3]

---

2. In a few cases, an amendatory statute will amend an earlier statute "to read as follows" and so provide a complete substitute and updated text. For example, see Public Law 93-445, which amended the Railroad Retirement Act of 1937 by completely rewriting its text, in the process renaming it the Railroad Retirement Act of 1974. 45 U.S.C. §§ 231 et seq. But soon after, Congress made additional cut and bite amendments to this new Act, so the 1974 text is no longer authoritative.

3. The problem is not a new one either. James Madison had planned to introduce the then-modern, if not radical, legislative drafting technique of interpolating amendments directly into the text of the U.S. Constitution, the primary legal text for federal law. He was not successful in doing so. Congress, for its first century or so, perhaps following this lead, would simply pass a new rule in a new statute. The new rule would prevail over the old rule as a later enactment. The earlier statute, though, was facially, if not substantively, left unchanged by the "amendment," so judges would just have to know it no longer applied as written, even though parts of it were impliedly repealed. Sometimes it was difficult to know how much of an older statute was still in force, given the lack of congruence between the application of the new rule and the old one. This is probably one reason the modern method of cut and bite amendments has proved so popular and almost altogether eclipsed the traditional common-law approach. However, that traditional approach is still used for constitutional amendments.



 

### *C. First attempt at codification—the Revised Statutes of the United States*

The problem was made more complex in the mid nineteenth century by a general American movement toward the "code" system of statute law. It seems to have been argued that the existing system gave the public too little usable notice of what the laws were (and perhaps the courts too great an ability to resolve ambiguities however they liked rather than as Congress intended). This movement resulted in a complete restatement and reorganization of federal statutory law in the Revised Statutes of the United States of America (hereinafter referred to as the "Revised Statutes of the United States," or simply the "Revised Statutes").

The enactment of the Revised Statutes of the United States was approved by the President on June 20, 1874.[4] Earlier statutes were repealed and the new Revised Statutes supposedly represented a complete statement of generally applicable federal law. It was intended that any amendments in the future would be made by changes to the Revised Statutes' text, a practice that had by then become the custom in most parts of the world, including the English-speaking "common-law" world.

So the Revised Statutes of the United States became just another law of the United States. Some parts of it are still in effect today, notably certain civil rights statutes, such as those "codified" (this turns out to be a loaded term that is not used to mean consistently the same thing, as we shall see later) in section 1983 and those near it in title 42 of the U.S. Code.

### *D. Complications*

When cut and bite amendments are made in a statutory common-law system, we have already seen that there is no formal document that shows the law as amended. In theory, anyone who wants can start with the original statute and each succeeding statute that makes the cut and bite amendments, and execute those amendments seriatim to create a text of the law as amended. We call those texts "compilations." Many of us are familiar with CCH or Prentice Hall, or with Collier's or West Publishing Company's compilations of commonly used statutes, such as the Internal Revenue Code, the bankruptcy law or the criminal code. (These various "codes," by the way, are not truly codes in the European sense, but the fact we often use that name indicates how strongly a definitive text is desired by users.)

---

4. See the Act of June 20, 1874, 18 Stat. 113, pt. 3, ch. 333. For a complete and detailed outline history of the statutes of the United States and their legal sources throughout its history, see *United States Statutes: Historical Outline and Source Notes*, Richard J. McKinney (2004) (available at http://www.llsdc.org/sourcebook/docs/us-statutes-outline.pdf).



 

There appears to have been no official regularly updated compilation of the Revised Statutes integrating the cut and bite amendments to the original text. This may have contributed to the Revised Statutes' general failure to wean Congress from Congress's earlier loose statutory ways.

### *E. A second attempt: the U.S. Code, a work in progress*

The Revised Statutes of the United States did not satisfy those wishing for reform in the way statutes were presented. Much of the bar, especially the New York state bar, continued to push for change. Acting through the House Judiciary Committee, advocates were able to establish, by the early twentieth century, an Office of Law Revision, which would be charged with bringing those laws enacted independently of the Revised Statutes into a single code with the Revised Statutes. This single code was called the United States Code. The Office of the Law Revision Counsel would periodically publish updated compilations showing the cumulative cut and bite amendments that Congress had made to earlier laws. The problem of authoritative compilations was finally addressed, for the first time in American history. Starting with those laws in the jurisdiction of the Judiciary Committee of the House, the new codifiers got off to a good start with the enactment as "positive law"—that is, a single statute or Act of Congress, several "titles" of this as-yet-incomplete U.S. Code.[5]

### *F. The varieties of legal effect of various parts of the U.S. Code*

In examining the U.S. Code, you will find at the front of each volume a listing of its "titles," some with asterisks and some without. Those with asterisks have been enacted into law as titles of the U.S. Code. Sometimes when someone says a title of the U.S. Code has been codified, this is what they mean. Like the Statutes at Large (the only official publication of the Acts of Congress, set forth seriatim in their native, as enacted, form), and for the same reason (namely that they were enacted as an Act of Congress), those titles are "legal evidence" of what are the laws of the United States (1 U.S.C. § 112 and 1 U.S.C. § 204). Notice these sections do not say "conclusive." Section 204 also makes the compilations updating the "enacted" or "codified" titles of the U.S. Code—cumulatively integrating the cut and bite amendments Congress has made to those titles—

5. And then things stalled again. While the process of "codification" continues, it is far from complete, and the original fifty-title framework for the U.S. Code seems increasingly burdened by changes in the way Congress divides national problems for legislative solution. So title 42, for example, has come to suffer from elephantiasis. The existence of a defunct title, title 6, made possible the incorporation of the "new" topic of homeland security without breaking the fifty-title structure, but that may be a process difficult to repeat.



 

"legal evidence" for their content. This could still be challenged by resort to the true statute version found only in the National Archives.

The other titles of the U.S. Code are in fact an attempt by the Office of the Law Revision Counsel to make sense out of and organize as a part of the U.S. Code those statutes that are not yet "codified" in it as positive enactments. This work, never passed by either House of Congress or signed by the President, is not technically the law of the United States. Nor are the updated compilations of those titles that the Office of the Law Revision Counsel from time to time makes. But by reason of that same section 204, they are "prima facie" evidence of what is the law of the United States.[6] However, the underlying statutes continue to be "legal evidence."[7]

As we have mentioned, the "codified" (in the sense of "enacted as positive law) titles of the U.S. Code are "legal" evidence of the laws of the United States, just as the Statutes at Large are. So you might think you could rely on "codified" titles of the U.S. Code as fully as you could on the statutes at large. However, in nearly every case,[8] Congress has, upon originally enacting a title of the U.S. Code, cautioned that it intends no substantive change in the laws so codified (and seemingly repealed). Presumably any apparent discrepancy or ambiguity in language in the codified title must be resolved by reference to the underlying and supposedly repealed mass of statutes brought into the codified title. Indeed, even where there is no discrepancy or ambiguity, in theory the underlying stat-

6. The Office of the Law Revision Counsel takes statutes, such as the Securities Act of 1933, and arranges them into titles, giving the sections new numbers and making various other form changes in them. Periodically, these "titles" of the U.S. Code are updated with the cut and bite amendments Congress has made to the original Act. Even though the presentation, section numbering, and other details are different, the United States Code version is therefore more up to date than the Statutes at Large version of the Securities Act as originally enacted. In some cases, people might say the Securities Act has been codified to title 15 of the U.S. Code, though this is a different use of the term "codification" than we have been making.

7. A number of cases deal with the effect of the placement of material from "uncodifed" statutes into those parts of the U.S. Code not enacted by Congress as positive law. *E.g.*, North Dakota v. United States, 460 U.S. 300 (1983) (classification decisions given no weight); Nashville Milk Co. v. Carnation Co., 355 U.S. 373 (1958) (an error made by the Law Revision Counsel has no effect); United States v. Welden, 377 U.S. 95 (1964) (recourse must be had to the original statutes when construing a section of the U.S. Code that has not been enacted into positive law).

8. Title 11 of the U.S. Code, dealing with bankruptcy, is an important exception. Also, on some occasions, Congress has reenacted an earlier title of the U.S. Code with substantive modifications, such as was the case with title 18 in 1948. CNA Fin. Corp. v. Donovan, 830 F.2d 1132 (D.C. Cir. 1987).



 

utes would trump the codified title![9] Needless to say, this creates yet another possibility for confusion in determining what are the laws of the United States.[10]

### *G. The bottom line on sources of federal statutory law*

So, to sum up, finding an authoritative copy of the laws of the United States is a tricky job. Only the National Archives has the real thing. The next best thing is a compilation made by applying the cut and bite amendments from amendatory statutes to a statute not yet codified. (Many commercial companies produce these, and in many areas they are used to such a great extent that errors in them are assumed to be in the "real" law of which they are unofficial compilations.) Not nearly as good, but often good enough, is to look to the U.S. Code in its current edition (but with care for recent enactments that are in force but found only in the Statutes at Large and not yet in the current edition of the Code or even its supplements) for laws in titles that have been codified, in the sense of enacted as such. Least authoritative, but often sufficient, are the versions of laws found in uncodified titles of the U.S. Code.

## Part II. Naming Conventions

Having established the authoritative texts of statutes, we have the context in which we can consider drafting conventions. Among the most important are those relating to the naming of subdivisions of a statute. As we have seen, federal law is a disparate collection of statutes enacted in differing styles, literally over the centuries. So it may come as a surprise that there are naming conventions about basic subdivisions of federal laws that have been (mostly) observed consistently over the entire range of statutes. However, it is not surprising that some laws, especially older ones, depart very substantially from the conventions, so caution must be used in applying them.

9. Sompo Japan Ins. Co. of Am. v. Union Pac. R.R., 456 F.3d 54 (2d Cir. 2006); United States v. Bhutani, 266 F.3d 661 (7th Cir. 2001); United States v. Ward, 131 F.3d 335 (3d Cir. 1997). I am grateful to Peter Lefevre for drawing these cases to my attention.

10. There are also sections in title 1 of the U.S. Code dealing with the effect of a compilation by Little and Brown (section 113) of the laws of the United States, a compilation few modern people have ever laid eyes on, and the effect of a compilation by the Secretary of State of the Treaties in Force of the United States (since these may, to the extent that they are self-executing, be fully as authoritative as a statute) (section 112a).



 

*Statutory Structure and Legislative Drafting Conventions: A Primer for Judges*

## A. *Sections*

Almost always, from the earliest days of the Republic, the text of a law, if divided at all, has been divided into sections. These sections either have the designation "section" (although for a while it was the convention not to have any designation for the first "section") or the designation "sec." (after the first section).Typically they are numbered with Arabic numerals, but in some old statutes this will not be so. Like every convention, these are sometimes violated. Still, the section is the most fundamental division of federal law, and almost all federal laws use it.

Some laws are so short they do not really have any subdivisions. Because of the custom of not designating the first section, some people decided these were "single section" laws, so now you will at times see a statute with a designation of a section 1, but no section 2. Probably this represents a misunderstanding of the structure of statutes, but it has become somewhat entrenched.

## B. *Subsections and paragraphs*

A section in turn is normally divided into subsections. These are designated by lowercase letters: "(a)," "(b)," etc. Each subsection is a complete sentence and idea within itself.

But sometimes the section is one complete idea, with several subdivisions, none of which is itself a full sentence. The subdivisions are meant to separate out partial sentence elements. These subdivisions of a section are called paragraphs—not subsections—even though they generally are not technically paragraphs, but are instead phrases or clauses. They are designated (usually) with Arabic numerals: "(1)," "(2)," etc.

An example might look like this:

Sec. 2. This section is supposed to convey—
    (1) the first idea;
    (2) the second idea; and
    (3) a third idea.

And yet, a paragraph can be a full, independent sentence or sentences when it is used as a subdivision of a subsection. That may have been its first use, and why it got the name. It might look something like this:

Sec. 2. (a)(1) This subsection is pretty complicated. It has a main idea.
    (2) It also has another idea that deserves its own exposition.

8

 

For now, in these illustrations, we have not used headings for the various parts. Headings are usually used now, but we will discuss that later. At this point it is easier to see the units without the headings.

So we have a section divided into subsections or sometimes paragraphs. The subsections divide into paragraphs. Paragraphs may have subparagraphs, designated usually with capital letters: "(A)," "(B)," etc.

## *C. Clauses*

In an ideal world, there would never be any further subdivisions. But in dense statutes, they are sometimes found. Usually they are called clauses and subclauses. A clause, like a paragraph, is not necessarily grammatically a clause. It is typically designated with a small Roman numeral, such as "(i)" or "(ii)." Subclauses use large Roman numerals, such as "(I)" or "(II)."

So you could get something that looks like this:

SEC. 2. IMPORTANT OVERALL TOPIC.

(a) In General—In a well-written statute, the main idea of the section will come first and be elaborated here.

(1) Sub-idea One.—If there are sub-ideas, they will show up looking something like this.

(2) Sub-idea Two.—There have to be at least two of them to make it worthwhile to do this. But either one of them can be divided further, like this:

(A) By this level of subdivision, the drafter may have stopped using headings; it is likely that further subdivisions, if needed—

(i) will be run-ons; and

(ii) will look something like this, and in a few cases will include their own subdivisions as follows:

(I) A ridiculously oversubdivided section can have these.

(II) It will always have to have more than one, though.

(B) You can't have a subparagraph (A) without a (B).

(b) Some Lesser, but Independent Idea.—Usually, the later subsections are for details that flesh out the main idea covered in the first subsection, such as exceptions, definitions, special rules, things like that.



 

In this example, you would say that section 2(a)(2)(A)(ii) has two subclauses, (I) and (II). Or you could say that clause (ii) of section 2(a)(2)(A) has two subclauses. Notice that when you combine a number of elements, you call the whole by the largest and first element in the combination: section 2(a)(2)(A)(ii), for example.

### *D. Bottom line in dealing with "small divisions"*

In most cases, the important nomenclature convention to remember is the difference between "subsections" and "paragraphs." At times, though, the decisions in cases can turn on the proper use of the nomenclature for smaller subdivisions.

### *E. Titles, chapters, and other divisions*

Most bills are divided into sections and their subdivisions, but some bills are rather too big for that, including omnibus bills with relatively unrelated topics combined together. These are divided into "titles," "chapters," and "subchapters," all relatively clearly labeled. Not all of these subdivisions may be used in any given bill, but sometimes all are. Occasionally, several different "Acts" of Congress are combined, each Act being called something like a "division." This is, thankfully, rare, and in most cases it is obvious from the labeling. So it causes little confusion even if it is aesthetically questionable.

### *F. Various styles, one nomenclature*

You may have noticed that in the examples I gave in the subdivision portion of this, I actually used two rather different styles. Mostly you will run into the "legislative counsel" style embodied in the longer example at the end of page 9, which has more headings, variations in typeface, and more indentations where there are subdivisions. But in a few cases you might run into the older "traditional style," shown in the first examples. It is characterized, usually, by fewer headings and less indentation. But the conventions about naming the subdivisions are the same in both styles; the main differences are in typeface and presentation.

### *G. Convention relating to cross references within a unit*

Sometimes you will find a cross reference in a law to another subunit in the same unit, such as another subsection in the same section, or another section in the same law. The convention is that mention of another subunit in the same unit does not require reference to the overall unit. Usually you will see "subsection (b)" rather than "subsection (b) of this section."

## Part III. Other Conventions That May Be Useful To Know

### A. *"Including" means "not limited to"*

It has become a convention in federal law that the term "including" means what it usually means in English. It is a nonexclusive "for instance" type of phrase. If I say I have some change in my pocket, including a penny and a dime, most people would expect that I might have some other coins as well. Few would think I meant to exclude that possibility. But in legal writing in general, there seems a worry that "including" means that what follows is a complete list of the elements. There are even a few federal laws that use the term "including but not limited to." The "but not limited to" should be thought of as surplusage. "Includes" is typically used in definitional sections. You might have a section that looks something like this:

SEC. 45. DEFINITIONS.

As used in this Act—

(1) the term "mother" means, with respect to a human, the woman who gave birth to that human; and

(2) the term "parent" includes mother.

Notice that paragraph (1) uses the word "means." That is like an equals sign in math. What follows is a full and final definition. But paragraph (2) uses the word "includes." Even by the context, you can tell it is not intended to equate "parent" with "mother," but leaves open the possibility, indeed probability, that others are parents as well. Very often, "includes" or "including" is used to bring into the coverage of the provision something that is rather counterintuitive. Perhaps you might find something like "The term 'firearm' includes any explosive device." While it might not make much sense in common speech, the intent is to provide the same rules for explosive devices that are provided for firearms, so this rather odd locution is used.



 

### B. *The doctrine of functus officio as applied to amendatory Acts*

Since the cut and bite amendment form has taken hold, it seems logical to recall that once the amendments made by an amendatory Act take effect, that Act is, to that extent, something of a spent force, almost a nullity. We can think of the amendatory Act as a sort of ship carrying passengers to the Act being amended. Once those passengers get out and go to that other Act, they are no longer really on the ship. Very occasionally, Congress will try to amend an amendatory Act that has taken effect. Kindly courts might wish to follow the evident intent by transferring those amendments to their real home, the Act amended, but this can be difficult if subsequent amendments to that Act change the context of the changes made in the earlier amendatory Act.

### C. *Definitions under title 1 of the U.S. Code*

There are a number of statutory default provisions that drafters of federal law often rely on, without referring to them by location in the law. These include the definitions and general provisions in title 1 of the U.S. Code; using "on the record after opportunity for a hearing" in connection with administrative rule making and adjudications; the avoidance of citation of civil venue and jurisdiction statutes; the provision for alternate and sometimes larger fines under section 3571 of title 18; and the convention that, in criminal statutes, the state of mind required for the conduct elements of the offense also applies to the circumstances and results elements of the offense. Drafters usually follow these conventions, but not always. When they do not, it is usually because someone has added into the law repetitive or surplus recitations. This can result from an attempt to reassure persons not as familiar with the defaults, or from simple inadvertence. Let's look at each individually.

Section 1 of title 1 of the U.S. Code provides a number of definitional conventions. There is a broad definition of "person" that includes most organizations and applies unless an individual law otherwise provides. The singular is deemed to include the plural and vice versa. Other definitions and provisions at the beginning of title 1 provide useful shortcuts for drafters, though sometimes traps for the unwary.

One such trap is the default definition of "person." This includes all sorts of groups and associations as well as natural persons. Combined with the rule, also set forth in section 1, that the singular includes the plural, this can create a much more sweeping provision than the casual reader might have expected. Congress often uses the word "person" when in fact they mean "individual." Since section 1 has an out, namely the exception "unless the context indicates otherwise," it may be necessary to apply this definition with caution.



 

Notice, too, that this definition of "person" does not include governmental entities, though it probably includes almost everything else. Yet some statutes are applicable to governmental entities as well as private ones. While it is not set forth as a definition, Congress has taken to using the term "entity" when it wants to include governmental entities.[11]

Other definitions in chapter 1 of title 1 are seldom noticed but could have a somewhat surprising effect. The term "vehicle" includes all forms of land transportation, but one is left to wonder what then is a "space vehicle" (section 4). The term "vessel" includes every "artificial contrivance used, or capable of being used, as a means of transportation on water" (section 5). I suppose a lot of things are capable of being used as flotation devices in a flood, such as perhaps an old wooden door passing by my roof as I try to escape, but in areas where there are no floods, it seems unlikely they should be considered vessels. Even in areas where there are floods, it seems unlikely that an old unused door stored in the attic should be considered a vessel. Once again, recourse would be needed to the context of the use of the term, but one wonders if these definitions are ever actually useful.

## D. Use of title 5 conventions

Chapter 5 of title 5 (a codified title) of the U.S. Code is popularly known as the Administrative Procedure Act, from its precodification embodiment as a separate statute. It provides a complete default system for many of the activities of administrative bodies, especially in rule making and adjudication, where executive agencies sometimes act in quasi-legislative or quasi-judicial modes. Though not every committee in Congress is aware of it, this body of law was intended to provide due process and uniformity in agency proceedings. Generally, the chapter provides for informal "notice and comment" rule making and simple adjudications, and the chapter that follows it in title 5 provides a fairly broad level of judicial review. In addition, the chapter also provides a more formal procedure as an option for rulemaking or adjudication, which leads to a somewhat more restricted judicial review. This more formal procedure is invoked merely by putting the words "on the record after opportunity for an agency hearing" in the new law Congress might be contemplating. Innocent as these words sound, they are full of legal effect. When applied to rule making, use of these magic words means that sections 556 (providing for very formal hearings) and 557 (relating

11. *See* Organizacion JD LTDA v. U.S. Dep't of Justice, 18 F.3d 91, 94–95 (2d Cir. 2001); Conner v. Tate, 130 F. Supp. 2d 1370, 1374–75 (N.D. Ga. 2001); Dorris v. Absher, 959 F. Supp. 813, 819–20 (M.D. Tenn. 1997); PBA Local No. 38 v. Woodbridge Police Dep't, 832 F. Supp. 808, 822–23 (D.N.J. 1993). I am grateful to Mark A. Jones for calling these cases to my attention.



 

to the contents of and how an agency will use the record established at the hearing) of title 5 apply instead of section 553(c), which provides a much less formal procedure, leaving many details to agency discretion. In the case of adjudications, the same sections apply with respect to hearings and records, making the adjudication into the equivalent of a judicial type trial.

Perhaps even more important than the procedure evoked by the simple "on the record after opportunity for an agency hearing" is the different scope of judicial review. In effect, the scope of review for a matter decided on the record after opportunity for an agency hearing is limited to whether or not the agency decision is "unsupported by substantial evidence on the record" taken as a whole. The convention is to use those words alone, without any reference to title 5. Since the full-bore formal proceeding is rarely used now, the fact that these words create a kind of springing use may be a trap for the unwary.

### E. *Reliance on title 28 conventions*

Another convention is based on the provisions in title 28 (chapters 85 and 87) providing default jurisdiction in U.S. district courts for the trial of most civil actions. In earlier times, when Congress created a new cause of action, it would also usually provide ad hoc provisions for jurisdiction and venue in the U.S. district courts. However, the enactment of chapters 85 and 87 has made it unnecessary to do this anymore. An added advantage of letting title 28 supply these details (jurisdiction, venue) is that they are likely to be more uniform than when done on an ad hoc basis.

This absence of statute-by-statute jurisdiction and venue provisions is less likely than some other omissions to trouble judges, however, since pleadings always must recite the jurisdictional provisions on which the case is based and the courts are very aware of the default provisions, such as section 1331 of title 28 (also a codified title, by the way).

The elimination of the amount-in-controversy requirement for federal cases is not always understood by congressional drafters, so you will sometimes find superfluous jurisdictional statements.[12] More troubling are superfluous venue provisions, as it is sometimes unclear whether they provide additional or exclusive venue, and they may leave out venue options that probably would have been included if the drafters had focused on that issue. Unfortunately, this is a case in which Congress sometimes fails to follow its own drafting conventions.

12. A few examples: 36 U.S.C. § 220505; Section 16 of the Deepwater Port Act of 1974 (33 U.S.C. § 1515); Section 4003 of Public Law 93-406 (29 U.S.C. § 1303).



 

### *F. Criminal fine conventions*

Another trap for the unwary is the combined effect of sections 3571 and 3559 of title 18 on possible fines for criminal offenses. There are a number of existing sections that purport to set maximum fines, and at times Congress inadvertently enacts additional ones. These seeming maxima may be superseded by the rules set forth in section 3571. The key rule (found in section 3571(b)), which is intended as a rule of construction to provide a uniform system of fines for federal offenses, says that the maximum fine is the higher of the maximum set by a specific statutory enactment and the general rule provided in section 3571 unless the specific statutory enactment overrules section 3571 by explicit reference to it (section 3571(e)).

One should also keep in mind section 3571(d), a little-noticed additional rule, which provides that in cases where the offense results in a gain or loss, the maximum fine can be increased over what it otherwise would be to an amount that is double that gain or loss.

For federal judges, much of this has been subsumed into the Sentencing Guidelines, but the evolving effect of those guidelines may require more recourse to the underlying statutory base for criminal penalties.

### *G. State-of-mind convention for criminal cases*

Another convention that is used in drafting, but is not codified in the statute law, also deals with criminal cases. That convention relates to the state of mind required with respect to various elements of an offense. In many cases, statutes use the formula "Whoever knowingly does X in circumstance Y with result Z shall be fined or imprisoned." It is clear that "knowingly" modifies the X, but perhaps less clear that the expectation is, unless otherwise stated, that "knowingly" also applies to Y and Z.[13]

---

13. One place where this convention is used is in 18 U.S.C. § 2241(c). In that section, the state of mind "knowingly" is explicitly applied to the conduct required for the offense, and through the convention would also apply to any circumstances and results that are required for the offense. This necessitated the addition of subsection (d), providing that in a prosecution under subsection (c) the government need not prove the defendant knew the victim was less than twelve years old. As stated in the report of the House Judiciary Committee, from which this section originated, "Absent this provision, the government would have had to prove that the defendant knew the victim was less than twelve years old, since the state of mind required for the conduct—knowingly—is also required for the circumstance of the victim's age." House Report 99-594 to accompany the Sexual Abuse Act of 1986. This convention may be grounded in the common-law doctrine relating to the "general intent" scienter requirement for criminal offenses. *See* United States v. Bailey, 444 U.S. 394 (1980).



 

There are some exceptions to this, most of them coming from a time before the convention was generally adopted or in statutes where the drafter was unaware of the convention. For instance, the crime of killing a federal officer during the conduct of that officer's duty does not require you know that the victim is a Federal officer or perhaps even that the officer is engaged in official duty. Undercover law enforcement officers were intended to be protected by the forerunner of this section (now found in an updated, and broader, version in 18 U.S.C. § 1114). The earlier version provided protections for a list of officers limited at first to law enforcement officers from named agencies, and made the killing of anyone on that list a crime. In that context it was relatively easy for the courts to decide that particular knowledge of which law enforcement agency the victim was employed by was not a required aspect of scienter, which had the effect of not requiring scienter for the fact the officer was an officer of the federal government. The current, much broader, language seems to be interpreted in the light of this earlier version.

The more common way of eliminating scienter for an element of an offense is simply to say so. The section of law defining the offense provides that the prosecution is not required to prove a state of mind with respect to whatever the element is.[14] Of course, in some cases this may raise constitutional issues.

Whether the convention that *scienter* for circumstances and results as well as conduct required for an offense applies needs to be considered on a case-by-case basis. However, it does apply in many cases, especially in newer laws, and some attention to the history of the section in question normally will resolve the issue.

### *H. Problems with "willful"*

The state of mind "willfully" is increasingly being avoided in federal statutes. Courts and commentators have noted its varied meanings and have strongly criticized it.[15] It has been used to cover everything from carelessness to intentional malice, and so is almost perfectly ambiguous. In most cases, the reality is that "knowingly" expresses the proper state of mind. Courts seem likely to infer its being the required state of mind even if it is not explicitly made so, and there may be some constitutional constraints on departing from it unless some nearly equivalent state of mind is provided, such as "with reason to believe."

---

14. Sections 2241(d) and 2243(d) of title 18 of the U.S. Code both have this format.

15. Spies v. United States, 317 U.S. 492, 497 (1943); United States v. Murdock, 290 U.S. 389, 395 (1933); United States v. Granda, 565 F.2d 922, 924 (5th Cir. 1978). See also the comments of Judge Learned Hand in the Model Penal Code and Commentaries, sec. 2.02 at 249 n.47 (Official Draft and Revised Comments 2005). I am indebted to Michael Volkov for these references.



 

## Conclusion

We have looked at some conventions that drafters of federal statute law currently use, at least most of the time in the context of the structure of federal statutory law. Readers should be cautioned that conventions change with language and usage over time, so this discussion of them will grow out of date. Conventions are not always followed, either because of ignorance or perhaps the age of the statute being considered. But starting with these conventions, a reader of statutes will have a better chance of gleaning the legislative intent that often hides deeply encrusted within the statute's off-putting verbal exterior.



 

# Considering the Courts: Statutory Interpretation

Chapter 3





 

*All new laws, though penned with the greatest technical skill, and passed on the fullest and most mature deliberation, are considered as more or less obscure and equivocal, until their meaning be liquidated and ascertained by a series of particular discussions and adjudications.*

**James Madison, *The Federalist* Number 37**

*The prophecies of what the courts will do in fact, and nothing more pretentious, are what I mean by the law.*

**Oliver Wendell Holmes Jr.**

*(1) Read the statute; (2) read the statute; (3) read the statute!*

**Justice Frankfurter's "threefold imperative to law students," as related by Henry Friendly, *Benchmarks* 202 (1967)**

60

 

Chapter 3

# Considering the Courts: Statutory Interpretation

## § 3.00 Introduction

As described in the Canadian case of *Regina v. Ojibway*, 8 *Criminal Law Quarterly* 137–139 (1965), a pony bearing a down pillow for a saddle was shot to put it out of its misery. The shooter was charged with killing a "small bird" in violation of the Small Birds Act, and the question on appeal was whether a pony was a "small bird" within the meaning of the act. The court held that it was.

"Statutory interpretation," the court observed, "has forced many a horse to eat birdseed for the rest of its life." For the full text of this case, see Appendix Six.

*Regina v. Ojibway* is a work of fiction, but a deft one—farfetched, and yet not completely absurd. Courts can and do read statutes in odd ways at times. As a drafter, you need to understand how and why that happens, so that you can draft, and advise your client, accordingly.

## § 3.01 Courts: The Most Important Audience

Some drafting projects never see the light of day, but most are intended to be read. Ultimately, the effect of a draft depends not on what you think the draft means or on what your client thinks the draft means, but on what the audience thinks the draft means.

To draft effectively, then, you need to get inside the mind of the audience and understand how the audience thinks. But who is the audience?



 

In drafting federal law, the most important audience (apart from the client) is the federal courts—and, in particular, the Supreme Court of the United States. Fortunately, it is not difficult to get inside the mind of the Court and understand how it thinks. The Court makes this process public in its published opinions; collectively, the process is known as statutory interpretation. (It is also known as statutory construction; the differences between the two terms are not great. For consistency's sake, this book uses "statutory interpretation" throughout.)

There are other audiences, of course. The draft will be read and interpreted by legislators, lobbyists, public officials, private individuals, industry leaders, journalists, and scholars, to name a few. In some ways these audiences are very different, but in two ways they are all alike: Each wants to know the effect of the draft, and each recognizes that the effect is ultimately determined by the courts, through judicial methods of statutory interpretation. The courts always have the last word, and the Supreme Court has the very last word: "We are not final because we are infallible, but we are infallible only because we are final." *Brown v. Allen*, 344 U.S. 443, 539 (1953) (Jackson, J., concurring). When you control how a court reads a text, you thereby control how others read that text as well.

Some who write about drafting have argued that a drafter does not need to be much concerned with statutory interpretation. Reed Dickerson, for example, argued as follows: "For the draftsman, many rules of interpretation are simply irrelevant. . . . They are irrelevant because the draftsman who tries to write a healthy instrument does not and should not pay attention to the principles that the court will apply if he fails." Reed Dickerson, *The Fundamentals of Legal Drafting* 54 (1965).

This is, to put it delicately, not the best advice. Suppose you were an appellate lawyer trying to convince a court that a statute means X. You probably would argue that the statute is clear and the plain meaning is X—but you must also be ready to argue that the statute, even if unclear, should be given the meaning X. In short, you need a fallback position. The suggestion that you should not have a fallback position in drafting is bizarre. Your job is to do all you can to give effect to the policy, not to rest on language that you think is clear.

Statutory interpretation applies at all times to all instruments, not just to those that are not, as Dickerson put it, "healthy." Indeed, it is used to determine whether an instrument is healthy in the first place. It is used to decide what a healthy instrument means, and what an unhealthy instrument means.

It is true that many principles of statutory interpretation are simply general principles about how best to read English prose. But many are not. Some are obvious, some are subtle, some are counterintuitive, some are traps for the unwary.

You can try to draft without paying attention to statutory interpretation. But rules of interpretation are like rules of the road: Drive on the right; stop on red; signal before turning; pedestrians have the right of way. If you don't know all the rules, sooner or later you will park in front of a fire hydrant or go the wrong way down a one-way street.

## § 3.02 What Kind of Judge?

Among those who write about drafting there is a curious debate about what kind of judge should be considered the primary audience. Can you safely assume that the audience is a "good-faith judge"—one who will give your words the benefit of the doubt—or should you assume that the audience is a "bad-faith judge"—one who will actively try to twist and evade your words?

This is sort of like asking whether you should be cynical or naive. It's not really a useful choice. You should be realistic.

The audience is almost certainly not a single judge. Perhaps if the Supreme Court were abolished and replaced by a single judge the question might be worth more study. But the fact is that a law is not what any one judge says it is, but what a majority of the nine justices on the Court say it is.

If it helps your process to have in mind a particular kind of judge, try the middle ground: Assume the judge is open-minded and skeptical. Do not assume the judge is sympathetic to you and your intended meaning. Thanks to you, the judge has to resolve a duel between warring lawyers—a duel that came about because your language is problematic. Do not expect the judge to cut you any slack.

Ultimately, the concern is not so much that a rogue court will invent an implausible meaning that mangles your statute. The concern is that a careful court, prodded by a persuasive attorney, or on its own initiative, will see a plausible meaning that you failed to see.



 

## §3.10 Judicial Power and Legislative Supremacy

The judicial power of the United States is vested by the Constitution in the Supreme Court of the United States and any other federal courts established by law.

The task of courts is to interpret and apply the law. As Justice Marshall famously put it, "it is emphatically the province and duty of the judicial department to say what the law is." *Marbury v. Madison*, 5 U.S. 137, 177 (1803).

The judicial power can be exercised only in cases and controversies. This means that the federal courts do not have power to issue advisory opinions. This also means that federal courts do not interpret statutes as an abstract exercise; they always have a particular case before them with a particular pattern of facts.

In resolving cases and controversies, a court actually performs three separate functions. First, the court finds which facts have been proven; second, the court interprets the relevant law; and third, the court applies the law as interpreted to the facts as found.

This chapter is concerned primarily with the second function, though the second and third functions sometimes blend together. A court interprets a statute in some cases because the language is unclear, and in other cases because the language, though clear, didn't anticipate (and doesn't squarely address) a controversy of the sort before the court.

### §3.11 The Power to Interpret

As a general matter, a court left to its own devices can interpret a statute using any technique that it likes. The court can consider the sound of a cat and the breath of a fish. Left to its own devices, a court can look to anything under the sun that it considers persuasive.

Courts have, for example, considered sources such as law review articles, history, social context, state law, and general principles of public policy. They occasionally invoke poetry or literature, such as the works of Shakespeare or Conan Doyle.

Of course, courts are not left entirely to their own devices. Most importantly, courts are bound by law to follow the Constitution and the laws of the United States.

Also, most courts are bound by custom—if not by law—to follow precedent. (Courts in a civil law system, such as the courts of Louisiana, are not.) Specifically, a court is bound to follow the precedents of courts that are higher in the judicial "chain of command." A court is not bound to follow the precedents of every higher court, but it is bound to follow the precedents of the higher courts to which appeals from its decisions are taken. Thus, each of the circuit courts is bound by the precedents of the Supreme Court, and each trial court is bound by the precedents of both the Supreme Court and one circuit court.

A court is not bound to follow the precedent of a lower court or of a court of the same level, including itself: No court is bound to follow its own precedents. As a result, the Supreme Court—having no higher court—is not bound to follow any precedents—its own or anyone else's.

That said, courts do not lightly overrule their own past decisions. This is known as the doctrine of stare decisis. "Very weighty considerations" underlie the doctrine, such as the need for laws to be clear and reliable, for disputes to be settled, and for faith in the judiciary to be maintained. See *Moragne v. States Marine Lines*, 398 U.S. 375, 403 (1970). The doctrine of stare decisis "is of fundamental importance to the rule of law." *Hilton v. South Carolina Public Railways Commission*, 502 U.S. 197, 202 (1991).

When interpreting the Constitution, the Court is somewhat flexible about overruling its past decisions, such as if the past decision is unworkable or the rationale for the decision no longer holds. In constitutional matters, what is most important to the Court is that it get the answer right (even if it takes several tries). The Constitution is not an easy document to amend, so society might be long stuck with a wrong answer if the Court did not overrule itself. See *Webster v. Reproductive Health Services*, 492 U.S. 490, 518 (1989) (plurality opinion).

A statute, on the other hand, is a relatively easy document to amend, so the Court is much less willing to overrule itself. What is most important to the Court is that once it reaches an answer, it abides by that answer. If Congress disagrees with that answer, "Congress remains free to alter what we have done." *Patterson v. McLean Credit Union*, 491 U.S. 164, 172–173 (1989).

The power to create specific techniques of statutory interpretation is seen as part of the judicial power. The Constitution does not require that specific techniques be created, but the courts, in their discretion, have seen fit to create them. Once created, a court can overrule them in much the same way as a court can overrule a statute, though—as with statutes—the courts have been reluctant to do so.

Remember, techniques of interpretation have generally not been enacted into law—a least not at the federal level. (In a fair number of states, some techniques—most notably, canons of construction—have been enacted into law.) Accordingly, techniques of interpretation reflect not the voice of the legislature but the ear of the judiciary. To the extent that applying a technique changes what the law would otherwise be, the legitimacy of the technique can be called into question.

Justice Breyer once pondered whether the Court could simply invent or adopt a new technique. "[C]an the Court simply adopt them?" he mused. "Where would it find the legal authority to do so?" He concluded that any newfangled techniques would "lack the legitimacy provided by continuous judicial use over many years." Stephen Breyer, "On the Uses of Legislative History in Interpreting Statutes," 65 *Southern California Law Review* 845, 870 (1992).

Could the Court adopt a new technique derived from continuous *drafting* use over many years? See § 3.13, relating to the *Koons* decision.

### § 3.12 Making Congress Follow the Techniques

Techniques of statutory interpretation are of great use to Congress—or so the Court claims. When courts consistently apply a set of techniques, laws are more reliable and certain, and the drafting of laws is more predictable and effective. It is of "paramount importance," the Court has stated, "that Congress be able to legislate against a background of clear interpretive rules, so that it may know the effect of the language it adopts." *Finley v. United States*, 490 U.S. 545, 556 (1989). (But see § 3.90, relating to Frank Horack.)

The Court not only supplies this background, but it presumes that Congress follows it: "It is presumable that Congress legislates with knowledge of our basic rules of statutory construction." *McNary v. Haitian Refugee Center, Inc.*, 498 U.S. 479, 496 (1991).

This is a powerful notion, but perhaps not as overbearing as at first it might seem. Courts have long presumed that everyone knows the law, and have long included Congress in that category. Thus, the Court presumes Congress is aware of existing law when it passes legislation. *South Dakota v. Yankton Sioux Tribe*, 522 U.S. 329 (1998). The Court presumes Congress is aware of how courts have interpreted a statute, *United States v. Alaska*, 521 U.S. 1 (1997), and the Court presumes Congress expects its statutes to be read in conformity with the Court's precedents, *Porter v. Nussle*, 534 U.S. 516 (2002).

In addition, the Court presumes Congress is aware of how administrative agencies have interpreted a statute. *Lorillard v. Pons*, 434 U.S. 575, 580–581 (1978). The Court even presumes that Congress is familiar with relevant scholarly writing. *Holloway v. United States*, 526 U.S. 1 (1999).

Thus, having presumed that Congress knows the results that courts reach, it is perhaps a small step to also presume that Congress knows the techniques courts use to go about reaching their results.

Whether this is a reasonable position for the Court to take is a fair question. Ironically, courts insist that Congress take into account how courts interpret statutes but by and large do not take into account how Congress drafts them: Courts are ambivalent about legislative history and almost never consult federal drafting manuals. (But see § 3.13, relating to the *Koons* decision.)

As a drafter, however, you must consider not what courts should do, but what they in fact do. Congress is on notice that the Court expects Congress to play by the Court's rules. Though not infallible, the Court has the last word.

### § 3.13 Tensions between Courts and Congress over Interpretation

Stereotypically, lawmakers think judges are mad or corrupt, and judges think lawmakers are illiterate or dense. These tensions have always been there and they will always remain. They are naturally present, and the Framers had them in mind when they separated judicial powers from legislative powers in the Constitution.

That said, tensions can be eased or they can be exacerbated. There is a generally accepted view that courts and Congress should work more closely together, or at least pay more attention to what the other is doing. See generally Robert A. Katzmann, *Courts and Congress* (1997).

Abner J. Mikva, who served not only in Congress but also as White House counsel and on the federal bench, cogently observed that courts and Congress share an "unawareness . . . of each other's game rules," and recommended that lawmakers (and drafters) pay more attention to how courts interpret statutes and, indeed, that court opinions applying principles of interpretation be distributed to drafters. Abner J. Mikva, "Reading and Writing Statutes," 28 *South Texas Law Journal* 181, 183 (1986).

This chapter is written with Mikva's recommendation in mind. Drafters should, indeed, pay more attention to how courts interpret statutes. Notably, however, that is only one part of his two-part recommendation.



 

Mikva also recommended that courts pay more attention to how Congress drafts laws. It seems fair to suggest that manuals specifying principles of legislative drafting be more widely consulted by courts.

In an important critique of how judges traditionally interpret statutes, Jack Stark, a longtime drafter for the Legislative Reference Bureau of the State of Wisconsin, noted that laws generally are written not by lawmakers but by drafters. Drafters generally apply a more or less universal set of conventions, such as that the word "shall" is used exclusively to require and the word "may" is used exclusively to authorize. Yet courts, Stark lamented, do not consider or apply these conventions. Jack Stark, "On Language Games and Statutory Interpretation: An Inside Narrative," 20 *Statute Law Review* 144, 150 (1999).

Perhaps that is changing. The Supreme Court in 2004 for the first time relied on the drafting manuals used by the House and Senate Offices of Legislative Counsel to interpret a statute: *Koons Buick Pontiac* GMC, *Inc. v. Nigh*, 543 U.S. 50 (2004). (The Court used the manuals, and other drafting guides, to determine that federal drafters conventionally give "subparagraph" a particular meaning, and applied that meaning.)

## § 3.14 Efforts by Congress to Regulate Interpretation

Congress regulates the interpretive process in many different ways, and there is no doubt that Congress has at least some power to do so. If Congress can fix rules of evidence and rules of procedure—and it is fairly well settled that it can—then Congress can probably fix rules of interpretation as well.

The simplest means by which Congress regulates meaning is by definition. Typically, a definition is in the form, "In this Act, the term 'X' means 'Y.'" Whenever a court encounters X, the court is supposed to give it the meaning Y, even if it would not normally do so. Notice, however, that definitions of this sort merely require this or that result; they do not tell the court how to interpret. They are better understood as rules of law, not interpretation.

A more nuanced means by which Congress regulates interpretation is by rule of construction. Unlike a typical definition, a rule of construction tells the court not merely what result to reach, but how to interpret. A typical rule of construction might provide, "This Act shall be construed liberally."

A good real-life example is section 103 of Public Law 94-136 (15 U.S.C. 2403), which provides, first, that it is the policy of the United States to use all practicable means and measures to stimulate a high rate of productivity growth and, second, that "the laws, rules, regulations, and policies of the United States shall be so interpreted as to give full force and effect to this policy."

Another is section 2 of the act of March 9, 1945 (popularly known as the McCarran-Ferguson Act; 15 U.S.C. 1012), which provides, "No Act of Congress shall be construed to invalidate, impair, or supersede any law enacted by any State for the purpose of regulating the business of insurance . . . unless such Act specifically relates to the business of insurance . . . ."

Still other examples are contained in chapter 1 of title 1, United States Code, which sets forth a number of rules, some of which (like definitions) dictate a result and some of which (like rules of construction) dictate a methodology. In the latter category are rules that the singular includes the plural (and vice versa), the masculine includes the feminine (but not vice versa), and the present tense includes the future tense (but not vice versa).

Some rules that are written as if they were rules of construction are, as with most definitions, better understood as rules of law. For two examples, look no further than the Constitution: The Ninth Amendment provides, "The enumeration in the Constitution, of certain rights, shall not be construed to deny or disparage others retained by the people," and the Eleventh Amendment provides, "The Judicial power of the United States shall not be construed to extend to any suit in law or equity . . . ." Though they use the word "construed," these rules require not that a methodology be followed but that a result be reached (or not be reached). Notice that in both examples you could strike "shall not be construed to" and insert "does not" without changing the meaning (and, indeed, that would probably be better drafting).

Rules of construction are often vague and rarely useful, and there are some who suggest that they unconstitutionally infringe on the judicial power. In any event, they are rarely invoked—at least the ones created by statute (the ones created by jurisprudence are invoked regularly). The example from 15 U.S.C. 2403, given above, seems never to have been applied in a published federal court decision, perhaps because courts find it vague, perhaps because courts find it unconstitutional or otherwise objectionable—or perhaps (as seems likely) because courts simply can't find it in the first place.

A more intrusive means by which Congress regulates interpretation is to tell the courts what they are required or forbidden to consider.

Here's one that seems innocent enough—section 19 of the act of June 25, 1948, which enacted title 18 of the United States Code and which is set forth in the notes at the very beginning of that Code, provides: "No inference of a legislative construction is to be drawn by reason of the chapter in Title 18, Crimes and Criminal Procedure, as set out in section 1 of this Act, in which any particular section is placed, nor by reason of the catchlines used in such title." Many of the laws that have enacted titles of the Code have similar language. Without this language, a court trying to make sense of an unclear section might try to glean meaning from the chapter in which it was placed and the catchline assigned to that chapter. But this language forbids a court from doing so. Can Congress do that? Is it constitutional?

A more interesting example is section 105(b) of the Civil Rights Act of 1991 (Public Law 102-166; 105 Stat. 1075; 42 U.S.C. 1981 note), which provides, "No statements other than the interpretive memorandum appearing at Vol. 137 Congressional Record S 15276 (daily ed. Oct. 25, 1991) shall be considered legislative history of, or relied upon in any way as legislative history in construing or applying, any provision of this Act that relates to *Wards Cove*—Business necessity/cumulation/alternative business practice." Can Congress do that? Is it constitutional?

But never mind whether that one is constitutional; what does it actually mean? Reading it casually one might think it means, "A court is required to consider this memorandum, and is forbidden to consider any other statements in the legislative record, in interpreting this Act." But on closer examination it says neither of these things. Literally, it forbids a court from relying on statements "as legislative history"—that is, by reason of its status as legislative history. It does not forbid a court from relying on statements for other reasons, such as for their inherently persuasive value. This is the sort of thing that happens when lawyers who are not drafters try to draft: The words grasp at meaning but do not grab it.

Remember, courts give weight to some statements because they are required to do so, such as the precedent of a higher court. But courts can give weight to any other statement merely because it has inherent power to persuade, such as the opinion of a sister court or lower court, or a law review article, or a line from Shakespeare. When read in a straightforward manner, that provision of the Civil Rights Act of 1991 forbids the use of a statement by reason of its status as legislative history, but does not forbid the use of a statement for any other reason—including its inherent power to persuade.

When read that way, the provision probably passes constitutional muster.



 

If Congress wants to disparage its own documents and tell the courts not to give them any special dignity, one would think Congress has the power to do so.

But it does beg the question of how the Court might respond if Congress tried more directly to tie the Court's hands. Suppose, for example, Congress passed a law to forbid the courts from applying a particular technique of interpretation. Would it be constitutional? The answer may vary from technique to technique. For one view, see Nicholas Quinn Rosenkranz, "Federal Rules of Statutory Interpretation," 115 *Harvard Law Review* 2085 (2002).

The Court has said the "power to determine the meaning of a statute carries with it the power to prescribe its extent and limitations as well as the method by which they shall be determined." *City of Chicago v. Morales*, 527 U.S. 41 (1999). That was in reference to the power of a state legislature, however; it does not necessarily apply to Congress.

Thus, while there are certainly boundaries, we do not yet know where they are.

## §3.20 The Overriding Goal: Determine the Intent of Congress

The Supreme Court does not publish an official treatise on statutory interpretation. Instead, the Court publishes piecemeal—a little bit in this case, a little bit in that one. Over time, the lessons from these cases accumulate and become more or less settled principles.

The overriding goal of statutory interpretation is to determine and give effect to the intent of Congress. More precisely, the intent sought with respect to an act is the intent of the Congress that enacted the act, and thus needs to be determined as of enactment.

Every other consideration must yield to that overriding goal. Statutory interpretation exists "to discover and not to direct the Congressional will." *Huddleston v. United States*, 415 U.S. 814, 831 (1974).

Beyond that overriding goal, however, there is not much you can hang your hat on. "Do not expect anybody's theory of statutory interpretation, whether it is your own or somebody else's, to be an accurate statement of what courts actually do with statutes. The hard truth of the matter is that American courts have no intelligible, generally accepted, and consistently applied theory of statutory interpretation." Henry M. Hart Jr. & Albert M. Sachs, *The Legal Process: Basic Problems in the Making and Application Of Law* 1169 (1994).

And one might fairly question the overriding goal. That is, one might fairly ask why the intent of Congress should trump the words of Congress. If the words accurately express the intent, then intent is redundant; if the words don't accurately express the intent, then Congress is being sloppy or misleading.

Should sloppy or misleading behavior be tolerated—even rewarded? Regardless, doesn't due process prefer a published word to a secret thought? The Court seemed to question its own reliance on legislative intent in *Lamie v. United States Trustee*, 540 U.S. 526, 542 (2004), when it said: "If Congress enacted into law something different from what it intended, then it should amend the statute to conform to its intent. It is beyond our province to rescue Congress from its drafting errors, and to provide for what we might think is the preferred result." (internal quotation marks and ellipses omitted). Whether that is a warning to be taken seriously remains to be seen.

One might also fairly ask whether Congress can ever be said to have an intent. Congress is a collection of hundreds of people in two separate chambers, each with individual intent. When Congress passes a law, however imperfect, it is reasonable to suppose that the intent of Congress was to pass that law, but any intent of Congress beyond that seems like wishful thinking.

But, then again, one must also ask what better alternative the Court should use. If not legislative intent, then what? Should courts take it upon themselves to make policy choices? Though state courts generally have the power to do so, federal courts do not. The legislative power is vested in Congress, not in the courts.

Suppose all the animals in a zoo agree on a policy of regular feedings, but they do not agree on what "regular feedings" requires. There is no "intent of the zoo," and trying to find it would do more harm than good. The regular feedings of a lion and a lizard are not the same. What seems best is to allow the policy to be applied on a case-by-case basis, using good judgment and common sense, based on the totality of the circumstances. Courts already do this sometimes, such as when a statute provides a general standard like "reasonable" or "good faith." Should courts do this more often? Do they already have the power to do so? If not, can Congress constitutionally give courts that power? Should Congress do so? The questions do not have quick and ready answers.

Because legislative intent can be problematic, courts sometimes speak instead about a statute's "purpose." Apparently, the distinction is that legislative intent asks why the particular Congress enacted the statute, while purpose asks why a reasonable Congress would have enacted the statute. Ultimately, though, it is a distinction without much difference, and courts tend to use the terms interchangeably. See discussion in Abner J. Mikva & Eric Lane, *An Introduction to Statutory Interpretation and the Legislative Process* 6–9 (1997).

## § 3.21 Rules of Thumb, Not Rules of Law

To achieve their goal—the goal of determining and giving effect to the intent of Congress—the courts apply a variety of techniques to shed light on what Congress most likely intended.

Some techniques are called "canons" or "maxims," others "principles" or "rules," but the labels are not of much practical importance. None of the techniques are rules of law (though some are derived, at least in part, from constitutional principles); most of them are simply rules of thumb—educated guesses about whether to draw an inference about legislative intent and, if drawn, how much weight to give it.

The Court has been candid about the limited utility of its techniques. Canons of construction, the Court has said, are "simply rules of thumb which will sometimes help courts determine the meaning of legislation." *Varity Corp. v. Howe*, 516 U.S. 489, 511 (1996). One canon pointing to one result is often countered by another pointing in the opposite direction. *Chickasaw Nation v. United States*, 534 U.S. 84 (2001). The use of legislative history, meanwhile, has been described as "the equivalent of entering a crowded cocktail party and looking over the heads of the guests for one's friends." *Conroy v. Aniskoff*, 507 U.S. 511, 519 (1993) (Scalia, J., concurring, attributing the statement to Judge Harold Leventhal).

When the various techniques all point toward the same result, the case is easy—and most cases are easy cases. When some techniques point toward one result and other techniques point elsewhere, a court has some serious work to do.

In any event, the various techniques are not binding and are not applied in a slavish or mechanical fashion. They are tools, not rules. The goal is not to apply the techniques, but to determine the legislative intent, and the techniques are subordinate to that goal:



 

> "However well these rules may serve at times to aid in deciphering legislative intent, they long have been subordinated to the doctrine that courts will construe the details of an act in conformity with its dominant general purpose, will read text in the light of context and will interpret the text so far as the meaning of the words fairly permits so as to carry out in particular cases the generally expressed legislative policy."
>
> *Securities and Exchange Commission v. C.M. Joiner Leasing Corp.*, 320 U.S. 344, 350–351 (1943).

For a drafter, the overriding lesson is to be aware of all the different techniques that a court might apply and to make sure that, when applied to your draft, the techniques point as consistently as possible toward a single result.

### § 3.22 Three Common Theories (Intentionalism, Textualism, and Pragmatism) and Their Limitations

To understand the limitations of the Court's techniques, it may help to understand some of the theory behind them.

No principle of statutory interpretation is etched in stone. Within the Court itself, there is often disagreement over how best to apply the various principles to a particular law or to particular facts. More broadly, there is also disagreement over what the principles should be.

Three common theories about the interpretation of statutes are intentionalism, textualism, and pragmatism. These are not the only theories, but they are a representative sample. These are not, mind you, theories about how courts do interpret statutes, but theories about how courts should interpret statutes. Each theory describes not how things are, but how things ought to be.

According to intentionalism, the Court should consider legislative and historical materials to determine why Congress enacted the law, and should apply the law in the way that Congress would have wanted. According to textualism, the Court should be concerned not with what Congress wanted, but only with what Congress said; the Court should consider the text and context only, and should apply the words that Congress wrote. According to pragmatism, the Court should consider the effects on society, and should apply the law in the way that the Court believes would produce the best effects on society.

In short, these three common theories can be summarized as follows:



 

What Did the Lawmakers Mean? (Intentionalism)
What Does the Law Mean? (Textualism)
What Should the Lawmakers Have Meant? (Pragmatism)

As a practical matter, the Court seems to operate as if it takes something from each of these theories. Even the most ardent intentionalist or pragmatist will recognize that the Court cannot take too many liberties with the plain text; even the most dedicated textualist will acknowledge a "scrivener's error" that should not be given literal effect. And so on.

Notably, all three theories agree that the starting point is the text itself; they disagree over the extent to which matters outside the text should influence its meaning. Because a drafter generally has no control over matters outside the text, there is little a drafter can do about them but be aware that they exist—and advise the client accordingly.

It has been said, pessimistically but perhaps realistically, that courts use statutory interpretation "not as approaches to be followed consistently from one case to the next, wherever they may lead, but as techniques to support a conclusion reached for other reasons." Robert J. Martineau, "Craft and Technique, Not Canons and Grand Theories: A Neo-Realist View of Statutory Construction," 62 *George Washington Law Review* 1, 40 (1993).

You do not have to be a cynic to recognize that the techniques are not used consistently. All you need to know is that there are nine justices and they are rarely unanimous:

> "Indeed, the same judges—even very great ones—give different emphasis at different times to the two souls that dwell within their breasts. Thus Holmes, whom Frankfurter quoted as saying of legislators, 'I don't care what their intention was. I only want to know what the words mean,' wrote also that 'the general purpose is a more important aid to the meaning than any rule which grammar or formal logic may lay down,' and even that 'the meaning of a sentence is to be felt rather than to be proved.' "
>
> Henry J. Friendly, *Benchmarks* 200 (1967).

Courts do more than woodenly apply techniques; at some point they run out of useful techniques and still do not have a clear answer. At that point, the serious business begins, and the courts consider everything they can, including policy. (Whether they admit in writing to doing so is another matter.) We should not be horrified when judicial officers exercise judgment; that is, after all, why they are called judges.

### § 3.23 The Plain Meaning Rule

Typically, the first step in the Court's analysis is to determine whether the language is clear or ambiguous. If clear, one set of rules applies; if ambiguous, another set. (Note that the Court uses "ambiguity" in the broad sense, to mean lack of clarity, rather than in the narrower sense described in § 6.11.)

At one time this determination was the crux of the case. To determine whether the language was clear, the Court would look only at that language. If clear, that was the end of the inquiry; the Court did not consult any matter outside the text itself. There was a safe harbor for clear language.

As one of the major Supreme Court decisions explained:

> "It is elementary that the meaning of a statute must, in the first instance, be sought in the language in which the act is framed, and if that is plain, and if the law is within the constitutional authority of the lawmaking body which passed it, the sole function of the courts is to enforce it according to its terms . . . . Where the language is plain and admits of no more than one meaning, the duty of interpretation does not arise, and the rules which are to aid doubtful meanings need no discussion."
>
> *Caminetti v. United States*, 242 U.S. 470, 485 (1917).

This rule—"if plain, game over"—was known as the Plain Meaning Rule. But the Court no longer follows this formulation, and the term has come to be used for a different rule not nearly as pivotal.

The old Plain Meaning Rule allowed for only one exception—after all, the "duty of interpretation does not arise" when the language was plain. The exception was when the plain meaning led to an "absurd result." Perhaps the most famous use of this exception is *Church of the Holy Trinity v. United States*, 143 U.S. 457 (1892), in which the Court considered a law that made it a crime to induce a foreigner to migrate to the United States "to perform labor or service of any kind." A church induced a foreign minister to migrate to the United States to serve as its rector. The Court held that this came within the plain meaning of the law, but produced an absurd result: Given the religious heritage of the United States (about which the Court went on at great length), the claim that Congress intended to punish a house of worship for hiring a foreign pastor, priest, or rabbi "cannot be accepted as correct." 143 U.S. at 472.

The old Plain Meaning Rule that informed the *Caminetti* decision in 1917 began to break down in the 1920s and 1930s. By 1940 it was no longer being applied. In a lengthy but important passage, the Court explained the breakdown of the old Plain Meaning Rule:

> "There is, of course, no more persuasive evidence of the purpose of a statute than the words by which the legislature undertook to give expression to its wishes. Often these words are sufficient in and of themselves to determine the purpose of the legislation. In such cases we have followed their plain meaning. When that meaning has led to absurd or futile results, however, this Court has looked beyond the words to the purpose of the act. Frequently, however, even when the plain meaning did not produce absurd results but merely an unreasonable one plainly at variance with the policy of the legislation as a whole this Court has followed that purpose, rather than the literal words. When aid to construction of the meaning of words, as used in the statute, is available, there certainly can be no rule of law which forbids its use, however clear the words may appear on superficial examination. The interpretation of the meaning of statutes, as applied to justiciable controversies, is exclusively a judicial function. This duty requires one body of public servants, the judges, to construe the meaning of what another body, the legislators, has said. Obviously there is danger that the courts' conclusion as to legislative purpose will be unconsciously influenced by the judges' own views or by factors not considered by the enacting body. A lively appreciation of the danger is the best assurance of escape from its threat but hardly justifies an acceptance of a literal interpretation dogma which withholds from the courts available information for reaching a correct conclusion."
>
> *United States v. American Trucking Associations, Inc.*,
> 310 U.S. 534, 543–544 (1940)
> (internal footnotes and quotation marks omitted).

By 1940, then, the old Plain Meaning Rule was dead. To determine whether the language was clear, the Court no longer used a "superficial examination" of the "literal words," but used all information available. The safe harbor for clear language was gone.

Not only that, but the exception for an "absurd result" was no longer the only exception. The Court would decline to follow the plain meaning in any case in which the result was "unreasonable" and contrary to the legislative purpose (or, more accurately, contrary to the Court's conclusion as to the legislative purpose).

By 1981, the Plain Meaning Rule was no longer even considered a rule of law. As the Court stated in *Watt v. Alaska*, 451 U.S. 259, 266 (1981): "The starting point in every case involving construction of a statute is the language itself. But ascertainment of the meaning apparent on the face of a single statute need not end the inquiry. This is because the plain-meaning rule is rather an axiom of experience than a rule of law, and does not preclude consideration of persuasive evidence if it exists." (internal quotation marks and citations omitted).

The Court sometimes describes the modern Plain Meaning Rule as a presumption. For example, in *BedRoc Limited, LLC v. United States*, 541 U.S. 176 (2004), the Court said: "The preeminent canon of statutory interpretation requires us to presume that the legislature says in a statute what it means and means in a statute what it says there."

Under the modern Plain Meaning Rule, the Court still asks whether the language is plain, but to answer that question looks not only at the language but at everything it considers persuasive. In short, the Court carries out a hunt for other meanings that, though not obvious from the text, are plausible once all things have been considered.

Thus, the modern Plain Meaning Rule no longer has many teeth, and no longer seems to serve much purpose. The choice it poses—clear or ambiguous—assumes that every text is either black or white, when in fact most texts are different shades of gray. The point at which, say, "battleship gray" is black and "harbor fog" is white is not always obvious, and reasonable people can disagree from case to case and text to text about whether that point has been reached. For example, all nine members of the Court once agreed that the civil RICO statute had only one plain meaning, but split 5–4 over what that meaning was. See *Sedima, S.P.R.L. v. Imrex Co.*, 473 U.S. 479 (1985).

Regardless, the lesson for a drafter is that—contrary to what Dickerson asserted in scoffing at statutory interpretation—a clear text does not ensure a clear result. There is no safe harbor for a good plain draft. The Court does not look solely at the text—and so neither can you.

What seems most practical in drafting is to treat plain meaning not as a toggle switch but as a sliding scale. The more clear the draft, the more likely the Court will apply it in a straightforward manner, rather than twist it to conform to the legislative history, the views of an agency, or any other matter outside the text.

### § 3.24 The Meaning of "Plain Meaning"

The plain meaning of a statute is the "ordinary or natural meaning." *Federal Deposit Insurance Corporation v. Meyer*, 510 U.S. 471, 476 (1994). Notably, the Court uses the ordinary meaning that prevailed when the statute was enacted, not when it is being interpreted. See *BedRoc Limited, LLC v. United States*, 541 U.S. 176 (2004) (interpreting "valuable minerals" in a 1919 mining law based on which minerals were valuable in 1919).

By natural meaning, the Court means not a literal meaning but a commonsense meaning. For example, in *Roschen v. Ward*, 279 U.S. 337 (1929), a law made it unlawful to sell spectacles unless an eye specialist "be in charge of and personal attendance at" the place of sale. Read literally, the law did not require the specialist ever to examine a patient. However, the Court denounced this literal reading as a "perversion"; obviously, the Court said, an examination is not required in every case, but the specialist has a duty in every case to decide whether one is necessary. There is, the Court said, "no canon against using common sense in construing laws as saying what they obviously mean." 279 U.S. at 339.

By ordinary meaning, the Court means the meaning in an "idiomatic sense": that is, "the same way that ordinary people in common usage might speak . . . any day of the week." *General Dynamics Land Systems v. Cline*, 540 U.S. 581 (2004). In that case, the Court held that "discrimination because of age" is "naturally understood" to refer to discrimination against those who are older, and does not include discrimination against those who are younger.

Plain meaning typically can be found by consulting a general dictionary. Some justices have been known to favor prescriptive dictionaries (which indicate how words should properly be used) over descriptive dictionaries (which indicate how words are actually used). See *MCI Telecommunications Corp. v.*



 

*AT&T Co.*, 512 U.S. 218, 228 n.3 (1994) (criticizing the use of a descriptive dictionary "for its portrayal of common error as proper usage").

### § 3.25 The Consequences of Plain Meaning

As discussed above, the old Plain Meaning Rule provided that the Court would determine whether meaning is plain based on the statutory text alone. Under the modern Plain Meaning Rule, the Court determines whether the meaning is plain based on all the evidence it considers persuasive.

Language does not have to be perfect to be covered by the Plain Meaning Rule. The meaning of the language must merely leave no doubt. For example, a law with punctuation errors can still have plain meaning. See *United States National Bank of Oregon v. Independent Insurance Agents of America, Inc.*, 508 U.S. 439, 463 and n.11 (1993) (despite punctuation problems, the "true meaning . . . is clear beyond question"). Likewise, a law with grammatical errors can still have plain meaning. See *Lamie v. United States Trustee*, 540 U.S. 526 (2004) (being awkward and ungrammatical "does not make it ambiguous").

Generally, a determination that the language is plain has several consequences.

First, the Court will not use certain categories of lesser evidence to change the plain meaning—though the Court may use lesser evidence to clarify and illuminate the plain meaning. Lesser evidence generally includes legislative history, headings, preambles, and other evidence not usually given much weight.

Remember, however, that the Court will use any evidence, including lesser evidence, to decide whether the meaning is plain. Indeed, the Court has said it is "error" not to do so. *Train v. Colorado Public Interest Research Group*, 426 U.S. 1, 9–10 (1976) (determining whether the meaning is plain without considering legislative history is error). Since that case, the Court has backtracked somewhat and said that legislative history need not be considered in all cases, but only in cases in which a party argues that the plain meaning of a law is demonstrably at odds with the intentions of its drafters. *United States National Bank of Oregon v. Independent Insurance Agents of America, Inc.*, 508 U.S. 439, 463 fn 11 (1993).

Second, an agency cannot interpret the language in a way that changes the plain meaning; if it tries to do so, the Court will not give that interpretation any *Chevron* deference. For more on *Chevron* deference, see § 3.62, "Agency Interpretation and *Chevron* Deference."



 

Third, the Court will ordinarily enforce the plain meaning "according to its terms." *Lamie v. United States Trustee*, 540 U.S. 526 (2004).

### § 3.26 When Plain Meaning Is Not Enforced

In some cases the Court will decline to apply the plain meaning and will apply another meaning instead.

The Court has emphasized that a departure from plain meaning is justified only in "rare and exceptional circumstances," *TVA v. Hill*, 437 U.S. 153, 187 fn 33 (1978), but the precise nature of those circumstances can vary.

The general principle appears to be that the plain meaning will not be followed if the plain meaning "will produce a result demonstrably at odds with the intentions of its drafters." *Griffin v. Oceanic Contractors, Inc.*, 458 U.S. 564, 571 (1982). If so, those intentions—not the plain meaning—must be controlling.

Thus, the plain meaning will not be followed if it would lead to an absurd result, or merely to an "odd result." *Public Citizen v. Department of Justice*, 491 U.S. 440, 454 (1989). Looking beyond the "naked text" for guidance is perfectly proper, the Court said, when the result it apparently decrees is "difficult to fathom," or where it "seems inconsistent with Congress' intention." 491 U.S. at 455.

In addition, the plain meaning will not be followed if it would render the statute unconstitutional, unless applying the plain meaning is "utterly unavoidable." *Branch v. Smith*, 538 U.S. 254 (2003). If a "serious doubt of constitutionality" is raised, the Court will determine whether an interpretation is "fairly possible" that avoids that doubt and, if so, will apply that interpretation instead. *Public Citizen v. Department of Justice*, 491 U.S. 440, 465–466 (1989).

And the plain meaning will not be followed if it would be contrary to the "spirit" of the statute. "It is a familiar rule that a thing may be within the letter of the statute and yet not within the statute, because not within its spirit, nor within the intention of its makers." *Church of the Holy Trinity v. United States*, 143 U.S. 457 (1892).

The *Holy Trinity* decision referred to a number of other situations that might also justify a departure from plain meaning. For example, though it is a crime to obstruct or retard a mail carrier, the crime does not apply when a sheriff arrests a mail carrier indicted for murder; though it is a crime to break out of jail, the crime does not apply when a prisoner breaks out because the jail is on fire.



 

Though the *Holy Trinity* decision made some very broad statements about when the Court can depart from plain meaning, the actual holding of the case is very narrow. The Court simply held that a general criminal law did not apply to a special situation not anticipated by Congress. (The other cases referred to in the decision followed the same pattern.) Had Congress considered the special situation it would (the Court concluded) have provided an express exception, so the Court corrected the oversight by providing an implied exception.

### § 3.27 When There Is No Plain Meaning

When a statute is ambiguous, all bets are off. The Court looks at everything it considers persuasive, deliberates thoroughly, and determines how best to read the statute. As always, the overriding goal is to determine and apply the legislative intent. See *United States v. Fisher*, 6 U.S. 358, 386 (1805) (when "the mind labours to discover the design of the legislature, it seizes every thing from which aid can be derived"); *Wisconsin Public Intervenor v. Mortier*, 501 U.S. 597, 611 fn 4 (1991) ("common sense suggests that inquiry benefits from reviewing additional information rather than ignoring it").

In deciding what Congress meant to do, the Court is guided by an assumption that Congress did not mean to do nothing. Unless Congress is merely restating the law—in which case the Court presumes that Congress intends not to change the law, see *Muniz v. Hoffman*, 422 U.S. 454 (1975)—the Court presumes that Congress intends its action to have real and substantial effect. See *Stone v. Immigration and Naturalization Service*, 514 U.S. 386, 397 (1995).

## § 3.30 Reading the Text of the Statute

The Court generally begins its analysis with the language of the statute. Starting with the statute has been called the "first principle" of statutory interpretation. *Mallard v. United States District Court*, 490 U.S. 296, 300 (1989).

Though the statute is the obvious starting point, many do not always start there. For that reason Justice Frankfurter once quipped, "this is a case for applying the canon of construction of the wag who said, when the legislative history is doubtful, go to the statute." *Greenwood v. United States*, 350 U.S. 366, 374 (1956).

Justice Frankfurter's droll chiding turned strangely prophetic when, just fifteen years later, his successors on the Supreme Court bench reasoned in one case as follows: "The legislative history . . . is ambiguous. . . . Because of this ambiguity it is clear that we must look primarily to the statutes themselves to find the legislative intent." *Citizens to Preserve Overton Park v. Volpe*, 401 U.S. 402, 412 fn 29 (1971). As Frankfurter would have been pleased to know, that statement has proven to be an isolated one.

The Court considers the text to be the most persuasive evidence of meaning and, as noted above, sometimes says there is a presumption that the legislature means what it says. After all, the text is the only form by which Congress, in its capacity as the constitutional legislature of the United States, directly expresses its intent. *Aldridge v. Williams*, 44 U.S. 9, 24 (1845).

## § 3.31 The Whole Act Rule

In reading the statute, the Court reads not only the word or sentence or provision that is in dispute, but the entire statute. This is known as the Whole Act Rule. As the Court has explained:

> "Statutory construction . . . is a holistic endeavor. A provision that may seem ambiguous in isolation is often clarified by the remainder of the statutory scheme—because the same terminology is used elsewhere in a context that makes its meaning clear, or because only one of the permissible meanings produces a substantive effect that is compatible with the rest of the law."
>
> *United Savings Association v. Timbers of Inwood Forest Associates*, 484 U.S. 365, 371 (1988).

Accordingly, in reading a statute, the Court is not guided by a single sentence or sentence fragment, but looks instead to "the provisions of the whole law," and also to its "object and policy," "structure," and "subject matter." *United States National Bank of Oregon v. Independent Insurance Agents of America, Inc.*, 508 U.S. 439, 455 (1993).

## § 3.32 Derive Meaning from Context

The meaning of a word should never be considered in isolation. Two giants of the law have given us two well-known similes that express this principle well.

First, in the words of Justice Holmes, "A word is not a crystal, transparent and unchanged, it is the skin of a living thought and may vary greatly in color and content according to the circumstances and the time in which it is used." *Towne v. Eisner*, 245 U.S. 418, 425 (1918).

Second, in the words of Judge Learned Hand, "Words are not pebbles in alien juxtaposition; they have only a communal existence; and not only does the meaning of each interpenetrate the other, but in all their aggregate take their purport from the setting in which they are used." *NLRB v. Federbush Co.*, 121 F.2d 954, 957 (1st Cir. 1941).

This general principle is embodied in a canon of construction known by its Latin name, *noscitur a sociis* (a thing is known by its companions). Like any other canon, it is not a rule of law but a rule of thumb, and is used to avoid giving a law "unintended breadth." *Jarecki v. G.D. Searle & Co.*, 367 U.S. 303, 307 (1961).

For example, in *Gustafson v. Alloyd Co.*, 513 U.S. 561 (1995), the Court interpreted the term "communication" in the phrase "any prospectus, notice, circular, advertisement, letter, or communication, written or by radio or television" not to mean any communication but only a communication "of wide dissemination." 513 U.S. at 575. Therefore, a "written communication" applied only to writings held out to the public at large, and not to an exchange of correspondence between two parties.

Likewise, in *Gutierrez v. Ada*, 528 U.S. 250 (2000), the Court interpreted the phrase "in any election" to apply only to an election for governor, rather than a general election, because the phrase was preceded and followed by references to gubernatorial elections.

### § 3.33 Assume Words Are Used Consistently

As part of the Whole Act Rule, the Court expects each term in the law to be used consistently. If Congress uses the same term in more than one place, the Court presumes that it has the same meaning in each place. *Ratzlaf v. United States*, 510 U.S. 135, 143 (1994). This rule is "at its most vigorous when a term is repeated within a given sentence." *Brown v. Gardner*, 513 U.S. 115, 118 (1994).

Conversely, if Congress uses one term in one place and a different term in another place, the Court presumes that each term has a distinct meaning. *Bailey v. United States*, 516 U.S. 137, 146 (1995).

Of course, these are presumptions, not requirements, and the Court has cautioned against applying them too enthusiastically. See *General Dynamics*



 

*Land Systems v. Cline*, 540 U.S. 581 (2004) ("The tendency to assume that a word which appears in two or more legal rules, and so in connection with more than one purpose, has and should have precisely the same scope in all of them, runs all through legal discussions. It has all the tenacity of original sin and must constantly be guarded against.").

## § 3.34 Assume Each Word Is Used for a Reason

As part of the Whole Act Rule, the Court expects that each clause and word in the law is included for a reason. The Court's duty is "to give effect, if possible, to every clause and word of a statute." *United States v. Menasche*, 348 U.S. 528, 538–539 (1955).

This is referred to sometimes as the "rule against surplusage," and at other times as the "rule against superfluities." A statute, the Court said, "should be construed so that effect is given to all its provisions, so that no part will be inoperative or superfluous, void or insignificant." *Hibbs v. Winn*, 542 U.S. 88 (2004).

However, this also is a presumption, not a requirement, and the Court may reject words as surplusage if inadvertently inserted or repugnant to the rest of the statute. *Chickasaw Nation v. United States*, 534 U.S. 84 (2001).

The Court has said it is "inappropriate" to apply the rule against surplusage when there are two ways to read the text—one that is plain but contains surplusage, and one that is ambiguous but free of surplusage. In such a case, the Court prefers the plain meaning, "since that approach respects the words of Congress." *Lamie v. United States Trustee*, 540 U.S. 526 (2004).

## § 3.35 Assume the Provisions Form a Coherent Whole

As another part of the Whole Act Rule, the Court expects all of the provisions of the statute to form a coherent whole.

For example, the Court presumes that when Congress uses particular language in one place and does not use that language in another place, the omission was intentional. *Keene Corp. v. United States*, 508 U.S. 200, 208 (1993).

Likewise, the Court presumes that when Congress uses a general provision in one place and a specific provision in another place, in apparent contradiction, Congress intends both to have meaning, with the specific qualifying the general. *Townsend v. Little*, 109 U.S. 504, 512 (1883). See also *State of Missouri v. Ross*, 299 U.S. 72, 76 (1936) ("special provisions prevail over general ones which, in the absence of the special provisions, would control"); *Fourco Glass Co. v. Transmirra Products Corp.*, 353 U.S. 222, 228 (1957) ("However inclusive may be the general language of a statute, it will not be held to apply to a matter specifically dealt with in another part of the same enactment . . . specific terms prevail over the general.").

### § 3.36 Purposes, Findings, Titles, and Headings

The Court places some parts of the text in the category of lesser evidence, which will not generally be used as a guide to meaning unless the law is ambiguous. In this category are purposes, findings, titles, and headings.

These parts of the text are considered lesser evidence because they are not used primarily to make law. Instead, they are used primarily as a convenience to the reader. Essentially, they are indirect evidence rather than direct evidence. That said, the Court does, on rare occasions, resort to these parts of the text to glean what it can about legislative intent.

A statement of purposes is perhaps the most useful form of lesser evidence. A statement of policy, a statement of findings, and a statement of the sense of Congress are all variations of the same idea. (See also § 4.47, "Commands That Are Not Mandatory: Hortatory, Precatory, and Directory.")

For an example of a case using a statement of purposes as a guide to meaning, see *Dole v. United Steelworkers of America*, 494 U.S. 26, 36–38 (1990) (where Congress did not mention disclosure rules in its "itemized and exhaustive" statement of purposes, that was "strong evidence" that the act did not apply to disclosure rules).

For an example of a case using findings as a guide to meaning, see *United States v. Turkette*, 452 U.S. 576, 588–590 (1981) (giving the RICO statute a broad interpretation in part because of the broad statement of findings). A preamble containing Whereas clauses is much the same as a statement of findings, and is treated in much the same way.

For an example of a case using a sense of Congress provision as a guide to meaning, see *Accardi v. Pennsylvania Railroad Co.*, 383 U.S. 225, 229 (1966) (in which the Court, interestingly enough, seemed to treat a sense of Congress as if it were actual law).

Be aware that the Court does not use the terms "title" and "heading" in the specific way that a drafter does. For example, in *Immigration and Naturalization Service v. National Center for Immigrants' Rights*, 502 U.S. 183, 189–190 (1991), the Court used what a drafter would call the heading of a clause as a guide to meaning, though the Court referred to it as the "title" of a "paragraph."

Regardless, it is fair to say that anything that a drafter might consider a title or a heading will be used by the Court as a guide to meaning when the meaning is in doubt.

This applies to long titles and short titles, as in *Caminetti v. United States*, 242 U.S. 470, 489–490 (1917). It applies also to section headings, as in *Almendarez-Torres v. United States*, 523 U.S. 224 (1998). It applies as well to chapter headings, catchlines, and any other part of the text that might be considered a title or heading in a general sense.

## § 3.37 Grammar and Punctuation

The Court generally applies ordinary rules of grammar in interpreting statutes. For example, in *United States v. Ron Pair Enterprises*, 489 U.S. 235, 241 (1989), the Court used the "grammatical structure" of a statute as a guide to meaning (concluding that the placement of commas created an independent clause). And in *Barnhart v. Thomas*, 540 U.S. 20 (2003), the Court applied the grammatical "rule of the last antecedent," according to which a limiting clause or phrase should ordinarily be read as modifying only the noun or phrase that it immediately follows. (For example, the Court said, a teenager told "you will be punished if you throw a party or engage in any other activity that damages the house" will be punished for throwing a party, whether or not the party damages the house.)

The Court also generally applies ordinary rules of punctuation in interpreting statutes. The meaning of a statute "will typically heed the commands of its punctuation." *United States National Bank of Oregon v. Independent Insurance Agents of America, Inc.*, 508 U.S. 439, 454 (1993). But if need be, the Court will "disregard the punctuation, or repunctuate," to render the true meaning of the statute. 508 U.S. at 462 (holding that certain quotation marks appeared in a statute only because of "scrivener's error").

## § 3.38 Placement in Code

An important exception to the general rule that meaning can be derived from context is that meaning is not supposed to be derived from the placement of a provision in the Code.

When a provision of an act is classified to the Code by Law Revision Counsel, the Court will "read it in the context of the entire Act, rather than in the context of the 'arrangement' selected by the codifier." *U.S. v. Welden*, 377 U.S. 95, 99 (1964).

When a provision is codified into a positive-law title, Congress typically requires—by law, in the act originally enacting that title—that no inference about a provision be drawn from the chapter in which it was placed or from the heading of that chapter. See section 19 of the act of June 25, 1948, which enacted title 18 (Crimes and Criminal Procedure) into positive law. That section is set forth in the notes at the beginning of title 18; similar requirements apply to other positive-law titles and are set forth in the notes at the beginning of those titles. It is not altogether clear whether these requirements also apply when a provision is later added to a positive-law title. Regardless, most people, and most courts, seem not to know these requirements are there.

## §3.40 Considering Other Statutes

Having considered the text of a statute, the Court will also consider the rest of the statutory context—that is, the body of law into which the statute fits.

Generally, the Court assumes that the new law is intended to fit into the body of law to form a consistent, coherent whole. This is much the same sentiment as in the Whole Act Rule, but it is applied in a somewhat looser, less rigid way.

### §3.41 Related Statutes

Courts do not interpret statutes in isolation, but in the context of the "corpus juris" of which they are a part. "The correct rule of interpretation is, that if divers statutes relate to the same thing, they ought all to be taken into consideration in construing any one of them." *Branch v. Smith*, 538 U.S. 254 (2003) (quoting from an 1845 Supreme Court decision). This technique is sometimes known as *in pari materia.*

Thus, if a term has a settled meaning in Statute A, and the same term is used in a related Statute B, the term will generally be read in B the same way it is read in A.

This applies, obviously, when Statute A was enacted first. Most people understand that intuitively.

But—and this may be counterintuitive—it also applies when Statute B was enacted first. That is, "if it can be gathered from a subsequent statute *in pari materia*, what meaning the legislature attached to the words of a former statute, they will amount to a legislative declaration of its meaning, and will govern the construction of the first statute." *Branch v. Smith*, 538 U.S. 254 (2003).

As the Court explained in *Food and Drug Administration v. Brown & Williamson Tobacco Corp.*, 529 U.S. 120 (2000): "At the time a statute is enacted, it may have a range of plausible meanings. Over time, however, subsequent acts can shape or focus those meanings. The classic judicial task of reconciling many laws enacted over time, and getting them to make sense in combination, necessarily assumes that the implications of a statute may be altered by the implications of a later statute." (internal quotation marks omitted).

For example, the Court added, "a specific policy embodied in a later federal statute should control our construction of the earlier statute, even though it has not been expressly amended." (internal brackets omitted).

## § 3.42 General Federal Laws

In addition to considering the immediately related statutes, the Court will also consider the broader context of general federal law. This is not limited to general definitions, though general definitions are perhaps the most important part of the broader context.

The most broadly applicable set of federal definitions is in chapter 1 of title 1, United States Code, sometimes referred to as the Dictionary Act. This chapter contains a series of definitions that apply to all federal law, unless the context indicates otherwise. If a law uses a term that is defined in the Dictionary Act, the Court will generally apply the Dictionary Act definition to that term.

For more on the Dictionary Act and how the Court interprets the phrase "unless the context indicates otherwise," see *Rowland v. California Men's Colony*, 506 U.S. 194, 199–200 (1993). In that case, the Court interpreted "context" to mean only the text of the law and related laws, and interpreted "indicates" in a very broad and flexible way. Nearly any reason, however slight, could "indicate" that the Dictionary Act definition should not apply.

Many other large organic laws contain definitions that apply to a large part of federal law. For example, section 101 of title 10, United States Code, contains a set of definitions that applies throughout that title of the Code.



 

### § 3.43 Earlier Versions of the Same Statute

When a statute has been amended over the years, the Court ordinarily does not care about the earlier versions. The starting point, the Court has said, is the existing statutory text "and not the predecessor statutes." *Lamie v. United States Trustee*, 540 U.S. 526 (2004). For that reason, the Court will generally look back at an earlier version only if the present version is unclear.

As an aside: This seems only partly right. When a statute is enacted as one public law and later amended by another public law, is it one law or two? There is a sense in which it is one new law—the first enactment as modified by the second enactment—and that is what the *Lamie* Court seemed to have in mind. But this "one new law" has never been enacted, as a single law, by Congress; the "one new law" is a splicing of two separate public laws, passed by two separate Congresses, each with a separate intent. So there is a sense in which the new law is really two laws—and that sense is the constitutional sense (in which a law is a measure that passes both chambers of Congress in identical form and is presented to the President), so perhaps it should not be dismissed.

For an example of a case in which the Court struggled mightily with how best to understand the statutory history, see *Koons Buick Pontiac GMC, Inc. v. Nigh*, 543 U.S. 50 (2004), in which an exasperated Justice Ginsburg, writing for the majority, said candidly: "The five separate writings this Court has produced demonstrate that [the statute] is hardly a model of the careful drafter's art." 543 U.S. 50 at fn 7 (2004).

### § 3.44 Resolving Conflicts between Statutes

Sometimes a statute does not meld seamlessly into an existing body of law. For a discussion of how the Court approaches inconsistencies and conflicts between statutes, see Chapter Nine, "Affecting and Amending Other Laws."

## § 3.50 Considering Constitutional Issues

Every Act of Congress is presumed to be constitutional. The Court does, however, consider constitutional challenges from time to time, and those challenges can color the way the Court interprets a statute in several ways.



 

## § 3.51 Avoiding Serious Constitutional Problems

Simply put, the Court will not interpret a statute in a way that renders it unconstitutional unless doing so is utterly unavoidable.

If a case can be decided on either statutory or constitutional grounds, the Court will—for "sound jurisprudential reasons"—decide it on the statutory ground and not reach the constitutional one. *Harris v. McRae*, 448 U.S. 297, 306–307 (1980).

Accordingly, the Court will not interpret a statute in a way that raises "serious constitutional problems." In such a case, the Court will choose some other plausible meaning that does not have the specter of constitutional difficulties hovering around it. *DeBartolo Corp. v. Florida Gulf Coast Trades Council*, 485 U.S. 568, 575 (1988). The Court will try every other plausible meaning to find one that saves the statute from being unconstitutional.

## § 3.52 When the Court Requires Clear Statements

There are certain matters that the Court treats with great delicacy. When Congress legislates in a way that may encroach on those matters, the Court requires that Congress be extremely precise. It is not enough, in these cases, for Congress to be plain; Congress must be more than plain.

When constitutional or other sensitive matters are at stake, the Court generally presumes that Congress does not intend to disturb the status quo. To overcome that presumption, Congress must state precisely its intention to do so. This is known as a "clear statement" rule. *Astoria Federal Savings & Loan Association v. Solimino*, 501 U.S. 104, 108–109 (1991).

Clear statement rules apply only when "weighty and constant" values are at stake. The purpose is to ensure that Congress "has in fact faced, and intended to bring into issue, the critical matters involved in the judicial decision." *United States v. Bass*, 404 U.S. 336, 349 (1971).

For example, a clear statement rule generally applies when a law would interfere in some way with state sovereignty, such as when it would abrogate the sovereign immunity of a state under the Eleventh Amendment (*Atascadero State Hospital v. Scanlon*, 473 U.S. 234, 243 (1985)), allow a state to be sued for damages (*Will v. Michigan*, 491 U.S. 58 (1989)), tell a state how to hire its judges (*Gregory v. Ashcroft*, 501 U.S. 452 (1991)), or impose a condition on the state's receipt of a federal grant (*South Dakota v. Dole*, 483 U.S. 203, 207 (1987)).

Similarly, the Court expects that Congress does not intend to preempt state law; the Court will not interpret a law in a way that preempts state law unless Congress makes the intent to preempt "clear and manifest." *Wisconsin Public Intervenor v. Mortier*, 501 U.S. 597, 605 (1991). Likewise, when Congress does not intend to preempt state law and provides a clear statement to that effect, the Court will apply that statement.

A clear statement rule also applies when a law would waive the sovereign immunity of the United States. *United States v. Mitchell*, 445 U.S. 535, 537 (1980).

A clear statement rule applies when Congress intends for a law to apply outside the United States (*EEOC v. Arabian American Oil Co.*, 499 U.S. 244, 248 (1991)), to apply retroactively (*Gozlon-Peretz v. United States*, 498 U.S. 395, 404 (1991)), or to apply without the possibility of judicial review or habeas review (*Demore v. Kim*, 538 U.S. 510 (2003)).

And a clear statement rule applies when a law that does not expressly apply to the President would, if applied to the President, pose a significant question regarding the President's constitutional functions. See *Franklin v. Massachusetts*, 505 U.S. 788, 800–801 (1992) (Court would require an express statement by Congress before assuming presidential actions could be reviewed for abuse of discretion under the Administrative Procedure Act); *Nixon v. Fitzgerald*, 457 U.S. 731, 748 fn 27 (1982) (Court would require an explicit statement by Congress before assuming President could be sued for damages).

Clear statement rules are like snowflakes—no two are exactly alike. One rule might require a "plain statement" of legislative intent; another might require that Congress make its intention "unmistakably clear in the language of the statute"; a third might require "express words to that effect." The basic message is the same: If you want to achieve a particular result, use words that make it unmistakably clear.

Some clear statement rules are more important than others. As the Court has explained, some clear statement rules are ordinary rules of construction, not required by the Constitution, while others are rules derived from constitutional law. *Hilton v. South Carolina Public Railways Commission*, 502 U.S. 197, 205–206 (1991). Allocating the various rules between these two categories is beyond the scope of this book.

### § 3.53 When the Court Requires Specific Findings

Another tack the Court has taken when confronted with a constitutional question is to require Congress to clearly articulate why Congress believes it has authority to act. The Court has indicated that Congress should preface a constitutionally questionable law with a formal statement of findings. If the findings are inadequate, the Court finds that the statute is unconstitutional.

For example, in *United States v. Lopez*, 514 U.S. 549 (1995), the Court struck down a prohibition on possessing a gun in a school zone, not being convinced that the activity substantially affected interstate commerce. The Court held open the possibility that the law would become constitutional if Congress revised it to include specific findings.

## §3.60 Actions by the President and Other Executive Officers

The legislative power is vested in Congress, but the executive branch has some say in how laws are made and interpreted. The Constitution authorizes the President to make legislative proposals, and requires that a bill not become law unless it is first presented to the President. In addition, Congress can (within certain limits), and does, delegate legislative power to executive agencies.

And, of course, every branch of the federal government must, to some extent, interpret the laws. The executive branch, for example, must interpret a law so that it can carry out the law properly. "Interpreting a law enacted by Congress to implement the legislative mandate is the very essence of 'execution' of the law." *Bowsher v. Synar*, 478 U.S. 714, 733 (1986).

### §3.61 Presidential Signing Statements

A bill can become law without the President's signature, if the President simply fails to return it within ten days after being presented with it. However, most Presidents sign most bills, and in the modern era most also provide a signing statement at the time of signing.

A signing statement is commonly used by the President to describe the likely effects of the bill, to identify constitutional concerns about the bill, and to explain how the executive branch will carry out the bill.

In addition, a signing statement is occasionally used to explain what the President believes the law means. This is sometimes referred to as "executive history," because it is more or less analogous to legislative history generated by Congress.

According to a memorandum of the Office of Legal Counsel of the Department of Justice, the use of signing statements for executive history appears to have originated (and their widespread use certainly began) in the Reagan administration, although "isolated examples can perhaps be found earlier." Walter Dellinger, Assistant Attorney General, "The Legal Significance of Presidential Signing Statements," Memorandum for Bernard N. Nussbaum, Counsel to the President (November 3, 1993).

In 1986, the memorandum relates, Attorney General Edwin Meese arranged to have signing statements published alongside legislative history in the U.S. Code Congressional and Administrative News to make sure that the President's interpretation of the bill would be recorded and available in the same manner as legislative history.

The Court apparently has never considered whether a signing statement should be given any weight. Several federal appellate courts have considered the question, however, and have given some weight to a signing statement. See *United States v. Story*, 891 F.2d 988 (2d Cir. 1989); *Berry v. Department of Justice*, 733 F.2d 1343 (9th Cir. 1984); *Clifton D. Mayhew, Inc. v. Wirtz*, 413 F.2d 658 (4th Cir. 1969). Whether the Court would follow this lead is uncertain, given that the Court is already ambivalent about using legislative history.

## § 3.62 Agency Interpretation and *Chevron* Deference

When Congress enacts a law that has more than one plausible meaning, the Court may conclude that Congress wanted the executive branch to have discretion over how best to resolve the ambiguity. If so, the Court will defer to the interpretation of the executive branch, as long as it is reasonable. This principle was first established in *Chevron U.S.A. v. Natural Resources Defense Council*, 467 U.S. 837 (1984), and therefore is known as *Chevron* deference or the *Chevron* doctrine.

When a Court defers to an agency interpretation under the *Chevron* doctrine, the Court does more than treat the interpretation with respect; the Court treats the interpretation as binding and conclusive.

Although the Court continues to refine and revise the *Chevron* doctrine, it appears that for *Chevron* deference to apply, five elements must exist.

First, the statute must be ambiguous. The Court will not defer to an agency interpretation if there is a plain meaning.

Second, Congress must have intended that the agency have discretion to interpret the statute. Evidence of intent can come from the text itself or can be implied.

Third, the agency doing the interpretation must be the agency responsible for "administering" the law. To qualify for this element, the agency must do more than frequently make use of the law; the agency must actually be responsible for carrying out the law. For example, the Department of Justice does not "administer" title 18 of the United States Code, even though that is the title relating to federal crimes and criminal procedure. (Title 18 is administered by the judicial branch, according to the Court.)

Fourth, the agency must adopt the interpretation through a formal, public process. Agency interpretations contained in policy statements, manuals, and guidelines do not qualify.

Fifth, the agency's interpretation must be reasonable. Note that the agency's interpretation is not required to be consistent with its past interpretation; an agency can adopt one interpretation and receive *Chevron* deference, and then adopt a new interpretation and receive *Chevron* deference again.

If *Chevron* deference does not apply to an agency interpretation, the Court will consider that interpretation on the same basis as it considers any other form of evidence—only to the extent that it has power to persuade.

## § 3.70 Actions by the Congress and Other Legislative Officers

In the search for legislative intent, the Court will consider a number of different types of evidence from the legislative branch. The most controversial type of evidence is legislative history, though the Court also has special rules for certain other types of evidence.

### § 3.71 Interpretation of Appropriations Acts

Most of the federal government is funded on a year-to-year basis through appropriations acts. Unlike legislation intended to make substantive law, an appropriations act is intended to allow the government to take money from the Treasury and spend it. The House and Senate each have procedures designed to keep substantive legislation separate from appropriations, although Congress with some regularity includes substantive legislation in appropriations acts.

The Court generally honors this distinction, however, and expects that



 

Congress does not intend to change substantive law with language in an appropriations act. The Court will permit such a change only if the intent to do so is clearly expressed. *TVA v. Hill*, 437 U.S. 153, 190 (1978); *United States v. Will*, 449 U.S. 200, 222 (1980).

A provision in an appropriations act is generally interpreted to apply for only one year—the fiscal year to which the appropriations act relates. If a provision is intended to apply beyond that year, that intent should be clearly expressed.

### § 3.72 Legislative History: Why It Is Problematic

Legislative history refers to the proceedings in Congress relating to a law before it was enacted. The legislative history includes official reports by congressional committees and official statements by members of Congress. More broadly, it also includes testimony at legislative hearings and the different versions of a bill's text as it was shaped by the legislative process.

Using legislative history as evidence of legislative intent is problematic for several reasons. A committee report is the view of only a handful of legislators of only one chamber; an individual statement is the view of only one member. And the more courts use legislative history, the more legislative history tends to be generated not to aid lawmakers but to influence judges, and that tends to subvert the entire process.

To a textualist, legislative history is so problematic that it should never be used. To others, legislative history is so problematic that, though usable, it should be taken with a considerable grain of salt. Accordingly, the Court generally turns to legislative history as a guide to meaning only when it must choose between more than one plausible meaning.

However, the Court sometimes turns to legislative history even when there is a single plain meaning, if only to confirm the plain meaning that it has already found. The Court has consistently said that legislative history can always be used as evidence of legislative intent, so long as it is not used to overturn a plain meaning. Under that reasoning, legislative history can be used to confirm or reinforce plain meaning. For a discussion of how agencies pay closer attention to legislative history than courts do, see *Congressional Deskbook*, § 10.72, "Legislative History."

Finally, in some cases the Court derives meaning not from legislative history, but from the absence of legislative history. For example, in *Koons Buick Pon-*



 

*tiac* GMC, *Inc. v. Nigh*, 543 U.S. 50 (2004), the Court reasoned that an apparently significant amendment to the Truth in Lending Act did not have any substantive effect, because there was "scant indication" in the legislative history that Congress meant to work a change. See also *Church of Scientology of California v. IRS*, 484 U.S. 9, 17–18 (1987) ("All in all, we think this is a case where common sense suggests, by analogy to Sir Arthur Conan Doyle's 'dog that didn't bark,' that an amendment having the effect petitioner ascribes to it would have been differently described by its sponsor, and not nearly as readily accepted by the floor manager of the bill."). The Court does not always do this, however; see *Whitfield v. United States*, 543 U.S. 209 (2005) ("Given the clarity of the text, mere silence in the legislative history cannot justify reading an overt act requirement, or a cross-reference to § 371, into § 1956(h)"); *United States v. Wells*, 519 U.S. 482, 496–497 (1997) (refusing to read a materiality element into the statute at issue based on silence in the legislative history); *Harrison v. PPG Industries, Inc.*, 446 U. S. 578, 592 (1980) (It "would be a strange canon of statutory construction that would require Congress to state in committee reports or elsewhere in its deliberations that which is obvious on the face of a statute.").

## § 3.73 Legislative History Compared with Post-Enactment Statements

There is a common misconception about why courts find legislative history useful as evidence of legislative intent. Many believe legislative history is used primarily because it reflects the views of lawmakers. Legislative history does reflect the views of some lawmakers, but that is not why legislative history is used.

Legislative history is used primarily because it was available to lawmakers and may have influenced their votes. The Court is under no delusion that the views expressed by some members in legislative history are an accurate sample of the views shared by all members. The Court does, however, recognize that the views expressed by some members can shape the views of other members and influence their votes. In short, legislative history matters not because it was said or written by lawmakers but because it was heard or read by other lawmakers.

This distinction is generally not discussed, but it appears most clearly in the Court's approach to post-enactment statements. A post-enactment statement is a statement made by a member after the enactment of a law about the member's motives and perceptions. A statement like this would be useful if the Court wanted to sample the views of members.



 

In fact, however, the Court almost never considers a post-enactment statement. As the Court has explained, a statement made after the fact "cannot possibly have informed the vote of the legislators who earlier enacted the law," and for that reason "there is no more basis for considering them than there is to conduct postenactment polls of the original legislators." *Pittston Coal Group v. Sebben*, 488 U.S. 105, 118–119 (1988) (post-enactment statements by key sponsors).

## § 3.74 Legislative History Compared with Subsequent Legislative History

A post-enactment statement is not the same thing as what is sometimes called "subsequent legislative history." The former term applies when lawmakers describe what their motives and understandings had been in enacting the law; the latter term applies when a committee, an individual member, or some other congressional entity describes what it understands a law to mean. You can think of a post-enactment statement as a form of first-party eyewitness testimony ("this is what we, this Congress, meant"), and of subsequent legislative history as a form of third-party interpretation ("this is what they, that Congress, meant").

Unlike a post-enactment statement, subsequent legislative history is occasionally given weight, though "subsequent legislative history will rarely override a reasonable interpretation of a statute." *Doe v. Chao*, 540 U.S. 614 (2004). But see *Seatrain Shipbuilding Corp. v. Shell Oil Co.*, 444 U.S. 572, 596 (1980) ("while the views of subsequent Congresses cannot override the unmistakable intent of the enacting one, such views are entitled to significant weight, and particularly so when the precise intent of the enacting Congress is obscure" [internal citations omitted]).

The Court is sometimes asked, in interpreting a law, to give weight to a decision by Congress not to adopt a proposed amendment to that law. The Court has repeatedly declined to do so. "Failed legislative proposals are a particularly dangerous ground on which to rest an interpretation of a prior statute," the Court has said, because the decision not to adopt the proposed amendment could mean so many different things. *United States v. Craft*, 535 U.S. 274 (2002).

Remember, too, that there is a distinction between subsequent legislative history and subsequent legislation, that is, subsequently enacted law. "Subsequent legislation declaring the intent of an earlier statute is entitled to great weight in statutory construction." *Loving v. United States*, 517 U.S. 748 (1996).

## § 3.75 Report Language

Legislative history includes the official reports generated in Congress in the course of the legislative process, such as a committee report or a joint statement of managers accompanying a conference report. (The conference report itself is not report language, but bill language, as discussed in § 2.31, "Resolving Differences by Amendment or Conference." In researching case law, however, you should be aware that court decisions often use the term "conference report" to refer to the joint statement of managers.) As with all types of legislative history, reports and joint statements are used with caution.

As between the two, the joint statement is more authoritative. Indeed, the joint statement is the most authoritative form of legislative history, because a joint statement not only is prepared by members of both chambers (who are specially appointed by the leadership of those chambers), but also must be voted on and adopted by both chambers. Thus, it is the only form of legislative history that is produced and considered by both chambers.

A committee report is inferior to a joint statement in two major ways: First, it is the product of only a single chamber; second, it is produced and considered at an earlier stage of the process. A committee report is, however, more authoritative than any form of legislative history other than a joint statement.

## § 3.76 Individual Statements

Legislative history includes statements made by members in the course of official proceedings, such as floor debate. An individual statement reflects merely the views and motives of the individual member, and the extent to which that statement may have influenced congressional intent is open to question.

An individual statement is less authoritative than a committee report, *Garcia v. United States*, 469 U.S. 70, 76 (1984), and will be disregarded if it conflicts with a joint statement or committee report. *United States v. Wrightwood Dairy Co.*, 315 U.S. 110, 125 (1942).

An individual statement will also be disregarded, even if made by a sponsor, if it conflicts with context and history. *General Dynamics Land Systems v. Cline*, 540 U.S. 581 (2004).

Accordingly, an individual statement generally carries weight only when there is no other legislative history available, such as when the statement relates to an amendment adopted on the floor. *Northeast Bancorp, Inc. v. Board of Governors*, 472 U.S. 159, 169–170 (1985).

When two or more individual statements are in conflict, the Court gives somewhat more weight to a statement made by a member in charge of the bill, such as a committee chairman, *United States v. St. Paul, Minneapolis & Manitoba Railway Co.*, 247 U.S. 310, 318 (1918), or a statement made by a sponsor of the bill, *Chrysler Corp. v. Brown*, 441 U.S. 281, 311 (1979).

The Court gives little, if any, weight to a statement made by an opponent of the bill, *Shell Oil Co. v. Iowa Department of Revenue*, 488 U.S. 19, 29 (1988).

When individual statements on the House side are in conflict with those on the Senate side, the Court gives greater weight to those from the chamber that originated the provision and to those from the chamber that produced a more definitive legislative history. *Steiner v. Mitchell*, 350 U.S. 247, 254 (1956).

### § 3.77 Hearing Testimony

Testimony at a legislative hearing does not receive any weight, with one important exception: When an executive agency actively sponsors a bill, the testimony of its officers during a legislative hearing on the bill is entitled to serious consideration. *Shapiro v. United States*, 335 U.S. 1, 12 fn 13 (1948).

Hearing testimony can also receive some weight if it can be shown that the language of the bill was revised in direct response to that testimony.

### § 3.78 Amendatory History

One might think that evidence of legislative intent could be found by comparing the version of the bill as enacted with versions of the bill at earlier stages in the legislative process.

However, the Court has held that a comparison of this sort is inconclusive, unless the change is explained elsewhere in the legislative history. *Fox v. Standard Oil Co.*, 294 U.S. 87, 96 (1935). But see *Babbitt v. Sweet Home Chapter of Communities for a Greater Oregon*, 515 U.S. 687 (1995) ("An obviously broad word that the Senate went out of its way to add to an important statutory definition is precisely the sort of provision that deserves a respectful reading."); *Doe v. Chao*, 540 U.S. 614 (2004) (rejecting a proposed interpretation because of "drafting history showing that Congress cut out the very language in the bill" that would have supported that interpretation).



 

### § 3.79 The Opinion of the Drafter

The last, but not least, category of legislative history is the opinion of the very person who drafted the law. In one notable case, the Court decided to give weight to a report prepared by the officer within the Department of Justice who, the Court said, "almost certainly drafted" the language at issue. The report explained the different parts of the bill. Though it was not made part of the public record, the Court reasoned that it was "likely that, at some point, the report was brought to the attention of the Congressmen considering the bill." Therefore, the Court—after first cautioning that "the ideas expressed therein should not be given great weight"—said that "it seems to us senseless to ignore entirely the views of its draftsman." *Kosak v. United States*, 465 U.S. 848, 856 (1984).

In a spirited dissent, Justice Stevens dismissed the report as "an internal Justice Department working paper" prepared fifteen years before the bill was finally enacted and dismissed the person who prepared it as "a lobbyist." He finished with a flourish that—even though it was not in a majority opinion—all drafters should take to heart:

> ". . . [W]e should be guided by the sensible statement that 'in construing a statute . . . the worst person to construe it is the person responsible for its drafting. He is very much disposed to confuse what he intended to do with the effect of the language which in fact has been employed.' *Hilder v. Dexter*, 1902. A.C. 474, 477 (Halsbury, L.C., abstaining). If the draftsman of the language in question intended it to cover such cases as this one, he failed."
>
> *Kosak v. United States*, 465 U.S. at 863–864 (Stevens, J., dissenting).

## § 3.80 Some Topics of Special Interest to Drafters

While there are many other topics that could be discussed, the remainder of this chapter focuses on a few topics that are of special interest to drafters.

### § 3.81 Definitions and Terms of Art

Drafters make frequent use of definitions. The Court has said that when a statute includes an explicit definition, the Court will follow that definition, even if it varies from the term's ordinary meaning. *Stenberg v. Carhart*, 530 U.S.



 

914 (2000). That assumes, of course, that the definition clarifies matters. If it does not, the Court will look elsewhere for meaning, including other parts of the text and the common law. *Raymond B. Yates, M.D., P.C. Profit Sharing Plan v. Hendon*, 540 U.S. 1 (2004).

Drafters sometimes also make use of terms of art. A term of art is a term that has an accepted meaning in a related law, in the common law, or in a specialized field to which the law relates. If the Court finds that a term is a term of art, the Court will apply that accepted meaning. See *Gustafson v. Alloyd Co.*, 513 U.S. 561 (1995) ("prospectus" is a term of art).

For example, if Congress uses a term with a settled meaning at common law, the Court assumes Congress meant to adopt the "cluster of ideas" behind that term, and interprets the term in that light. *Beck v. Prupis*, 529 U.S. 494 (2000) (turning to the well-established common law of conspiracy to interpret the term "conspire"). To identify or interpret a term of art, the Court sometimes consults a specialized dictionary, such as a law dictionary or medical dictionary.

## § 3.82 Narrow Interpretations and Broad Interpretations

There are some policies that the Court openly favors and some that the Court openly disfavors. When a law implicates one of these policies, the Court interprets the law not in an evenhanded way, but with a thumb on the scale.

The technique is usually characterized as a "presumption." The presumption typically will not disturb a single plain meaning if there is one, but will be used to help the Court choose among plausible meanings.

**Broad Interpretation.** When the Court favors a policy, the Court generally interprets the law "broadly" or "liberally." For example:

The Court has said that "remedial legislation" should be interpreted broadly. *Tcherepnin v. Knight*, 389 U.S. 332, 336 (1967). But this particular presumption is so vague (what is "remedial legislation," anyway?), has come under such criticism, and is so infrequently applied, that it is unclear whether it still carries any weight as a general principle.

A statute providing benefits to a class of people should be interpreted in favor of the beneficiaries. See *King v. St. Vincent's Hosp.*, 502 U.S. 215, 220 fn 9 (1991) (benefits to members of the Armed Forces); *Montana v. Blackfeet Tribe*, 471 U.S. 759, 766 (1985) (benefits to Indians).

Federal statutes that are intended to fill a void in local law enforcement should be interpreted broadly. *Moskal v. United States*, 498 U.S. 103 (1990).



 

**Narrow Interpretation.** When the Court disfavors a policy, the Court generally interprets the law "narrowly" or "strictly." For example:

> Statutes establishing evidentiary privileges should be interpreted narrowly, because privileges impede the search for truth. *Pierce County v. Guillen*, 537 U.S. 129 (2003).
>
> Statutory procedures for removal should be interpreted strictly. *Syngenta Crop Protection, Inc. v. Henson*, 537 U.S. 28 (2002).

And perhaps the most important category of laws interpreted narrowly are laws relating to crime and criminal procedure. When interpreting these laws, the Court applies what is called the "rule of lenity." According to the rule of lenity, when there are two rational readings of a criminal statute, one harsher than the other, the Court chooses the harsher only when Congress has spoken in clear and definite language. *McNally v. United States*, 483 U.S. 350, 359–360 (1987). The Court will resolve any ambiguity in the statute in favor of the defendant. *Hughey v. United States*, 495 U.S. 411, 422 (1990). Likewise, the Court assumes that a state-of-mind requirement applies to each element of a criminal offense, unless Congress clearly indicates otherwise. *United States v. X-Citement Video, Inc.*, 513 U.S. 64, 72 (1994).

## § 3.83 Congress Does Not Mumble

The Court sometimes makes a sweeping generalization about how Congress operates and uses that generalization as a guide to meaning (or, perhaps, as a signal to Congress).

In some cases the generalization seems to be descriptive—describing how Congress does in fact operate. In other cases the generalization seems to be prescriptive—describing how the Court would like Congress to operate.

A generalization of this sort is not unlike when a teacher (a Vermont schoolmarm, perhaps?) generalizes to a student, "Students in this class do not mumble." Whether that statement is a description or a command, the student gets the message—mumbling is not tolerated.

The Court's generalizations about Congress often come across this way. "Congress does not mumble," the Court seems to be saying, tapping a ruler in its palm.

Some examples:



 

> "Congress, we have held, does not alter the fundamental details of a regulatory scheme in vague terms or ancillary provisions—it does not, one might say, hide elephants in mouseholes." *Whitman v. American Trucking Associations, Inc.*, 531 U.S. 457, 468 (2001). Thus, Congress did not make a radical change in the law in a provision purporting to be a technical or conforming amendment—or so the Court held. *Director of Revenue of Missouri v. CoBank, ACB*, 531 U.S. 316, 323 (2001).
>
> If "Congress had meant to set a counterintuitive limit on authority to act, it would have said more than it did." *Barnhart v. Peabody Coal Co.*, 537 U.S. 149 (2003).
>
> "Where Congress intends to refer to ownership in other than the formal sense, it knows how to do so." *Dole Food Company v. Patrickson*, 538 U.S. 468 (2003).
>
> "When Congress has wished to create such an addition to the law of copyright, it has done so with much more specificity." *Dastar Corp. v. Twentieth Century Fox Film Corp.*, 539 U.S. 23 (2003).
>
> "If Congress intended the term 'demonstrates' to require that the 'burdens of production and persuasion' be met by direct evidence or some other heightened showing, it could have made that intent clear by including language to that effect." *Desert Palace v. Costa*, 539 U.S. 90 (2003).
>
> "Congress could have conditioned the entire subsection (g)(4)(A) as applying only to 'a person entitled to recovery.' That, of course, is not what Congress wrote." *Doe v. Chao*, 540 U.S. 614 (2004).

It is hard to see how a generalization of this sort would apply in a particular case, to a particular statute. But the Court's willingness to use these generalizations reinforces the notion that the Court will look anywhere it likes in its search for meaning (§ 3.11), including its sense about how Congress does (or should) draft. And because the Court pays attention to how Congress drafts, poor drafting of one law can cause damage to the entire statute book (§ 9.70).



 

## § 3.84 How the Court Interprets a List

When the Court interprets a list of items, it uses two time-honored techniques as a guide to meaning. Both are canons of construction known by their Latin names.

The first technique, *noscitur a sociis* (a thing is known by its companions), was discussed above (§ 3.32). It stands for the general proposition that a word should be interpreted in context with other words. If the context is a list of items, the items should be interpreted in light of one another, that is, "words grouped in a list should be given related meaning." *Dole v. United Steelworkers of America*, 494 U.S. 26, 36 (1990).

The second technique, *ejusdem generis* (of the same kind), is simply a narrow and specialized version of the first technique. It stands for the specific proposition that when Congress ends a list of specific items with general words, "the general words are read as applying only to other items akin to those specifically enumerated." *Harrison v. PPG Industries, Inc.*, 446 U.S. 578, 588 (1980).

For example, when a law refers to "contracts of employment of seamen, railroad employees, or any other class of workers engaged in interstate commerce," the general words, "any other class of workers engaged in interstate commerce," do not mean all classes of workers engaged in interstate commerce. Instead, they mean only classes of workers like seamen and railroad employees. What classes are those? The Court's answer was "transportation workers." *Circuit City v. Adams*, 532 U.S. 105, 114–115 (2001).

The technique of *ejusdem generis* is related not only to *noscitur a sociis*, but also to the principle that Congress uses each word for a reason (discussed in § 3.34, "Assume Each Word Is Used for a Reason"). In the *Circuit City* case, if the Court had given the general words a broad meaning, that broad meaning would swallow up the other items in the list. The Court assumes that "seamen" and "railroad employees" are not idle examples but guides to meaning.

For another example of *ejusdem generis* in action, see *Washington State Department of Social & Health Services v. Guardianship Estate of Keffeler*, 537 U.S. 371 (2003). In that case, the Court considered a law that referred to "execution, levy, attachment, garnishment, or other legal process" and determined that the general words, "other legal process," should be understood to mean a process much like execution, levy, attachment, and garnishment. For that reason, the general words cover only a process that uses a "judicial or quasi-judicial mechanism."



 

As always, these techniques are tools, not rules. The Court will not use these techniques to overturn a plain meaning and will not apply them when the legislative intent appears to be to the contrary.

### § 3.85 The Court's Reluctance to Imply Additional Exceptions

Sometimes the Court is asked to create an implied exception to a general rule. When Congress has already created one or more express exceptions, the Court is reluctant to imply additional ones.

This technique is sometimes known as the rule against implied exceptions, but more often by its Latin name, *expressio unius est exclusio alterius* (the inclusion of one is the exclusion of others).

As with any technique, the Court will not apply this technique if legislative intent is to the contrary. Beyond that, there is some confusion about exactly when and how this technique is applied.

The Court has been known to apply this technique to a law that has only one exception. For example, in *TRW Inc. v. Andrews*, 534 U.S. 19 (2001), the Court considered a general statute of limitations that was subject to a single exception (for cases involving willful misrepresentation), and decided that Congress implicitly excluded the possibility of other exceptions, such as a discovery rule.

Likewise, in *Christensen v. Harris County*, 529 U.S. 576 (2000), the Court considered a law providing that an employee may use compensatory time unless the employer's operations would be unduly disrupted, and decided that the one basis given—undue disruptiveness—was the sole basis on which an employer could deny the use of compensatory time.

However, the Court at times has said that the technique applies only when there are "two or more" exceptions that are part of an "associated group or series," justifying the inference that the items not mentioned were excluded by deliberate choice, not inadvertence. *United States v. Vonn*, 535 U.S. 55, 65 (2002). For example, "the enunciation of two exceptions does not imply an exclusion of a third unless there is reason to think the third was at least considered." *Barnhart v. Peabody Coal Co.*, 537 U.S. 149 (2003).



 

## §3.90 Conclusion

This chapter covers a lot of ground. The contention here is that a drafter needs to be familiar with this ground to draft effectively, and to advise clients effectively.

When a court interprets a statute, one of the questions it asks is why Congress drafted it the way it did. When you draft a statute, one of the questions you should ask is how a court will interpret it. If this chapter accomplishes nothing else, it should impress upon you that this is not an easy question to answer. What was said in 1949 by Frank Edward Horack Jr. largely remains true today:

> "If courts believe, as they say, that legislatures are presumed to know of past judicial decisions and that statutes are drafted with a knowledge of them, they must recognize that they have given legislative draftsmen poor guides for future action. To be sure, the draftsman knows that if his statute is held to be penal it will be strictly construed, while if it is considered to be remedial the interpretation will be 'liberal'; that if he uses enumeration he must face the rule of *ejusdem generis*; while if he uses words of general import the statute may be 'void for vagueness.' But he does not know when the court will determine that one set of rules is applicable and when the other. For him the rules of statutory construction are at best, meaningless; at worst, they are unseen and 'extraconstitutional obstacles' that he must avoid if possible."
>
> Frank Edward Horack Jr.
> "The Disintegration of Statutory Construction"
> 24 *Indiana Law Journal* 335, 347 (1949).

Perhaps the single most important lesson to be gleaned from this chapter is that it is not enough to use clear language in isolation: The Court does not read language in isolation. The Court interprets statutes holistically, assuming that a particular statute is a small coherent system within a body of federal law that is a large coherent system. To ensure that your draft has the effect the client wants, you need to draft not only clearly, but holistically: Your draft should work as a coherent whole and it should fit into the general body of law in a coordinated manner.

It is sometimes said that a drafter creating a statute is like an architect or engineer creating a building. Yes, but that only goes so far. A drafter is also like a mechanic, fitting a statute into a body of law like a mechanic fits a part into a machine.

This chapter should also impress upon you that the Court does not simply apply a literal reading of the text. The Court will look for meaning from any source it finds persuasive, including the many techniques it uses for guessing what Congress meant. You need to anticipate the sources and techniques the Court might apply, and draft (and advise) accordingly.

The task can be daunting; the techniques used by courts can be bewildering. You may be tempted to throw up your hands in frustration. "Loose judicial reading makes for loose legislative writing. It encourages the practice illustrated in a recent cartoon in which a senator tells his colleagues 'I admit this new bill is too complicated to understand. We'll just have to pass it to find out what it means.' " Felix Frankfurter, "Some Reflections on the Reading of Statutes," 47 *Columbia Law Review* 527, 545 (1947). Avoid that practice if you can, and do not get discouraged.

Finally, you should always bear in mind that a court interprets a statute in some cases because Congress was unclear, and in other cases because Congress didn't anticipate the question before the court. To best serve your client, you need to anticipate not only the typical controversies that might arise, but also the atypical ones. For a discussion of how to do so, see Chapter Four, "Thinking Through the Policy."



 

# A Guide to Federal Grant Statute Drafting

By Malcolm S. Mason

From
Drafting Federal Grant Statutes:
Studies in Administrative Law and Procedure 90-1

Administrative Conference of the United States (ACUS)
Office of the Chairman

*Table of Contents is on Page 5*

 

## A GUIDE TO FEDERAL GRANT STATUTE DRAFTING

By Malcolm S. Mason

Senior Fellow, Administrative Conference of the United States

### *Preface*

Loren Smith, Chairman of the Administrative Conference of the United States, now Chief Judge, United States Claims Court, and his successor as Chairman of ACUS, Marshall Breger, and the staff of the Conference, particularly Stephen Babcock, Jeffrey Lubbers and Charles Pou, Jr., have been enthusiastically helpful and supportive.

The Advisory Board members have been similarly helpful in supplying approaches, comments and constructive criticism.

Schnader, Harrison, Segal & Lewis and Paul Dembling of that firm have been very helpful in providing facilities and services in support of this project. Paul G. Dembling has served as a member of the Advisory Board. The word-processing staff of Schnader, Harrison, Segal & Lewis, especially Ed Grzyb and Anna Gaskins, have been patient and helpful.

The National Assistance Management Association has been very helpful and its Board members, officers, and several past Presidents have participated actively.

Members of Congressional staffs have participated in discussions of the project and have supplied valuable suggestions and documentation. Among others who have participated in meetings and discussions and have supplied materials, may be mentioned: Dr. Margaret Wrightson, formerly Majority Staff Director, Subcommittee on Intergovernmental Affairs (Senate), and Ms. Donna Fossum, formerly with the Committee on Government Operations (House).

A member of the HHS Departmental Grant Appeals Board, Judy Ballard, and a member of the Staff of the Board, Terrie Gale, have assisted in the research, through the courtesy of the Board Chair, John Settle, a member of the Advisory Board.

Professor Morell E. Mullins of the School of Law, University of Arkansas at Little Rock, has recently published a very practical and sagacious handbook on statutory drafting, focusing on state law drafting (see Bibliography, Appendix). He has been both helpful and generous in his detailed and insightful criticism.

 

## NOTE ON 1 U.S.C. 1

Attention is called to 1 U.S.C. 1, Rules of Construction:

"(3) words importing the masculine gender include the feminine as well."

If I sometimes write "the lawyer, he" or "the draftsman, he" I intend to imply no priority of masculine lawyers against feminine lawyers or of masculine draftsmen as against feminine writers of legislative drafts. In many cases where I write "the lawyer, he" or "the draftsman, he" the rest of the sentence includes a suggestion that "the lawyer, he is confused" or "the draftsman, he has confused us". Little would be gained by insisting on equal grammatical recognition for women.

## DESCRIPTION OF THE PROJECT

The Conference has undertaken a study on problems in the drafting of federal assistance statutes, intended to lead to the preparation of a guidebook.

The objective of the study is to encourage clear, precise drafting of grant and assistance-related statutes.

It is not the purpose of the study to develop guidance on statutory drafting generally but to focus on aspects related to grant statutes.

It is also not the purpose of the study to develop a treatise on grants generally but to focus on aspects of the grant institution and practices that significantly affect the drafting of the statutes.

It is, further, not the purpose of the study to support particular goals of substantive policy, but to assist policy-makers in the development of statutes which are, as nearly as possible, effective in achieving the policy-makers' substantive policies, whatever they may be.

It is hoped that the outcome will help produce better-crafted assistance statutes, reduce divergences, improve agency administration, and avert needless uncertainty and litigation.

 

## ADVISORY GROUP

(1) Professor Richard B. Cappalli
Temple University School of Law

(2) Robert Coakley
Office of Senator Lawton Chiles

(3) Paul G. Dembling
Schnader, Harrison, Segal & Lewis

(4) James E. Frech
Arthur E. Anderson & Co.

(5) Thomas Hadd
Grants Information and Analysis Branch Chief
Environmental Protection Agency

(6) Malcolm S. Mason
Consultant

(7) Bruce D. McDowell
Acting Director
Government Policy Research
Advisory Commission on
Intergovernmental Relations

(8) Richard Parsons
Senior Attorney
General Accounting Office

(9) Paul Posner
Senior Executive Service Candidate
General Accounting Office

(10) Charles Pou, Jr.
Senior Staff Attorney
Administrative Conference of the U.S.

(11) Norval D. (John) Settle, Chair
Departmental Appeals Board
Department of Health & Human Services

(12) Dr. Margaret Wrightson
formerly Majority Staff Director
Senate Subcommittee on
Intergovernmental Affairs

 

**TABLE OF CONTENTS**



 

**8 Studies in Administrative Law and Procedure**



 

# I. INTRODUCTION

## A. ARE GRANT STATUTES GENERALLY WELL DRAFTED?

Are grant statutes well drafted? Some are. Too many, though, are ambiguous, raise questions, and create unnecessary disputes and litigation. Worst of all, some lead to results different from what the drafter intended. "[O]ften Congress cannot be heard clearly because its speech is muffled."[1] While there are necessarily subjective elements in such a judgment, a consensus of experienced observers in the field and significant empirical evidence cited herein support it.

Great drafters may be born, but some simple rules and reminders can lead to better drafting.[2] Several of these have special relevance to statutes in the field of federal assistance. This Guidebook seeks to set them forth, and discuss special problems facing drafters of grant laws.

## B. SOME EXPERT ASSESSMENTS INDICATE THAT GRANT STATUTES ARE OFTEN NOT CLEAR

A fundamental problem is that such statutes often lack explicitness on eligibility, on the range of administrative discretion, on the purposes for which funds may be used, on the presence or absence of federal controls or restrictions, and on provision for evaluating the results. Other goals often not met are avoidance of overinvolve-ment in the details of the regulatory function, and stan-dardization of language to insure consistent interpretation.[3]

---

[1]Frankfurter, *Some Reflections on the Reading of Statutes*, 47 COL.L.R.527, 535-6.

[2]Among classic writings on the subject are Dickerson, Legislative Drafting (Boston, Little Brown, 1954, reprinted by Greenwood Press, 1977), and Hirsch, Drafting Federal Law (Department of Health and Human Services, Office of the General Counsel, Legislation Division, 1980) which focuses more directly on assistance statutes. An extensive bibliography will be found below in Chapter V.

[3]Many of these points are discussed *infra*. They are made by *DEMBLING in the context of the following general comment (at 305):

 

The Advisory Commission on Intergovernmental Relations (ACIR), a broad and bipartisan body that has done significant research in grant problems, comments with insight on influences in the structure and operation of Congress that tend to interfere with good design of grant programs:

> In practice difficulties arise in obtaining Congressional respect of statutory design criteria. Congress may feel impelled to take action on a problem before sufficient knowledge and expertise is acquired to draft a bill meeting these criteria in all regards. . . .Congress may choose to ignore one or more principles of sound statutory design for its own coalition-building purposes. This reason may be why it combined several incompatible objectives into a single program under the small business loans portion of the Economic Development Administration Act. . . . [*E.g.*, to attract new industries or expand old ones in areas of low employment, but not to subsidize competitors against industries in the area]. (p. 70)
>
> Anxious to respond to needs, Congress is often not sure what will meet those needs. Sometimes, out of honorable impulses, it seeks many good but incompatible objectives in the same piece of legislation. (p. 73)[4]

---

VIII. Legislative Concerns

While there are some efforts for consolidating and understanding the flow of information regarding federal assistance programs to the public, there has not been a uniform approach to grant and federal assistance legislative drafting by the Congress. There is no common thread to be discerned regarding the various statutes which are enacted dealing with federal assistance programs. There has been no common structure to these statutes. Each program is authorized by a statute which uses it own language. No common set of definitions has emerged.

Citations in short form such as "*DEMBLING" are spelled out more fully below in the Bibliography (Appendix), where they are identified by the initial *.

Examples of vagueness, lack of standardization, over-intensive regulation, will be cited later in this chapter and in later chapters.

[4]ACIR, in *Categorical Grants: Their Role and Design*, A-52, undated but apparently 1978, Chapter III, The Role of Congress. *Cf.* Kozinski, Remarks

 

•Cappalli, 2:04, p. 6, comments:

> While the "proper" size and nature of national government involvement in the socioeconomic problems of America is essentially a political judgment, the efficiency and effectiveness of what is considered appropriate by our political processes is or should be a nonpartisan concern. To phrase it another way, it is essentially a concern of all people and parties to have that program run well. Yet, the disjointed and incremental congressional process was incapable of generating a systematic appraisal of the "style" and "structure" of federal assistance.[5]

## C. SOME EXAMPLES CONFIRM THAT VIEW

There are many indications of room for improvement. One such symptom of drafting deficiency is the discovery - not as unusual as it should be - that a statute just enacted must promptly be amended because its provisions direct action that the Congress did not in fact intend.

Family Educational Rights and Privacy Act, Education Amendments of 1974, 88 Stat. 484, 57, *amending* 438 of the General Education Provision Act, 20 U.S.C. 1232g, August 21, 1974, attempted to define the rights of students and their parents to information about their school records and to privacy of those records. In seeking to define both rights of access to information and rights to privacy, the Congress undertook a delicate task and the drafter stepped on his own toes.[6]

---

at January 9, 1986 joint luncheon of Federal Bar Association Capitol Hill and Pentagon Chapters, reported in FBA Government Contracts Section Newsletter February 1986, p. 7.

[5]*Cf.* •*Current Trends*, 35 FED.. BAR J. 163 at 186: ". . . there is a growth of particular statutory impingements on the operations of grant-making agencies which tend to express valid concerns but often are written without an appropriate broad framework so that they may lack balanced protections and may be counterproductive."

[6]No sooner was the law enacted than it became apparent that it would not do what Congress intended and in some ways, particularly in the relations of parent and child, might do just the opposite. Before the year was out, Congress enacted several pages of detailed changes, P.L. 93-568, 2, 88 Stat. 1855, December 31, 1974; retroactive to November 19, 1974. At the same time and probably for a similar reason, P.L. 93-568, 3,

 

Similarly ill-drafted is the Pucinski Amendment which deals with the same problem as the Administrative Procedure Act rulemaking provisions 552 and 553 (particularly, no rulemaking without 30 days advance publication in the Federal Register) but omits the carefully balanced protections of 552(a)(1) and 553(b)((A) and (B) and (d) (1)(2) and (3), which provide, as the Pucinski amendment did not, for cases of actual notice, for cases where good cause exists for departure, and for distinction between substantive rules and interpretive rules and for rules that recognize an exemption or relieve a restriction.[7]

## D. THE SUPREME COURT REPEATEDLY FINDS GRANT STATUTES NOT CLEAR

The Supreme Court has repeatedly commented on the poor drafting of grant statutes that have come before it. For example:

*Board of Ed. of City Sch. Dist. etc. v. Harris*, deals with a grant program to assist states in moving toward desegregation and turns on whether discrimination is measured by intent or effect.[8]

---

amended 901a of the Educational Amendments of 1972, 20 U.S.C. 1681, retroactive to July 1, 1972. Prohibiting educational programs receiving federal assistance from discriminating on grounds of sex, the Congress was dismayed to find it had curbed the YMCA, the YWCA, social fraternities, and other traditionally one-sex organizations which it considered benign.

[7]But *cf.* Sky, *Rulemaking in the Office of Education*, 26 AD. L. REV. 129 (1974), and Sky, 62 VA.L.REV. 1017 (1976), *Rulemaking and the Federal Grant Process in the United States Office of Education. See* Economic Opportunity Act of 1964, 623, as amended (1972), 42 U.S.C. 2971 ; *See Local 2677 v. Phillips*, 358 F.Supp. 60, (D.D.C. 1973) at 81-82; *contrast Local 2816 v. Phillips*, 360 F.Supp. 1092, 1100 (N.D. Ill., E.D., 1973). *cf.* General Provisions Concerning Education, Title IV of P.L. 90-247, as amended by P.L. 91-230, P.L. 92-318 (renumbered) and P.L. 93-380, 432(b), 20 U.S.C. 1232(b), which recognizes the need for qualifying the absolute terms of the old 431(b), but modifies it in a way that requires notice of proposed regulation to the pertinent Congressional Committees and the absence of disagreement by the committees and notice to the Speaker of the House and President of the Senate of final regulation and the absence of a concurrent resolution of disapproval. In addition, there is to be submission of schedules, of planned final regulation. The complexity of this raises questions of practical expediency in addition to the constitutional problems involved in the "legislative veto".

[8]444 U.S. 130, 100 S.Ct. 363 (1979) The central issue involved the ineligibility provisions of Section 706(d)(1)(B) of the 1972 Emergency School Aid Act, 86 Stat. 354, as amended, 20 U.S.C. Sections 1601-1619, repealed and simultaneously re-enacted, with amendments not material here, by Title VI of the Education Amendments of 1978, P. L. 96-561, 92 Stat. 2252, 2268, effective September 30, 1979. The re-enactment is recodified as 20

 

The Court, although sharply divided on the result, was unanimous in finding the statute inadequately clear.

Justice Blackmun, writing for the Court, quoting the ineligibility provisions said:

> The mere reading of this language [sec. 706(d)(1)(B) ineligibility provisions of 20 U.S.C. 1601(o) 1972 Emergency Aid Act] reveals that it suffers from imprecision of expression and less than careful draftsmanship. The first portion clearly speaks in terms of effect or impact. The second portion, arguably, might be said to possess an overtone of intent. There is nothing specifically indicating that this difference exists or, if it does, that it was purposefully drawn by Congress . . . . (444 U.S. at 138-139).[9]

Justice Stewart, writing for himself and two other dissenting Justices, said:

> Since the meaning of 706(d)(1)(B) is thus concededly ambiguous, it is necessary to look

---

U.S.C. Sections 3191- 3207 (1976 ed., Supp. II). On this form of amendment, *see* discussion, *infra*, Ch. III, "Special considerations in Drafting Amendatory Grant Statutes - Leave a track." Sections 3191-3207 in turn were repealed. P.L. 97-35, Title V, Subtitle D, Ch. 2, Subch. E, 587(a)(1), 95 Stat. 480, codified at 20 U.S.C. Section 3863.

The provision in question made a school district ineligible for assistance if it has, after June 23, 1972, had in effect a practice which results in the disproportionate demotion or dismissal of personnel from minority groups or "otherwise engage[s] in discrimination . . . in the hiring, promotion, or assignment of employees." The issue was whether intent to discriminate or only a disparate impact is required to bar the school district. The majority held that discriminatory impact is the standard by which ineligibility is to be measured, relying on its perception of the overall structure of the Act, the legislative history and its reading of the section which it acknowledged was imprecise and not carefully drafted. The dissent reached the conclusion that a racially discriminatory motive or intent in the school district's faculty assignment policies was required to bar the school district. It differed from the Court on its perception of the overall structure of the Act, on the legislative history and on its reading of the language of the critical section, but agreed that the language was ambiguous.

[9] Later in the opinion he said:

While perhaps it might be possible to theorize and to parse the language of 706(d)(1)(B), as the Board so strongly urges, in such a way as to conclude that impact alone is sufficient for ineligibility with respect to 'demotion or dismissal,' but intent is necessary with respect to 'assignment of employees,' we conclude that the wording of the statute is ambiguous. This requires us to look closely at the structure and context of the statute and to review its legislative history. (444 U.S. at 140).

 

> beyond the statutory words in order to ascertain their meaning (444 U.S. at 154).

Since the impact-or-intent issue involved in *Harris* was a well-known matter of debate and did not come as a surprise, we may conclude that if the Congress had a legislative purpose and wished to resolve it, greater clarity should have been achievable.

If it had intended the result reached by the Court, it might have said "or otherwise engaged in practices in the hiring, promotion or assignment of employees of the agency having a discriminatory impact with respect to race, color, or national origin, whether or not there is independent proof of discriminatory intent." If it had intended the result reached by the dissenters, it might have said "or otherwise engaged in practices in the hiring, promotion, or assignment of employees of the agency, with intent to discriminate on the basis of race, color, or national origin."

Of course, from the Congress' failure to do that, it does not follow that it was careless or incompetent. There are often reasons other than carelessness or incompetence why a legislator will accept ambiguities in a statute. An issue may not be ripe for legislative resolution and insistence on clarity in details may sometimes result in a failure to enact a program believed to be overall desirable. Circuit Judge Abner J. Mikva's comment, reflecting his experience as a Congressman as well as a Judge, is:

> We certainly should not be critical of ambiguity of language. Sometimes that is the only way a bill can pass--by sloughing over the hard parts and dulling the bright lines we would like to see.[10]

Nevertheless, the case is a reasonable reminder to statute writers that, unless you are obfuscating deliberately, it is possible and sometimes desirable to be clearer than the drafter of the ESAA was in the view of both sides of the Court.[11]

---

[10]Mikva, *Reading and Writing Statutes*, 28 S. Tex. L.R. 181, 187 (1986). *Cf.* Frankfurter, *op.cit.*, n.1, *supra*, at 528: "Moreover government sometimes solves problems by shelving them temporarily. The legislative process reflects that attitude. Statutes as well as constitutional provisions at times embody purposeful ambiguity or are expressed with a generality for future unfolding." *See* also *infra* text at n.19.

[11]Other examples abound, as the reader will see in later sections. *United States v. Locke*, 471 U.S. 84, 105 S.Ct. 1785 (1985), involved the problem of defining a deadline in a statute not in the field of grants but in a closely allied field. The case is discussed at some length in "Current

 

Developments, Vol. 21, No. 1, Fall 1985, p. 6. "Late Filing of Mining Claims". The statute, the Federal Land Policy and Management Act, P.L. 94-579, 43 U.S.C. 1701-1784, required that to protect substantial rights, miners file an annual notice "prior to December 31."

In *Locke*, the local Office of the Bureau of Land Management had told the miners that filing their claims on December 31 would be good. (Uncontradicted affidavit). The miners, who were actively working their valuable claim, flew to the Regional Office and filed on December 31. In April they were informed that, filing on December 31, they were a day late and had forfeited their claim. A majority of the Court said this was the result Congress intended, but the whole Court clearly viewed the statute as badly written.

The Court's opinion by Justice Marshall, at 1793 referred to ". . . the fact that Congress might have acted with greater clarity or foresight . . ." Justice O'Connor, concurring, at 1802, referred to "a poorly worded statutory deadline."

Justice Powell, dissenting, at 1802, said "the statutory deadline is too uncertain to satisfy constitutional requirements" and cited with approval the adverse comments of the separate dissent by Justice Stevens. Justice Stevens, with whom Justice Brennan joined, referred to circumstances that cast doubt both on the care with which Congress drafted 314 and on its meaning (1806 cited by Justice Powell at 1803) and called the statute "at least, ambiguous." At 1805, citing his dissent in *Delaware*, 430 U.S. 93, 97, 97 S.Ct. 911, 925, Justice Stevens underlines "the unfortunate fact that Congress is too busy to do all of its work as carefully as it should." At p. 1805 at n. 3 and p. 1806, citing Sherwood article in ROCKY MOUNTAIN MINERAL LAW INSTITUTE, he speaks of "inartful draftsmanship"; at 1807 he comments: "Plain language, . . . indeed"; at 1807 "an awkwardly drafted statute"; at 1808: "poorly drafted statute"; at 1810: "an ambiguous statute."

The United States, appellant, concedes that "[i]t may well be that Congress wished to require filing by the end of the calendar year and that the earlier deadline resulted from careless draftsmanship."

Did Congress really intend the result of the *Locke* case? The majority do not question that. The opinion of the Court simply argues in substance: That's what they said and they have the power to do it. Justice Stevens dissenting, believed the actual intent of Congress was to permit filings up to the end of the calendar year. Justice Powell, dissenting, comments (at 1803): "This is certainly the more reasonable interpretation of congressional intent and is consistent with all the policies of the Act."

The Department of the Interior, when the statute was new, understood the "prior to December 31" language to permit filing on December 31. The Bureau's local office, when consulted in this case, still understood it that way. Time of filing was clearly not very important to the Department since it would accept a letter received as late as January 19 (43 C.F.R. 3833.0-5m) and only in April informed the claimants they were late. This looks like an artificial issue.

Still, if Congress really wanted a December 30 filing deadline, what should it have done? It could have said "before the close of business December 30." More likely, there was no real need for this unusual deadline and the drop-dead language of the statute should have been softened. There is no indication that national land policy suffers from filings that are so marginally delayed.

 

In *Dixson v. United States,*[12] the question was whether officers of a private nonprofit corporation, not a federal agency nor a federal grantee, not even a grantee of the grantee, but only a sub-sub-grantee administering and expending federal community development block grants, are "public officials" for purposes of the federal bribery statute, 18 U.S.C. 201(a). The opinion of the Court, at 1177, notes:

> As is often the case in matters of statutory interpretation, the language of section 201(a) does not decide the dispute.

The dissent, at 1183, refers more vigorously to the "ambiguity," "facial ambiguity," "ambiguous coverage of the statute."

In other instances, where Congress wanted a statute on bribery or related economic offenses to apply to non-federal employees, it has said so expressly.[13] If it wanted that result it might have said so expressly here. If, as I believe, it did not want that result, it might have said so expressly also. It should be noted that if a federal statute does not apply, state statutes would presumably make the same conduct an offense under state law and the Congress may well have been satisfied with that result. If so, it is difficult

---

[12] 465 U.S. 482, 104 S.Ct. 1172 (1984), discussed in *Current Developments, vol. 19 No. 4, Summer 1984, p. 16, and vol. 22, No. 1, Fall 1986, pp 11-13.

[13] *See* *Current Trends, 35 FED. BAR J. at 167-168, 179-180. There is a long history of Congressional action that provides where necessary specific criminal statutes where it wants criminal sanctions rather than apply to grants broad general criminal statutes. By enacting the specific statutes, Congress showed that it did not understand the general statute to apply. Examples are 42 U.S.C. 1396h (kickbacks, bribes, or rebates in medicaid programs) recently strengthened by the Medicare and Medicaid Patients and Program Protection Act of 1987, P.L. 100-93, August 18, 1987; 18 U.S.C. 874 (kickbacks from public works employees on work financed by loans or grants from the United States); 42 U.S.C. 2703 (embezzlement or kickbacks and related misconduct in economic opportunity grant programs, repealed as part of general revisions of Economic Opportunity Act, P.L. 90-222, Title III, 301, *see* 1304; *see* 42 U.S.C. 2971(f), P.L. 97-35, Title VI, 6836). *See* 18 U.S.C. 665, theft or embezzlement in CETA program. *See also*, Job Training Partnership Act, section 182, amending 18 U.S.C. 665, Pub. L. 97-300; note also 436 dealing explicitly with the application of provisions of federal law to enrollees in the Job Corps. Robert Carmody has called my attention also to 18 U.S.C. 666 added by Pub. L. 98-473, Title II, 1111, Oct. 12 1984, 98 Stat. 2149. This action was proposed precisely to provide a specific statute instead of relying, as the Supreme Court did, on a general one of questionable applicability. Senate Report No. 98-225, p. 369 in 1984 U.S. CODE CONG. AND ADM. NEWS 3182 at 3510-3511.

 

to expect the Congress to anticipate the Court's reading of the statute, so the drafting may not be seriously at fault. I believe the Court was poorly informed. It may however, be appropriate for Congress to enact a general grant framework which announces that unless the contrary is clearly expressed, a grantee is not an arm, agent, or instrumentality of the federal government, its records are not records of a federal agency, its torts are not federal torts and its personnel are not federal employees or federal officials.[14]

*Pennhurst v. Halderman*,[15] involved the question whether a federal "bill of rights" for the retarded actually established substantive rights for the retarded and gave them a cause of action when they were denied those rights in an institution established by the State using federal grant funds. The Court held it did not. Justice Blackmun, concurring in part and concurring in the judgment, referred, at 1547 to "this confused and confusing legislation." Justice White, however, with whom Justices Brennan and Marshall dissented in part thought the statute "plain enough to me" (at 1550). Opinions can and do differ on such matters, but on questions of private rights of action, it would be well for drafters to consider greater explicitness.[16]

*Board of Educ., etc. v. Rowley*,[17] involved the question whether the Education for the Handicapped Act, which states as a condition for receiving federal assistance, the providing of free appropriate public education entitles a deaf child to a sign-language interpreter in the classroom. The opinion notes:

> We are loath to conclude that Congress failed to offer any assistance in defining the meaning of the principal substantive phrase used in the Act. It is beyond dispute that, contrary to the conclusions of the courts below, the Act does expressly define "free appropriate public education": [in terms of "appropriate"].

---

[14] Current Trends, 35 FED. BAR J. at 179-180.

[15] 451 U.S. 1, 101 S.Ct. 1531 (1981)

[16] This view was underlined by Justice Powell, joined by the Chief Justice, concurring in *Guardians Ass'n v. Civ. Serv. Com'n of City of N.Y.*, 463 U.S. 582, 608-9, 103 S.Ct. 3221, 3236 (1983): "Congress, for reasons of its own, all too frequently elects to remain silent on the private right-of-action question. The result frequently is uncertainty and litigation as to available remedies without clear legislative guidance."

[17] 458 U.S. 172, 102 S.Ct. 3034 (1982).

 

> ... Like many statutory definitions, this one tends toward the cryptic rather than the comprehensive, but that is scarcely a reason for abandoning the quest for legislative intent.... (458 U.S., at 187-188)
>
> Noticeably absent from the language of the statute is any substantive standard prescribing the level of education to be accorded handicapped children.... (458 U.S., at 189)
>
> When the language of the Act and its legislative history are considered together, the requirements imposed by Congress become tolerably clear. (458 U.S., at 203).

In calling the requirements "tolerably" clear, the Court, "loath to conclude that Congress failed to offer any assistance in defining the meaning of the principal substantive phrase used in the Act," was hardly awarding a commendation. The Court held that the lower courts should not have concluded, as they did, that the Act requires the provision of a sign- language interpreter, and reversed and remanded. Justice Blackmun, although reaching the same result, stated that he read the legislative history and goals of the Act differently (458 U.S. at 210). Justice White, dissenting, with Justice Brennan and Justice Marshall, expressed the view that the majority opinion contradicts itself, the language of the statute and the legislative history and disregards congressional intent (458 U.S., at 212).[18]

It must be acknowledged that the Supreme Court is not the most reliable evaluator in this field. Most Justices' awareness of the problems of grant operation is unfortunately minimal. The Court sometimes finds or says it finds unclear a statute that more experienced, equally disinterested observers find clear enough. The Court similarly finds or says it finds statutes plain and clear that others may find murky. Nevertheless, statutes are usually not written to provoke litigation. While Court pronouncements are not absolute tests of the clarity of a

[18]Note that the Congressional failure (if it is a failure) to define "appropriate" better (appropriate is defined in terms of appropriate) may have been wise. I do not intend to prejudge questions of that kind. This may be the best way to break new ground. But if the drafters knew what they wanted and could get the bill passed, perhaps better drafting was possible.

 

statute, when the Court repeatedly says statutes are unclear and difficult to interpret -- and especially when both majority and minority in the same case say so, -- there is good reason to look carefully at the draftsmanship.

### E. AMBIGUITY IS SOMETIMES DELIBERATE AND SOMETIMES JUSTIFIED BUT SHOULD BE HELD TO A REASONABLE MINIMUM

As previously noted some statutes are deliberately vague or ambiguous: Precision may be premature in the development of a new social program.[19] Precision of expression moreover might lose the possibility of gaining a majority.[20] It is a fair question whether such vague statutes should be enacted, but it does happen, and no guidebook on drafting will cure deficiencies that are introduced intentionally.[21] Indeed, when a clear statute cannot be enacted, a drafter may show exceptional skill in writing one ambiguous enough to gain the votes of legislators on both sides of the issues involved. These skills are reserved for a more advanced course.

---

[19] *See* Frankfurter, *op.cit. supra*, n.1., at 528, and n.10. *supra*. *See* Cleveland, The Future Executive, Harper & Row, 1972, p. 34: "... look sharp to see whether clarity or ambiguity serves the system better". *See* *Current Developments, vol. 22, No. 1, Fall 1986, p. 12 Comment C. *See* Mason, Separate Statement on ACUS Rec. 74-2, 3 ACUS 38, 42.

[20] ACIR, Categorical grants, A-52, *op. cit. supra*, n.4, at pp. 71 and 73 suggests:

> Modifications that destroy good design features are probably the easiest changes made in the coalition - building process. . . . Most importantly, during the coalition - building process to achieve enactment, preferred design features are frequently compromised.

Clarity is one of the design features often so sacrificed.

It is not only in legislative drafting that this kind of compromise occurs:

Chief Justice Hughes once said that he tried to write his opinions clearly and logically, but if he needed the fifth vote of a colleague who insisted on putting in a paragraph that did not 'belong', in it went, and let the law reviews figure out what it meant. Rehnquist, THE SUPREME COURT: HOW IT WAS, HOW IT IS (William Morrow, New York, 1987), p. 302.

[21] James J. Kilpatrick, *The Idea Is to Communicate*, Washington Post, Monday, Nov. 18, 1985, Op-Ed: "...sometimes we write for the pure pleasure of turning a pretty phrase; sometimes we draft tax law. Most of the time we write in the hope of being clearly understood." *Cf.* *Hirsch, p. 30: A draftsman may seek a degree of vagueness for reasons of policy; unnecessary vagueness should not be inflicted on his client because of the draftsman's ineptness.

 

### F. WHO SHOULD BE INTERESTED IN GRANT STATUTE DRAFTING PROBLEMS?

Drafters of grant statutes are not only the legislators and their staffs, but also agency legislative and program personnel, who originate many programs, and representatives of potential recipient and beneficiary groups who may be affected favorably or adversely by grant legislation. Advocates and courts interpreting statutes in the grant field may benefit by greater familiarity with the drafting problems involved in writing the statutes.

This Guidebook eschews substantive preconceptions. It seeks to be content neutral. It is not, however, neutral about the value of the grant institution, properly used. Whatever your substantive goals, you should know how to use the tools available to write them into effective legislation. Doing so requires an awareness of the grant as an institution that has evolved a distinctive character. Drafters must know, for example, that a grant is assistance to an autonomous recipient. They should understand when it is more effective to use grants rather than other techniques, why a grant is sometimes said to be like a contract and why it can be harmful to adopt this line of thought.

Features of our grant system include:

(a) Local governance in certain areas is protected.

(b) Pluralism is a goal.

(c) Operational independence is preserved.

(d) Delegation is characteristic.

(e) Grants are a congressional monopoly: No grant without statute.

(f) When made to a state, a grant is an arrangement between sovereigns.

Major changes are going on in the field of grants. Whereas in the 35 years beginning about 1950, grants grew from about $2 billion annually to about $175 billion, Reagan Administration policy and harsh fiscal facts have recently caused this explosive growth to level off and may even cause it to reverse.[22] Some decreases and program terminations have already occurred.

---

[22] Reliable figures for the amount of grant funds are very difficult to get. The most readily available, such as the Budget Special Analyses are for various reasons incomplete and possibly misleading. *See* for example, •Current Developments, Vol. 20, No. 1, Fall 1984, *The Size of the Grant Budget*, p. 7; No. 2, Winter 1985, *Breul's Figures for the Size of the Grant Program*, p. 10.

 

Current Administration policy (1988) favors cutting down the number of grant programs, not only reducing them in dollar amount but consolidating separate programs and converting some to block grants,[23] or other forms of assistance.

While we can expect that there will be fewer, smaller grant programs in the near future, these trends hardly represent watershed changes that will lessen the importance of the grant process.[24]

Factors indicating that grants will continue to represent a major federal activity are these:

(1) They take advantage of an efficient and largely fair federal tax system.

(2) They avoid growth of an even more massive federal bureaucracy.

(3) They permit local choices as to how best to deal with problems of national scope that nevertheless require or are seen to require adjustment to local circumstances, such as police, education, medicine, publication, welfare, research.

(4) In the absence of federal support, many grantees such as universities would turn to alternative courses that are limited and potentially detrimental: state funding, private-sponsored research, tuition increases.

(5) Without federal support, research levels and important service levels will be reduced.

(6) Federal funding can protect autonomy where it is essential. Where it is necessary to "fight city hall", you can't expect city hall to fund you.

Many existing programs will be reauthorized, usually modified as a result of congressional oversight and changed goals. In all likelihood, new grant programs will be enacted from time to time.[25] In any event, grants have a variety of

---

[23]Discussed below at Ch. II, 2, Types of grants.

[24]This question was addressed in an extended discussion of *Zero-Funding the Grant Technique*, *Zero Funding Grant Supported Activities*, *The Uniqueness of the Grant Approach* and *Two Basic Questions*, *Current Developments, Vol. 14, No. 2, January 1979, P. 14 *ff*.

[25]Thus, the Safe Drinking Water Acts Amendments, P.L. 99-339, June 19, 1986, adds a demonstration grant program; the Mentally Ill Individuals Act, P.L. 99-319, May 23, 1986 also adds a new grant program; the Excellence in Minority Health Education and Care Act, P.L. 100-97, August 18, 1987, creates a grant program for health professionals schools; the Stewart B. McKinney Homeless Assistance Act, P.L. 100-77, July 22, 1987, creates several related grant programs.

The "Orphan Drug Amendments of 1988," P.L. 100-290, sec. 3, extends and continues a small grant program. April 18, 1988. The Child Abuse Prevention, Adoption, and Family Services Act of 1988, P.L. 100-294,

 

advantageous features, serve valid governmental purposes and will survive.

As noted by the Supreme Court in *United States v. Orleans*:

> Federal funding reaches myriad areas of activity of local and state governments and activities in the private sector as well.[26]

There are activities that will not be done as well, or not at all, if left to diverse private sources or local authority alone. Here is an example: Rational use of energy resources is a pressing national need. Yet the short term local interests of each consumer and each community may pull against the long run national interest of all consumers and all communities.[27] Only national action can deal with this problem.

To form a sound judgment of whether grants are appropriately to be used in a particular case, we must look at two questions: (1) what should be federally supported (and, because federally supported, can be steered or regulated for major federal goals) as opposed to state or local or only privately supported? (2) If federally supported, what should be done by grant as against being done by federal government directly, "in-house", or by contract or by other techniques?

The answer to the second question turns on what can be done best or what should be done on a local level.[28]

Certain activities are felt in American tradition to be properly local. To federalize them would wrench strongly

---

April 25, 1988, restructures previous activities and creates new grant programs.

The Augustus F. Hawkins - Robert T. Stafford Elementary and Secondary School Improvement Amendments of 1988, P.L. 100-297, April 28, 1988, reauthorizes existing programs and creates new grant programs.

The Civil Rights Restoration Act of 1987, P.L. 100-259, March 22, 1988, corrects recent decisions of the Supreme Court, cutting across major grant programs.

[26]425 U.S. 808, 817 (1976).

[27]Another example is the interstate highway system. *See, e.g.*, NATIONAL COUNCIL ON PUBLIC WORKS IMPROVEMENT, FRAGILE FOUNDATIONS (Final Report to the President and Congress), February 1988, Criteria for Evaluating Public Works Roles, pp. 81-86, Highway Roles, pp. 87-89. *See* review of (Netherlands) Committee for the Development of Policy Analysis, *The Subsidy Instrument*, November 1975, in FBA FEDERAL GRANTS COMMITTEE NEWSLETTER, October 31, 1975, par. 5.

[28]*Cf.* FBA Federal Grants Committee Check List on the Uses of Grants in the Energy Field, June 14, 1977, pp. 3 *ff.*, 8 *ff.*

 

held beliefs that have some validity and have, in any case, more force than their actual merits justify as a mere pragmatic matter. We do not want a federal police force, a federal education system, a federal practice of medicine, a federal newspaper. We believe that welfare laws should be in important respects responsive to locally divergent situations. We know that creative research needs autonomy in the conduct of the research.[29] When these feelings are involved, the federal government will not appropriately conduct the program itself nor by contract, but will use other techniques of which grant is a principal example.

Thus, grants belong to the area where two inconsistent trends cross: where the problem requires national action rather than local, but our policy perceptions nevertheless call for local control and adjustment to local circumstances. Both pulls may sometimes be satisfied by a federal grant to encourage local action in a direction broadly defined by national goal considerations. Where both of these inconsistent crossing needs are not present, the appropriateness of the grant technique should be questioned and zero-funding of a grant approach is probably a correct outcome. Where both are present and are of substantial importance, serious consideration should be given to the possible effectiveness of the grant technique and a decision for funding may be justified if the goal is important enough, the cost acceptable, and the benefits and costs of alternative techniques less compelling.

The grant system will change. It may, by some measures -- dollar amount, number of different programs -- shrink, but it has not outlived its usefulness and is not at the edge of disappearing. It should be understood by those who determine its size, shape and other characteristics. This includes legislators and legislative staff, executive department staff, advocates, the courts, lobbyists and representatives of those who may be affected by grant programs. It is a distinctively American governmental device that will continue to be needed and is worth handling better than it has been in the past.

---

[29] *Cf.* Smith, *Judicialization: The Twilight of Administrative Law*, 85 Duke L.J. 427, 445 (1985): "You can do many things by threat or promise, but you cannot create or invent by that method . . . creativity and invention can spring only from the individual human mind, while law operates at the level of society."

 

## II. PLANNING AN ASSISTANCE PROGRAM

Before the drafting of a grant statute begins, the program itself should be planned: its goals and subgoals, its structure, its social and administrative techniques. A drafter may sometimes be the policy-maker. More often a drafter is a technician aiding the policy-maker. Yet there is an unavoidable overlap between the role of policy-maker and drafter. When it is possible, it is desirable that the drafter participate from the beginning of the planning of the program: the drafter should understand fully the policy that is to be effectuated and should be in a position to point out early that there are options that should perhaps be considered or that have been left undecided. The drafter must know the techniques to be employed; should judge whether they are likely to effectuate the policy goals; and has a responsibility to inform the policy-maker, if necessary, when the techniques to be employed may not be those best calculated to achieve the policy goals, that others are available to achieve them better.

This is a give-and-take that should, if possible, start early in the process. Planning a grant statute begins with the planning (or with helping to clarify the planning) of the program.

In this Chapter we shall examine some leading considerations in planning a grant program. In the next Chapter, considerations in planning the statute. The order of topics is, broadly speaking, an appropriate chronological sequence of topics as they should be given attention or as they affect successive stages in the operation of an assistance program:

A. The choice of instrument.

1. Is the program to be a grant program as opposed to a direct federal operation?

2. Should the program instrument be a grant or a contract?

3. Why should it matter whether one instrument or the other is used?

4. If the program is to be assistance, is the instrument to be a grant or cooperative agreement?

B. Types of grants.

C. Various programs in addition to grants have assistance elements.

 

D. Grants in context

1. A grant program need not and generally does not stand alone.

2. Good grant statute drafting calls for at least consideration of setting the purposed grant statute in a context of such other activities, and adjusting the various elements to each other.

E. The constitutional basis for grants.

F. Grants are a Congressional monopoly.

G. The administering office

1. If a program is to be a grant program, who should administer it?

2. It is recommended that absent clear reasons to the contrary, grant authority should normally be conferred on agency heads with express or implied power of delegation rather than on specified subordinates.

H. How much discretion should be left to the Executive?

I. What should be the funding mechanics of the program?

J. What is the intended class of recipients?

K. Should there be a requirement for local sharing in the costs?

L. Should there be a requirement for maintenance of local effort?

M. No-Supplant: Should there be a requirement that federal funds not be used to supplant local effort?

## PLANNING AN ASSISTANCE PROGRAM

### A. CHOICE OF INSTRUMENT

1. IS THE PROGRAM TO BE A GRANT PROGRAM AS OPPOSED TO A DIRECT FEDERAL OPERATION?

"Grant programs represent a means for the governance of our society which is rooted in a pluralistic conception of the value of drawing on both private and governmental sources."[1]

For convenience, the word "grant" will be used throughout to include both grants in the narrower sense and related assistance instruments, except where the distinction is

[1] Leventhal, Cir. J., in *Forsham v. Califano*, 587 F.2d 1128, 1138 (D.C. Cir., 1978), *aff'd. Forsham v. Harris*, 445 U.S. 169 (1980).

 

important and made clear by the context as it is in Section A4, *infra*. A principal advantage is that "grant" is not only the more usual instrument but the term most commonly used in such general discussion as Judge Leventhal's comment quoted above.

A drafter may be called upon to develop grant legislation for a program that is not best accomplished by grant, or to develop non-grant legislation for a program that would be better achieved by grant. The line is not always distinct, but the guiding principle is clear:

2. USE A GRANT WHEN TWO CONDITIONS ARE PRESENT:
   a. There is an important federal purpose to be served.
   b. There are also local concerns that should share in shaping the remedy for the problem perceived, and should be encouraged to supply drive, imagination, creativity, modification to local circumstances.

Both must be present. If both are not present in a significant degree, something other than a grant is likely to be a better choice. For example, the food stamp program at an early stage allowed for modification from state to state to permit adjustment to local circumstances and local perceptions. The statute's declaration of policy expressly stated that

> the Nation's abundance of food should be utilized cooperatively by the States, the Federal Government, and local governments to the maximum extent practicable to safeguard the health and well-being of the Nation's population and raise levels of nutrition among low-income households.[2]

Increasingly, however, uniform federal regulations overwhelmed the areas for local variation. Administratively, OMB then correctly determined that this was not really a grant program.[3]

---

[2]Act of August 31, 1964, P.L. 88-525, 2.

[3]Budget of the United States Government Special Analyses 1977, at 260; 1989, at H-12. The Congress apparently had envisioned and intended some such result, because it progressively withdrew from its policy statements first, "to the maximum extent practicable" and then the whole reference to the cooperative action. Compare Act of August 31, 1964, *supra*, with Act of January 11, 1971, P.L. 91-671 1; Act of September 29, 1987, P.L. 95-113, Title XIII, 1301 (7 U.S.C. 2011).

 

Differences between a grant program and a direct federal program are illustrated by two major health care programs. Medicaid is a grant program; Medicare is not (Titles XVIII and XIX of the Social Security Act). Both are, broadly speaking, parallel systems for providing medical services to wide classes of beneficiaries. Medicaid provides assistance to states which wish to make medical services meeting the standards of the Act available to eligible beneficiaries.[4] Medicare, not a grant program, is part of the Social Security system directly administered in theory by the Federal Government.[5] In practice, the States may serve as agents for the Federal Government, so the external resemblance of the two systems is close. The distinction between the two systems -- one a grant program, one not -- makes sense if it is desired that the medical services for those who are eligible because of lack of resources (Medicaid) be administered in a way that effectively allows each state to measure for itself the cost of services to be provided and in a significant way to adjust, to its own conditions and its own perceptions, the style and kind of medical services program. If not, this should be a federally administered program like the medical services for those eligible by having qualified for social security (age or disability rather than indigence).[6]

If the two conditions described above at the beginning of this section are present and grant is chosen as the program instrument, that implies a commitment on the part of the Federal Government to respect for local initiative, planning, preferences, ways of operating that should be honored. Accordingly, the legislation should not be drafted in a way which allows the Federal Government to run the program,

[4]Medicaid supports state and local efforts to provide health services to roughly 25 million low-income residents, with roughly $37 billion of Federal assistance, which is somewhat more than half of the total cost. *See* FY 1988 Special Analyses H-12; 1989, B-15, H-10; Budget, FY 1990, at 5-115; The FY 1991 estimate for Medicaid federal payments has increased to $45 billion, *id.* FY 1991 at A-208, A-719.

[5]Medicare is expected to serve about 33 million persons, aged, disabled, or suffering from end-stage renal disease. It is expected to cost very roughly $95 billion, FY 1989 Budget 5-114, and 6g-35. Budget FY 1990 at 5-123; *cf.*, Budget FY 1991 at A-721-724 (changes of format make comparison with past years difficult). This is before the Medicare Catastrophic Coverage Act of 1988, P.L. 100-360, which was estimated to provide revenues exceeding outlays until 1990 (Cong. Budg. Off. Estimate, U.S. CODE CONG. & ADMIN. NEWS, August 1988, p. 803, 904.) That Act was almost entirely repealed, P.L. 101-234, as of Dec. 31, 1989.

[6]In fact there are proposals to terminate Medicaid as a grant program and substitute a federally administered program. *E.g.*, Remarks by Senator Dave Durenberger to the National Assistance Management Association, March 8, 1983, 2 Assistance Management, No. 1 December 1983, 6, 8.

 

dominate the program, or intrude beyond need. The statute should be written on the assumption of respect for grantee autonomy.[7]

3. SHOULD THE PROGRAM INSTRUMENT BE A GRANT OR A CONTRACT?

If the purpose is acquisition of goods and services for the Federal Government, the program should be a contract program; although this should be obvious, in practice it has not always been done that way. If the purpose is assistance, it should not be a contract program but a grant program (or, see below, a cooperative agreement program. As noted earlier, the term "grant" is used for convenience to cover both grants and cooperative agreements except when the difference is important.). This is the distinction made by the Federal Grant and Cooperative Agreement Act [P.L. 95-224, 41 U.S.C. 501, recodified at 31 U.S.C. 6301] It is not a perfect distinction, but it is a workable one. What is "assistance" (also called "a public purpose of support or stimulation") is not defined, and perhaps is not quite definable. The key to what is "assistance", however, is that assistance respects the autonomous goals of the recipient and encourages them rather than directs or compels or dominates them.

4. WHY SHOULD IT MATTER WHETHER ONE INSTRUMENT OR THE OTHER IS USED?

It matters because contracts of the Federal Government are the subject of elaborate rules, statutory and regulatory, that are in many important respects inappropriate to the grant relationship.[8] The contract rules are designed to

[7]Wallick, *Why Grants? Why Not Direct Federal Program?*, p.5, in ABA National Institute, "Focus 77, Public Contracts and Grants From Local and Federal Perspectives", April 21-22, 1977:

> Why grants--Why not let the federal government manage the programs directly? The answer is not, I submit, merely for the purpose of providing two layers of bureaucracies where one would suffice. Consequently, I suggest there should be a rebuttable presumption against any statute or regulation which further limits local initiative or difference. Their need and value must be quite clear and convincing before they are adopted.

[8]Some of these distinctions may be summarized:

Government contracts normally provide for cost plus a profit. Grants normally provide cost minus a cost-sharing.

Contracts are normally subject to objective competition based, in the case of formally advertised contracts, primarily on price or, in the case of negotiated contracts, on efficiency and effectiveness. Grants are subject to

 

operate in areas of entrepreneurial competition, which is untypical for grants. They are designed to minimize certain abuses that have been encountered in government procurement which do not generally arise in grant situations. They express generally an arms-length relationship between contracting parties which normally is not appropriate to grants. Contracts and grants, moreover, have in intangible but real ways developed cultural styles of their own. Confusion of these styles creates undesirable misunderstanding.[9]

---

no competition or to a subjective competition not based on price and not even necessarily on efficiency; the poorest supplier may sometimes be preferred because it most needs help.

Contract specifications are normally clear and the goal is to make them precise. Grant specifications often and appropriately are general and vague.

Contracts are subject to strict rules of advertising, bidding, bid protest. Grants are subject to no rules or looser rules of advertising and application. Generally, in grants, there is no provision for protest by A if A is rejected in favor of B. The qualified best bidder has a right to the contract. A qualified applicant has a right to a grant of the mandatory type but not to a grant of the discretionary type.

The Government may unilaterally terminate a contract for its convenience. The contractor may not unilaterally terminate for its convenience. The Government may not unilaterally terminate a grant for its convenience, but the grantee may do so.

The Government has remedies for a contractor's failure to perform or for poor performance. Specific performance is available to the extent normally provided in private transactions. The Government generally has no remedy for grantee's failure to perform or for poor performance except that unauthorized expenditures may be recovered. Specific performance is generally not available to the Government as grantor, except perhaps on civil rights issues.

*Quantum meruit* may be available in contract cases. It is often said that *quantum meruit* is not available in grant cases (but *see* Southern Illinois University - Carbondale, HEW DGAB Docket No. 78-5, Decision No. 49, October 31, 1978 esp. at 5-8).

Some of these contrasts are noted, discussed, and qualified in •Highlight 2-4; Mason, Administrative Review of Performance, Payment and Termination Controversies, 1-2, in ABA National Institute, April 21-22, and May 11-12, 1977 "Focus 77, Public Contracts and Grants from Local and Federal Perspectives"; •Current Trends at 166-168, 187-189.

[9]Mason, in ABA National Institute, *supra*, n.8:

> Procurement contracts are dominated by the ethos of the market place; cold, hard-boiled, arms-length most-bang-for-the-buck relations in competition for the award, in supervision and enforcement of the deal. Not always, but typically so. Procurement contracts deal mostly with what can be counted and measured, the abstract, the impersonal, the formalized. A mile of road, a ten story building, a thousand desks, a million vaccinations.

 

It matters also because experience has shown that administrative officers, if permitted to do so, will often misuse one instrument for the other in order to escape from restrictive contract rules in a procurement situation by calling the arrangement a grant, or to escape from specific grant consequences in a grant situation by calling the arrangement a contract.[10]

---

> Grants are dominated by the spirit of assistance: hot, enthusiastic, personalized, concrete, concerns about people, services to people with faces, names, ages, needs. Instead of a procurement contract, grant administration accepts the spirit of partnership, and grantee autonomy in place of bought and paid for control.

These differences of style are particularly visible in the important field of scientific research. Much of the most important results of Nobel prize winners, for example, were their failure to do what they set out to do. If they had had grants, the grants would have been glorious successes. Had they had contracts, they would simply have turned in failures. Examples are the work of Penzias and Wilson who got the Nobel award for failing in the task they had undertaken, namely to construct and calibrate a radiation receiver of sufficient precision and so free of adventitious distortions as to show no excess radiation above that received from identified targeted sources of radiation; and the work of Michelson who got the Nobel award for failing in the task he had confidently undertaken, to set up an interferometer with sufficient precision, eliminating instrumental causes of inaccuracy, so as to measure the difference in the speed of light in the direction of the earth's movement from that across the direction of the earth's movement. *See* *Current Developments, Vol. 20, No. 1, Fall 1984, p. 7, "Luria's Slot Machine"; *cf.* Vol. 21, No. 2, Winter 1986, p. 11, "The Joking Physicist."

[10]P.L. 95-224, the Federal Grant and Cooperative Agreement Act of 1977, February 3, 1978, Sec. 2(a)(1),(2),(3):

> Sec.2.(a) The Congress finds that --
>
> (1) there is a need to distinguish Federal assistance relationships from Federal procurement relationships and thereby to standardize usage and clarify the meaning of the legal instruments which reflect such relationships;
>
> (2) uncertainty as to the meaning of such terms as "contract", "grant", and "cooperative agreement" and the relationships they reflect causes operational inconsistencies, confusion, inefficiency, and waste for recipients of awards as well as for executive agencies; and
>
> (3) the Commission on Government Procurement has documented these findings and concluded that a reduction of the existing inconsistencies, confusion, inefficiency, and waste is feasible and necessary through legislative action.

 

For these reasons the Federal Grant and Cooperative Agreement Act drew the distinction between acquisition and assistance. It is not a perfect distinction, but it is a useful and broadly desirable one and should be respected at least until substantial experience with the Act has been accumulated.

New statutes should, as a matter of course, accept the distinction drawn by this general statute. They should not needlessly contradict it nor needlessly repeat its provisions.

### 5. IF THE PROGRAM IS TO BE ASSISTANCE, IS THE INSTRUMENT TO BE A GRANT OR COOPERATIVE AGREEMENT?

The Federal Grant and Cooperative Agreement Act distinguishes between them in terms of whether substantial involvement is anticipated between the executive agency and the recipient (cooperative agreement) or not (grant) (sec. 5(2) and 6(2)).[11] Cooperative agreements, in practice, seem largely employed to fudge the application of grant rules.[12] It

[11]P.L. 95-224, February 3, 1978, originally codified as 41 U.S.C. 501-509, recodified with some amendments as 31 U.S.C. 6301-8. The appropriate use of grants is now specified in 6304 and of cooperative agreements in 6305.

[12]The Act directed OMB to study these questions and to issue interpretative guidelines (sec. 8 and 9 of original Act). The OMB did not make effective use of this opportunity. OMB, Managing Federal Assistance in the 1980s (March 1980). *See*, *Current Developments, Vol. 15. No. 4, July 1980 p. 6. Agencies that wish to smuggle some contract characteristics into an assistance relationship, or otherwise avoid application of grant rules they find troublesome, or on the other hand to avoid contract rules by making a grant instead of a contract, are able to take advantage of the lack of clear guidance to do what the Act intended to prevent their doing. A GAO analysis of the OMB guidance and of agency practice makes the following points: Agencies Need Better Guidance For Choosing Among Contracts, Grants, and Cooperative Agreements GGD-81-88, September 4, 1981:

> [B]ecause Federal officials are not systematically examining assistance relationships in selecting either grants or cooperative agreements, there is no certainty that officials are limiting requirements in assistance awards to those consistent with the intended relationship....
>
> [W]e found several actual or proposed assistance awards which we believe should have been procurement contracts. Most of the proposed or actual awards were cooperative agreements. (p.8)....
>
> Two years after OMB issued its guidelines, officials of Federal agencies, OMB, and we, ourselves, do not clearly understand what a cooperative agreement is for. (22)...

 

may be questioned whether the provision for cooperative agreements in fact serves a useful purpose.[13] The Office of Management and Budget, instructed to study and provide guidelines on this matter, has had an opportunity, but did not use it, to propose a clearer definition which today still does not exist. Notwithstanding the broader advice given above (Sec. A.4) not to tamper unnecessarily, Congress might therefore usefully consider eliminating this verbal category or proposing a sharper definition. Drafters may well note the possible problems if a proposed statute should use the cooperative agreement as its model instrument.

**B. TYPES OF GRANTS**

If the program is to be a grant program there are several distinguishable types of grants to be considered: mandatory grants which give the grantor agency limited discretion and discretionary grants which give the grantee less entitlement.

A grant statute may define a class of eligibles and may provide that an eligible who chooses to participate shall be entitled to receive a specified amount of grant or a grant in an amount determined by a formula contained in the statute. Because the right to receive the grant (and the duty on the part of the executive to make the grant) is fixed by the statute, the program is generally called *mandatory* or, sometimes, an entitlement. When the amount is set by formula, the grant is called a formula grant. Most mandatory grants are formula grants and most formula grants are mandatory. Typically, the recipient of a mandatory grant is a state. Often (but the trend is perhaps away from this), a condition of a mandatory grant program to states will be the submission of a State Plan conforming to the statute. In that case, the grant may be called a State Plan grant. Most mandatory grants are State Plan grants and most State Plan grants are mandatory.

---

> Currently there are no standard operational differences between grants and cooperative agreements.... The operational consequences of choosing a grant or a cooperative agreement are presently so unclear that some officials consider the choice to be a distinction without a difference (54)." These comments remain valid.

*See also* Parker, *95-224* [the Federal Grant and Cooperative Agreement Act] *Doesn't Work, So What's Next?*, 3 ASSISTANCE MANAGEMENT No. 1, Spring 1986.

[13]•Current Developments, Vol. 14, No. 1, October 1978, p. 6.

 

The formulas for many of these grants have often depended on the amount the State chooses to spend for the statutory grant purpose: the federal government reimburses (or advances on the basis of an estimate) a portion, defined by the formula, of what the State spends. Such grants are called open-ended. They tend to create awkward problems of interpretation and for obvious reasons of fiscal stringency they are becoming less frequent than they were some decades ago.[14]

In contrast, a grant statute may leave to the discretion of the administering agency whether to make a grant or not. Such programs are called *discretionary*. In most cases discretionary grant programs permit the administering agency to determine in its discretion not only whether a grant should be made but what should be the size of the grant, within the limits of the available appropriation and of any statutory requirement to spread the awards amongst the states or among other classifications. (An Administrator should not channel all the awards towards his home State or his alma mater). Provisions for such spreading may look something like a formula fixing the exact amount of a mandatory grant but fix instead only the ceiling for the total of all the discretionary grants going to recipients in a particular state or of a particular kind: an example of the latter provision would be a requirement that a certain share of all grants go to rural recipients or to institutions of higher education. Most discretionary grant programs require the submission of an application describing in some detail a particular proposed project and are therefore called "project" grants. With limited funding, applications may be weighed against the merits of other applications, but the process of grant competition is more subjective and generally less structured and less price oriented than is the case with competed procurement.[15]

---

[14] DERTHICK, UNCONTROLLABLE SPENDING FOR SOCIAL SERVICES GRANTS, The Brookings Institution 1975, esp. at 106. An effort to escape from some of these problems is Title XX of the Social Security Act. Title XX of the Social Security Act, providing a "cap" for social services that will receive federal matching, was an attempt to deal with a runaway expansion of expenditures which the Congress blamed in part on HEW's failure to impose limits. *See* Legislative History of P.L. 92-512, Title III, State and Local Fiscal Assistance Act of 1972, 3 U.S. CODE CONG. & ADMIN. NEWS '72 pp. 3937-8; Legislative History of P.L. 93-647, Social Services Amendments of 1974. 4 U.S. CODE CONG. & ADMIN. NEWS '74 p. 8135. Title XX was later further revised by P.L. 97-35, the Omnibus Budget Reconciliation Act of 1981, Title XXIII, Subtitle C. 2352(a).

 

Some hybrids exist. For example, a program may call for mandatory grants to the states out of which sub-grants shall be made to local governments or other recipients within the state at the discretion of the state, or at the discretion of the state with federal approval.[16]

Grant programs ordinarily define the purposes for which the grant funds may be used. If the purposes are defined with some narrowness, the program is called "categorical".[17] If it is defined more broadly, it is called a "block" grant.[18] If defined very broadly it may be called revenue sharing, or general purpose fiscal assistance. Special revenue sharing is a term sometimes used for programs that impose some restriction on the area of use but are still very broad. Such programs may be regarded as block grants or as something

---

[15]*See* n.8, *supra*. *Cf.* *Settle and Yamada, The Award Process, at 66 and 72.

[16]Examples are 42 U.S.C. 300 w(c)(2), Preventive Health and Health Services Block Grant; P.L. 98-377, August 11, 1984 207(b)(1)(A), 20 U.S.C. 3967, Education for Economic Security Act, Catalog 84.164.

[17]An example of a categorical program is P.L. 99-605, the Refugee Assistance Extension Act of 1986, 8(2)(A).

> The Director [of the Office of Refugee Resettlement, HHS]. is authorized to make grants to States for assistance to counties and similar areas in the States where, because of factors such as unusually large refugee populations.... there exists and can be demonstrated a specific need for supplementation of available resources for services to refugees. (B) Grants shall be made available under this paragraph -- (i) primarily for the purpose of facilitating refugee employment and achievement of self-sufficiency...."

[18]An example of a block grant is 42 U.S.C. 300x *ff.*, the Alcohol and Drug Abuse and Mental Health Services Block Grant. These grant funds may be used for:

> (1) planning, establishing, maintaining, coordinating, and evaluating projects for the development of more effective prevention, treatment, and rehabilitation programs and activities to deal with alcohol and drug abuse; and (2) grants to community mental health centers in accordance with section 1916(c) and grants to community mental health centers for the provision of the following services: (A) Services for chronically mentally ill individuals.... (B) Identification of severely disturbed children and adolescents....(C) Identification and assessment of mentally ill elderly individuals... (D) Services for identifiable populations which are currently underserved in the State... (E) Coordination of mental health and health care services provided within health care centers. Amounts provided for the activities referred to in the preceding sentence may also be used for related planning, administration, and educational activities.

 

intermediate between block grants and general revenue sharing. The lines here are not sharply drawn.

The principal line of distinction for operating purposes is between mandatory grants and discretionary grants. For budget purposes, the General Accounting Office regards the principal line of distinction in grants as that between block and categorical grants.[19]

---

[19]The General Accounting Office classification is indicated by the following excerpts from A GLOSSARY OF TERMS USED IN THE FEDERAL BUDGET PROCESS (March 1981).

> GRANTS
>
> Assistance awards in which substantial involvement is not anticipated between the Federal Government and the State or local government or other recipient during the performance of the contemplated activity. Such assistance is not limited to a State or local government as in the case of grants-in-aid. (*See* P.L. 95-224, Federal Grant and Cooperative Agreement Act of 1977.
>
> The two major forms of Federal grants are block and categorical. Block grants are given primarily to general purpose governmental units in accordance with a statutory formula. Such grants can be used for a variety of activities within a broad functional area. Examples of Federal block-grant programs are Omnibus Crime Control and Safe Streets Act of 1968, Comprehensive Employment and Training Act of 1973, and assessment of severely mentally disturbed children and Housing and Community Development Act of 1974, ad the 1974 Amendments to the Social Security Act of 1935 (Title XX). Categorical grants can be used only for a specific program and are usually limited to narrowly defined activities. Categorical grants consist of formula, project, and formula-project grants.
>
> Formula grants allocate Federal funds to States or their subdivisions in accordance with a distribution formula prescribed by law or administrative regulation. Project grants provide Federal funding for fixed or known periods for specific projects or the delivery of specific services or products. (*See also* Cooperative Agreement; Grants-in-Aid.)
>
> GRANTS-IN-AID
>
> For purposes of the budget, grants-in-aid consist of budget outlays by the Federal Government to support State or local programs of governmental service to the public. Grants-in-aid do not include purchases from State or local governments or assistance awards to other classes of recipients (*e.g.*, outlays for research or support of Federal prisoners). (*See also* Cooperative Agreement; Grants; Revenue Sharing.)
>
> REVENUE SHARING
>
> Federal funds distributed by formula to State and general-purpose local governments with few or no limits on the purposes

 

## C. VARIOUS PROGRAMS IN ADDITION TO GRANTS HAVE ASSISTANCE ELEMENTS.

Examples include loans, loan guarantees, insurance, direct training. To the extent that they resemble grants, some of the considerations applicable to the drafting of grant statutes are worth taking into account. Each, however, has some elements of difference and some historic incrustation of its own that makes the drafting factors at least traditionally different.[20]

---

for which the funds may be used and few restrictions on the procedures which must be followed in spending the funds. (*See also* Grants-in-Aid.)

850 GENERAL PURPOSE FISCAL ASSISTANCE
Federal aid to State, local, and territorial governments that is available for general fiscal support. Also included are grants for more restricted purposes when the stipulated purposes cross two or more major budgetary functions and the distribution among those functions is at the discretion of the recipient jurisdiction rather than the Federal Government. It includes payments in lieu of taxes, broad-purpose shared revenues, general revenue sharing, and the Federal payment to the District of Columbia. Payments specifically for community development or social service programs are not included in this function.

851 General Revenue Sharing
The general revenue sharing program.

852 Other General Purpose Fiscal Assistance
All other programs in this function, which are mainly shared revenues, counter-cyclical fiscal assistance whenever there is such a program, and the Federal payment to the District of Columbia.

Another influential classification is ACIR's *A Typology of Federal Grants*, in A-52, CATEGORICAL GRANTS: THEIR ROLE AND DESIGN (approved May 6, 1977) pp. 5-9.

[20]The range of these programs is suggested by a classification made in the Catalog of Federal Domestic Assistance, (6-88) p. X.

Types of Assistance

Currently, programs in the Catalog are being classified by GSA into 15 types of assistance. (Cooperative Agreements as a type of assistance is used for programs administered under that mechanism. However, the definition does not appear in this section.) Benefits and services of the programs are provided through seven financial types of assistance and eight nonfinancial types of assistance. The following list defines the types of assistance which are available through the programs. Code letters below (A through O) which identify the type of assistance) will follow program titles in the Agency Index,

 

Applicant Eligibility Index, the Functional Index, Deadlines Index, and in the list of added programs.

A Formula Grants -- Allocations of money to States or their subdivisions in accordance with a distribution formula prescribed by law or administrative regulation, for activities of a continuing nature not confined to a specific project.

B Project Grants -- The funding, for fixed or known periods, of specific projects or the delivery of specific services or products without liability for damages for failure to perform. Project grants include fellowships, scholarships, research grants, training grants, traineeships, experimental and demonstration grants, evaluation grants, planning grants, technical assistance grants, survey grants, construction grants, and unsolicited contractual agreements.

C Direct Payments for Specified Use -- Financial assistance from the Federal government provided directly to individuals, private firms, and other private institutions to encourage or subsidize a particular activity by conditioning the receipt of the assistance on a particular performance by the recipient. This does not include solicited contracts for the procurement of goods and services for the Federal government.

D Direct Payments with Unrestricted Use -- Financial assistance from the Federal government provided directly to beneficiaries who satisfy Federal eligibility requirements with no restrictions being imposed on the recipient as to how the money s spent. Included are payments under retirement, pension, and compensation programs.

E Direct Loans -- Financial assistance provided through the lending of Federal monies for a specific period of time, with a reasonable expectation of repayment. Such loans may or may not require the payment of interest.

F Guaranteed/Insured Loans -- Programs in which the Federal government makes an arrangement to indemnify a lender against part or all of any defaults by those responsible for repayment of loans.

G Insurance -- Financial assistance provided to assure reimbursement for losses sustained under specified conditions. Coverage may be provided directly by the Federal government or through private carriers and may or may not involve the payment of premiums.

H Sale, Exchange, or Donation of Property and Goods -- Programs which provide for the sale, exchange, or donation of Federal real property, personal property, commodities, and other goods including land, buildings, equipment, food and drugs. This does not include the loan of, use of, or access to Federal facilities or property.

 

**D. GRANTS IN CONTEXT**

1. A GRANT PROGRAM NEED NOT AND GENERALLY DOES NOT STAND ALONE.

The program has as its goal the effectuation of a federal purpose in a context in which local participation is considered important. In effectuating that federal purpose, the Congress may appropriately draw on a panoply of weapons. It may assist local undertakings by grant, but it may at the same time, within its constitutional powers, direct local action or forbid certain contrary local actions. It may direct the federal executive agencies to serve the same

---

I Use of Property, Facilities, and Equipment -- Programs which provide for the loan of, use of, or access to Federal facilities or property wherein the federally-owned facilities or property do not remain in the possession of the recipient of the assistance.

J Provision of Specialized Services -- Programs which provide Federal personnel to directly perform certain tasks for the benefit of communities or individuals. These services may be performed in conjunction with nonfederal personnel, but they involve more than consultation, advice, or counseling.

K Advisory Services and Counseling -- Programs which provide Federal specialists to consult, advise, or counsel communities or individuals, to include conferences, workshops, or personal contacts. They may involve the use of published information but only in a secondary capacity.

L Dissemination of Technical Information -- Programs which provide for the publication and distribution of information or data of a specialized technical nature frequently through clearinghouses or libraries. This does not include conventional public information services designed for general public consumption.

M Training -- Programs which provide instructional activities conducted directly by a Federal agency for individuals not employed by the Federal government.

N Investigation of Complaints -- Federal administrative agency activities that are initiated in response to requests, either formal or informal, to examine or investigate claims of violations of Federal statutes, policy, or procedure. The origination of such claims must come from outside the Federal government.

O Federal Employment -- Programs which reflect the government-wide responsibilities of the Office of Personnel Management in the recruitment and hiring of Federal civilian agency personnel.

 

goals by contract activities or by direct activities inhouse. It may also encourage certain action by providing tax incentives ("tax expenditures").

2. GOOD GRANT STATUTE DRAFTING CALLS FOR AT LEAST CONSIDERATION OF SETTING THE PROPOSED GRANT STATUTE IN A CONTEXT OF SUCH OTHER ACTIVITIES, AND ADJUSTING THE VARIOUS ELEMENTS TO EACH OTHER.

For example, a program that gives formula financial assistance to states that undertake programs of energy conservation may be a part of a more comprehensive program (in the same statute or not) that affords loan guarantees for the opening of new fuel sources, requires manufacturers to meet energy efficiency targets, undertakes federal research, gathers energy data, authorizes government purchase of petroleum for a petroleum reserve, calls for federal government officials to abstain from over-use of official automobiles, permits price fixing, authorizes limited anti-trust exemptions, provides tax incentives, and so on.

## E. THE CONSTITUTIONAL BASIS FOR GRANTS

The drafter of course must operate within a constitutional framework. The principal source of authority for grants is the "spending power", Article I, Section VIII, cl.1: "To...provide...for the general welfare of the United States" reinforced by the "necessary and proper" clause, (I, VII, cl.18):" To make all laws which shall be necessary and proper for carrying into execution the foregoing powers, and all other powers vested by this Constitution in the Government of the Untied States, or in any department or officer thereof." This authority is, of course also supported by the individual substantive powers that may be relevant: to regulate commerce, provide for the common defense, to declare War...raise and support Armies...provide and maintain a Navy...make Rules for the Government and Regulation of the land and naval forces...provide for calling forth the Militia... organizing, arming, and disciplining, the Militia... and so on. It may be limited, of course, by other provisions of the Constitution (seem obvious but some untested) such as Amendments I (establishment of religion), X (reserved powers of the States).[21]

---

[21] *South Dakota v. Dole*, ___ U.S. ___, 107 S.Ct. 2793 (June 23, 1987), sustained the validity of the Minimum Drinking Age (attached as a condition to highway funds grants), against a contention that this was a matter reserved to the states under the Twenty-First and Tenth

 

## F. GRANTS ARE A CONGRESSIONAL MONOPOLY

Only Congress may authorize a grant program. The fact that a program may be seen by the Executive as being desirable does not authorize the Executive to make a grant unless Congress has provided the authority by statute.[22] Article I, section IX, cl.7 provides: "no money shall be drawn from the Treasury, but in Consequence of Appropriations made by Law..." Article IV, section 3, provides: "...The Congress shall have Power to dispose of and make all needful Rules and Regulations respecting Territory or other Property belonging to the United States...

## G. THE ADMINISTERING OFFICE

### 1. IF A PROGRAM IS TO BE A GRANT PROGRAM, WHO SHOULD ADMINISTER IT?

Grant authority can of course be granted to the President, who will delegate it. Much more commonly however, authority is granted by statute directly to the head of an agency, who will normally delegate it within the agency.[23] Authority is sometimes split: this usually does

---

Amendments. Current Developments, Vol. 23, No. 1, Fall 1987, "A Right to Drive Alcoholized."

[22]This may seem obvious but it is not always obvious. *See* *Current Trends, 169. In Legis 50/The Center for Legislative Improvement, HEW DGAB Docket No. 76-17, Dec. No. 48, September 26, 1978, then Vice President Ford made a suggestion (it was apparently heard by some agency officials as an order) that a program he found desirable be funded. Inadequate attention was paid by the funding agency to whether there was statutory authority for funding. *See* DGAB Dec. p. 2 and Order to Show Cause in the case file, p. 6. The Board, although aware of the issue, found that the case could be disposed of without confronting this embarrassing issue. The facts are something of an aberration. The rule that grants are validly made only as authorized by statute is safely established and in general respected. In contrast, it is generally accepted that contracting is an inherent power; contracts entered into by Federal officers may be valid without legislative authorization. *See, e.g., Van Brocklin v. Anderson*, 117 U.S. 151, 154, 6 S.Ct. 670, 672 (1886); MCBRIDE & TOUHEY, GOVERNMENT CONTRACTS (Matthew Bender, 1987), 1.10; GOVERNMENT CONTRACT LAW (Procurement Associates, Covina, California, 1984) 1.1.

[23]Paul Dembling, in drafting the National Aeronautics and Space Act of 1958, placed the functions and authorities of the organization in the "Administration" rather than in the "Administrator." 42 U.S.C. 2473. Of course, the Administrator is given direction over the Administration. 42 U.S.C. 2472. Mr. Dembling comments, "This was done primarily to obviate the problem of delegability. It also made delegation a simple administrative matter." Letter to Charles Pou, Jr., ACUS, February 23, 1988. This is a model worth considering.

 

not work although it may satisfy political needs sometimes. A special trap is the giving of grant authority by statute expressly to a subordinate within an agency.[24] This may sometime be done deliberately, but it may sometimes occur inadvertently. In either case, the result is often confusion of administration: the subordinate has direct statutory power and tends to believe that the discretion and responsibility are his. The agency head, having organizational supervision over the subordinate tends to believe that control over the discretion and some of the responsibility are his.

2. IT IS RECOMMENDED THAT ABSENT CLEAR REASONS TO THE CONTRARY, GRANT AUTHORITY SHOULD NORMALLY BE CONFERRED ON AGENCY HEADS WITH EXPRESS OR IMPLIED POWER OF DELEGATION RATHER THAN ON SPECIFIED SUBORDINATES.

## H. HOW MUCH DISCRETION SHOULD BE LEFT TO THE EXECUTIVE?

In an ideal world, perhaps, Congress would define the goals of its grant programs and the money limits, and give

---

The more usual model of conferring power on the Administrator will also work well if clear and express powers of delegation are provided. The Peace Corps, for example, has had a history of structural changes, into ACTION and out again. Its Act now confers authorities on the President, 22 U.S.C. 2502 and 2509, but provides: "The President may exercise any functions vested in him by this Act through the Director of the Peace Corps. The Director of the Peace Corps may promulgate such rules and regulations as he may deem necessary or appropriate to carry out such functions, and may delegate to any of his subordinates authority to perform any of such functions." 22 U.S.C. 2503(b).

P.L. 97-113, the International Security and Development Cooperation Act of 1981 (December 29, 1981), also provides, 601(d)(2): "The Director of the Peace Corps shall continue to exercise all the functions under the Peace Corps Act or any other law or authority which the Director was performing on December 14, 1941." The intention of this provision to protect the then existing authority of the Director is spelled out in the Conference Report, p. 76 (1981 U.S. CODE CONG. & ADMIN. NEWS, 2489 at 2513). In consequence, there has been little need since then for active consideration of delegations. (Telephone conversations, September 1988, with John Scales, General Counsel, Peace Corps). There is a complication in this pattern. Since the Peace Corps operates abroad by agreement with foreign countries, it is almost unavoidable that the President and the Secretary of State retain recognized authorities that may cut across at times those of the Director of the Peace Corps. Although split authority, it is suggested in the text (Section G.1 at note 24), is ordinarily not desirable, the reasons for this split are quite clear.

[24] *See* Chapter III, sec. 5, Establishment of Administering Office.

 

the Executive broad powers to carry out the program goals within the money and other applicable limits. This may be a good general prescription for legislation. It is particularly relevant to grant programs because they generally operate in very complex fields (medicine, education, scientific research, environmental pollution, social welfare) where adjustments must be made to changes in circumstances and where initial perceptions of the problem to be solved are rarely sufficiently detailed and balanced: wisdom comes with living.

It is the legislative function to sketch the elevation and side views of a proposed construction, but not to draw the blueprints or hammer the nails. Those are functions of the executive. There is therefore good sense in suggesting that grant statutes be broad in their terms and leave much to administrative discretion.

Unfortunately, there is a great deal of history of administrative discretion being used in directions contrary to what the Congress expected and intended. There is also a great deal of history of administrative discretion being abdicated: there is a well-known bureaucratic drive to take no unnecessary initiative. Both of these tendencies, in opposite directions, disappoint the Congressional purpose. As a result, the Congress often believes it necessary to write more detailed instructions. Undesirable results often follow.

One of the undesirable results of over-specific statutory instructions is that they typically discourage executive impulses to use common sense when it is called for: 'if the Congress has spelled out its wishes, let us follow them -- it is safer and easier than to run the risks of fitting our actions to the underlying statutory purpose.' By taking the responsibility of spelling out its wishes, the Congress reinforces the bureaucratic impulse, which is there in any event, to abdicate discretion. Examples abound. One illustration may suffice.

As part of the "War on Poverty", Title I of the Elementary and Secondary Education Act of 1965 authorized expenditures to improve the education of children in low-income areas. The Office of Education construed the statute as generally restricting Title I assistance to school attendance areas having a percentage of low-income children at least as high as the district-wide average. As a general rule for starting an approach to the complex problem of distributing limited funds, this was not unreasonable, but specific concrete applications of this general rule plainly were unreasonable.

 

Assume two schools in the State, one very poor with 30 percent of its enrollment poor, one distinctly less poor with 15 percent of its enrollment poor; the less poor school may qualify for assistance because it is in a relatively wealthy district with a district average of 10 percent poor while the very poor school is disqualified because it is in an extremely poor district with a district average of 35 percent poor. In this situation, the general rule, which is administrative, not statutory, is not reasonable. The administrators should have had enough common sense to modify their rule, but institutional common sense is not very common in many bureaucracies.[25] The Congress rightly thought this administrative application absurd. In 1974, the House Committee on Labor and Education said, "the special needs of the educationally disadvantaged child and programs to meet their needs must be locally devised... [I]t was never intended by the Act to render any school with a 30% concentration ineligible."

Faced with this appropriate admonishment, the Office of Education amended its rules to correct the precise horror case put by the Committee, but did nothing to correct its basic wrong-headed approach. In 1977, testimony before the relevant House Subcommittee showed that there were still "schools in relatively affluent counties receiving Title I assistance with no more than 5% Title I children while schools in Baltimore City with 25-30% Title I children are excluded from this program."

Congress, commenting again adversely on the inflexible targeting rules of the Office of Education regulations, now amended the Act, administrative good sense having defaulted and admonishment having failed. The 1978 amendment provided that any school attendance area would be eligible if at least 25 percent of its children were from low-income families.

This kind of congressional action, getting into the mechanical details of administrative rulemaking is undesirable and should not be made necessary. It is particularly undesirable when it is a response to unwise rulemaking because it polarizes the relationship of legislature and administrative agency and reinforces the worst tendencies of bureaucracy: if Congress is going to spell out these details, we will take it at its exact word,

---

[25]This history is reviewed in *Bennett v. New Jersey*, 470 U.S. 632, 105 S.Ct. 1555 (1985), esp. in dissenting opinion by Justice Powell, 470 U.S., at 646. The legislative history and the case are discussed in •Current Developments, Vol. 20, No. 4, Summer 1985, p. 17, but that discussion contains an arithmetic slip for which I am responsible; it is revised here.

 

follow blindly and refuse to go an inch beyond or to use a pinch of common sense salt. Persistent wrongheadedness by an administrative agency, unfortunately encouraged by too crude efforts at correction, gives little scope for a healthier relationship. If Congress specifies, "don't eat the grass", the agency develops an appetite for daisies ("you didn't tell me not to eat the daisies").

Is there a solution? There is no easy one, but a general pattern of conduct can be suggested.

- Start by assuming that the agency head does have good sense, and give the agency broad discretion.
- Be explicit about goals and try to be clear that specific rules that clearly do not serve the goals should yield.
- Do not make statutory prescriptions for agency heads more specific or more mandatory in tone or terms than is really necessary to guide the agency.
- Supplement the statutory definition of goals with realistic oversight, which, again, should emphasize serving goals more than watching specific mechanical rules.

Once the specific rules get the upperhand, Caligula can appoint his horse consul because the rules didn't mention the obvious presupposition of humanity.[26]

## I. WHAT SHOULD BE THE FUNDING MECHANICS OF THE PROGRAM?

There are two principal patterns of funding for grants. Mandatory, state plan, formula grants are typically funded in advance, often quarterly on the basis of expenditure estimates, submitted by the grantee, of its probable

[26] *Cf.* Lon L. Fuller, Anatomy of the Law (reprinted 1976, Greenwood Press, Westport Conn.) 62. Some other examples of these problems have also been commented on in •Current Developments, *e.g.*, Vol. 20, No. 4, Summer 1985, "Who will educate the educators"; and at some length in Ohio Department of Public Welfare, HEW DGAB Docket No. 78-50-OH-HC, Dec. No. 66, October 10, 1979, p. 3 *ff.* In that case, involving the Medicaid system (Title XIX, Social Security Act) requirement for annual medical review of patient care (Section 1903(g)(1)(D)), "The medical review requirement was for sometime after its enactment substantially or wholly unenforced by HEW. After an expression of Congressional displeasure, HEW reversed its practice and went to the opposite extreme of strict literal enforcement of the same provision. (H.R. Rep. No. 393-Part II, 95th Cong., 1st Sess. 84, 85 (1977); S. Rep. No. 453, 95th Cong., 1st Sess. 40, 41 1977). This overreaction was required neither by Congressional intention nor by a sound interpretation of the law." *Ibid.* 3.

 

entitlement, subject to later correction after actual expenditure reports are submitted and subject to other adjustments (occasionally pluses, more often minuses) for exceptional performance or defective performance).

Discretionary project grants are typically funded, also in advance, on the basis of projected cost budgets. Money not validly spent in accordance with the grant conditions may be returnable to the agency but often is carried over for use in a later year after submission of new budget projections.

Although grants must, of course, be made out of appropriated funds and must be awarded for a present need (not for the shelf, not for a program to begin next fiscal year or two years from now), it is entirely proper to make awards this year out of this year's appropriation for a project starting this year, even though the money will be expended over several years. HHS has regularly made grants for research projects, particularly in NIH, intended to last several years. The projects are approved on a multi-year basis but funded by successive annual grants. These grants are made with notice that there is a recommendation only, not a commitment of future funding.[27]

## J. WHAT IS THE INTENDED CLASS OF RECIPIENTS?

The nature of the prospective recipients governs some basic assumptions of accountability and other relationships. If the proposed recipients are states, it is well to remember that the grant is an arrangement between sovereigns.[28] Intergovernmental comity plays a role that is not involved where the recipient is, say, a non-profit corporation created to apply for and receive federal grants. What would be

[27]This system was modified by the Office of Economic Opportunity which invented the "program year" system under which the initial grant was made of an amount estimated to last a year but susceptible in theory of being available indefinitely. Successive awards were then made, without advance commitment to do so, of new amounts for any estimated amount needed in addition to the available carryovers. The NIH system is better known but still inadequately understood. It is described in more detail in •Mason and Dembling, Federal Grant Litigation, 30 The Practical Lawyer No. 7 (October 15, 1984) pp, 57-59; Missouri Health and Medical Organization, HEW DGAB, Docket No. 77-24; Rejection of Appeal, June 21, 1978, pp. 3-6 and 8-9; Southeast Philadelphia Community Corporation, HEW DGAB, Docket No. 79-75, Rejection of Appeal, Sept. 24, 1979. See also, in •Current Developments, Vol. 20, No. 4, Summer 1985, p. 18 "NIH Multi-Year Grants", discussion of a recent controversial departure by NIH from its usual pattern of funding.

[28]Noted *supra*, Ch. I, p. 15. On the whole subject of this section, *see also* Ch. III, section 7, Authorization of Assistance.

 

appropriate and prudent administration in the latter case, might be unsuitable meddling in the former. States are appropriately assumed to be financially stable, accountable, entitled to use their own fiscal and auditing procedures as far as possible. Local governments and United States Territories, as well, are reasonably indulged to some extent, on similar assumptions, although history does show some large local governments to have engaged in questionable bookkeeping and to have been at the brink of bankruptcy at various times, recently.

Educational institutions have ancient traditions of academic independence; unnecessarily to infringe these creates frictions that can sometimes be avoided with benefit to both sides. Hospitals and other non-profits provide different problems again. Among non-profits, it may be wise to distinguish between those that have independent financial stability and those that do not.[29] In a small number of cases, individuals and profit-seeking entities may be eligible for grants.

It is said that spokesmen for Indian Tribes consider that it is demeaning to receive a "grant" and more dignified to receive a "contract." This may be an overgeneralization, but it is an element to inquire into and consider. It is also said (notably, for example, in the energy field) that profit-making corporations prefer to receive assistance by contract because their administrative mechanisms and personnel are geared to deal with contracts and do not understand grants.

There are provisions for international assistance. Again distinctive considerations come into play: it is unavoidable that, if you wish to extend the aid you must accept a large measure of respect for national sensitivities.

The OMB Circulars have distinguished some of these cases: State and local governments (A-128, Audits; A-102, Grants and Cooperative Agreements; A-87, Cost Principles); Non-profit organizations (A-122, Cost Principles); Educational Institution (A-88, Indirect Cost Rates, Audit, Audit follow-up); Educational Institutions, Hospitals and Other Non-Profits (A-110, Administrative Requirements).

The Catalog of Federal Domestic Assistance contains an Applicant Index that identifies for each program the eligibility of some of these categories of potential grantees (1989 edition, AEI-1).

---

[29]*See, e.g.*, HEW, A Program for Improving the Quality of Grantee Management, Vol. II, Financially Dependent Organizations (1970).

 

**K. SHOULD THERE BE A REQUIREMENT FOR LOCAL SHARING IN THE COSTS?**

The grant is intended to encourage grantee initiative. There should therefore be assurance of sufficient grantee involvement to stimulate and trigger local initiative. Unless counter-balancing values of sufficient importance are clearly present, the grant program should be designed to meet this threshold test: there should be a requirement or an assurance that the grant recipient will make a significant investment in the program.

In addition to helping to assure a realistic local involvement, the local share requirement has a leveraging effect. It makes a limited amount of federal money go further by the requirement that grantee money be added to the undertaking.

The local investment is usually measured by money or money equivalent. It may be expressed as a requirement for contribution of a non-federal share towards the whole cost of the grant activity or, equivalently, as a limitation on the permissible federal share of the whole cost.[30] Some grant programs call for the grantee to supply from non-federal

---

[30]For an example of belt-and-suspenders, expressing the requirement both ways, *see* P.L. 100-77, the Stewart B. McKinney Homeless Assistance Act, July 22, 1987, sec. 601, Grant Program for Certain Health Services for the Homeless:

> (e)(1)(A) The Secretary [of Health and Human Services] may not make a grant under subsection (a) to an applicant --
>
> (i) in an amount exceeding 75 percent of the costs of providing health service under the grant; and
>
> (ii) unless the applicant agrees that the applicant will make available, directly or through donations to the applicant, non-Federal contributions toward such costs in an amount equal to not less than $1 (in cash or in kind under subparagraph (B)) for each $3 of Federal funds provided in such grant.

A simpler local share example is P.L. 100-4, the Water Quality Act of 1987, February 4, 1987, 514(a):

> The Administrator is authorized to make a grant to the San Diego Water Reclamation Agency, California [does "authorized" here mean "directed"?] to demonstrate and field test for public use innovative processes which advance the technology of wastewater reclamation and which promote the use of reclaimed wastewater. (b) The Federal share of grants made under this section shall be 85 percent of the costs of conducting such demonstration and field test.

 

sources a half, or a third, or a quarter, or a fifth, or a tenth of the funds needed to carry out the program.[31]

In place of money contributions, grantees may generally contribute the use of space or equipment, or services. Special rules for the valuation of such "in-kind" contributions, and special safeguards against possible abuse (particularly by over-valuing the contributions in kind), are generally provided in regulations and need not be in the statute. The services of volunteers (doctors, nurses, teachers aides, crossing guards, bookkeepers) form an important part of the Head Start program, for example, and fully demonstrate the reality of the local involvement in a typical Head Start project.[32]

When such contributions in kind are not permitted, the requirement is said to be for a "hard match".[33] This tends to make for inflexibility that may not always be desirable.

---

[31]Research programs often do not have a statutory requirement for a specific non-federal share, but agencies have sometimes been directed or encouraged administratively to require some non-federal share, such as one percent or five percent, depending on such factors as the special benefits to the grantee from the project itself or from the equipment to be acquired in connection with the project. *See, e.g.*, former OMB Circular A-100 (FMC 73-3).

[32]Head Start became a very successful nationwide program under the Office of Economic Opportunity. Its complicated statutory history traces to the Economic Opportunity Act of 1964, as amended by section 215 of the Economic Opportunity Amendments of 1966, 80 Stat. 1462. After numerous amendments, the Economic Opportunity Act was repealed, 42 U.S.C. 9912(a) effective October 1, 1981, but Project Head Start was continued by the Head Start Act, P.L. 97-35, Title VI, Subtitle A, ch. 8, subch. B, 635, 95 Stat. 499. 42 U.S.C. 835(b) provides "... Non-Federal contributions may be in cash or in kind, fairly evaluated, including plant, equipment or services." *See also* the almost identical provision in P.L. 98-377, the Education for Economic Security Act, August 11, 1984, 309(a)(2) The Federal share for each fiscal year shall be 50 per centum. (3) The non-Federal share of payments under this title may be in cash or in kind, fairly evaluated, including plant, equipment or services.

Very similar language is used in the Stewart B. McKinney Homeless Assistance Act, July 22, 1987, sec. 601, *supra*, n.30, at (e)(1)(B).

[33]A leading example of "hard match" was LEAA, P.L. 96-157, the Justice System Improvement Act, sec. 2, amending Title I of the Omnibus Crime Control and Safe Streets Act of 1968, 401(b)(2)(A) [42 U.S.C. 3741(b)(2)(A)], "The non-Federal portion of the cost of such program or project shall be in cash." This section was tacitly repealed and replaced, but see the similar provision in P.L. 98-473, further amending Title I of the Omnibus Crime Control and Safe Streets Act of 1968, new sec. 403(b)(2).

A letter from Betty Jo Christian has called my attention to the "Section 18" formula grant program providing capital and operating funds for public transportation in nonmetropolitan areas, 49 U.S.C. 1614 (1982), and furnished a memorandum by Kenneth J. Pierce of her office which illustrates some of the problems that arise in connection with programs of

 

Exceptionally, funds supplied by the federal government under one program may be used as the non-federal contribution under another. This is specially provided for in a few statutes.[34] Unless expressly authorized, it would generally not be acceptable.[35] While this practice does not necessarily defeat the purposes of the non-federal share

---

this kind. The statute requires, with respect to operating expenses, at least a 50% local contribution and, of that, at least 50% must come solely from undistributed cash surpluses, replacement, or depreciation funds or reserves available in cash or new capital. 1614(e). Thus, half the local contribution must be "hard match." The remaining half of the local contribution may be soft match and may apparently include funds originating in other federal grant programs to the extent that is not prohibited, or in contribution of services.

A sample question: if a grantee busline contracts with the grantee of, say, a Head Start program to transport its children or with a program for the elderly to transport its clientele, may the contract payment then be used by the busline grantee as "hard match?" Federal Highway Administration and UMTA staff apparently first considered that the proceeds of such service contracts could be used as hard match. UMTA staff then changed its view and decided that such service contract payments could be used for soft match, not for hard match. This is qualified by considering a fund that pools both Federal and non-Federally-derived funds on the assumption that non-Federal funds flow first and to the extent that such funds are in the pool may be used as hard match. Still later UMTA staff, it appears, proposed to treat service contract payments even from an agency receiving no federal funds as ineligible for the hard match. This shifting view seems to indicate that the underlying grant statute is not clear in an area where real problems exist. I suspect that the complexities envisioned by staff go beyond anything the Congress could have anticipated. It is possible that the statute itself is more complicated than any realistic intention of the Congress required. I believe that left to itself, agency staff might not have been as tough as Congress wanted but would have been nearly as tough and much simpler and straightforward. Perhaps a simpler statute and a better oversight process might have worked better. [For the statements of staff position, I rely on Mr. Pierce and documents he quotes from].

[34]P.L. 100-4 the Water Quality Act of 1987, February 4, 1987 Sec. 202(f): Notwithstanding any other provision of law, Federal assistance made available by the Farmers Home Administration to any political subdivision of a State may be used to provide the non-Federal share of the cost of any construction project carried out under Section 201 of the Federal Water Pollution Control Act.

The contrary is expressly directed in the Stewart B. McKinney Homeless Assistance Act, *supra*, n.30, at (e) (1)(B): Amounts provided by the Federal Government, or services assisted or subsidized to any significant extent by the Federal government, may not be included in determining the amount of such non-Federal contributions.

[35]GAO, Principles of Federal Appropriation Law (June 1982) pp. 13-26. OMB, Circular A-110, Attachment E, b.(5); and common rule issued in connection with A-102, ___.24(b)(1). 53 Fed. Reg. 8088 at 8092. A-110 is expected to be revised in a parallel format.

requirement, it should not be authorized without careful attention to the relation of means to end.

**L. SHOULD THERE BE A REQUIREMENT FOR MAINTENANCE OF LOCAL EFFORT?**

Since the grant is planned to encourage local action rather than offset local funding, it should be reflected in an increase, not a diminution of grantee activity. This is normally measured by the amount of money spent. There is therefore often a requirement that the grant recipient shall spend in the grant year for the grant purposes not less than it was already spending for the purposes (in the preceding year, perhaps, or in the average of two, or of three, preceding years. This requirement is called Maintenance of Effort (MOE).[36] It has a measurable test for compliance: dollars spent per year. The Maintenance of Effort requirement is related to the non-federal share requirement, but is not the same requirement. Suppose that a grant project contemplates $100,000 of total cost: $80,000 of federal funds supplemented by a 20% non-federal requirement; that is $20,000 of local funds to make a total of $100,000. Now suppose that the grantee has already been spending $40,000 of its own funds for the grant purpose. A contribution of $20,000 will satisfy the non-

[36]*E.g.*, P.L. 99-570, October 27, 1986, Title XII, the Commercial Motor Vehicle Safety Act of 1986, 12005(e)(1). The Secretary [of Transportation] may not make a grant to any State under this section unless such State agrees that the aggregate expenditure of funds of the State and political subdivisions thereof, exclusive of Federal funds, for testing of operators of commercial motor vehicles will be maintained at a level which does not fall below the average level of such expenditure for its last two fiscal years preceding the date of this Title [Note that by fixing the test period as preceding the date of the statute, the provision avoids a ratchet effect that would result from a test period preceding the date of the grant: in the latter case each succeeding grant year might raise the level required but could not lower it. Note, also, that in fixing the test period in terms of the State's own fiscal year, the provision simplifies the determination of the required level even though it may introduce disparities from state to state with different fiscal years].

Contrast P.L. 98-473, October 12, 1984, 660, amending the Juvenile Justice and Delinquency Prevention Act of 1974, adding a new Title IV, Missing Children, 406(c) [42 U.S.C. 577(c)]. In order to receive assistance under this title for a fiscal year, applicants shall given assurance that they will expend, to the greatest extent practicable, for such fiscal year an amount of funds (without regard to any funds received under any Federal Law) that is not less than the amount of funds they received in the preceding fiscal year from State, local and private sources. *See infra*, text at n.38.

 

federal share requirement but it will not satisfy a maintenance of effort requirement. To meet the MOE requirement, the grantee must spend at least $40,000 of its own funds, receiving only $60,000 of federal funds to make a $100,000 total project, or must spend $40,000 of its own funds, receiving $80,000 of federal funds to make a $120,000 total project, in either case substantially exceeding the non-federal share requirement.

A trap: requirements of MOE are generally desirable because they help assure that the grant serves the basic grant purpose of encouraging certain forms of local action instead of encouraging local abdication in reliance on federal funding. In certain cases, however, they can be counter productive. MOE requirements should not be so rigidly drawn as to force counter productive results. An example is the city which undertakes an experimental program that proves successful and by its success helps the enactment of a national grant program to carry out similar undertakings. It may have done this with the aid of a one-time foundation grant.[37] A strict maintenance of effort requirement in the federal grant statute might have the perverse effect that the one city that had the foresight, the initiative and the interest to start the program rolling might now be the only city in the country excluded from carrying on after federal funds are available. This can hardly be the federal intent, and if it is not, it would be unfortunate if the statute were so written as to compel or encourage that result.

Another trap: the ratchet effect. If each year the grantee must maintain the previous year's level of effort, the required amount may continually increase. It can go up but must not go down. Be clear about whether you want that result or want maintenance only of the level established before any federal grant.[38]

---

[37]*See, e.g.*, Bloomfield College Cooperative Education Program, HEW DGAB Docket No. 78-4, Decision No. 82, February 22, 1980, esp. at 2-3. This problem is sometimes helped in part by including in an MOE provision such a phrase as "excluding expenditures of a non-recurring nature." *See* for example, P.L. 92-157, the Comprehensive Health Manpower Training Act of 1971, 104(a) amending the Public Health Service Act 770(f), 773(d); P.L. 92-158, the Nurse Training Act of 1971, 3(b) and 4(a) amending the Public Health Service Act, 805(c) and 806(e)(1)(B).

[38]*See* Juvenile Justice and Delinquency Prevention Act of 1974, *supra* n.36.

 

## M. SHOULD THERE BE A REQUIREMENT THAT FEDERAL FUNDS NOT BE USED TO SUPPLANT LOCAL EFFORT?

If a grant program simply transfers an activity from a local budget to a federal budget, it does not satisfy the basic purpose of grant programs to stimulate local action and does not face the fiscal reality of a federal budget that needs to be controlled. If such a transfer is prevented by a requirement of maintaining a previous dollar level of expenditure, that is maintenance of effort, discussed in the previous section. There is, however, a quite different approach to this problem that is not often clearly understood.

A statute may require the grantee to give an assurance that grant funds will be used to "supplement, not supplant" the activities grantee *would carry on* in the absence of federal funding.[39] The purpose is clearly similar to that of the maintenance of effort rule, but the operation is quite different. This is often not understood.

Note, to begin with, the conditional expression "would carry on". This does not permit the same objective, measurable, test presented by a maintenance of effort rule. It is not a requirement that can be monitored by an accountant and that sort of enforcement should not be expected.

The No-Supplant rule is normally essentially precatory. It is sometimes said, incorrectly, that it is wholly unenforceable and should therefore not be used.[40] That is

---

[39]*E.g.*, Preventive Health and Health Services Block Grant, 42 U.S.C. 200 w-4(c).

> As part of the annual application required by subsection (a) of this Section, the chief executive officer of each State shall certify that the State--
>
> (4) Agrees that Federal funds made available under Section 300w-2 of this title for any period will be so used as to supplement and increase the level of State, local, and other non-Federal funds that would in the absence of such Federal funds be made available for the programs and activities for which funds are provided under that section and will in no event supplant such State, local, and other non-Federal funds;..."

Very similar but not identical provisions are in P.L. 98-377, the Education for Economic Security Act, 209(b)(6), and P.L. 99-570, the Anti-Drug Abuse Act of 1986, October 17, 1986, 4126(a)(2)(G).

[40]*See, e.g.*, Comptroller General, Report to the Congress, Proposed Changes in Federal Matching and Maintenance of Effort Requirements for

 

not correct. No-Supplant does have teeth, but mainly at the inception of a project when the agency can and should ask whether the applicant has planned a budget realistically and in good faith so that it is not relying on federal funds to replace local funding.[41]

If the budget is properly prepared, the agency can get a reasonable assurance at the beginning of the project that the grantee is not planning to withdraw its own support and rely on federal support. After that stage, absent flagrant bad faith, the bookkeeping of state and local fiscal systems does not make it rewarding to attempt to identify whether specific expenses have been supplanted. Failure to understand this leads to bad legislative drafting, bad regulatory drafting, wasted effort in grant monitoring and unnecessary nuisance to grantees.

A potential trap in this area is that failure to distinguish clearly between the Maintenance of Effort approach with its auditor's perspective and the No-Supplant approach with its management perspective often leads to apparently confused mixtures of the two in the same statute.[42] Clarity of thought, here as elsewhere, is desirable in drafting statutes.

---

State and Local Governments, GGD-81-7, December 23, 1980, esp. at 54-57.

41 *Cf.* St. Landry Parish School Board, HEW DGAB, Docket No. 75-4, Dec. No. 17, May 28, 1978, 5 *ff.*

42 An example of such a hinny is the Education of the Handicapped Act, amended by the Rehabilitation Act Amendments of 1986. 20 U.S.C. 1413(a)(9)(B) requires State plans to provide satisfactory assurance that Federal funds made available "will be so used as to supplement and increase the level of State and local funds expended for the education of handicapped children and in no case to supplant such State and local funds", subject to a waiver provision. 20 U.S.C. 1414(a)(2)(B)(ii) requires applications for grants by local educational agencies and intermediate educational units to provide satisfactory assurance that Federal funds expended by local educational agencies and intermediate educational units "shall be used to supplement and, to the extent practicable, increase the level of State and local funds expended for the education of handicapped children, and in no case to supplant such State and local funds." These provisions, slightly different from each other for no apparent reason, are both clearly supplement -- no-supplant clauses. They lack, however, the classic conditional clause: "that would be expended in the absence of such federal assistance", so it is possible to call them MOE clauses. They also lack, however, the precision of a comparative basis to be expected of a maintenance of effort clause.

P.L. 99-506, the Rehabilitation Act Amendments of 1986, Sec. 1005 is captioned Maintenance of Effort and provides: Notwithstanding any other provision of the Education of the Handicapped Act, the Secretary and the State educational agency, in the case of Section 614(a)(2)(B) (ii) of that Act [20 U.S.C. 1414(a)(2)(B)(ii), quoted above], shall not include expenditures made from an accrued fund reserve surplus after July 1, 1983, and prior to October 1, 1985, which are used for services for handicapped children.

 

The whole record betokens very loose conception and very loose expression of intent with respect to maintenance of effort and no-supplant. The 1986 amendment is what physicians sometimes call "a beautiful case". It is probable that the drafter knew what was meant, and it seems possible that insiders, having heard discussion, knew what was meant, but it seems impossible for an uncommitted outsider to draw any intelligible meaning from the words of Section 1005. Although the section is captioned "Maintenance of Effort," the sponsors of the provision referred to it as providing an exception to a "non-supplanting" clause, remarks of Senators Eagleton and Danforth, 132 CONG. REC. No. 115, pp. S12100-1 (September 8, 1986). What is an accrued fund reserve surplus? Nothing in either the amended or the amending Act gives a clue. Are the Secretary and the State educational agency not to "include expenditures from an accrued fund reserve surplus" in the "Federal funds expended" or in the "State and local funds expended"? This was a Senate amendment. The Conference Report offers some but very little help. Going back to its original submission, it turns out that this amendment was cobbled to fit the feet of the St. Louis Special School District, of St. Louis County, MO. Once that is understood it hardly matters what the statutory language, but it would all have been clearer if the statute had said so. The purpose seems to be quite avowable: the School District had led the country in providing education for the handicapped and would have been penalized unfairly if required to maintain after enactment of the Education of the Handicapped Act its exceptional effort in the period 1983-1985. On the other hand, if the language of the Education of the Handicapped Act had been a standard no-supplant provision, and had been correctly understood, the problem would have disappeared or would have required no more than some kind words in a Committee report or a planned floor interchange. On the propriety of not enforcing literal MOE provisions against grantees who have been unusually forthcoming, *see supra*, text at n.37.

 

## III. PLANNING A GRANT STATUTE

In the previous chapter, we have considered the planning of the grant program itself, an operation that should normally precede the planning of the grant statute which will authorize the program. We now examine the statute-planning. The following sequence of discussion is intended to parallel a typical line of examination that assists good statute drafting. The suggestions made in this chapter are intended primarily not as prescriptions for drafting but as invitations to ask certain useful key questions.

HOW SHOULD A GRANT STATUTE BE STRUCTURED

There are great variations from one grant statute to another, not always a result of considered choice. *Dembling[1] deplores the failure to develop a uniform approach, a common structure, a common set of definitions, a parallelism of expression where parallel results are intended. Dembling also deplores the failure to develop general statutes which would give a common framework to grant programs that do not deliberately depart from a common structure.

Nevertheless, some common elements of structure are developing. The following is a suggested outline that may serve both as a tentative order of topics for a typical grant statute and as a checklist for consideration in planning the statute.

### A. OUTLINE OF A TYPICAL GRANT STATUTE

Sec. 1. Short Title
Sec. 2. Table of Contents
Sec. 3. Findings and Purposes
-- State your sources of power explicitly
-- State your purposes explicitly
Sec. 4. Definitions [and herein other questions of language]
-- Anticipate litigation

---

[1]*Dembling, p. 305. This and other publications referred to by short titles or author's name only are identified in Chapter IV, *infra*, with full citations.

 

-- Define your terms
-- *Plain language* can be a trap
-- Borrowed language and borrowed provisions
-- A danger in cut and paste
-- Standardization
-- Remember that your proposed statute is intended to affect live people

Sec. 5. Establishment of Administering Office
-- A trap: Who's the boss?
-- The problem of micromanagement
-- Overdemanding rules

Sec. 6. Authorization of Appropriations

Sec. 7. Authorization of Assistance
-- Do not unnecessarily or inadvertently direct state or local governments or private bodies to act through structures or particular officers that the State (or local government or private body) would not choose for itself.
-- Be explicit about eligibility
-- Be explicit about intended beneficiaries
-- Think about flow-through of grant rules to sub-grantees and contractors under grants.
-- Administrative discretion
-- Provide explicitly for discretion
-- Deal explicitly with questions of federal preemption
-- Be explicit about last dollar provisions
-- Autonomy

Sec. 8. Allotment formula
Sec. 9. State Plan provisions
Sec. 10. Discretionary grant provisions
Sec. 11. Conditions of assistance
Sec. 12. Accountability, Audit, Monitoring provisions
Sec. 13. Sanctions and Incentives
Sec. 14. Rulemaking power
Sec. 15. Administrative and Judicial Review Provisions
-- Administrative
-- Judicial
-- Disallowance and non-conformity

Sec. 16. Provisions for relationship to allied programs (investigations and study, inhouse activity, contract activity, regulatory activity, educational activity)
Sec. 17. Report to Congress
Sec. 18. Repealers, saving harmless, severability, sunset and miscellaneous provisions
-- Check up periodically on existing statutes

 

Sec. 19. Effective date.[2]

**B. SPECIAL CONSIDERATIONS IN DRAFTING AMENDATORY GRANT STATUTES**

**C. SOME SUGGESTIONS FOR GENERAL STATUTES**

These topics are discussed in this chapter in more detail.

**A. OUTLINE OF A TYPICAL GRANT STATUTE**

**Sec. 1. Short Title**

It is customary to start a major statute with a short title. Often the "short title" is not short enough to be a convenient form of citation--the principal reason for having short titles. Let your short title be descriptive but let it be short. Good short titles, for example, are:

P.L. 79-404, the Administrative Procedure Act
P.L. 88-499, the Administrative Conference Act
P.L. 99-308, the Firearm Owner's Protection Act
P.L. 99-323, the Presidential Libraries Act of 1986
P.L. 99-371, the Education of the Deaf Act of 1986
P.L. 99-372, the Handicapped Children's Protection Act of 1986
P.L. 99-398 the Klamath Indian Tribe Restoration Act
P.L. 99-399, Titles I through IV, the Diplomatic Security Act.

More questionable are:

P.L. 99-319, the Protection and Advocacy for Mentally Ill Individuals Act of 1986.
P.L. 99-554, the Bankruptcy Judges, United States Trustees, and Family Farmer Bankruptcy Act of 1986.

[2]This outline is the result of melding the structures of several grant statutes I consider well organized. Generally similar outlines, with differences of detail, are offered by •Cappalli 1.11 and by •Hirsch, p. 11 *ff.*, in both cases with discussion of each topic.

 

Fairly good is P.L. 99-570, the Anti-Drug Abuse Act of 1986, but Subtitle I, G has a short title of its own (Sec. 1301), the Controlled Substances Import and Export Penalties Enhancement Act of 1986, that seems unwieldy without clear necessity.

> P.L. 99-252, the Comprehensive Smokeless Tobacco Health Education Act of 1986 might have been served by amputation of several words. Perhaps Smokeless Tobacco Act would have been enough, or Smokeless Tobacco Education Act, or Smokeless Tobacco Health Act.
> P.L. 99-519, the Asbestos Hazard Emergency Response Act of 1986 should probably have been pruned. Asbestos Act, or Asbestos Hazard Act might have sufficed.

Often, as in several of the statutes cited above, the short title includes a year. Occasionally, the year is necessary in order to differentiate members of a series of laws with the same subject. In many cases, the year is not necessary and may prove confusing.[3] For example, P.L. 95-224, An Act to distinguish Federal grant and cooperative agreement relationships from Federal procurement relationships, and for other purposes, has a short title provision "That this Act be cited as the 'Federal Grant and Cooperative Agreement Act of 1977'". It became law February 3, 1978. The reference to 1977 in the short title can only confuse. P.L. 99-264, the White Earth Reservation Land Settlement Act of 1985 provides for allotment of land and for cash grants. It became law on March 24, 1986. Several words in the short title seem inessential, including "of 1985". P.L. 99-504, the Nebraska Wilderness Act of 1985, became law on October 20, 1986. P.L. 100-259, the Civil Rights Restoration Act of 1987, became law on March 22, 1988; the over-optimistic short title does not help clarity.

### Sec. 2. Table of Contents

In a complex statute, a Table of Contents is a desirable addition. This normally follows the short title.[4]

---

[3]•Hirsch, p. 11, recommends both the elimination of unnecessary year references and keeping short titles short. He gives an excellent example of a puffy short title: P.L. 88-164, the Mental Retardation Facilities and Community Mental Health Centers Construction Act of 1963.

[4]For example, P.L. 99-272, the Comprehensive Omnibus Budget Reconciliation Act of 1986, Section 1 includes the Short Title, followed by a Table of Contents listing 20 Titles. P.L. 99-433, the Goldwater-Nichols Department of Defense Reorganization Act of 1986, Section 1(a) contains

 

### Sec. 3. Findings and Purposes

Many grant statutes contain one or several provisions setting forth Congressional findings and a statement of the purposes of the legislation. When done thoughtfully, this is good practice.

-- *State your sources of power explicitly*

Much effort is spent by judges, advocates, agencies, grantees, speculating about whether Congress in a particular enactment was relying on the welfare clause, the commerce power, the XIVth Amendment, or some combination of those and other powers.[5] Unless there is a reason to refrain from identifying the source of power, it will add to understanding and economy to specify the source.

Early in the development of a statute affecting federal assistance, it will be useful to consider the source of power relied on and probably the desirability of stating it explicitly.[6]

---

the "short title", Section 1(b), the Table of Contents identifying 48 sections, 6 titles. Incidentally, either "Goldwater-Nichols Act" or "Defense Reorganization Act" might have been enough as a short title. P.L. 99-498, the Higher Education Amendments of 1986, Section 1(a) has the Short Title, Section 1(b) explains that references to "the Act" are to the Higher Education Act of 1965, Section 1(c) identifies 43 sections, 10 titles, and 255 new or revised sections of the Act. P.L. 100-4, the Water Quality Act of 1987, Section 1(a) has the Short Title, Section 1(b), the Table of Contents identifying 72 sections and 5 titles. P.L. 100-297, the Augustus F Hawkins - Robert T. Stafford Elementary and Secondary School Improvement Amendments of 1988, Section 1(a) gives the "short title," 1(b) the table of contents, which runs to 10 pages of 8-point type for a statute of 301 pages of 10 point type.

[5] *E.g., Pennhurst State School and Hospital v. Halderman*, 451 U.S. 1 (1981) turned on the question whether Congress was acting under the XIVth Amendment or the spending power. The court said (at 15): "In discerning Congressional intent, we necessarily turn to the sources of Congress' power to legislate, namely, Congress' power to enforce the Fourteenth Amendment and its power under the Spending Clause to place conditions on the grant of federal funds."

[6] *See* chapter II, section E on basic constitutional principles. The tensions between the constitutional provisions conferring powers on Congress and those reserving powers to the states and the people has resulted in some recent flip-flops of the Supreme Court in adjusting that balance with respect to the commerce clause, *Garcia v. San Antonio Metro. Transit Authority*, 469 U.S. 528, 105 S.Ct. 1005 (1985), overruling *National League of Cities v. Usery*, 426 U.S. 833, 96 S.Ct. 2465 (1976), (*but see* p. 852, n.17 on the spending power clause). *National League* overruled *Maryland v. Wirtz*, 392 U.S. 183 (1968): Full circle in 17 years. These fluctuations have been present but have not recently been so dramatic with respect to the general welfare clause.

 

-- *State your purposes explicitly*

This helps in interpretation of language that may be unavoidably somewhat ambiguous, and steers the result in the direction the legislature may have actually intended.

Particularly is this true of statements of the substantive goals of a grant program. In addition to these substantive goals some elements of other goals may be present, and sometimes less openly avowed because of political sensitivity. Among these are the financing of a program for the ulterior purpose of getting revenues collected federally into local hands; this happens but is generally not declared except in the case of general across-the-boards revenue sharing. Sometimes a purpose of general support to an institution - minority colleges, for example - may be plainly stated (and it is useful to do so in order to avoid misunderstanding). More often it is probably part of the intention of grant programs, but not directly said. Grants normally carry conditions. These may be classified as conditions imposed to protect the substantive program to which they relate; conditions imposed to protect the federal interests necessarily involved because federal funds are being disbursed (the State and local Hatch Act to help prevent federal funds being used for partisan purposes,[7] and civil rights[8] conditions are in this class); conditions imposed for their own sake, the grant serving as a vehicle. In the third class of conditions, the grant offers a carrot to do what the recipient cannot legitimately be coerced into doing.[9]

The degree of disclosure will vary, but disclosure is generally good drafting, and a fair description of at least the substantive goal is clearly appropriate.

The meaning of a statute is to be looked for in all the parts together and in their relation to the end in view.[10] Therefore state your purposes.

The general purpose is a more important aid to the meaning than any rule which grammar or formal logic may

---

[7]5 U.S.C. 1501 *et seq.*

[8]P.L. 100-259, the Civil Rights Restoration Act of 1987 (March 22, 1988), explicitly amends the principal Civil Rights Acts affecting grants.

[9]Some commentators do not regard this category as constitutionally valid. *See, e.g.,* Note, *Taking Federalism Seriously: Limiting State Acceptance of National Grants*, 90 YALE L.J. 1694 (1981). But *see* *Current Developments, Vol. 23, No. 1, Fall 1987, p. 8, *A Right to Drive Alcoholized.*

[10]Cardozo, J., in *Duparquet v. Evans*, 297 U.S. 216, 218 (1936).

 

lay down.[11] Therefore, if you do not wish to be misunderstood, state your purposes openly and clearly.

There is sometimes a disposition to regard Findings and Purposes provisions as empty rhetoric. Sometimes they are, because done perfunctorily. When they are, they do little good and may do harm, because loose language carelessly included may lead to unintended views of the "legislative intent." But when they are written, as they should be, with deliberate attention, they are valuable parts of the statute. This is as true of grant statutes enacted under the welfare clause as of regulatory statutes under the commerce clause.[12]

Explicit statements of findings and purpose can be very valuable in a welfare clause statute as well as in others because they not only show the constitutional basis of the statute but show the path to the correct interpretation of its provisions. A good example of this is found in the Economic Opportunity Act of 1964, as amended. That statute, founded on the welfare clause, provided a set of anti-poverty measures. Both the Act as a whole and some of the individual titles were headed by careful findings and statements of purpose. When the question arose whether a Community Action Agency, organized to receive grants under this Act, was an armed instrumentality, or agent of the United States, whether its personnel were federal employees, its torts federal torts, its property federal property, the explicit Congressional statements, reinforced by other contemporary statements, which reflect the intended autonomy of the grantees were successfully used,

---

[11]Holmes, J. in *U.S. v. Whitridge*, 197 U.S. 135, 143 (1905). Although this was written in the context of "an addition made in new circumstances to a form of words adopted many years before," it is more broadly applicable, and Frankfurter so cites it, *Some Reflections on the Reading of Statutes*, 47 CoL.L.R. 527, 538 (1947).

[12]*Hirsch (p. 11) believes that

> Findings and statements of purpose may be useful, in a bill founded on the commerce clause, to bolster the constitutional validity of provisions to regulate intrastate commerce. Beyond this -- in bills based on the welfare clause, for example -- they serve no significant legal purpose.

This is one of the few points on which I disagree with Hirsch.

 

by government attorneys who were appropriately instructed, to resist such claims.[13]

*Cappalli 1.11 suggests that the Statement of Findings and Purpose "provides the 'spirit' with which courts and administrators should approach the difficult task of interpreting ambiguous language found within the statute and applying such language to the myriad facts of life." He adds, however, that in *Pennhurst State School and Hospital v. Halderman*, 451 U.S. 1, "the Supreme Court repelled an effort to create substantive rights out of such congressional oratory." In *Pennhurst*, in fact, the Court relied expressly on the "exhaustive statement of purposes" in 42 U.S.C. 6000(b)(1) (1976 ed., Supp. III), 451 U.S. at 11-12 and 18, to conclude that Congress did not intend "to require the states to fund new substantive rights." It therefore held that a separate section, then 42 U.S.C. 6010, called "Congressional findings respecting rights of developmentally disabled" did not intend to make recognition of such rights a condition of funding. It is 6010 that Cappalli refers to as congressional oratory, but any inference based on this case that congressional statement of findings and purpose ( 6000) are of no importance seems mistaken. [14]

Often the plan of a statute evolves during drafting and during the successive steps of clearance, hearing, redrafting that it may go through. When that happens, the thoughtful use of the findings and purposes provisions includes going back to reexamine whether they still mesh with the bill as it emerges.[15]

### Sec. 4. Definitions [and herein other questions of language]

---

[13]One exception, where the standard brief prepared for the purpose was not used, was *U.S. v. Orleans* in the Court of Appeals, Sixth Circuit, 509 F.2d 197 (1975). The government lost, but the case was reversed by the Supreme Court, 425 U.S. 807, 96 S.Ct. 1971 (1976), when an argument giving more stress to the statute's Statements of Purpose was developed. *See* Brief for the United States, *U.S. v. Orleans*, No. 75-328, October Term, 1975, esp. pp. 12-13. *See* *Current Trends, at p. 180, n. 100.

[14]Section 6010, incidentally, has since been repealed and replaced by Section 6009, a frequent and unnecessarily confusing procedure. *See infra*, this chapter, Part B, "- Leave a track".

[15]Professor Mullins (*see* Preface, *supra*, and *see* Bibliography, Ch. IV, *infra*), has suggested in a letter to Charles Pou, Jr., ACUS, February 12, 1988, "Ideally, the 'purpose' statement should be among the last provisions finally drafted." My own preference is for drafting the purpose statement at the beginning because it guides the drafting, but this is largely a matter of taste and circumstances. Professor Mullins rightly emphasizes that in any event the drafter always should adjust the purpose statements to reflect substantial changes in substantive provisions that may have occurred.

 

-- *Anticipate litigation*

It is a chastening and often healthy experience for a person wielding power to be challenged in court. It often produces a degree of courtesy and consideration, fairness and rationality that sometimes is lacking without it. An agency head whose steel has been so tempered in early career will be stronger for it. A similar tempering is needed for the sponsor of legislation. A basic tool for the strengthening of any lawyer's work, and especially a drafter's, is the testing of the draft in litigation either in fact or, better, in a professional's anticipatory imagination.

Regulatory statutes (say, securities laws, for example) are often written under close observation by professional representatives of affected industries, and the drafters often are acutely aware that the statute may be tested in litigation. This leads to a more careful approach than would otherwise be taken, and to a bill that has undergone a kind of adversary challenge during the drafting process.

Grant statutes are often not watched as carefully nor by the same kind of professional representatives.[16] The proposers of such statutes often feel that they are proposing something that is obviously good and that will be generally approved, and they do not anticipate challenge. They may watch with care those portions of the bill that contain dollar signs, but sometimes treat other provisions of the bill as atmospheric and rhetorical and not worth sharp study. This may be a mistake. The result may be that language in the parts of the bill which have no $ sign is vague and fuzzy, possibly even contradictory of other parts, and the bill is enacted. Once enacted, the language has a life of its own and may prove mischievous.[17]

---

[16] I am indebted to John Bell, a skilled craftsman in the writing of grant statutes, for emphasizing this contrast in a private conversation.

[17] Perhaps the classic case of how statutory language may have a life of its own is the provision in Title II of the Economic Opportunity Act of 1964 which defines a community action agency as one "...which is developed and conducted with the maximum feasible participation of residents of the areas and members of the groups served..." MOYNIHAN, MAXIMUM FEASIBLE MISUNDERSTANDING (The Free Press, New York, 1969), traces the substantial impact this language had on American society in the decade or so following its enactment. *See* esp. MAXIMUM, p. 97: "For this purpose [shaking things up] the all-but forgotten term 'Maximum feasible participation' was decisive". That impact was wholly foreign to the recognizable intent of the drafters (MAXIMUM, p. 87, 180) the Congress who passed it, (MAXIMUM, p. 91..."Congress made it clear to anyone who wished to take note that it did not expect the antipoverty program to be a disruptive influence".), and the President who signed it (MAXIMUM, p. 143). It entered the statute with "no public discussion" (MAXIMUM, p. 90-91).

 

-- *Define your terms*

Grant statutes often use terms that require definition. Perhaps grant statutes have somewhat more need for explicit definitions than many other kinds of statute. This is not, however, intended as encouragement for multiplying definitions beyond need. Professor Mullins comments,[18] "Felix Cohen had something worthwhile to say about definitions -- '[A] definition is useful if it insures against risks of confusion more serious than any that the definition itself contains.'"[19]

Standard questions for the drafter include what to define, where to define (beginning, end, or as you go along, alphabetically or in some other order), how to define, and what to do about definitions in a statute that amends another statute.

Hirsch and other writers give advice on this subject. *Hirsch (p. 12) has some good advice, for example, on the value of definitions that assume the dictionary meaning and clarify the penumbra - for example: "the term 'physician' includes an osteopathic practitioner as determined under the law of the state in which he is practicing". *Hirsch also warns of the danger of Pickwickian definitions -- for example: the term 'bribery' was defined in a bill (not enacted) to include all amounts received by a federal employee as compensation for any service (including his federal pay check? Yes, including his federal pay check, but another provision exempted receipt of his federal paycheck from the penalty provisions). Someone found that definition convenient and clever, but it is bad drafting.[20]

Statutes sometimes give no definition of terms that look as though they represent simple concepts but in fact give a simple appearance to very complex notions. This is illustrated by significant disputes in the medicaid program, involving the terms "expended" and "overpayment."[21]

---

[18]Letter to Charles Pou, Jr., ACUS, February 12, 1988.

[19]F. Cohen, *Transcendental Nonsense and the Functional Approach*, 35 Col. L.R. 809, 836 (1935).

[20]*Mullins, p. 95, also warns against "special hazards of defining a term in a manner *too* inconsistent with conventional usage. The conventional or established usage of a term is a powerful force. The conventional meaning of a term exerts a kind of gravitational pull on the drafter, and the reader, who are constantly tugged, psychologically, toward reverting to use the term in its customary sense."

[21]Section 1903(a)(1) of the Social Security Act provides that the State is entitled for each quarter to payment of the Federal medical assistance percentage (itself defined in a very elaborate formula) "of the total amount expended during such quarter as medical assistance under the State plan."

 

Plausible differences of interpretation have involved many states and millions of dollars.[22] The Departmental Grant Appeals Board's results in these cases generally reflect the outcome the Congress probably would have wanted had the question come up in advance, although as a result of the poor drafting of the statute, the reasoning is somewhat forced. The lack of definition has created substantial unnecessary costs in uncertainty, delay and litigation. Assuming the intent was indeed what the Board thought it was, the Congress should have defined "expended" to show that it required an effective parting with money, and should have defined "overpayments" to show that it includes payments which the Secretary determines are in excess of the appropriate payment and should have specified that amounts recovered by the state from third parties are of course to be treated promptly as overpayments. It is true that the field is a difficult one and no statute can be written immune from cavil, but better clues to intent could have been left.

Another example: the Job Training Partnership Act refers to "recipient" in several sections. The term is not defined. Sometimes it seems to mean the State, sometimes the Governor of the State, sometimes a sub-grantee. There are sections where within a single section the term seems to

---

"Medical assistance" is defined in Section 1905(a) as "payment of part or all of the cost of covered care and services."

The term "expended" in 1903(a)(1) is not defined.

Section 1903(d)(2) provides that payments, based on estimated quarterly expenditures, shall be reduced "to the extent of any overpayment . . . which the Secretary determines was made . . . for any prior quarter . . ."

The term "overpayment" in 1902(d)(2) is not defined unless 1903(d)(3) is an implicit definition. Section 1903(d)(3) provides: "The pro rata share to which the United States is equitably entitled, as determined by the Secretary, of the net amount recovered during any quarter by the State or any political subdivision thereof with respect to medical assistance furnished under the State plan shall be considered an overpayment to be adjusted under this subsection."

[22]*See* GAO, STATES SHOULD INTENSIFY EFFORTS TO PROMPTLY IDENTIFY AND RECOVER MEDICAID OVERPAYMENTS AND RETURN THE FEDERAL SHARE, HRD-80-77. California Department of Health Services, HHS DGAB Decision No. 244, December 31, 1981 (appealing $18,000,000 disallowance in federal financial participation, "FFP"); California Department of Health Services, HHS DGAB Decision No. 619, January 28, 1985 ($6,746,437 of FFP). At least nine states have had substantial problems. Other states involved in appeals of more than a million dollars each include Massachusetts (No. 262) New York (Decisions Nos. 261 and 311), Arkansas (No. 423). At least five such disputes have gone to court.

 

have different meanings.[23] Was this shifting usage intentional? Probably not. Would the problem have been cured by a definition of "recipient." Probably yes.

-- *Plain language can be a trap*

It seems to be an obvious value that statutes (and rules) should be written in plain language the man in the street can understand. But when you deal with a complex idea and shirk the complexities because your language will then not be "plain" you are not solving your problem, nor the Administrator's problem, nor the problem of the affected public.

•Hirsch correctly says (p. 32):

> There is a limit to how simply a complex idea can be expressed. That a statute is hard to understand is not always a compelling criticism; what shames the draftsman is a statute that he has made unnecessarily hard to understand.

"Plain writing" has become so much an approved goal that it has fallen into the classic trap of promoting language that seems plain by Flesch index (simple, straightforward sentences, no long or obscure words) but fails to communicate. Drafters, seeking to write plain, too often suppress the complicating detail that is essential to real working clarity.[24]

-- *Borrowed language and borrowed provisions*

---

[23]*See*, for example, Sections 164(a)(2); (d); (e)(1); (2), and (3); 165 (a)(1); and 166(a). Cited in •Current Developments, Vol. 21, No. 2, Winter 1986, p. 14.

[24]In drafting government definitions of poverty levels, for example, OEO, ordinarily outstanding in its effort and success in communication, wilfully suppressed a statement as to whether income levels were meant to be gross or net, and if net, net of what, whether capital transactions counted or did not, whether the value of services received counted or did not count, and so on. This was done to avoid cluttering up the regulation with what would be perceived as complexity. Thus, what was unspoken often exceeded in significance what was spoken, and a particular income level was defined, in effect, as $3,750 plus or minus an undefined amount that may be more than $3,750. That may be plain writing, but it is also plain foolishness. This example is taken from •Grant Rulemaking, pp. 51-52. The problem is also noted in the Grant Rulemaking field in •Current Developments, Vol. 16, No. 12 January 1985, p. 5.

 

Take advantage of language which has been interpreted by the courts and administrative tribunals.[25]

When words have acquired traditional meanings, to use them in a distinctively different sense is dangerous, but invention of new terminology may be puzzling. These are common problems, particularly troublesome in the grant field.

New words sometimes have value when it is deliberately intended to create a new concept and to dramatize it by giving it a new name.

*-- A danger in cut and paste*

"Borrowed language" must not be confused with an unthinking exercise in cut-and-paste. To borrow language from another statute is acceptable if indeed the implications of same structure, same intent, same background, are really intended. Too often, however, the borrowed language is chosen on a very hasty and superficial impression that "that language seems to have something to do with what we want to do, and it has been used before: so let's use it." This can be harmful. An area in which it seems to be common is in the drafting of maintenance of effort provisions.[26]

*Mullins (p. 11) correctly notes: "THE DRAFTER SHOULD NEVER MINDLESSLY COPY THE MODEL. THE DRAFTER SHOULD APPROACH THE MODEL AS IF IT WERE A FIRST DRAFT WHICH NEEDS REVISION. (Usually, it does.)"

*-- Standardization*

Several writers have pointed out that the language of grant statutes varies immensely from statute to statute, apparently without any intention that the difference of language convey a corresponding difference of meaning.[27]

---

25*Dembling, p. 305.

26*See* discussion of maintenance of effort, Ch. II, Section L.

27*Dembling, for example, says, p. 305:

> Each program is authorized by a statute which uses its own language. No common set of definitions has emerged. Such basic terms as "grant," "grant-in-aid," "grant agreement," "subsidy," are used in different ways in different statutes. One statute bears little resemblance to another statute which may encompass similar conditions. Advantage is not taken by using language which has been interpreted by the courts and administrative tribunals. Variations in assistance programs occur because of a lack of uniformity in drafting standards, not

 

Reed Dickerson, one of the leading authorities on the drafting of laws, has said[28]

> The cardinal rule of all drafting, sometimes called 'the draftsman's golden rule,' can be stated in four words: Use your terms consistently. For one thing, don't vary your terminology when referring to the same thing.*** And don't do the converse. Don't use the same term to refer to different things.*** Consistency is a *sine qua non* of all effective communication.[29]

Grant statutes, both individually and especially taken as a group, often violate both branches of this golden rule: they use different words to mean the same thing and the same word to mean different things.[30]

The time has come for greater uniformity and standardization. Perhaps the best way to do this is to enact one or more general statutes providing definitions and a framework which other grant statutes thereafter should incorporate or treat as incorporated and should depart from only upon a clear showing of a need for different definitions and a different framework. Such general statutes will accomplish a great simplification and clarification of the grant field.[31] Even before this objective is achieved the discussions involved in attempting it will be valuable in directing draftsmen towards the goals of simplification, clarification and elimination of unnecessary variations.

-- *Remember that your proposed statute is intended to affect live people*

When statutes get too abstract and too complex it is easy to lose the sense that people bleed when cut. An example:

---

necessarily because of congressional intent." *Cf.* •Cappalli, 1.11.

[28]Dickerson, *How to Write a Law*, 31 NOTRE DAME LAW. 14, 24 (1955).

[29]Quoted in Ray Forrester, *Truth in Judging: Supreme Court Opinions As Legislative Drafting*, 38 VANDERBILT L.R. 463, 467-8 (1985).

[30]A thesaurus of words are used in various statutes and occasionally in the same statute to mean "grant": "assistance," "award," "pay," "federal participation," "agreement," "contract," "support." For an example of the same word used to mean different things, *see* Job Training Partnership Act, *supra*, at n.23.

[31]*See* discussion of general statutes, *infra*, C. Some Suggestions for General Grant Statutes.

 

42 U.S.C. 1396a (Medicaid): State plans for medical assistance.

(a) Contents. A State plan for medical assistance must--***

(1) ...
(2) ...
(3) ...
(4) ...
(5) ...
(6) ...
(7) ...
(8) ...
(9) ...
(10) provide--***

(a) ...
(b) ...
(c) that if medical assistance is included for any group of individuals described in section 1905(a) who are not described in subparagraph (A), then--***

(i) ...
(ii) ...
(iii) ...
(iv) if such medical assistance includes services in institutions for mental diseases or intermediate care facilities for the mentally retarded (or both) for any such group, it also must include for all groups covered at least the care and services listed in paragraphs (1) through (5) and (17) of section 1905(a) or the care and services listed in any 7 of the paragraphs numbered (1) through (17) of such section;***

except that (I) the making available of the services described in paragraph (4), (14), or (16) of section 1905(a) to individuals meeting the age requirements prescribed therein shall not, by reason of this paragraph (10) require the making available of any such services, or the making available of such services of the same amount, duration, and scope to individuals of any other ages,..."[32]

In a statute which governs the lives of people who are old, sick, poor, and mentally retarded, as this does, this draftsmanship reinforces unnecessarily and unwisely a

[32]The first sentence of this statute takes 14 1/2 pages as printed in USCS and includes 140 numbered or lettered sub-, subsub-, and subsubsub-clauses.

 

tendency to abstract, artificial, dispositions of the living people affected.[33]

### Sec. 5. Establishment of administering office

Often, but not always, the administration of a grant program is conferred by statute on a particular administrative agency with authority to make rules. The agency may be independent or established within an existing agency.

In principle, authorization to make grants could be given to the President, who would delegate. More commonly, it is made to the head of a Department or independent agency, who will usually delegate it. When a special office is created, the grant-making and rule-making powers are likely to be lodged in the new office.

Provisions for the establishment of agencies vary greatly according to their purpose and situation. Much of the variation, however, comes from a lack of a standard model. Good patterns are hard to find. The drafter may wish to explore Title 5 U.S.C. generally, and a sample agency such as the Department of Housing and Urban Development, 42 U.S.C. 3531-3541, or the National Science Foundation, 42 U.S.C. 1861 ff. for suggestions. Perhaps the best thought out pattern is that of the Office of Economic Opportunity, P.L. 88-452, 78 Stat. 508. Although the agency is no longer alive and the statute is old enough to create a risk of anachronism, it provides nevertheless a useful checklist of items to consider.[34]

---

[33]Contrast *Bell, p. 4, "According to Congress itself in a law enacted many years ago, statutes are to be divided into basic units called sections, each of which "shall contain, as nearly as may be, a single proposition of enactment." *See* 1 U.S.C. 104, Act of July 30, 1947, Ch. 388, 61 Stat. 634. The provisions of 42 U.S.C. 1396a, of which a fairly typical excerpt is quoted in the text, and in particular the provisions relating to institutions for mental institutions and intermediate care facilities for the mentally retarded, have given rise to a substantial amount of dispute and litigation. It is difficult to say with certainty that the Internal Revenue Code style is the cause of the disputes but I believe it has contributed to them.

[34]The personnel employment provisions, for example, were written before major revisions of the federal personnel laws. The provision for advisory committees was written before the Advisory Committee Act. For such reasons, it is not recommended that this statute be parroted, but that it be used to suggest topics for inclusion. The following is a list of catch phrases to indicate the contents of the Act: Sec. 601. Office of Economic Opportunity. There is hereby established in the Executive Office of the President the Office of Economic Opportunity -- headed by a Director who shall be appointed by the President, by and with the advice and consent of the Senate. -- Deputy -- three Assistant Directors. -- Provision for transfer of the Office elsewhere in the executive branch -- compensation. Sec. 602.

 

*-- A trap: Who's the boss?*

The drafter must consider this carefully: To what extent is it intended that the officer who directly receives grant authority shall have a discretion free of the normal agency supervision? This question, if not answered, can cause confusion or unnecessary tensions within the agency. If such discretion is intended, it should be given with care and thoughtful attention to these problems.

An example may be the Food and Drug Administrator who sometimes seems to rule a palatinate largely independent and disdainful of the Secretary of Health and Human Services.[35] Another example may be the

---

Authority of Director -- (a) to appoint personnel -- (b) employ experts -- (c) appoint advisory committees -- (d) with the approval of the President, arrange with and reimburse the heads of other Federal agencies for the performance of any of his functions, delegate and authorize redelegation -- (e) utilize, with their consent, the services and facilities of Federal agencies without reimbursement, and of State agencies -- (f) accept money or property by gift -- (g) accept voluntary and uncompensated services -- (h) allocate and expend, or transfer to other Federal agencies for expenditure, funds available -- (i) disseminate data and information -- (j) adopt an official seal which shall be judicially noticed -- (k) deal with, complete, rent, renovate, sell, properties acquired -- (l) collect or compromise all obligations -- (m) expend funds for printing and binding, for rent -- (n) establish such policies, standards, criteria, and procedures, prescribe such rules and regulations, enter into contracts, make payments in advance or by way of reimbursement, with necessary adjustments on account of overpayment or underpayments, and generally perform such functions and take such steps as he may deem to be necessary and appropriate to carry out the provisions of the Act. Sec. 604. Economic Opportunity Council (of agency heads). Sec. 605. National Advisory Council (public representatives). Sec. 611. Coordination of related programs.

[35]Commissioner Frank Young assures me that if this comment about FDA was correct at one time, as I believe it was, it no longer is. He says

> We are and do function as part of HHS. The confusion results from the fact that certain functions are delegated from the Secretary to the Commissioner. In our most recent administrative plan (Action Plan Phase III), we focus even more closely on our Health Function. We are now viewing our responsibilities as (1) Public Health Problem Prevention, (2) Public Health Problem Identification and (3) Public Health Problem Resolution. In my tenure as a Commissioner I have kept the Department informed and as required fully involved in decisions. Therefore, I would reject the concept that we function outside of the Department. Particularly important delegated functions include product evaluation and enforcement.

 

Commissioner of Social Security.[36] These are necessarily subjective judgments, but come from long and fairly close observation. Drafters should be aware that this generally unintended distortion of agency relationships happens, and should prefer (unless otherwise instructed) to name the head of the Department as the authority for grants.

-- *The problem of micro management*

Administration of a grant program involves a natural tension between legislature and executive and between both and the recipients. Grant programs are often complex in their technical nature (consider, for example, a project of basic scientific research, or one of research on the effect on the liver of certain blood components, or for the provision of medical services in a poverty area, or for supplying school lunches to school children). They are often affected by complex and controversial scientific or economic or social

---

[36]*See* Chapter II, sec. G, If a program is to be a grant program, who should administer it? *See* Smith, *Judicialization: The Twilight of Administrative Law*, 85 DUKE L.J. 427, 448 (1985), commenting on the semi-autonomy of such organizations as FDA and SSA.

At the swearing-in of a new Commissioner of Social Security, the new Commissioner, who had been an Assistant Secretary of Health, Education, and Welfare, gracefully accepted words of praise from the Secretary and added that he felt a sense of loss in leaving the Department. How much effect on practical problems this sense that the Social Security Administration was not part of the Department would have, is hard to determine, but there seems litle doubt that it had some and may have helped explain some of the frictions encountered between headquarters staff and Administration staff. The draftsmanship of the Social Security Act is not at fault here; it clearly gives the operating power to the Secretary. Congress has been concerned for many years about the independence of the Commissioner on Aging and the Administration on Aging within the HEW (now HHS). It has provided that the Commissioner shall report to the Office of the Secretary (why not to the Secretary? perhaps to allow for action by the Undersecretary, but "Office" opens the door wider), but shall administer his functions through the Administration on Aging (42 U.S.C. 3011, 3030bb, 3058b, 3058c(c)). The Secretary shall not approve or require any delegation of the functions of the Commissioner to any other officer not directly responsible to the Commissioner. The continuing struggle may explain the following amendment which plainly goes overboard. P.L. 98-459, the Older Americans Act Amendments of 1984, 413, adding new 433 to the Older Americans Act of 1965 [42 U.S.C. 3037b] "(a) The Commissioner shall be responsible for the administration, implementation, and making of grants and contracts under this title and shall not delegate authority under this title to any individual, agency, or organization." The Commissioner has a large staff. He must and does delegate. Is it possible to believe that Congress meant what Congress said? When consulted about this provision, Dr. Samuel Johnson replied, "I would never listen to it, if it made me such a fool."

 

or political factors. It is difficult or impossible to spell out in advance by legislative directive how they are to be conducted. Not surprisingly, the Congress often finds itself disappointed in the actual conduct of programs that it (somewhat vaguely perhaps) had anticipated would operate otherwise.[37]

A frequent response to such disappointment is to spell out, in an amendment to an existing statute, or in future statutes, more detailed and positive directions, or in other ways to attempt to control the Executive's discretion or the recipient's autonomy.[38]

Such efforts are often self-defeating. The effective administration of a grant program may require executive discretion, including discretion to be wrong. The achievement of grant goals calls for recipient independence including the right to be wrong. Too vigorous an effort by the legislature to engage in micro-management often runs

---

[37]*See Bennett v. New Jersey*, 470 U.S. 632, 105 S.Ct. 1555 (1985), and discussion, *Current Developments, Vol. 20, No. 4, Summer 1985; Ohio Department of Public Welfare, DGAB Docket No. 78-50-OH-HC, Decision No. 66, October 10, 1979.

Edith Green, then an influential Congress Member (Member of the 84th through 93rd Congresses, 3rd Oregon District, member of appropriation, and education and labor committees), insisted successfully on including in the Economic Opportunity Act of 1964, as amended, a provision giving first option to local governments as grantees of community action grants. A year later she was bitterly outraged to find that local governments had not received the large flow of community action grants she had anticipated. The reasons were simple. Where community action programs existed, the vast majority of local governments had already painfully worked out compromises that they did not wish to reopen. It is, moreover, rare that local governments have, under their own state laws, the powers that were required under the Act to qualify as a community action agency. Local governments' counsel knew it and knew that they could not sign the required certification that their governments were qualified, so local governments generally did not apply, notwithstanding Representative Green's insistence that they were to have priority. Representative Green was disappointed, but she need not have been. This example is not unique but is unusually clear. At the time of this development I was a member of General Counsel's staff of OEO. I have checked my recollection with Donald Baker, then General Counsel, later Counsel for Employment and Training, Health & Safety, Human Resources, Labor-Management Relations, Pensions, House Committee on Education and Labor. *See* 210(d), added in 1967 Amendments to the Economic Opportunity Act: Director may designate if State or political subdivisions are not willing to be designated. Powers required of a community agency are in 210, 211, 212.

[38]*See* n.37, *supra*, *Bennett* case, *Ohio* case.

 

aground in the real world in which grant programs must operate.[39]

In the grant field, micro-management is wrong in principle because it seeks to delimit the discretions and autonomy that are essential to a well-organized grant program. It has a special adverse effect in that an executive agency, faced with overly specific directives from the Congress, often protects itself by blind and rigid application of the rules imposed on it.[40] The result is typically a program that is less effective, less fair and unnecessarily expensive.

-- *Over-demanding rules*

Is there room for common sense in grant administration? One might think the answer would be "yes, of course". Yet there are valid reasons why common sense must be confined. Common sense is not in fact very common and rules that control free floating common sense are introduced to assure regularity, visible even-handedness, and objectivity. There is a legitimate tension between the appropriate respect for those rules and the appropriate recognition that there are situations where rules must bend for extraordinary circumstances and extreme cases.[41]

It is not possible to state general rules of law with the absolute precision that would justify a totally rigid enforcement. A general statute must necessarily be read with at least a minimum element of common sense that recognizes extraordinary circumstances and extreme cases to which it does not apply. Where the reason for the rule stops, an ancient legal maxim teaches us, the rule stops.[42]

---

[39]*See* •Current Trends, XV, *Increasing Legislative Oversight and Legislative Tinkering*, 35 FED. BAR J. 163, 186 and esp. 187 n.124, with several examples.

[40]*See* •Current Developments, Vol. 20, No. 4, Summer 1985, p. 15 "Who will educate the educators." This reaction is probably more common in the grant field than aggressive defiance or stubborn evasion.

[41]An example, fairly typical of many, is this: a state, grantee under the Medicaid program is required to inspect regularly the facilities that supply services (hospitals, nursing homes). Finding laxity in the agency's enforcement of this inspection program, Congress directed a specific schedule of annual inspections, with sanctions for non-compliance. What happens in the event of severe storms, creating a state of emergency, making road travel impossible, if some inspections are thereby delayed a month? HEW thought it was required by law to impose a sanction. *See* HEW DGAB, Ohio Department of Public Welfare, Docket No. 78-50-OH-HC, Decision No. 66, October 10, 1979, pp. 3-5.

[42]The need to give recognition to appropriate exceptions is often stated, but unfortunately often overlooked and should therefore be emphasized. As

 

In general, statutory directions, particularly those addressed to administrative agencies, are intended to be construed reasonably in light of their purpose; the authority of the agency to make (with thoughtful care) common sense adjustments to extreme and oppressive instances is normally to be assumed.

This is one of the most difficult areas for statutory drafters to deal with. When broad and loose guidance is given it may lead to creative government but it may lead to discretion run riot. When tight, narrow direction is given, it may lead to a foolish or willful rigidity such as both HEW and the Office of Education (now Department of Education) often exhibited in the past.[43]

A way out is difficult to find but elements of the solution may include

---

Harlan, J. stated the matter in *Amalgamated Assn. of St. E. R. & M. C. Emp. v. Lockridge*, 403 U.S. 274 (1971), with respect to the preemption doctrine, that doctrine "is, like any other purposefully administered legal principle, not without exception." 403 U.S. 274, 297.

Douglas, J. dissenting in *NLRB v. Seven-Up Bottling Company*, 344 U.S. 344, (1953) noted: "There are exceptions to most general rules; and the Board [NLRB] should be the guardian of the exceptions as well as the formula itself." 344 U.S. 344, 353. The majority agreed with the dissenters on the importance of recognizing exceptions where circumstances make application of a general rule to a particular situation "oppressive and therefore not calculated to effectuate a policy of the Act". 344 U.S. 344, 349.

Judge Leventhal emphasized in a thoughtful decision:

> The agency's discretion to proceed in difficult areas through general rules is intimately linked to the existence of a safety valve procedure for consideration of an application for exemption based on special circumstances. WAIT Radio v. FCC, 418 F.2d 1153, 1157 (D.C. Cir. 1969).

*Cf. Gulf Oil Corporation v. Hickel*, 435 F.2d 440, 447 (D.C. Cir. 1970). *Cf. also National Broadcasting Company v. United States*, 319 U.S. 190, 207, 225 (1943); *United States v. Storer Broadcasting Company*, 351 U.S. 192, 204-5 (1956).

*See also* Davis, Discretionary Justice, pp. 25-26:

> Rules alone untempered by discretion, cannot cope with the complexities of modern government and of modern justice.

*Cf.* Gardner, *The Procedures by which Informal Action is Taken*, 24 AD.L.R. 155, 159-160, 165 (1972),

> ...no man is wise enough to devise any rule, however narrow its scope and rich its obvious appeal, which can uniformly be applied...

43*See* *Current Developments, Vol. 20, No. 4, Summer 1985, at 15, *Who will educate the educators*, and 17, *Education Again*.

 

- avoidance by drafters of micro-management that is not really necessary,
- coupled with explicit recognition in drafting of elbow-room for discretion (by responsible officials),
- coupled with a freer and better oversight process that creates more two-way communication between Congress and the Executive; the legislative veto was never a solution because it worked as a club not a telephone.

**Sec. 6. Authorization of appropriations**

It is customary for grant statutes (and often other statutes as well) to contain an authorization of appropriations.[44] There is no constitutional requirement for this, and its absence from an enacted statute does no harm. The provision represents a customary adjustment between the interests of the Congressional committees that have jurisdiction over the substance of the statute and those that have jurisdiction over appropriations. To permit the substantive committees to have their say on the size of appropriations and to hold hearings on that question if they should wish, the custom is to include an authorization of appropriations, setting, presumably, a ceiling and a suggested amount, but not authorizing expenditures until an appropriation has been enacted. An appropriation made without an authorization would be perfectly valid but may

---

[44]*E.g.*, P.L. 99-519, the Asbestos Hazard Emergency Response Act of 1986, Sec. 4(a) amending section 512 of the Asbestos School Hazard Abatement Act of 1984 (P.L. 98-377; 20 U.S.C. 4011 *et seq.*): "In addition, for such purposes there are authorized to be appropriated out of the Asbestos Trust Fund established by Section 5 of the Asbestos Hazard Emergency Response Act of 1986 $25,000,000 for each of fiscal years 1987, 1988, 1989, and 1990."

P.L. 99-551, the Domestic Volunteer Service Act Amendments of 1986, amends the Domestic Volunteer Service Act of 1973 by adding: "(1) There is authorized to be appropriated to carry out part A of title I (except section 109) $25,000,000 for fiscal year 1989. (2) There is authorized to be appropriated to carry out section 109(c)...." etc

P.L. 99-590, Title I, amends the Wild and Scenic Rivers Act (16 U.S.C. 1274), providing (sec. 103(a)), grants to the city of Fort Collins for a study, and specifying (d) "FUNDING--There are hereby authorized to be appropriated up to $150,000 to carry out the provisions of this section."

 

be delayed by a point of order.[45] Often, the authorization of appropriation is reduced to a gesture:

> "There are hereby authorized to be appropriated such sums as are necessary to carry out this Act."[46]

Drafting techniques are, of course, influenced by the complexities of the current budget process. Although this is an important technical matter, it is beyond the scope of this book. It is desirable, however, that the drafter of grant statutes be alerted to the importance of these complexities.[47]

---

45*See* House Rule XXI.2(a), Rules of the House of Representatives, House Doc. No. 98-277 (98th Cong. 2d Sess.); Senate Rule XVI, Senate Manual, Sen. Doc. 98-1(98th Cong. 2d Sess.).

46*E.g.*, P.L. 99-576, the Veterans Benefits Improvement and Health-Care Authorization Act of 1986, Sec. 224 (Revision of State Home Construction Grant Program) (a) amends 38 U.S.C. 5033(a) to read: "There are hereby authorized to be appropriated such sums as are necessary to carry out this subchapter through September 30, 1989."

47Donald Hirsch (*see* Bibliography) in a letter to Charles Pou, Jr., ACUS, January 18, 1988, calls attention to this:

> "Particularly since the enactment of the Congressional Budget Act of 1974, the selection (or replacement) of funding mechanisms has been among the more sensitive issues in the development (or amendment) of financial assistance programs. A draftsman must be prepared, today, to explain to the policymaker the fiscal and tactical implications of this selection....
>
> "To take a simple example, consider a federal loan guaranty program, such as the Guaranteed Student Loan Program in title IV-B of the Higher Education Act of 1965.
>
> "The draftsman must be aware that a loan guaranty program is "credit authority" within the meaning of section 3(10) of the Congressional Budget Act of 1974. Therefore the draft bill must contain language to provide that the program may be "effective for any fiscal year only to such extent or in such amounts as are provided in appropriation Acts." Section 402(a) of the CBA. If it fails to contain this language, the bill may be struck down by a point of order on the floor of either House.
>
> "It might be useful if the draftsman knew that the amount of a loan guaranty is not "budget authority," as that term is used in the annual Budget of the United States. In discussing the desirability of a limit on outstanding guarantees (for example, in meetings with OMB), the draftsman may point out that the volume of such guarantees does not inflate the budget numbers.

 

"Finally, although this may seem a bit arcane, for purposes of sequestration under Gramm-Rudman-Hollings a loan guaranty ceiling will be reduced by the uniform percentage applied to the sequesterable outlay base. BUT if the program has NO ceiling (for example, the status of the VA Guaranteed Home Loan Program in 1986) then OMB will administratively IMPOSE a ceiling for purposes of sequestration. If the imposed ceiling is too low, the administering agency will then have to propose legislation to increase it. [FN. The OMB ceiling imposed on the VA Guaranteed Home Loan Program for purposes of fiscal 1986 sequestration was $6 billion too low and had to be raised legislatively.] This peculiarity bears on the desirability and size of the ceiling for a new guaranty program. Alerting policy officials engaged in the development or amendment of a guaranty program to this issue is the responsibility of the draftsman.

"Let's take the more complicated example of an appropriated entitle-ment, such as Medicaid or AFDC. To draft such a program, or speak to its formulation, the draftsman must keep in mind a few fundamentals:

"Unlike a true entitlement, such as the Old-Age, Survivors, and Disability Insurance Program ("social security"), an appropriated entitlement must be funded annually. But unlike a non-entitlement formula grant program (*e.g.*, the Community Services Block Grant Act, where the formula allocates only the amount appropriated) the appropriation for an appropriated entitlement is much like an estimate. That is, the grantee state is legally entitled to reimbursement without regard to the size of the appropriation. Of course, nothing is paid unless it is appropriated. Consequently, should the amount that the United States owes to a state exceed the available appropriation, the United States would be compelled to default. In its turn, the grantee state might find itself forced to curtail assistance to the ultimate program beneficiary. For these reasons the draftsman should write the bill to anticipate, and perhaps facilitate, the use (in later-enacted implementing appropriations bills) of language to avoid an appropriations short-fall. [F.N. For example, he might draft a provision authorizing advance appropriations or advance funding, or both. Although such provisions are not technically required under congressional rules, appropriations committees act as though they are. In other words, they are unwilling to employ such devices to fund new statutes in the absence of authorizing language in the statute.]

"The executive branch policy maker must be informed that the size of the program, when enacted, will not be controllable through the appropriations process (exclusive of the special case of Gramm- Rudman-Hollings sequestration).

"Congressional consideration of legislation proposing new appropriated entitlements is subject to various rules contained in section 401 of the Budget Act ("Bills Providing New Spending

 

**Sec. 7. Authorization of assistance**

This is the heart of a grant statute. The structure of the assistance program itself is discussed above in Chapter II. When mandatory programs are intended, the provision typically reads: "The Secretary [or the Administrator] shall make grants..." [or "shall pay", or "is authorized and directed"].[48] When discretionary programs are intended, the provision typically reads: "The Secretary may make grants...".[49] Of course, sometimes "shall" is used where

---

Authority"), including a rule as to when such a program may go into effect. [FN. The treatment of appropriated entitlements as meeting the Congressional Budget Act's section 401(c)(2) definition of "spending authority", although universally accepted, has given OMB hemorrhoids under Gramm-Rudman. The reason: if a program creates spending authority, GRH-mandated procedures (the so-called "Gradison baseline") for estimating program outlays for a fiscal year (in anticipation of sequestration) generate a significantly larger number than if the program did not create spending authority. Therefore, in the FY 1987 joint OMB/CBO sequestration report, in the face of a CBO dissent (not to mention OMB's own acceptance of appropriated entitlements as spending authority in the FY 1986 sequestration report), OMB chose to reinterpret the CBA to exclude appropriated entitlements from the CBA definition of "spending authority". Congress responded with a "Clarifying Amendment Respecting Appropriated Entitlements", section 101(b)(6) of the recent Balanced Budget and Emergency Deficit Control Reaffirmation Act of 1987, specifically including appropriated entitlements in section 401(c)(2), at least for purposes of GRH references. There is no question that the Parliamentarian of either House would rule that section 401 of the CBA applies to appropriated entitlements.]

"For purposes of reconciliation, the budget resolution will instruct the pertinent authorizing committees rather than the appropriations committees (contrary to the situation vis-a-vis discretionary grant programs). This is a matter of interest to agency legislative liaison.

"Some of this may seem like esoterica, but it is the bread and butter of people who make a living out of the drafting of grant programs (or, more commonly these days, the amending of grant programs)."

[48] P.L. 100-4, the Water Quality Act of 1987, Sec. 212(a). Subject to the provisions of this title, the Administrator shall make capitalization grants to each State for the purpose of establishing a water pollution control revolving fund.

[49] P.L. 100-4, the Water Quality Act of 1987, Sec. 406(g)(1). The Administrator is authorized to conduct or initiate scientific studies, demonstration projects, and public information projects... For the purposes of carrying out this subsection, the Administrator may make

 

"may" is meant.[50] That is an old problem. It is not desirable, but may have recently found some apparent justification in concerns about impoundments. Assuming that some part of the program is intended to be of the mandatory, formula, state plan type, the statute will normally include a section providing an allotment formula and a section stating the state plan requirements.[51] Where some part of the program is of the discretionary type, there is likely to be a separate section or several for discretionary grant provisions.[52] Major programs, of course, often include both kinds of grants.

> -- *Do not unnecessarily or inadvertently direct state or local governments or private bodies to act through structures or particular officers that the state (or local government or private body) would not choose for itself.*

Grant statutes often assume, or require, or exert pressure towards particular arrangements within state or local governments. For example, they may call on the governor of the state or a mayor to take certain action which from a state point of view may belong more appropriately to the legislature or to an agency within the state designated by state (or local) legislation. They may require certain functions to be placed within a particular agency - a "single state agency," the Health Department, the State Administration on Aging - while the state may consider a different allocation of powers appropriate.[53] Sometimes

---

grants to State water pollution control agencies, institutions, organizations, and individuals.

[50]P.L. 99-158, the Health Research Extension Act of 1985 revises Sections 472-476 of the Public Health Service Act, using the word "shall", to provide grants to individuals to enable them to accept traineeships and fellowships; to physicians; to appropriate public or private nonprofit medical libraries; to existing public or private nonprofit medical libraries; to public or private nonprofit institutions of higher education and individual scientists. In most of these cases it seems highly unlikely that "shall" was used wittingly. For example, Sec. 475(a). The Secretary, with the advice of the Board [of Regents of the National Library of Medicine] *shall make grants to and enter into contracts with* existing public or private nonprofit medical libraries...[emphasis added]. It cannot have been intended that existing libraries have an entitlement nor that they are to receive both grants and contracts. In all probability "may" or "is authorized to" would have expressed this better.

[51]*See* sections 8 and 9, *infra*.

[52]*See* section 10, *infra*.

[53]*See* text *infra* at n.57.

 

such provisions raise federal constitutional questions; more often, the Congressional power may be clear but the wisdom of this federal disturbance of state arrangements may be less clear. Such provisions may clash with state constitutional provisions or interpretations but on such issues the state must yield (assuming that the federal grant program is a valid exercise of the general welfare power and the conditions appropriately clear and that other provisions of the federal constitution are not an independent bar).[54]

-- *Be explicit about eligibility*

> Executive agencies should not have to address highly political issues such as who is eligible to receive funds from a certain program. The Congress should be explicit on eligibility. In the absence of adequate definitions of eligibility in a statute, there should be a clear understanding as to the range of administrative discretion to include or exclude categories of recipients.[55]

This is good advice, often not followed.

-- *Be explicit about intended beneficiaries*

This includes explicitness about eligibility, but it goes further. Grant funds given to eligible recipients often are intended to benefit primarily certain classes of non-recipients. For example, funds granted to a health center may be intended primarily to benefit the community, the sick of the community, or the poor of the community. This is often worth defining. If the health center in fact emphasizes its training function, which primarily benefits, in the first instance, a medical school and its young physicians rather than service to the community, that may be contrary to the Congressional intent. In the short run, the training or service emphasis can be quite different. What is best in the long run calls for difficult judgments Congress may not have intended to leave to the parochial judgment of this grantee. Again, the center may turn out to

---

[54]State of N.C. *ex rel. Morrow v. Califano*, 445 F.Supp 532 (1977), *aff'd.* 435 U.S. 962, 98 S.Ct. 1597 (1978), where the State claimed that to comply with federal grant conditions requiring a certificate of need for the construction of hospitals would violate the State constitution. *Cf. South Dakota v. Dole*, __U.S.__, 107 S.Ct. 2793, 2796 (1987).

[55]•Dembling, p. 305. *See also*, Chapter II, Section 10, What is the intended class of recipients?

 

serve primarily the sick in a sub-community who are not poor rather than the entire community or the sick in the poorer sub-community. Did Congress intend to leave this to grantee's choice? A statute can give a strong or weak indication of intent on those matters.

When identifying the intended beneficiaries, drafters should also consider the extent of the rights intended to be conferred. Are they to have a right to be consulted? A right to a hearing if dissatisfied? And to a court appeal? A right to be heard in opposition to benefits given to others? Those things need not always be spelled out, but if they are not, the sponsors of the legislation may be surprised by the outcome in the courts and will have only the drafter to blame.[56]

*-- Think about flow-through of grant rules to subgrantees and contractors under grants*

When grants are made to eligible recipients, many conditions may be imposed on the recipient. The recipient is often expected or permitted to make subgrants or contracts to perform part of the grant work. Which of the conditions imposed on the grantee must be complied with by the subgrantee or by the contractor under a grant? And who decides? If the grantee is required to make reports to the grantor in a specified format, must the subgrantee make parallel reports to the grantee in the same format? May the grantee decide what reports it wants from the subgrantee in order to meet the requirements of the grant? This is the flow-through problem. It is a difficult one. It has in the past been subject to OMB guidance. For a number of reasons,

---

[56]*See* Section 15, *infra*, Administrative and Judicial Review provisions.

 

the OMB guidance was unsatisfactory. OMB recognizes this and is in the process of making a comprehensive revision.[57]

The drafter of a grant statute may reasonably leave this matter to OMB. This will have the virtue of reinforcing an effort at uniformity. The OMB approach, however, whether good or bad, is necessarily somewhat abstract. It pursues a goal of a particular kind of uniformity and a goal of devolution of authority to States, in an across the board manner that reflects little of the variations of grant structures and purposes.

The drafter of a grant program should be aware that this is a currently controversial problem and should make an informed judgment as to whether flow-through problems should be left to the current and the evolving rules or need guidance in a particular direction.

-- *Administrative discretion*

A theoretical pattern of government calls for basic policy to be set by legislation, but executed by an administrative agency with broad discretion to set the detailed rules that are only adumbrated by the legislative policy. That discretion includes a discretion to recognize exceptions to general rules that often cannot be anticipated at the point of legislation but are essential to the achievement of reasonable results.

For example, many federal grant statutes require grantee states to perform the grant under a single State agency.[58]

---

[57]OMB Circular A-102 (State and local Governments) has been revised; A-110 (Non-profit institutions) par. 5, is now being revised. *See* OMB Notice of Review of A-102, 49 Fed. Reg. No. 118 (June 18, 1984); Lasker, *OMB Circular A-102: Has Its Time Passed*, 2 Assistance Management No. 1, December 1983, p. 3; *Symposium, "Rethinking A-102,"* 2 Assistance Management No. 2, June 1984. OMB seeks to foster a particular concept of federalism by improving the authority and flexibility of states, although some grant programs may represent efforts by the federal government to strengthen the authority and flexibility of units of government below the State level. The OMB approach is certainly defensible and may be desirable, but it is not the only rational approach to these problems. *See* Circular A-102, Uniform Administrative Requirements for Grants and Cooperative Agreements to State and Local Governments, 53 Fed. Reg. 8034 (March 11, 1988), Preamble at 8035, "flow-down", Common Rule at 8087.

[58]*See* discussion *supra*, text at n.53. An example is 42 U.S.C. 602. State plans for aid and services to needy families with children;

(a) Contents. A State plan for aid and services to needy families with children must--...

(3) either provide for the establishment or designation of a single State agency to administer the plan, or provide for the

If the Congress determine that the single State agency approach is sound, it should also recognize that there are circumstances where a single State agency requirement may become a strait jacket and where the purposes of the single State agency requirement can be achieved as well or better without enforcing the requirement. In such circumstances, the federal grant-making agency should be authorized to waive the requirement upon a convincing showing of the desirability of a waiver. That waiver power should either be implicit in the structure of the statute or should be explicit. In fact, single State agency requirements are generally subject to an explicit waiver authority.[59]

-- *Provide explicitly for discretion*

This pattern is one that should be considered whenever a grant-making agency is given instructions that are mandatory in form: discretion is likely to be desirable. Authority to grant waivers, exemptions, deviations, is apt to be needed. Where there is doubt, it should ordinarily be considered implicit, but explicit authority should be considered by the drafter.[60]

-- *Deal explicitly with questions of federal preemption*

Preemption by federal law is, of course, something that occurs in many fields, and causes doubts and problems often. It is a problem of special difficulty in the grant field

---

establishment or designation of a single State agency to supervise the administration of the plan;....

[59]31 U.S.C. 6404. Use of existing State or multimember agency to administer grant programs

Notwithstanding a law of the United States providing that one State agency or multimember agency must be established or designated to carry out or supervise the administration of a grant program, the head of the executive agency carrying out the program may, when requested by the executive or legislative authority of the State responsible for the organizational structure of a State government --

(1) waive the one State agency or multimember agency provision on an adequate showing that the provision prevents the establishment of the most effective and efficient organizational arrangement within the State government; and

(2) approve another State administrative structure or arrangement after deciding that the objectives of the law authorizing the grant program will not be endangered by using another State structure or arrangement. (Sept. 13, 1982, P. L. 97-258, 1, 96 Stat. 1007).

[60]*See also* Chapter II, Section H, How much discretion should be left to the Executive?

 

because of two factors. (1) Grants contemplate recipient autonomy and preemption should therefore not be too readily assumed[61] and (2) grant statutes are often not clearly drafted.

In *King v. Smith*,[62] Alabama's "substitute father" regulation was held invalid on the ground that it defines "parent" in a manner inconsistent with 406(a) of the Social Security Act.

In *Rosada v. Wyman*,[63] the Supreme Court, with some complaint about the uncertainty of the federal statute[64] held New York's standard of need in the Aid to Families with Dependent Children program to be invalid because of conflict with the federal statute.

The Administrative Conference has recommended:[65]

> "1. Congress should address foreseeable preemption issues clearly and explicitly when it enacts a statute affecting regulation or deregulation of an area of conduct...."

That is good advice for grant statute drafters as well.

-- *Be explicit about last dollar provisions*

Grant programs are sometimes intended to provide safety-net funding supplementing other sources of funding. In some health programs, for example, if the patient has a medical insurance, the grant is to be used to pay costs beyond what the insurance will pay. The grant is intended

---

[61] *See* "Current Trends, 35 FED. BAR. J. 163, at 178, VIII. Irradiation of the Supremacy Clause.

[62] 392 U.S. 309 (1968), esp. at 333, 88 S.Ct. 2128, 2141, n.34: "There is of course no question that...any state law or regulation inconsistent with such federal terms and conditions is to that extent invalid." Although HEW, charged with administering the Act, had objected to the Alabama regulation, the grounds of its objection were not those that made the regulation objectionable to the Court. *See Douglas, J.*, concurring, *ibid.* at 335.

[63] 397 U.S. 397, 90 S.Ct. 1207 (1970).

[64] 397 U.S. at 412; 90 S.Ct. at 1218.

[65] ACUS Rec. 84-5, Preemption of State Regulation by Federal Agencies, 1984 ACUS 27, and background report by Richard J. Pierce, Jr., at 517. *See also* 14 (ACIR) INTERGOVERNMENTAL PERSPECTIVE, Vol. 14, No. 1, Winter 1988, p. 23, Federal Preemption of State and Local Authority.

 

to be the "last dollar".[66] This is in contrast with Medicare, for example, (not a grant program) which in some cases pays the first dollar and is then supplemented by any private insurance.

This is a complex issue and Congressional intent is not always clear. It is useful for the drafter to seek or make an articulate decision on the intent or a deliberate decision to leave the decision to the administering agency.

-- *Autonomy*

It has been stated earlier that the essence of the grant relationship is the autonomy of the grantee on substantive essentials.[67]

This does not mean that there are not many and important qualifications, conditions that crimp the grantee's autonomy. There are. Autonomy is not perfect and cannot be. A complex set of intergovernmental and other tensions in our system must be accommodated. Nevertheless, autonomy is at the heart of the relationship and when grant

---

[66]Example: 42 U.S.C. 1396(a) State plans for medical assistance [Medicaid] (a) A State plan for medical assistance must--...(25) provide (A) that the State or local agency administering such plan will take all reasonable measures to ascertain the legal liability of third parties to pay for care and services... (b)...treat such a legal laiblity as a resource...and (c)... where such a legal liability is found to exist after medical assistance...seek reimbursement for such assistance to the extent of such legal liability;...

Another example: 42 U.S.C. 254c Community Health Centers--(e) (2) Except as provided in subsection (d)(1)(B), the Secretary may not approve an application for a grant under subsection (d) unless the Secretary determines...that (E) the center has made or will make and will continue to make every reasonable effort to collect appropriate reimbursement for its costs in providing health services to persons who are entitled to insurance benefits under title XVIII of the Social Security Act, to medical assistance under a State plan approved under title XIX of such Act, or to assistance for medical expenses under any public assistance program or private health insurance program...

[67]*See* Chapter I, Who should be interested in grant statute drafting problems, and II, 1. The choice of instrument. This has been recognized in legislation, such as the Federal Grant and Cooperative Agreement Act, 31 U.S.C. 6304; by the executive, for example, when food stamps were reclassified by OMB from grants to benefits because the federal control had increased (The Budget, FY1977, Special Analyses, p. 260, *see also* Catalog 10.551); by the courts, *see, e.g., Forsham v. Califano*, 587 F.2d 1128, esp. at 1138. "The reference to 'an *autonomous* grantee' is a core concept" (1978), *aff'd.* sub. nom. *Forsham v. Harris*, 455 U.S. 169, esp. at 180 (1980),"reflecting the same regard for the autonomy of the grantee's records as for the grantee itself", *U.S. v. Orleans*, 425 U.S. 807 (1976); and by writers, *see e.g.*, •Cappalli, 1.07; •Current Trends, 35 FED. BAR J. 163, 166, *I. The Black Letter Law.*

 

statutes are written, it is well to ask of each provision that impairs autonomy: is this necessary, worth the cost, and consistent with the basic intention of the program?

### Sec. 8. Allotment formula

Allotments are instructions for the distribution of available funds to the several states or other recipients. Among the purposes of such allotments are to provide assurance against undue concentration of grants to particular states or regions because of favoritism (or somewhat less reprehensible reasons such as ease of administration) and "to alleviate disparities in the fiscal resources at the state and local levels."[68]

The term "allotment" has a fairly clear meaning. So does "distribution" or "distributing." This process is also sometimes called "allocation" or "apportionment." These terms are often used seemingly interchangeably by statutes and agencies. It might be desirable to standardize them and use them consistently.[69] "Allocation" is often used to identify distributions of authority to obligate funds within an agency and distribution of funds to classes of activity (so much to educational services, so much to research) rather than distribution of funds to recipients. "Apportionment" is often used to identify distribution of authority to obligate funds over time (for example, by quarters) notably by OMB under the Antideficiency Act. For that reason, this text prefers the term "allotment" for the distribution of funds to states and other recipients. Whether this particular usage or another should be adopted, however, is less important

---

[68] GAO, GRANT FORMULAS, A CATALOG OF FEDERAL AID TO STATES AND LOCALITIES (GAO/HRD-87-28) p. 12.

[69] GAO, GRANT FORMULAS, n.68, *supra*, at p. 413 has a glossary which defines Allotment: An amount of funds received by a grant recipient;

Allocation: A distribution of funds among grant recipients, arrived at by applying a formula to specific program funds available;

Apportionment: A division of available funds, among activities, projects, or objects (or a combination thereof), based on a formula.

A footnote comments that the Federal Highway Administration uses the terms differently.

GAO, although giving the terms specific meanings in the glossary, uses them more loosely in its text (*e.g.*, "allocations" and "allotments," pp. 45, 86, 98, 100, 282, 354; "apportioned" p. 176, 210, 232. Of course, this usage is influenced by the fact that the statutes use the terms inconsistently and the agencies from which GAO gathered its information did so too. GAO's earlier A GLOSSARY OF TERMS USED IN THE FEDERAL BUDGET PROCESS (March 1981) at pp. 33-35 gives quite different definitions for these terms. Statutes use them without definition, again with apparently different meanings.

 

than the recognition that inconsistency now prevails and could be reduced.

In mandatory grant statutes, the entitlement of each state or other recipient may be specified by dollar amount[70] or by a statutory fraction of the amount that becomes available.[71] These formulas are sometimes very complex.[72]

---

[70]*Cf.* P.L. 97-328 (Mary McLeod Bethune Council House), a single recipient assistance statute:

> Sec. 3...the Secretary of the Interior is authorized and directed to enter into cooperative agreements with the National Council of Negro Women... Sec. 5...there are authorized to be appropriated $100,000 to provide financial assistance under section 3.....

*See also* P.L. 99-590, amending the Wild and Scenic Rivers Act (16 U.S.C. 1274), providing grants and technical assistance to the city of Fort Collins, and authorizing $150,000 to be appropriated for that purpose.

[71]For example, P.L. 1004, the Water Quality Act of 1987, sec. 206, amending sec. 205(c) of the Federal Water Pollution Control Act: "...Sums authorized for such fiscal years shall be allotted in accordance with the following table:

'States
Alabama.................. .011309
....
Virgin Islands........... .000527'"

[72]GAO, GRANT FORMULAS, *supra* note 68, has a valuable survey of formulas used in allotments in 142 programs representing 87 per cent of all federal grants-in-aid. GAO sought to use a common terminology across programs and translated the gist of the process into algebraic terms. One example: p. 158, Solar Energy and Energy Conservation Bank (CFDA 14.550) (12 U.S.C. 3614 and 3615): Allocations are made to states. Each state's allotment is made in proportion to (FY 1985) the product of a need indicator and an incentive factor.

Allocations to states that are new to the program are raised to a minimum of $120,000 if the initial formula allotment is below that amount. Other participating states are guaranteed a $20,000 minimum.

**Mathematical Structure:**

STATE SHARE = (NEED*INCENT)/SUM OF NUMERATOR

where,

NEED = .50* (.50* LOINCHH+.30* MODINCHH+.20* HIINCHH)+ .50*ENERGY

INCENT = 1.0+[P*(.10*BTUSAVE+.10*INVEST+.50*EXPEND+ .30*COMMIT)]

**Definitions:**

All data elements in the need factor are expressed as a percent of the largest state (i.e., largest state = 100 percent):

LOINCHH = number of households in each state with incomes 80 percent or less of state median income MODINCHH = number of households in each state with incomes between 80 and 150 percent of state median HIINCHH = number of households in each state with incomes above

 

Typical allotment provisions take account of such things as the population of the states, the number of poor persons or of children of poor families attending school or of miles of highway or of passengers emplaning at a particular airport. They often provide for a minimum grant or for a save-harmless provision if a State would receive under the formula less than it had been receiving.[73]

Sometimes the formula is left to be worked out by the agency, with Congress giving only an indication of elements to be considered.[74]

---

150 percent of state median ENERGY = amount of energy consumed per household in a state, in BTUs

All data elements in the incentive factor (INCENT) are rated on a scale from 0 to 5:

BTUSAVE = BTU savings as a percent of grant subsidy in prior 24 months (in each state)

INVEST = dollars invested in subsidized projects as a percent of grant subsidies in prior 24 months (in each state)

EXPEND = proportion of obligated grant funds expended in prior 24 months

COMMIT = state's proportionate share of grant funds expended in the prior 24 months

P = penalty factor, where the incentive factor is reduced by 5 percent for every 10 percent of other federal funds used to subsidize the matching requirement for this program. The minimum penalty is 5 percent; the maximum is 50 percent. (P = 1.0 if no other federal funds are used).

[73]*See* Solar Energy and Energy Conservation Bank, *supra*, n.58. Vocational Education State Planning and Evaluation (CFDA 84.121), 20 U.S.C. 2306-2309, 2311, hold harmless through FY 1984, minimum allotment of 40%, maximum 60%. Local Rail Service Assistance (CFDA 20.308, 49.1654(h)), no state gets less than 1%. Alcohol and Drug Abuse and Mental Health Services Block Grant (CFDA 13-992), 42 U.S.C. 300x-1a, all states held harmless at 1984 level. Older Americans Program: Planning Coordination Evaluation and Administration of State Plan (CFDA 13.633A), 42 U.S.C. 3028(b), minimum allotment for the states, District of Columbia and Puerto Rico is 1/2% or $300,000 or FY 75 allocation, whichever was greater.

[74]*E.g.*, 16 U.S.C. 1456a(c)(3)(A) The Secretary shall make grants to any coastal state to enable such state to prevent, reduce, or ameliorate any unavoidable loss in such state's coastal zone of any valuable environmental or recreational resource, if such loss results from the transportation, transfer or storage of coal or from alternative ocean energy activities.

(B) Such grants shall be allocated to any such state based on rules and regulations promulgated by the Secretary which shall take into account the number of coal or alternative ocean energy facilities, the nature of their impacts, and such other relevant factors deemed appropriate by the Secretary.

42 U.S.C. 300 j--2(a)(4) "...the Administrator shall, in accordance with regulations, allot the sums appropriated...among the states on the basis of population, geographical area, number of public water systems, and other

 

Allotments are sometimes also established for discretionary project grants with the intention of steering the selection of grantees so that there is a fair distribution among the states.[75]

In drafting allotments, here are some questions to be considered:

Will the proposed formula tend to produce the intended results?

Does the proposed formula treat similarly those similarly situated?

Does it treat differently those differently situated? Does it, for example, give more to those who have more need and less to those who have less need? Does it give more to those who furnish a greater effort? Does it give less to those less likely to benefit?

No rule of appropriate action is being offered here: These are questions that it is often useful for technicians to ask. The policy answers are for the policy makers.

How do you estimate the total expected program costs? For a medical program do you look to statistics of illnesses? Or do you count total population on the assumption that illnesses will run in proportion, or poverty, on the assumption that with poverty, illnesses and need for treatment increase? If the program deals with homelessness, if reliable measures are lacking, what do you use as a measure for distributing funds?

Are the factors that are used really relevant to the distribution that is wanted or valid surrogates for relevant factors?

Is the formula unnecessarily complicated? Many seem to be.

Would there be administrative economy in adopting formula elements already used in other statutes rather than requiring the gathering of a new set of data only slightly different from those already being gathered? An imaginary example: If one agency gathers data on the number of houses that are substandard in any of three ways (no running water, no hot water, no sewage system), should another agency be directed to get data on the number of homes that lack running water? Perhaps yes, if the fact of running water is essentially significant, but perhaps no, if the existing data will probably give closely the same result.

---

relevant factors...." *cf.* Catalog, *supra*, p. 287 State Public Water System Supervision Program Grants (66.432).

[75]Head Start (CFDA 13.600), 42 U.S.C. 9853(b).

 

Are the data needed to apply the formula available and clearly identified? Will they be available on time to be used when they are needed? Formulas based on census data have sometimes run into trouble because the census data were, perhaps unavoidably, delayed.[76]

Will the data elements used withstand litigation challenge? (Formulas based on census data recently ran into trouble because minority group spokesmen claimed their number had been undercounted, affecting the amount of grants their areas would receive.)[77]

---

[76]GAO/HRD-87-109 BR, Block grants, Proposed Formulas for Substance Abuse, Mental Health Provide More Equity, is an example of specific analysis of a proposed formula. The GAO catalog *supra*, gives not only examples but surveys of the kinds of data sources looked to. Cf. for example of congressional concern, 1980 CQ Almanac 229 ("Congressional Reapportionment") on the use of the 1980 census for computing congressional representation - objection to the counting of aliens in the state populations. Use of the census for allotting grant funds was not at that point objected to but was objected to elsewhere by minority representatives. *See* GAO/GGD-87-99FS, July 1987, Decennial Census, Coverage Evaluation and Adjustment Activities.

[77]Moynihan, Maximum Feasible Misunderstanding, *supra*, n.17, comments, p. 198:

> The Bureau of the Census, one of the truly noble institutions of the Federal government, has quietly been transforming its decennial survey into a continuous measurement process. Much room remains for improvement. (In 1960, some 10 percent of the nonwhite population was missed, with proportions twice that and more among young adult males.)

The 1980 Census was challenged by nearly two dozen lawsuits claiming that the census severely undercounted urban blacks and Hispanic populations. New York City, for example, believed the undercount costs it $26 to $52 million a year in federal grant money and a U.S. House seat. Seven years later, these lawsuits were unresolved. For the 1990 Census, OMB questions the inclusion of about half of the 70 long-form questions involving housing, work, and fertility. The Census Bureau, some grant-making agencies, housing groups and others have protested. OMB "labeled as 'nonsense" implications by some critics that OMB has an ideological motive for its objections--a desire to reduce the scope of housing programs, for example, by reducing data on housing." Washington Post, *Census Bureau Looks to 1990 As Lawsuits Over 1980 Linger*, Wednesday, August 19, 1987 (Federal Page). Expert on Undercount [Dr. Barbara Bailar] Quits Census Bureau [hearsay that she believed that political factors may have entered into an October 30 decision by the Commerce Department that forbids an undercount adjustment of 1990 census figures]. Washington Post, The Federal Page, December 18, 1987. *Cf.* OMB Watch, Action Alert, July 1988, "1990 Census Housing Information Still at Risk". *Cf. also*, OMB Watch, Monthly Review, Vol. 4, No. 6, June 30, 1988, OIRA Puts the Brake On Bus Industry Census. No opinion is expressed here on the propriety or wisdom of these OMB decisions: what is relevant is that the drafter should not too readily assume that statistics needed for a formula will be available.

 

**Sec. 9. State plan provisions**

Many mandatory grant programs require States to submit for approval a State plan setting forth how the State proposes to conduct the program. The typical condition for approval is compliance of the plan with specified requirements. Ordinarily, there will be opportunity for States to obtain review if their plans are turned down.

The "Medicaid" statute may be taken as a sample (not a model) State plan statute. It illustrates a pattern of state plan provisions duplicated in several other similar statutes. It also reflects some common defects in the drafting of such provisions, including inordinate length and complexity and additional difficulty resulting from incorporation by reference of provisions from other statutes which add up to a lack of clarity.

Paraphrased and sharply cut, 42 U.S.C. 1396a can be outlined as follows: It requires a State plan for medical assistance (Medicaid) to cover in an approved way these topics:

(a) 1. application to all parts of the State (plans that serve only "downstate", for instance, are not acceptable)

2. State financial participation. (This must not be prejudiced by local inabilities to carry part of the burden)

3. hearing for those denied assistance

4. personnel practices (merit basis, training, protection against conflict of interest by major employees)

5. single state agency

6. reports to the Secretary

7. safeguards against disclosure of confidential information

8. accessibility of assistance to applicants

9. maintenance of standards

10. eligibility of individuals and required categories of service

11. cooperative agreements with state agencies

12. examination to determine whether an individual is blind

13. payment rates

14. non-imposition of enrollment fees

15. coordination with medicare

16. availability of assistance to residents when out of state

17. income standards for eligibility

18. compliance with 42 U.S.C. 1396p with respect to liens

 

19. safeguards for simplicity of administration and best interests of recipients.
20. special provisions for patients over 65 in mental institutions
21. special provision for patients over 65 in public mental institutions
22. staff standards
23. patients' freedom of choice of provider
24. consultative services
25. third party liability (last dollar)
26. special provisions for inpatient mental hospital services
27. agreements for record keeping
28. special provision for skilled nursing facilities
29. licensing of administrators
30. utilization review (to assure economy)
31. written plan of care and periodic inspections in skilled nursing facilities
32. direct payment to patient, with exceptions
33. review of plans of care
34. provision for certain services before application
35. disclosure of ownership of providers
36. publicity for surveys of facilities
37. prompt payment procedures
38. disclosure of subcontractors
39. barring of persons involved in false provider claims
40. use of uniform reporting system
41. notification by State of actions to terminate providers
42. audit
43. notification of availability of screening services
44. certification of need for inpatient services
45. mandatory assignment of rights of medical support owed to recipient
46. income and eligibility verification [some "notwithstanding" clauses]

(b) plan shall not be approved if it contains an age requirement of more than 65 years, a resident requirement excluding any resident of the State, or a citizenship requirement excluding any citizen of the United States.

(c) nor if it will reduce aid under State plans under Titles I, X, XIV, or XVI.

 

(d) performance of medical and utilization review services by delegation
(e) grandfather clause for family eligibility
(f) effective date of plan
(g) [repealed]
(h) [repealed]
(i) termination of certification of facilities
(j) waiver in American Samoa

The whole of this takes over 19 pages as printed in USCS. A single subsection (10) alone occupies 3 pages. Whether this is too long depends of course on whether the content is really appropriate and necessary and cannot be expressed clearly in less space.

Some of these provisions serve a valid purpose in permitting each State to shape its own program its own way, within broad federally-imposed limits. That is consistent with the basic function of grant programs. For example, under (2), a State may elect to pay all of the non-federal share of the costs of the program from its own funds. The State, if it chooses to pay less than all, may require cities or counties to contribute, but it must still pay at least 40 percent of the non-Federal share itself. In addition, it must provide for a distribution of funds from both Federal and State sources for carrying out the State plan on an equalization or other basis which will assure that the lack of adequate funds from local sources will not result in lowering the amount, duration, scope or quality of care and services under the plan. This serves a federal goal of uniformity of services throughout the State, but leaves to the State substantial room for devising its own fiscal arrangements.

In contrast, under (12), if it is necessary to determine whether an individual is blind, there shall be an examination by a physician skilled in diseases of the eye or by an optometrist, whichever the individual may select. There is no room here for variation in plans from state to state as there is in (2). Why is it part of a state plan? This may be a sensible requirement but, as state plan boilerplate, it surreptitiously introduces a federal legislative requirement that belongs elsewhere in the statute.

Similarly (35) requires that the State plan "provide that any disclosing entity (as defined in section 1124(a)(2) receiving payments under such plan complies with the requirements of section 1124". Read by itself this is wholly uncommunicative. Referring to section 1124, we find a requirement to be imposed by regulation or contract of certain disclosures of ownerships by "disclosing entities". That term is defined in a passage that takes almost a full page and involves eight further incorporations by reference, including several back to Title XIX (Medicaid). The section is probably intelligible with effort, but the effort required seems excessive. Is it necessary? In any case, since the requirement is to be imposed by the Secretary and the State has no room for tailoring a plan in this respect to local preferences, why is it in a State plan section?

It may be felt that requiring the inclusion of certain provisions in a plan that is nominally the State's own plan and signed by its officers discourages State evasion, but it is very doubtful that either the States or the courts consider a clause more binding in honor because the State is required to say it than if it were merely imposed by federal law. If desired, a State could be asked to certify that it is aware of Sections -- through -- and will comply with them. In any case, simpler and clearer drafting can be achieved by breaking out these substantive requirements that are imposed by federal law without room for State variation.

Some considerations in the drafting of State plan provisions:

(1) The multipage single sentence style is neither necessary nor desirable. It can be done more simply:

Along these lines, for example:

"Sec. 100. A State plan shall comply with the standards of Sections 120 through 150.

Sec. 101. A State plan shall expressly refer to and incorporate expressly or by reference the standards of Sections 170 through 190.

Sec. 120. A State shall pay out of its own funds not less than 40% of the non-Federal share of the costs of the programs.

Sec. 121. If the State requires contribution to the costs of the program from local sources, it shall nevertheless assure that the lack of adequate funds from local sources will not result in lowering the amount, duration, scope, or quality of care and services under the plan. For this purpose, in the event that the State requires such contribution, it shall provide for a distribution of funds from both Federal and State sources for carrying out the state plan on an equalization or other basis which will provide this assurance."

 

(2) Surreptitious substantive law should come out of the closet. Subsections (12) and (35) discussed above are examples of such surreptitious substantive law.

(3) Are we sure we need State plans at all? To the extent that significantly different approaches by the several states are desired, yes - let the State set out its plan. But boilerplate? Let it be imposed by fiat or, if thought necessary, adopted by explicit reference.

### Sec. 10. Discretionary grant provisions

A discretionary grant provision will usually read something like: "The Secretary may make grants..." Of course, "shall" is sometimes used for "may"; but, in general, should not be.[78] The characteristic of a discretionary grant program is normally that the agency has discretion both as to whether to make a grant to the applicant or not and, if so, for how much (within the limits of appropriations, allotments, apportionments).

The process leading up to the award of a grant need not be spelled out, but it sometimes is. Congressional guidance may touch, for example, on any of the following points:

-- Preliminary public participation in the shaping of programs and priorities.[79]

-- Announcement of availability, award process, priorities.[80]

-- Review of applications. Some agencies use referees or peer review panels.[81] These are sometimes required by statute.

-- Competition. The amount of available funds is limited. Grants will be made to a selected group, normally much fewer than the total number of applicants. It is desirable that all potential grantees be given fair notice of the availability of the grants and of their opportunity to apply and that the applications be evaluated in an objective, competent manner.[82] This may be called competition but it is quite different from

---

78 *See supra*, text at n.50.

79 ACUS Rec. 71-4 Minimum Procedures for Agencies Administering Discretionary Grant Programs, para. 2, Development of Criteria by Rulemaking, and supporting study by Kurzman, 2 ACUS 181, 185.

80 ACUS Rec. 71-3 Articulation of Agency Policies, and supporting report, 2 ACUS 175; Rec. 71-4 *supra*, n.65, para. 1, Public Notice; Rec 74-2, Procedures for Discretionary Distribution of Federal Assistance, and supporting study by Gilhooley, 3 ACUS 422.

81 ACUS Rec. 71-4, *supra*, n.79, para. 3, Avoidance of Conflict of Interest; *Settle and Yamada, The Award Process, 59, 66.

82 *See* ACUS Rec. 71-4, *supra*, n.79.

 

the usual federal procurement competition which requires that the lowest price bid by a responsive responsible bidder be accepted.[83] Grant goals are not necessarily best served by market competition as to price. The identity of the applicant, its need sometimes more than its ability, the importance of its acquisition of capacity that it does not have, its creativeness, its enthusiasm, and other factors may be more important then its ability to underbid rivals.

-- Award. Technical questions of appropriations law and of revocability may attend the question of precisely when, or by what act, a grant is made. It is rare that this question is directly considered by Congress and it is not essential that it be considered. Confusion may, however, result from inadvertent tampering with the process.

-- Renewal. Once a grant has been made, there may be some expectation of renewed awards, perhaps some equity of renewal. There is a general trend toward recognizing, at least by favorable procedural treatment, the expectation of renewal. Congress has sometimes reflected this trend. In some instances, Congress has explicitly denied an expectation of renewal. In any case, it is well for drafters to inform themselves of the pattern of grant-making that exists in practice in the particular field. For example, in medical research it is common to anticipate three, five, or seven years of renewals as normal for a major undertaking. For technical considerations of appropriations law (an agency is generally forbidden to make a commitment of future appropriations), the agency makes as clear as it can that while it contemplates future awards to permit say a seven year project to be completed (assuming the availability of funds, satisfaction with grantee's effort, and no serious change of circumstance) it does not make a present commitment to make further awards. This is a difficult line to walk gracefully. Courts have not always understood.[84] An occasional error on the

[83]The Job Training Partnership Act, Sec. 402, dealing with migrant and seasonal farmworker programs calls for procedures consistent with standard competitive government procurement policies. This appears to reflect a misunderstanding of the considerations referred to in the text. *See* *Current Developments, Vol. 21, no. 2, Winter 1986 at p. 14.

[84]An instance of such failure of a court to understand is *Southern Mutual Health Association v. Califano*, 574 F.2d 518 (D.C. Cir. 1977). Contrast *Missouri Health and Medical Association v. United States*, 641 F.2d 870 (Ct. Cl. 1981). For detailed discussion of the problem, *see* Missouri Health and Medical Organization, HEW DGAB Docket No. 77-24, Rejection

 

part of the agency has helped to reinforce misunderstanding. If statutes are not to create or increase confusion, it is desirable that drafters writing statutes in this field be aware of the mechanics of the system.

It is well to consider, in planning a grant statute significant differences in the style of activity intended. Grant statutes that contemplate construction of facilities will be and should be different from those offering services to a specified population. Grant statutes encouraging basic research, applied research, social research demonstration projects, or providing general support to institutions, or other activities will all be different. The more the drafter understands of the structure and practices in the field in which the grant is made, the better the draft is likely to be, even if there should be no explicit incorporation of such knowledge. Sometimes knowledge aids a drafter in not thinking that knowledge isn't needed.

### Sec. 11. Conditions of assistance

Most conditions of assistance are imposed by agency regulations but a number are set forth by statute, particularly those that are called "cross-cutting" conditions which apply to all grants or broad classes of grants. An example of a condition framed to fit a particular grant program is the Nurse Education provision for recapture of funds granted for construction of facilities which then cease to be used for the training purposes for which they were intended, or are then used for sectarian instruction or religious worship, or cease to be owned by a public or nonprofit school.[85]

In the case of foreign assistance, it is not considered possible or not considered tactful to impose conditions explicitly on foreign independent sovereigns. Accordingly, a virtual condition is imposed: the result is sought to be reached in a more round-about way by directing the

---

of Appeal, June 21, 1978, pp. 5-6 and 8-9; Group Health Association of Northeastern Minnesota, HEW DGAB Docket No. 79-62, Rejection of Appeal, September 7, 1979, pp. 3, 7-9; Southeast Philadelphia Community Corporation, HEW DBAG Docket No. 79-75, Rejection of Appeal, September 24, 1979, pp. 2-5; Mason and Dembling, *Federal Grant Litigation*, 30 THE PRACTICAL LAWYER No. 7, October 15, 1985, pp. 55, 57-59. To avoid possible misunderstanding, I wish to note that I was not a member of the DGAB when its Chairman made the decision reversed in Southern Mutual Health, nor did I draft the regulation there misconstrued by the Court.

[85]P.L. 99-92, the Nurse Education Amendments of 1985, Title VIII, amending 42 U.S.C. 296c.

 

President or the Secretary of State to assure that the foreign government complies with the intended condition, without expressly imposing a condition on the recipient.[86]

Cross-cutting conditions, applying to all grants or some wide category of grants cover such matters as public employee standards (the Hatch Act on partisan political activity was an early example of a cross-cutting condition),[87] availability of records, labor standards, environmental protection, and rules against discrimination in programs funded in part by federal grants.[88]

Conditions imposed by statute are often reinforced by requiring the grantee to sign an "assurance" of compliance. This may serve the purpose of compelling articulate awareness of the condition, but may also create some

---

[86] *E.g.* P.L. 99-8, The African Famine Relief and Recovery Act of 1985, provides for grants to private and voluntary organizations and international organizations for famine relief. Sec. 5(c) is what I call a virtual condition that the foreign government of the countries to which aid is directed shall not allow assistance to be diverted to other purposes or other population groups than those intended. This is expressed by a requirement: "That the President shall ensure that adequate procedures have been established so that assistance pursuant to this Act is provided to the famine victims for whom it is intended." *Cf.* 22 U.S.C. 2394a: a virtual condition that the officials of the recipient country shall not extort or receive improper payments. If they do, the President when he learns of it is to report the fact to Congress with "a recommendation...as to whether the United States should continue a security assistance program for that country." *Cf. also* 22 U.S.C. 2370(c), no assistance to a country that does not pay its debts to a United States person (unless the President finds otherwise on national security grounds); (e) suspension of assistance to nations that nationalize or expropriate American property, repudiate American contracts or impose discriminatory taxes or exactions or conditions (unless the President grants a waiver for reasons of American national interest); (h) foreign aid not to be used to assist Communist-bloc activities; (i) or preparing for aggressive military efforts; (j) the President shall consider terminating assistance where there is destruction of United States property; (o) consideration to excluding countries which seize or impose sanctions against United States fishing vessels fishing in international waters; (q) or default in principal or interest payments on loans (unless the President decides otherwise on national interest grounds); Sec. 2371, the President shall terminate assistance to any government which grants sanctuary to international terrorists (unless he finds national security to require otherwise).

[87] *Oklahoma v. United States Civil Service Commission*, 330 U.S. 127 (1942).

[88] An inventory of cross-cutting requirements, including both statutory and non-statutory provisions, is set out in OMB, Managing Federal Assistance in the 1980s (Report pursuant to the Federal Grant and Cooperative Agreement Act of 1977 (P.L. 95-224) p. 20 ff. This inventory is also set out in *Cappalli, App. 11-B, following his discussion of grant conditions.

 

ambiguity about the source of authority for enforcement--is it the underlying statutory conditions or the assurance.[89]

Some questions to be considered in drafting statutory provisions for grant conditions:

-- Is a statutory provision necessary? Is the matter not one that can be safely and more efficiently left to agency rule-making?

-- Is the matter not already covered by a general statute? For example, there is a general statute against discrimination in grant programs on grounds of race, color, or national origin.[90] If a new grant statute provides its own provision on the subject (more than a mere incorporation of the general rule by reference) it runs the danger of implying that the general rule does not apply. The specific provision will often be less detailed, less balanced by necessary qualifications. Its presence in the statute may thus defeat its own purpose.[91]

### Sec. 12. Accountability, audit, monitoring provisions

When monies of the United States go to grantees for the purposes of a grant program, it is a legitimate concern of the Congress that they be used for the intended grant purposes, not diverted to other improper purposes, nor even diverted to purposes proper in themselves but different from those contemplated by the grant conditions.[92]

---

[89]*See* •Cappalli 11.22 "-- Coutu-Type Grant Strings." *Universities Research Ass'n v. Coutu*, 450 U.S. 754 (1981), held that Davis-Bacon Act does not confer upon an employee a private right of action for back wages under a contract that has been administratively determined not to call for Davis-Bacon work and which therefore does not contain a prevailing wage stipulation. Reading the case very broadly, •Cappalli uses the expression"-- Coutu-Type Grant Strings" to refer to grant conditions which are not enforceable unless expressly included in the grant documents, in contrast with conditions that are enforceable by strength of the statute imposing them.

[90]P.L. 88-352, Title VI, 42 U.S.C. 2000d *et seq.*

[91]The Job Training Partnership Act is an example of this danger. *See* •Current Developments, Vol. 21, No. 2, Winter 1986, pp. 13-14 and Vol. 23, No. 1, Fall 1987, pp. 8, 19-20. *Cf.* •Grant Rulemaking, pp. 48-49 on the "Pucinski" amendment, which created problems for the same reason: displacement of a well-constructed general statute (the APA) by an incompletely thought out provision covering some of the same ground.

[92]Grantees charged with improper expenditures often argue that the money, although diverted, was nevertheless used for good purposes broadly consistent with the policies of the statute. Although this argument may be heeded in a doubtful case, and may moderate the sanction, it is generally unavailing as a defense where the violation is clear. In State of Minnesota

 

In order to protect the integrity of such grant expenditures, there are general statutes assuring the maintenance of appropriate records (while discouraging excessive record keeping requirements), and access of appropriate government representatives (the Comptroller General, and the various agency Inspectors General), and requiring audits and inspections and reports to be made and submitted by certain major grantees.[93] In addition, specific grant programs often have provisions calling for similar or specially tailored audit and monitoring procedures.[94] Self-auditing and self-evaluation are often used in grant programs.[95] This is a useful device. Drafters should be aware, however, that too often reports are required but never used.[96]

Some considerations in drafting accountability provisions:

---

Department of Public Welfare, HEW DGAB Docket No. 75-15, Decision No. 26, August 17, 1976, the State conceded that funds awarded under the Crippled Children's Services Program for Year B were expended for Year A services in violation of the Federal Health Grants Manual incorporated by reference in the grant. The State argued, however, that all grant monies were used for Crippled Children's Services expenses. The Board rejected this argument, noting that the requirements

> relating to the use of current year grant funds for current year services are not arbitrary bureaucratic devices for Federal meddling in state service programs. The purpose of this requirement, simply stated, is to try to insure, in a world in which there are simply not enough funds available to provide all necessary services to all children or other persons in need, a rational process by which funds which are available are allocated to priority needs as identified by the grantee agencies... A failure by a grantee to plan and monitor its projected expenditures by reference to a set of articulated priorities within fiscal year limitations as to available funds will likely lead to expenditures benefitting some with lesser needs at the expense of others with greater needs.

[93]31 U.S.C. 6503 (b) (records of grants to States); former 7107(c) and (d) (joint management funds, expired February 3, 1985 pursuant to 7112); 7304 (availability of records - block grants; P.L. 95-452, the Inspector General Act of 1978, as amended, 5 U.S.C. App. 6; the Single Audit Act of 1984, 31 U.S.C. 7501 *et seq.*; OMB Circular A-128 (1985); *see* Paperwork Reduction Act, P.L. 96-511, as amended, 44 U.S.C. 3501-3520 (1982), esp. 3502(4) and (16), and 3504, ACUS, Federal Administrative Procedure Sourcebook (1985) 771 *ff.*

[94]*E.g.*, 42 U.S.C. 1785 (Child Nutrition, participating institutions shall keep accounts and records which shall be available for inspection); 42 U.S.C. 4592 (Alcohol Abuse, recipients shall keep records which shall be available to the Secretary and the Comptroller General).

[95]*See* •Current Trends, 35 Fed. Bar J. at 185 (XIII. Increasing Use of Grantee Self-Evaluation).

[96]*See* •Monitoring Grantee Performance, 84 n.15, 16.

 

(1) If a general statute covers the matter, enacting a specific provision in a specific grant program may be undesirable. If there is an applicable Single Audit Act, why put an audit provision in a statute providing grants to States? The result may be confusion. There may be an implication that the general Single Audit Act does not apply. The specific provision may lack balancing qualifications that the Single Audit Act worked out.

(2) Is the matter not safely left to agency rule making?

(3) If a provision is desirable in spite of the preceding points, is it written with a realistic understanding of the practices of the field and of what is obtainable and necessary from grantees that have well-established accounting systems of their own or well-established disdain or lack of competence for otherwise normal record-keeping.[98]

### Sec. 13. Sanctions and incentives

When monitoring of grant performance shows violations of grant terms, there is a panoply of possible response to use. A grant statute may direct some of these or may encourage flexible response by the agency. The drafter should be aware of possible alternatives.

A first response should often be the offering of help by the agency to the grantee to help grantee set its house in order. This may be very informal. When it is more formal it is sometimes called technical assistance and sometimes capacity building. Authorization of such assistance is often desirable.

---

[97]P.L. 98-502, the Single Audit Act of 1984, 31 U.S.C. 7501 *ff.* requires states and local governments receiving sufficiently large grants to have an audit made meeting certain standards.

[98]The academic world, for example, finds it very artificial to make records that purport to distribute the time of a researcher to specific projects. Creative work does not readily fall into specific boxes of time. A researcher working on ten projects does not dream and let his imagination range from 9:15 to 10 A.M., prepare to teach from 10:15 to 11, work on project A from 11:15 to 12, teach from 1:15 to 2 and work on project B from 2:15 to 3. Efforts to make the researcher report his time in such units create friction and do not work. OMB Circular A-21, in its earlier form especially, has lead to much academic protest. *See, e.g.*, *BARNES & CATTELL, Grants to Educational Institutions, 245, esp. at 257, Impact of Federal Grant-Related Regulations on the Recipient Institutions; Thomas, *Reporting of Faculty Time: An Accounting Perspective*, 215 SCIENCE (January 1982) 27. Physicians, similarly, are often accustomed to instructing nurses to make certain file entries. It is difficult to discipline them into making the entries by their own hand.

 

Further informal enforcement techniques include reproof and warning. These generally do not require explicit statutory authorization. A further step might be public disclosure of deficiencies and of appropriate corrective action.[99]

More formal action includes:

-- disallowance of costs improperly incurred may be imposed and the funds involved withheld or recovered.[100] A form of sanction peculiarly suited to grants that are normally renewed is an adjustment of next year's grant to take account of improper spending in this year's grant.[101]

-- additional reporting requirements or other grant conditions on the grant may be imposed, for example, the requirement of a countersignature on checks, or a limitation on the rate of withdrawal of funds. Such additional grant conditions may not generally be imposed on a current grant without grantee's consent unless the power to do so has been expressly reserved in the original grant or is expressly conferred by

---

[99]ACUS Rec. 71-9, Enforcement of Standards in Federal Grant-in-aid programs, D. Range of Sanctions, and supporting study by Professors Tomlinson and Mashaw, 2 ACUS 531. But note Rec. 73-1 urging restraint and caution in the use of adverse agency publicity, and supporting study by Professor E. Gellhorn, 3 ACUS 17, 67.

[100]This should be obvious but it has been controversial at least until the Debt Collection Act, P.L. 97-365, P.L. 98-167, ACUS, Federal Administrative Procedure Sourcebook (1985) 211 *ff.* An indication of the controversy and misunderstanding on this point is *State of New Jersey, Dept. of Ed. v. Hufstedler*, 662 F.2d 208 (3rd Cir., October 13, 1981, *reh. den.* December 17, 1981), *reversed and remanded, Bell v. New Jersey*, 461 U.S. 773, May 31, 1982, discussed in •Current Developments, Vol. 17, No. 3, Spring 1982, pp. 3, 10; Vol. 19, No. 2, Winter 1984, p. 16.

[101]The Economic Opportunity Act, as amended by the Economic Opportunity Amendments of 1967, Sec. 243 (then 42 U.S.C. 2835) authorized as one alternative in disallowance cases "a commensurate increase in the required non-Federal share of the costs of any grant or contract with the same agency or organization which is then in effect or which is entered into within twelve months after the date of disallowance." *See* Sencland Community Action, Inc., HEW DGAB Decision No. 21, June 25, 1976, pp. 2-3; Head Start of New Hanover County, Inc., Decision No. 65, September 26, 1979. In a number of mandatory grant statutes, the grantee receives an advance quarterly payment based on an estimate. This amount may then be adjusted in a later quarter when the new estimate will be "reduced or increased to the extent of any overpayment or underpayment ...for any quarter." Overpayments may result from inaccurate forecasting, of course, but apparently may also result from violations of grant terms. *See* Minnesota Department of Human Services, HHS DGAB Decision No. 653, June 7, 1985.

 

statute.[102] The inclusion of such authorization in a statute should not lightly be adopted however. It is not recommended because it would impair, in most cases excessively, the autonomy of the grantee, tending to make it illusory.

-- additional conditions may, when appropriate, be added to the next award to the grantee instead of to the current grant.

-- where necessary, in the case of serious violations, and particularly if there is reason to anticipate further serious violations, there may be a termination of the current award for cause.[103]

-- suspending the grant is possible in urgent cases pending a determination; this should normally be understood not as an alternative sanction but as a procedural step similar to a temporary injunction[104]

-- in sufficiently serious cases, a grantee, or specified personnel of the grantee, may be debarred for a period of time from receiving (or working on) future grants.[105]

-- specific performance or mandatory injunction is rarely if ever appropriate. This recommendation is, however, controversial.[106]

-- a criminal sanction may appropriately be included for certain classes of violation that merit it.[107]

---

[102]*Pennhurst State School & Hospital v. Halderman*, 451 U.S. 1, 25, 101 S.Ct. 1531, 1544 (1981): "Through Congress' power to legislate under the Spending Power is broad, it does not include surprising states with post-acceptance or 'retroactive' conditions." *See* *Current Developments, Vol. 18, No. 1, Fall 1982, 17-18 (Openness in Government: HHS Won't Explain); No. 2, Winter 1983, 6 (Openness in Government: HHS Still Won't Explain); No. 3, Spring 1986, 6.13 (Openness in Government: HHS Is Not Going to Explain).

[103]For cause: Grants should not be terminated for the convenience of the government. The assertion of a power to do that would make the grant essentially illusory. *See* *Current Trends, 35 FED. BAR J., at 167 n.25.

[104]A suspension should normally be prospective. *See* discussion of this point in National Urban Indian Council, HHS DGAB Decision No. 710, December 5, 1985.

[105]E.O. No. 12549, February 18, 1986, 51 FR 6730. In the case of violations of non-discrimination provisions, 42 U.S.C. 2000 d-1 contains a limited debarment provision.

[106]*See* Ch. II, n.8. *See* *Current Trends, at 167 n. 24 ("I. The Black Letter Law"), 177-279 ("Increased Federal Controls"), 179 ("VIII. Irradiation of the Supremacy Clause). ACUS Rec. 71-9, Enforcement of Standards in Federal grant-in-Aid Programs, D, Range of Sanctions, lists injunctive action to require fulfillment of "assurances". The authority for this and its appropriateness is questionable and in any case limited. *But see* Tomlinson and Mashaw, *supra* n.99..

[107]General statutes in this area include 18 U.S.C. 201-224 (bribery, conflicts of interest), 231 (false claims), 245 (intimidation), 286

 

-- civil penalties or reductions of assistance may be imposed.[108]

-- graded partial sanctions, such as diminution of the rate of federal financial participation, may be used as sanctions for unsatisfactory performance.[109]

-- a counterpart to graded sanctions is the holding out of incentives for sound performance and good results.[110]

---

(conspiracy to defraud the United States), 287 (false claims, again), 1001 (false statements). Examples of criminal provisions for specific grant statutes are 18 U.S.C. 874 (kickbacks in construction grant programs), 42 U.S.C. 1396 h (b) (kickbacks, bribes or rebates in Medicaid programs). The history of Congressional action providing explicit criminal provisions for specific grant statutes argues against construing general statutes broadly to reach grant programs not clearly covered by them, contrary to the result reached in *Dixson v. United States*, 465 U.S. 482, 104 S.Ct. 1172 (1984) which applied, on an interpretation of supposed Congressional intent, a general statute against bribery of "public officials" to the bribery of employees of a non-profit corporation sub-grantee of a city receiving a housing grant, calling them "public officials." The bribery, of course, could and should have been punishable under state law and perhaps under 18 U.S.C. 286 and 1001. •Current Developments Vol. 21, No. 3, Spring 1986, 14-15. This is an area where it may be appropriate for Congress to express its intent more strongly, perhaps by a general statute.

[108]*See* ACUS Rec. 72-6, Civil Money Penalties as a Sanction, and supporting study by Professor Goldschmid, 2 ACUS 896. This recommendation does not intend to cover grants (*ibid.* 67 n.4) but *cf.* Rec. 71-9, *supra*, on Grant-in-Aid programs. *See also* Rec. 79-3, Agency Assessment and Mitigation of Civil Money Penalties and supporting study by Diver, 1979 ACUS 203. Provisions for reduction of the level of assistance as a sanction for violations of conditions come close to the civil penalty notion. Thus highway assistance may be reduced in amount if a state highway official takes an active role in partisan on politics, or if the state's laws permit minors to buy liquor. *See* discussion of *South Dakota v. Dole*, ___U.S.___, 107 S.Ct 2793 (1987) and *Oklahoma v. United States Civil Service Commiss.*, 380 U.S. 172 (1947) in •Current Developments, Vol. 23, No. 1, Fall 1987, p. 8 (*A Right to Drive Alcoholized*). *See also* next footnote on graded sanctions.

[109]The Medicaid program requires grantees to maintain an effective program of medical review. In the absence of a satisfactory showing of such a program, federal financial participation in the costs of the program ("FFP") is reduced according to a formula set out in 1903(g)(5) of the Social Security Act, 42 U.S.C. 1396b(g)(5). A sample calculation of this reduced FFP is set out in Arkansas Department of Human Services, HHS DGAB Decision No. 735, March 28, 1986. *See* •Current Trends, at 178 n.94.

[110]*See* ACUS Rec. 71-9, Part E ("Other Performance Incentives") and supporting study by Professors Tomlinson and Mashaw, 2 ACUS 531, esp. at 622. *See* 29 U.S.C. 1602 (Job Training Partnership Act, 6% of State allotment to be used by the Governor to provide incentive grants for programs exceeding performance standards). *Cf. also* 1582 (Presidential awards for outstanding achievement by the private sector). Under the Medicaid program, states are required to enforce third-party liabilities, thereby diminishing the government costs of the program. An incentive of

 

-- transfer of grants from an offending grantee to another.[111]

Some considerations in the drafting of sanctions and incentives provisions:

(1) Sanctions in grant programs usually punish the wrong people. If a state violates Medicaid rules, for example, will you cut off the State? It is the indigent sick who will be hurt.[112]

(2) The agency may need flexibility to compromise and use indirection. Suppose that the world's greatest bio-medical researcher, who has developed early tests for major diseases and developed vaccines for some of them, simply will not, cannot, keep neat books; there is no thought that funds are improperly diverted, but time, money, property, just are not regularly and properly recorded, -- do you want the agency to refuse to fund him and lose for the world the research he is outstandingly capable of performing? A statute could direct that, but it may not be the wisest course. It may be desirable to leave the agency free to cajole, to offer help, to require passing the funds through a mutually satisfactory responsible university, or develop other methods of dealing with this problem case. If, instead of requiring the agency to cut him off, you allow the agency to fund him, but require it to obtain satisfactory records nevertheless, you may find that, to achieve that,

---

15% of such collections is provided for collection efforts made by a political subdivision of the state or by one state for another. 1903(p), 42 U.S.C. 1396b(p). *See* New York State Department of Social Services, HHS DGAB Decision No. 628, March 19, 1985. The purpose and theory of the reduction provision and of amendments to it are discussed in detail in Effect of DEFRA Amendments on Utilization Control Disallowances, HHS DGAB Decision No. 655, June 7, 1985. A similar but perhaps broader incentive is contained in the Aid to Families with Dependent Children, 42 U.S.C. 658(a).

[111]ACUS Rec. 71-9, Part D5.

[112]*See* *Current Trends at 178 n.93. In the context of a Revenue Sharing program (currently not available), Tomlinson and Mashaw make the significant suggestion that sanctions incurred for violation of a categorical program, instead of being applied to that program, be applied to the revenue sharing amount thus assuring continuance of the categorical program but inducing compliance with federal standards, nevertheless, by tightening the purse strings. *Op. cit.*, n.110, at 622. On the general problem of sanctions, Tomlinson and Mashaw note but reject the possible sanctions of authorizing civil or criminal punishment of the individual state or local officials who willfully violate federal standards; federal rating of state or local officials on the basis of compliance, affecting their career opportunities; removal of offending state and local officials; federal take-over and operation of offending programs (this last has been experimented with by OEO and perhaps others.)

 

excessive machinery of control has to be piled on. Room for breathing, a softer approach, may be justified by the interests at stake, and should not be unnecessarily precluded.

(3) In drafting sanctions provisions, remember that you cannot command compliance. You can cut off aid. You can encourage compliance. But ordering compliance may be ordering the tide to halt.

(4) When sanctions are imposed it is important to provide a mechanism for review. This is required by fairness. It is also expedient because, where no review mechanism is provided, affected persons will nevertheless seek to obtain review and courts will be strongly inclined to provide review, making up a mechanism if possible.[113] The costs to the government and the affected public in this unsystemized hunt for a remedy are unnecessarily high.[114]

(5) You can and should recognize the value of incremental change. A pattern that the drafter should have in mind and that the agency should have in mind is this: when unsatisfactory performance is observed on the part of a wide class of grantees, the soundest response is not necessarily to match performance against standards and impose sanctions for shortcomings. Often, dealing with sovereign states or other autonomous grantees, you must recognize the possibility that your standards were not properly set if many grantees do not seem able to comply, and you must be willing, sometimes, to seek not perfect performance but increasingly better performance.[115] Agencies should put in place (none seem yet to have done it)[116] and drafters should encourage, a dynamic process that moves incrementally towards better performance, taking stock of results periodically, recognizing deficiencies, and taking steps that will

---

[113]*See* •Current Trends, *The Blunt Instrument*, 35 FED. BAR J. 163 at 183-4.

[114]ACUS Rec. 82-2 "Resolving Disputes Under Federal Grant Programs"; supporting study, Steinberg, *Federal Grant Dispute Resolution*, MEZINES, STEIN, GRUFF, ADMINISTRATIVE LAW, Ch. 53 & 54. *See infra*, Section 15, Administrative and Judicial Review Provisions.

[115]•Monitoring Grantee Performance p. 82 *ff.* ("Dynamic Process of Grant Management") and 96 *ff.* ("Feedback").

[116]•Current Developments, Vol. 19, No. 3, Spring 1984, p. 8 notes such a process undertaken by Wisconsin to improve incrementally its management of social service grant programs. Federal agencies do not appear to have done so in a systematic way.

 

improve, if not necessarily perfect, grantee's (and agency) performance.

**Sec. 14. Rulemaking power**

Grant statutes should be simple, when that is possible. But even when they go to the opposite extreme (as, for example, the Social Security statutes often do), there is no possibility that even the most elaborately spelled out statutory rules can fully and satisfactorily deal with all the problems that will be confronted in the administration of the statute. The Congressional work load is too great to permit the full elaboration of rules by Congress. It is not likely that many members of Congress will have the necessary expertise in the substantive problems of a particular, often very technical, field (nor is there any reason why they should have -- they have a quite different task). There are often cross-currents of thought about what relatively are details which, if they were to be definitively articulated in the bill itself, could prevent enactment of a statute that both sides regard as desirable. The operation of a statute after its enactment almost always discloses problems that were not and could not be anticipated. The Congress is too unwieldy a body to respond quickly and flexibly to unforeseen problems of application. That is what the administrative agency is there for.

It is thus desirable that after defining goals as clearly as possible and suggesting approaches as strongly as possible, the writing of specific substantive rules be left to the agency. It is so obvious that an agency charged with administering a grant program should have such rulemaking power that the power ought to be presumed even if not expressed. Since the making of substantive rules is seen as a delegation of legislative power, however, it is not safe to rely on that obvious need. A grant statute should contain an express authority to make rules.

The authority to the agency to make substantive rules can, and ordinarily should, be granted in very simple terms. A complicated structure of rulemaking authorization invites litigation.[117] Sometimes much more elaborate provisions or

---

[117]Professor Mullins, commenting on a draft of this book, letter to Charles Pou, Jr., ACUS, February 12, 1988, calls attention to *In re Permanent Surface Min. Regulation Litigation*, 653 F.2d 514 (D.C. Cir. 1981). The authority to "publish and promulgate such rules and regulations as may be necessary to carry out the purposes and provisions of this Act" was sufficient, but parties challenging the rulemaking were able to point to twenty-one specific rulemaking provisions. These provisions, authorizing particular topics or kinds of rules, supported a colorable, although in the

 

more stringent provisions are imposed.[118] While these may be needed, their possible disadvantages are worth a second thought before they are used. Among these additional provisions are the following:

-- "Pucinski-type" provisions that require publication of proposed rules.[119] Publication is already required by the Administrative Procedure Act with careful qualifications. Duplicating the APA with all the qualifications should be unnecessary, while duplicating it without all the qualifications may be unwise.[120]

-- "Wait-and-see" provisions that require submission of proposed rules to Congressional committees may serve as substitutes for the legislative veto, which has

---

end rejected, argument that the agency's substantive rulemaking power was limited to the more specific provisions. *See, supra,* section 4, "Definitions--Anticipate Litigation."

[118]P.L. 96-294, the Energy Security Act, June 30, 1980, 94 Stat 611 illustrates both the simple and the (perhaps unnecessarily) complex.

Professionally simple: 260, adds a new title XX to the Food and Agriculture Act of 1977. Section 2001 [7 U.S.C. 1435] (a) 12) "The Secretary [of Agriculture] may issue any regulations necessary to carry out the provisions of this subsection."

Inflated: 408 (d), referring to small-scale hydropower initiatives, "The Secretary [of Energy] shall take such action as may be necessary to assure the establishment *** of such rules and regulations as may be necessary to fully implement his responsibilities under title IV of the Public Utility Regulatory Policies Act of 1978 and the amendments thereto made by this section.

Less simple: 520, relating to financial assistance for solar energy systems, "***the Board [of Directors of the Solar Energy and Energy Conservation Bank in the Department of Housing and Urban Development] shall issue such final rules and regulations as the Board determines are necessary to carry out this subtitle, including rules and regulations to assure that there will be no fraud in the provision of financial assistance through grants under this subtitle***."

Complex: 565 adds to the National Energy Conservation Policy Act a new section 712 consisting of some 30 lines of print authorizing rules on the content and implementation of state energy conservation plans for commercial buildings and multifamily dwellings. Publication and opportunity for comments and a delay of publication of final rules of 45 days from publication of proposed rules are required. The last two lines are again quite simple: "The Secretary [of Energy] may prescribe any other rules necessary to carry out the provisions of this title." Little if anything more seems necessary.

[119]Amendments sponsored by Rep. Roman Pucinski to many grant statutes required advance publication of rules and guidelines. There are several versions of the basic provision. *See* •Grant Rule Making, at 48 n.16 and 49 n.18. Sky, *Rulemaking in the Office of Education,* 26 AD. L. REV. 129, 131 (1974); Sky, *Rulemaking and the Federal Grant Process in the United States Office of Education,* 62 VA. L. REV. 1017, 1019 n.7.

[120]•Grant Rule Making at 48-49.

 

now been generally recognized as invalid in view of the Supreme Court's opinion in *Chadha* and its decisions in a string of related cases.[121]

-- Provisions that require identifying the agency's source of authority. Such identification is often called for by good practice. When, however, it is made a blanket requirement, it is often honored in a perfunctory way that serves no useful purpose and defeats the intention of the statute.[122]

-- Provisions that require rules to be published within a specific period of time. These provisions are sometimes a response to an agency's failure to issue rules with reasonable promptness.[123] The agency may need and perhaps deserve the pressure, but often such requirements are an over-reaction. It may be impossible for the agency to comply, it distracts limited resources to this task from possibly more valuable tasks, and it encourages the drafting of rules that are not as well thought out as they should be.

Major general statutes that govern the issuance of rules and that ordinarily do not require reduplication include the APA,[124] the Regulatory Flexibility Act,[125] and the Paper Work Reduction Act.[126]

### Sec. 15. Administrative and judicial review provisions

-- *Administrative*

If a person dealing with the government feels ill-treated, the government should provide a readily accessible recourse to resolve the disagreement if possible. This is especially the case in the field of grant law since a characteristic of the grant process is its reliance on the enthusiasm of the grantee, an enthusiasm that will be dampened if a feeling is permitted to grow that grantees may be ill-treated without

[121] ACUS, Legislative Veto of Agency Rules After INS v. Chadha, (1984).

[122] *Grant Rulemaking, at 49.

[123] *Ibid.* ACUS, A Guide to Federal Agency Rulemaking (1983) 85. ACUS Rec. 78-3, Time Limits on Agency Actions, and supporting study by Tomlinson, Report on the Experience of Various Agencies with Statutory Time Limits Applicable to Licensing or Clearance Functions and to Rulemaking, 1978 ACUS 119, esp. at 233 *ff.*

[124] 5 U.S.C. 551-554. ACUS Federal Administrative Procedure Sourcebook (1985) 3 *ff.*

[125] 5 U.S.C. 601-612. Sourcebook 901 *ff.*

[126] 44 U.S.C. 3501-3520. Sourcebook 771 *ff.*

 

recourse. Grantor agencies should furnish a recourse, informal by preference, readily accessible and seen to be fair, independent and knowledgeable.[127]

It is not essential that the recourse be provided by explicit statute. Agency rule-making authority is sufficient basis for establishing a resolution process. The best model was created without statute.[128]

Congress has, however, in many cases, preferred to provide explicitly for the establishment of such mechanisms. These range from fairly general provisions for "reconsideration" or "hearing"[129] to establishment of a specific institution with detailed provisions for its make-up, powers, and procedures.[130]

Agencies are generally aware, or should be, that the absence of an acceptable mechanism not only impairs the grantor-grantee cooperation that is desirable, but encourages resort to the courts with resulting costs of litigation in time and manpower and decision by a tribunal necessarily less sensitive and aware of the goals and difficulties of the program. The existence of a mechanism that is seen to be fair and informed encourages courts to feel less compelled to accept jurisdiction or, if they do, then to review on a standard that gives greater weight to the administrative result. An agency that is not prepared to stand the test of informed independent review within its own house impairs the quality of its own work and invites more strenuous judicial supervision.

In planning a disputes resolution provision, it is important to distinguish types of dispute. These are most readily recognized by considering the time line on which they occur: pre-award disputes, post-award disputes, renewal disputes.

---

[127]Rec. 82-2, "Resolving Disputes under Federal Grant Programs," and supporting study Steinberg, *Federal Grant Dispute Resolution* in MEZINES, STEIN, GRUFF, ADMINISTRATIVE LAW, ch. 53 & 54. *See supra*, Section 13, Sanctions and Incentives, text at n.113.

[128]HEW DGAB, created by Secretary Weinberger and placed, for independence, in the Office of the Under Secretary. The author, having been the first full time Chairman of the Board, acknowledges a bias but believes this represents a consensus of informed opinion. Wallick and Chamblee, *Bridling the Trojan Horse*, 4 JOUR. OF COLL. AND UNIV. LAW 241 (1978) at 277.

[129]42 U.S.C. 1316 (Social Security Act), (a)(2) "reconsideration" with "hearing" for conformity issues, (d) "reconsideration" for disallowance issues; in fact HHS provides a hearing for both.

[130]P.L. 95-561, Nov. 1, 1978, Sec. 1232 established the Education Appeal Board. P.L. 100-297, sec. 3501, April 28, 1988, substituted an Office of Administrative Law Judges.

 

Pre-Award Award Post-Award Renewal

(1) Pre-award disputes are primarily of the type: "we should have gotten a grant and didn't." Occasionally they are of the type: "they should not have gotten a grant and did." If all such disputes were to be afforded statutory review, the burden would be enormous since the number of applicants for grants far exceed the number of grants that can be made. In limited areas, however, Congress has provided review mechanisms.[131] Short of full review, there are the possibilities of lesser recourse such as provisions for announcement of standards and priorities and disclosure of reasons, where assignable, for making or not making an award[132] (complicated by problems of protecting the confidentiality of comments by peer reviewers).[133]

(2) Post-award disputes may concern such matters as refusal to grant a waiver that grantee has applied for, disallowances of costs alleged to be incurred in violation of grant terms, voiding or terminating a grant for serious deficiency in the application or performance. These are the primary concerns of most grant dispute resolution processes.

(3) Renewal disputes depend on the increasingly strong recognition of an expectation that grants of a renewable kind will be renewed, absent strong grounds to the contrary: the Head Start program is an example.[134]

Each of these three types of disputes brings special considerations into play that should not be ignored.

Some considerations in planning a statutory grants disputes resolution process:

(1) Should there be a statutory provision at all, or anything more than a broad authorization? Cannot the matter be safely left to the agency?

---

[131] Steinberg, *op. cit., supra,* n.127, 53.02 [3][a] n.25 notes that the Department of Justice and the Legal Services Corporation have such pre-award review. There are others, *e.g.*, the Job Training Partnership Act, 29 U.S.C. 1576, 1578.

[132] ACUS Rec. 71-4, Minimum Procedures for Agencies Administering Discretionary Grant Programs, and supporting study by Kurzman 2 ACUS 181; Rec. 74-2, Procedures for Discretionary Distribution of Federal Assistance, and supporting study, by Gilhooley, 3 ACUS 422.

[133] *See Wu v. National Endowment for Humanities*, 460 F.2d 1030 (5th Cir. 1972).

[134] 42 U.S.C. 9836(c), 9841(3).

 

(2) If there is to be a provision, how much detail is necessary or wise?

(3) While establishment of a process is healthy and desirable, imposition of statutory rules may force procedures too costly and often too formal for the benefits. Weigh this in considering the requirements that are to be imposed.

(4) A requirement for more than very informal discussion of the denial of discretionary grants may quickly overwhelm the agency's resources.

(5) Expectations of renewal are, appropriately, getting stronger over a long time-span, but disputes concerning disappointed expectations should be recognized as different in kind from terminations and other sanctions for grantee misconduct.

(6) Independence of the Board or other disputes-resolution institution is important. Legislation can perhaps encourage it, but there is little that legislation can do to assure it. Unless the value of independence is perceived by agency heads and effectively protected by them, it will not happen. The ALJ model, however useful in other contexts, while it protects independence, invites the very things that grant dispute resolution should seek to avoid: judicialization, overformalism, hearing officials' lack of commitment to and understanding of the goals of the program.[135]

(7) A disputes resolution process can be a precious resource for spotting the areas of administration that give rise to the "hospital cases." This opportunity for recognizing deficiencies and preventing them in the future should not be wasted by agency policy makers nor by Congressional oversight committees. Avoid writing appeals provisions that so emphasize a quasi-judicial character of agency grant appeals boards as to preclude their contribution to good policy making.[136]

-- *Judicial*

---

[135]*See* Mason, *Administrative Law -- Reality or Red Tape?*, 40 RIVISTA JURIDICA DE LA UNIVERSIDAD DE PUERTO RICO 91 (1971).

[136]*See* •Monitoring grantee performance 79, 98. *Cf.* ACUS Rec. 87-7, A New Role for the Social Security Appeal Council, and supporting study by Koch and Koplow, *The Fourth Bite at the Apple: A Study of the Operation and Utility of the Social Security Administration's Appeals Council*, 1987 ACUS Vol. I, 625, esp. at 748, "What is important to the traditional structure of the typical government agency, however, is a self-conscious appellate authority, which deliberately attempts to look past the run of case-by-case determinations and extrapolate into more generally-applicable policy.".

 

Judicial review of grant disputes will take place whether specifically authorized by the grant statute or not, but there are a number of questions of importance that can be specified by legislation that are often left unclear. Attention to them in drafting a grant statute is worthwhile.

Among these are: Who has standing? If a grant is made (or refused), to X (or made and then terminated), shall X's employees be permitted to obtain review (apart from X itself)?[137] Members of the class of contemplated ultimate beneficiaries of the grant to X (for example, patients in a hospital)?[138] Organizations purporting to represent the class of ultimate beneficiaries? Rival applicants for the same grants? Concerned members of the public? The Supreme Court has commented on a frequent failure of Congress to give guidance on this type of question.[139]

In what court shall review be provided, district court or court of appeals? State court or federal court? It should be remembered that the grantee is ordinarily a creature of state law and in a dispute between grantee and subgrantee or grantee and employee, or grantee and ultimate beneficiary, the primary issues may be state law questions rather than federal grant law questions. State court jurisdiction may sometimes be appropriate.

What level of deference to the administrative action? The Administrative Procedure Act standard (5 U.S.C. 706) is often adequate and drafters' efforts to create special standards of judicial review may create confusion.

What distinctions between review of different types of grant disputes?

There are some general statutes partly covering the field of judicial review: the Administrative Procedure Act, the Debt Collection Act. To what extent do these need supplementation in particular cases?

*-- Disallowance and non-conformity*

When a grantee violates the rules of a grant, expenditures improperly made by the grantee may be disallowed, either by the grantor's refusal, after appropriate notice and opportunity for any appeal provided, to pay the federal

---

137 *Cf. Apter v. Richardson*, 510 F.2d 351 (CA7, 1975).

138 *O'Bannon v. Town Court Nursing Center*, 447 U.S. 773, 100 S.Ct. 2467 (1980).

139 *See, e.g., Guardians Ass'n v. Civ. Serv. Com'n of City of N.Y.*, 463 U.S. 582, 579 and esp. concuring opinion at 608, 103 S.Ct. 3221, 3230, 3236 (1983), quoted *supra*, Ch. I, n.16.

 

share, or by action to recover federal share already advanced. When the grantee violates the rules in fundamental ways, or systematically, or on a large scale, that may constitute a non-conformity of its plan to the statute or a substantial non-conformity of its actions to its plans, and the grantee may be disqualified from participation. In some grant statutes, particularly those that are part of the Social Security Act, this larger disqualification, because its consequences are expected to be more important, are attended with more elaborate procedural protection for the grantee. A disallowance may have "reconsideration" by the Secretary and informal procedures voluntarily offered by the grantor, and a possible recourse to the Federal District Court.[140] A non-conformity may have a statutory provision for "reconsideration" by the Secretary (that is, in practice, by the Secretary's delegate), an express right to a "hearing" and an express right of appeal by petition directly to the Federal Court of Appeal and possible recourse to the United States Supreme Court.[141]

Because of this different level of protection, grantees, challenged for improper expenditure, sometimes take the somewhat paradoxical position: this is not just a little matter of a disallowance, this is the big violation, a non-conformity, therefore the grantor cannot proceed against us just for the improper expenditure.

---

[140] 42 U.S.C. 1316; 45 CFR Part 16, App.A. *See State of Conn., Dept. of Income Main. v. Heckler*, 471 F.2d 1052, 1055 (1984), *aff'd.* 471 U.S. 524, 528, 105 S.Ct. 2210, 2212.

[141] 42 U.S.C. 1316(a)(2), and (3),(4) and (5). *See Gardner v. State of Alabama, Dept of Pensions & Security*, 385 F.2d 804 (CA5 1967) *cert. den.* 389 US to 46 (1968).

It should be noted that the contrast between 42 U.S.C. 1316(a), providing expressly for court review (in the Court of Appeals) and possible recourse to the Supreme Court, and 1316(d), which does not expressly contemplate any court review, gives rise to a possible argument that Congress intended there to be no court review in the case of disallowance under 1316(d). The argument is formally a good one, since it may be said that Congress having the court-review question in its mind pointedly omitted provision for it in subsection (d). The argument is unrealistic, however in view of the large amounts often at stake ($100 million in *Gardner*, which is not unusually large) and the importance of the question to the States and the affected public. This suggests that the omission of reference to court review in subsection (d) may have been a drafting negligence. In any case, the Administrative Procedure Act supplies a remedy. *See* Connecticut case, *supra*, n.140; *Bowen v. Massachusetts*, ___ U.S. ___, 108 S. Ct. 2722 (1988); "Bowen and the Nichomachean Ethic," 24 Pub. Cont. Newsl., No. 2, winter 1989.

 

Wrangling about whether a violation is specific enough to base a disallowance or general enough to base a non-conformity proceeding is non-productive. It is desirable that either a clear test be provided for distinguishing between disallowance and non-conformity, or that the distinction be eliminated, or that grantor (or, if preferred, grantee) be given explicitly the power to determine which set of procedures are to be followed.

**Sec. 16. Provisions for relationship to allied programs**

Good grant programs usually do not stand alone nor should they. If the grant program is for research, there may be and usually are, related research programs carried on by the government in its own laboratories with its own personnel and programs carried on for the government under contract, and possibly also related research carried on without grant support by institutions and businesses outside the government. If the grant program is for a public service, there may be related grant programs supporting research or experimental efforts to improve the service. There may be regulatory controls intended to supplement the encouragement provided by the grant program. There may be efforts at public education to make the results of the service programs or research programs more fruitfully utilized. There may be loans, loan guarantees, tax benefits. It is useful in writing a grant statute to consider the coordination and relationships of these multiple approaches to common goals. Sometimes a coordinating body or authority is provided. Often this is unnecessary, but it is appropriate to consider whether it is desirable and if so, to include statutory provisions.

**Sec. 17. Report to Congress**

It is customary to aid Congressional oversight and public information by requiring the filing of an annual report to Congress.

**Sec. 18. Repealers, saving harmless, severability, sunset and miscellaneous provisions**

A number of miscellaneous provisions are often part of a grant statute: It may be necessary to repeal existing provisions in the same field. If changes are made in the amount of support, there is often a provision saving harmless present recipients now getting more support than they would under the new statute.[142] If there is a possibility that a provision of the statute may be held unconstitutional or otherwise invalid, it is often provided that the remaining provisions of the statute are severable and shall remain in effect.[143] This should not be done, of course, unthinkingly: If the controversial provision is the essence of the statute, it is not necessarily desirable (in the event that it be cut out) to keep the remaining provisions intended merely to support it.

Provisions are often included giving a determined life-span to the program so that it does not automatically perseverate without fresh consideration by the Congress of the value of the authorized program.[144] The danger, here, is that Congress has not always acted within the time limits it has itself set.[145] This leads to severe undesirable strains in the administration of a program which, it may be determined in the end, should continue, but which, because Congress has not acted, could not, in its planning, count on continuation.

---

[142]*See, e.g.,* the Medicaid provisions of the Omnibus Budget Reconciliation Act of 1986, sec. 9421, 100 Stat. 2065, amending sec. 9528 of the Consolidated Omnibus Budget Reconciliation Act of 1985, but providing that during FY 1987 the amendment "shall not apply to a State if the effect of applying the amendments would be to reduce the amount of payment made to the State under that section." *See also* save harmless provisions noted under Section 8, *supra*, allotment formula, n.73.

[143]*E.g.*, 20 U.S.C. 4073 [The Equal Access Act for students who wish to conduct a forum in a school receiving federal financial assistance]: If any provision of this title or the application thereof to any person or circumstances is judicially determined to be invalid, the provisions of the remainder of the title and the application to other persons or circumstances shall not be affected thereby. *Cf.* 42 U.S.C. 4591 (Alcohol Abuse): If any section, provision, or term of this Act is adjudged invalid for any reason, such judgment shall not affect, impair, or invalidate any other section, provision, or term of this Act, and the remaining sections, provisions, and terms shall be and remain in full force and effect.

[144]*E.g.*, P.L. 100-87, Subtitle C - Job Training for the Homeless, 741 "The provisions of this subtitle other than section 740 [Amendments to the Job Training Partnership Act] shall terminate on October 1, 1990."

[145]As of December 21, 1987, the current one-day stop-gap measure funding the government once more came to an end. The newspapers barely mentioned this fact. When they did, they often said that government "technically" comes to a halt. That we can call this a technicality is eloquent of how routine this practice has become. It is no way to run a railroad. OEO, HEW and other agencies over many years have suffered repeated stop-and-go crises that destroy efforts at rational planning because of absence or threatened absence of program authorization renewals and appropriations. *Cf.* *Current Trends, 35 FED. BAR J. at 162, III. Improvements in the Appropriations Process.

 

-- *Check-up periodically on existing statutes*

Because grant programs have grown helter-skelter, it is desirable that existing programs be reviewed from time to time (and that future programs be subject to sunset provisions or to similar review) in order to determine whether the program meets its purposes, whether it is still necessary, and whether changes should be made. Such review is provided for in P.L. 90-577, 601, 602, 603, 31 U.S.C. 6507, 6508, which directs review every 4 years by the appropriate Committees and, on request of an appropriate Committee, by the Comptroller General and the ACIR. Although the statute does not explicitly say so, this review could also be an occasion for improving the draftsmanship of statutes that are retained on the books.[146]

**Sec. 19. Effective date**

It is not necessary but often thought desirable to specify an effective date for the statute.[147] This is most often felt to

[146]Emogene Trexel points out in a letter, March 19, 1986, that

> language in grant statutes can become obsolete over time and through improved practices. For instance, commingling of federal funds used to be prohibited. Now, local governments are required to 'pool' federal funds to avoid unnecessary draw-downs of cash.

This is an example of the kind of thing periodic check-ups should watch out for.

[147]Day certain. P.L. 100-77 (Homeless Assistance, Title VIII, Subtitle A, Sec. 803(b): The Amendment made by this section shall become effective on July 1, 1988.

Discretionary date. *ibid.*, sec 809(b): The amendments made by this section shall become effective and be implemented as soon as the Secretary of Agriculture determines is practicable after the date of enactment of this Act...

Date measured from date of enactment. idem; ...but not later than 160 days after enactment of this Act.

P.L. 100-17, Title IV, the Uniform Relocation Act Amendments of 1987, sec. 418: The amendment made by section 412 of this title (to the extent such amendment prescribes authority to develop, publish, and issue regulations) shall take effect on the date of the enactment of this title. This title and the amendments made by this title (other than the amendment made by section 412 to such extent) shall take effect on the effective date provided in such regulations but not later than 2 years after such date of enactment.

Retroactive. P.L. 100-50, the Higher Education Technical Amendments Act of 1987, approved June 3, 1987, sec. 27: The amendments made by this Act shall take effect as if enacted as part of the Higher Education Amendments of 1986 [which was effective generally on enactment, October 17, 1986].

 

be needed in an amendatory statute. The major trap is that the statute may require various time consuming steps that cannot be accomplished within the time available. This problem may be especially acute for programs that have their own well-established calendar. For example, educational programs often begin in September and commitments are often made the previous spring. It is not helpful to authorize a new program in November or even in August, intended to start that Fall. If grants must be made within a current fiscal year but the statute does not become effective until late in the year, appropriations not fixed until still later, then apportionment, allotment, allocation, notice of availability, publication of proposed rulemaking, final rulemaking, receipt of applications, evaluation of applications, award of grants may require the impossible to be done with indeliberate speed.[148] Drafters should be aware of the problem and avoid it, or perhaps temper the first year's wind to the tender lamb by not requiring impossible action to be completed within the initial year.

## B. SPECIAL CONSIDERATIONS IN DRAFTING AMENDATORY GRANT STATUTES

### -- Leave a track

The fact that a statute is an amendment to an existing statute creates problems of tracking. Consider, for example, the lawyer who has long familiarity with the Federal Grant and Cooperative Agreement Act of 1977, P.L. 95-224, Feb. 3, 1978, 92 Stat. 3, 41 U.S.C. 501. Looking up the text in 41 U.S.C. to focus on a particular problem, he finds a line that says: "Repealed." This is a terrible experience. "What? Repealed? I didn't know that." Of course, he takes a deep breath and studies further and finds that the text, essentially unchanged, is now in 31 U.S.C. Or try the Intergovernmental Cooperation Act of 1968, P.L. No. 90-577, 82 Stat. 1098, 42 U.S.C. 4201 (1976)(?). Look it up in 42 U.S.C.. "Repealed." After a deep breath, you find a piece of it in 31 U.S.C.

Statutes that make small amendments to existing statutes and recompile them, often do not leave as clear a track as they could and should. The reason seems to be a drafter's superstition that it is inelegant to be clear and

148The first year of Head Start was an example of a crash program that worked, but often it will not work. When forced by statute (as was not I believe the case with Head Start) it more often than not will not work. Last minute summer job programs present similar problems.

 

direct. How would it hurt, for example, to replace the statute that has been moved with a bracketed note that says: "[Moved with minor amendments to Title 31]"? An official note, not leaving it to an annotator. It wouldn't hurt and it would help, but drafters seem to believe that there are intrinsic proprieties in drafting that override clarity and helpfulness.

Leave a track.

**-- Is redesignation necessary?**

A more complex problem: if you must repeal a subsection (d), do you redesignate (e) as (d)? If you must insert a new section after subsection (c), do you call the new section (d) and redesignate (d) as (e)? If you do either, you will create confusion for the lawyer who thinks he is familiar with old subsection (d). Peacock, Notes on Legislative Drafting (REC Foundation 1961) would totally scrap the practice of redesignation, and he clearly has a strong point. *Hirsch, 27 points to the "havoc it would create, for example, if section 501(c)(3) of the Internal Revenue Code of 1954, dealing with organizations eligible for exemption from income tax, were periodically redesignated."

Hirsch[149] takes a less extreme view than Peacock. Peacock says, don't redesignate. Hirsch says: "the larger the subdivision and the older the statute the more you should try to avoid redesignation." (p. 28).

**-- An amending statute may need a different approach than an original statute**

Many rules or counsels of good practice in the drafting of free-standing statutes do not apply or do not work the same way when the statute to be drafted is an amendatory statute.

The drafter of an amendment must work with an existing structure. He is not as free as the original drafter in writing what he believes is a logical and understandable structure. If he is not making a comprehensive revision, he must work with the structure he finds.

Curiously, however, as *Hirsch points out (p. 23), organizing an amendment to follow step by step the structure of the original Act may deprive the amending bill

[149] In this section, I draw very freely from *Hirsch's Chapter IV, Amending a Statute, which calls attention clearly and helpfully to many of the problems of the amendatory statute.

 

of internal coherence. If for example one purpose of the amendment is to add one target to a group of targets, it may not be good amending practice to follow the structure of the original Act by (1) amending the Act's "Findings and Purposes", then (2) amending the definitions, then (3) amending the State Plan Requirements, then (4) amending the Research and Demonstration Projects section.

"Ordering those amendments in the bill as they are ordered in the Act," *Hirsch points out, "and separating them from each other by unrelated amendments, will make it difficult to discover the draftsman's purposes and how he carried them out . . . . [S]uch a structure, moreover, may place minor technical amendments in a bill's introductory sections while burying major program changes in the rear.

"Good drafting practice calls for grouping amendments by subject."

*Hirsch recommends a "modular construction," grouping amendments by subject, and shows that it has advantages not only in the clarity of the bill but in the outcome of a bill that may be further amended or may be adopted only in part. (p. 23).

In the case of amendments to a complex statute, it is unlikely that the drafter will be aware of all the places in that statute and in other statutes that involve cross-reference to the section being amended. Hirsch gives the example of section 218 of the Social Security Act, 42 U.S.C. 418 as it stood in 1980, which deals with voluntary agreements for the social security coverage of state and local employees. This section is referred to at least six times in two free-standing public laws, at least eight times in various parts of the Internal Revenue Code, and in at least six other sections or sectional subdivisions buried in a title that runs to several hundred pages. Peacock says, similarly, "But no draftsman can, and, as far as we know, none has even tried to accomplish the impossible task of assuring that he has run down all possible existing citations or references anywhere in the whole wide legal and administrative world." (Peacock, p. 42; *Hirsch, p. 27). Citations, it is true, are now becoming accessible by computer but redesignated sections complicate that approach and less direct reference may elude computer search.

Unless you happen to be an expert in the particular problem both in detail and broad perspective, how do you know whether proposed amendments achieve the results you intend. *Hirsch's advice: "Second Rule of Statutory Construction: CONSULT AN EXPERIENCED PROGRAM ATTORNEY." (p. 22). My amendment to Hirsch's advice:

 

but not after midnight on the eve of mark-up, an unfortunately common practice.

Particularly troublesome are amendments that amend invisibly. *Hirsch gives as a striking example a proposed enlargement of the Poultry Products Inspection Act (71 Stat. 441; 21 U.S.C. 451) which, had it become law, would have made that Act apply to domesticated rabbits without however actually amending the Act. What reader of the Poultry Products Inspection Act thereafter would have understood that feathers means pelt? (*Hirsch, p. 28). Another telling example in *Hirsch is the National Housing Act which appears to fix the maximum rate of interest on home mortgages insurable by HUD at six percent (section 203(b)(5)). But Public Law 90-301, without amending 203(b)(5), allows the Secretary to fix maximum rates to meet the market. (*Hirsch p. 28).

In general, "Notwithstanding any other law..." or "Notwithstanding the provisions of section...", unless used with special care, are invitations to trouble.[150]

### C. SOME SUGGESTIONS FOR GENERAL GRANT STATUTES

There now exist a small number of statutes that apply to grants generally, unless expressly excluded by particular grant statutes. Among these, the principal one is the Federal Grants and Cooperative Agreements Act of 1978 (now recodified in 31 U.S.C. sec. 6501 ff). Also relevant are the Paperwork Reduction Act,[151] Federal Claims Collection Act[152] and the Debt Collection Act,[153] the Administrative Procedure Act which in part exempts grants from its rulemaking procedures but nevertheless applies to many grants because the administering agencies have agreed to waive the exemption.[154] Anyone drafting grant statutes should be familiar with these statutes.[155]

---

[150]*Hirsch, p. 28.

[151]P.L. 96-511, December 11, 1980, 44 U.S. Code 3501 *et seq.*

[152]P.L. 89-508, July 19, 1966, 31 U.S.C. 3711(a)-(e).

[153]P.L. 97-365, October 25, 1982; P.L. 98-167. November 29, 1983, 5 U.S. Code 552 a (b) and (m), 5514; 18 U.S.C. 1114; 26 U.S.C. 6103, 7213; 28 U.S.C. 2415(i); 31 U.S.C. 3701, 3711(f) 3716-3719.

[154]5 U.S.C. 551-59, 701-06, 1305, 3105, 3344, 5372, 7521. On the waiver of the rulemaking exemption, *see* ACUS, A GUIDE TO FEDERAL AGENCY RULEMAKING (1983) 26-27.

[155]They are conveniently collected with commentary and related materials in ACUS, FEDERAL ADMINISTRATIVE PROCEDURE SOURCEBOOK (1985).

 

Some further topics are worth considering for general legislation. The purpose would be to set forth a general approach to grant problems of a kind that repeat themselves, to save repetition of frequently occurring matters in each grant statute, to avoid unintentional variations in phrasing (which can lead to inferences that substantive differences were meant when they were not), and to resolve doubts that have troubled the Courts, administrators, grantees, and beneficiaries.

Here is an outline of some considerations that might go into such a general statute. They are offered to stimulate thinking on a subject which seems to have received little thought so far.

Definitions: A list of standard definitions that would apply to all grant statutes unless the contrary is clearly indicated.

Some basic notions of grant law that would apply to all grant statutes unless the contrary is clearly indicated:

A grantee is not (by reason of being a grantee) an arm, instrumentality, or agent or agency of the United States.

Its employees are not (by reason of its being a grantee) employees or officials of the United States.

Property held by the grantee is not (by reason of its being a grantee) property of the United States.

Money held by the grantee is not (by reason of the grant) money of the United States. Even money received pursuant to the grant, once it is validly transferred to the grantee is not money of the United States. Grant funds include funds held by the grantee required to be committed to the purpose of the grant, both those received from the United States and those required to be supplied by grantee. The United States does, however, have a residual interest or resulting trust in its favor of its proportionate share of grant funds and property bought with grant funds.

Grantees are generally expected to meet with their own funds or property or with funds or property derived from sources other than the United States, a share of the grant costs. If that share is specified by a statute, and grantee fails to supply this required non-federal share, the proportionate amount of federally supplied funds may not be validly expended by grantee. If they are expended nevertheless, grantee is obligated to return to the United States that amount of federally supplied funds spent, that is necessary to bring actual local share into the required ratio.[156] the proportionate amount of federally supplied funds. This, and other requirements, may, however, generally be waived by the grantor agency for good cause shown. Similarly, the grantor agency may, if a grant is renewed, authorize an adjustment of the non-federal share that will permit the required non-federal share to be supplied over a two year period instead of a one year period. (Perhaps a three year period?)

The grantor agency shall generally be authorized to waive any fringe requirement on a finding that the interests of justice and the purpose of the rule will be served by a waiver. Such waivers shall be reported to the Congress forthwith if they involve a matter greater than a specified amount.

Provisions in statutes requiring that activities paid for with local funds shall be supplemented not supplanted by the grant funds require good faith performance and shall be reflected in budget and plans submitted by the grantee in advance of operation. They do not contemplate enforcement by financial audit.

Provisions in statutes requiring maintenance of a previous level of effort require good faith performance and do contemplate enforcement by financial audit. They are, however, like most requirements, subject to waiver for good cause shown. In particular, a grantor agency shall generally have discretion to waive maintenance of effort provisions where the recent level of effort of the grantee is distorted by special nonrenewable grants from non-federal sources or special effort by the grantee intended to fund an experimental program or to launch early a program expected or reasonably hoped to be later funded in part by a federal grant program.

Agencies administering grants are authorized to establish grant appeals boards (or to arrange for the services of grant appeals boards established by other grant making agencies). Procedures should where possible emphasize the informal and the possibility of employing alternative methods of dispute resolution. The independence and competence of such boards shall be assured. The experience of such

[156] Sample calculations and alternatives are discussed in "Recovery of Education Grant Funds Misspent or Accounted for Improperly," 25 Pub. Cont. Newsl., no. 1, fall 1989, at 10. A sample case: statute calls for an 80:20 ratio. Grantee draws down and spends the federal 80, but puts up only 10 of local share. Grantee is to pay back to the United States 8, so that the net federal contribution will be 72, local contribution 18. The ration 72:18 = 80:20.

 

boards shall be looked to as a source of information leading to improved grant administration procedures and methods.

Every grant making agency shall periodically review its results and make plans for improved administration.

 

# IV. REFERENCE MATERIALS

## A. OVERVIEW AND BRIEF PRELIMINARY SUGGESTIONS

This chapter contains, following this overview and the quick starting suggestions:

Part B. Two comprehensive bibliographies:

1. Related to grants
2. Related to drafting, and

Part C. A list of acronyms and other abbreviations us ed in the body of the book or often encountered.

Before plunging into the Bibliographies, which, although not exhaustive, are fairly extensive, it may be helpful to have a quick sketch of selected materials that will be found particularly useful for the drafter dealing with grants.

Items marked in the Bibliography with an initial * are those cited in the body of this book by an author's name or other short title, where they are also marked with an *. As you run through the list, watch out for the asterisks. They identify a set of materials that will be of major help to the drafter of grant statutes. Lack of an asterisk does not imply that the work is not very useful. It means only that the work did not happen to be cited often enough to call for a short title or that it seemed clearer to cite the work by full title.

Treatise: There is one treatise on grant law, *Cappalli, 3 volumes with annual updates.

One-volume book: A leading one-volume book on grant law is the ABA Public Contract Law Section *Federal Grant Law.

Leading articles include *Current Trends, a comprehensive review, and *Current Developments, a quarterly comment; articles on special topics by George Brown and by the several contributors to *Federal Grant Law, of whom the most prolific include Madden, Wallick, Dembling, Gavin, who are Chairman and Past Chairmen of the ABA Public Contract Law Section.

A useful guide to grant law news is Federal Grants Management Handbook supplemented by monthly reports.

ACUS Recommendations and studies are very useful on procedural aspects of grants. The recommendations are published in the Federal Register, in 1 C.F.R. 305, and in the Conference's Annual Report. Both the recommendations and the supporting studies are published in annual bound volumes. The studies often appear also as law review articles. ACUS publishes a comprehensive Bibliography.

ACIR studies, emphasizing the structural aspects of grants to State and local governments, are published in monograph form. ACIR also publishes a quarterly journal, Intergovernmental Perspective.

Comptroller General Decisions and GAO Reports often contain valuable information about particular programs and problems. Also very useful to the drafter are GAO general studies such as Principles of Federal Appropriations Law; Grant Formulas, A Catalog of Federal Aid to States and Localities (GAO/HRD - 87-28); Federal Funding, Information on Selected Benefit/Mandatory Spending Programs (GAO/AFMD - 88-31FS).

The *Catalog of Federal Domestic Assistance is a very important resource.

Most of the major law reviews carry materials dealing with grants from time to time. Specialized law reviews and non-legal journals may be helpful, especially on particular technical problems. It is possible to give only some sketchy materials of this sort as suggestions:

Administrative Law Review
American Journal of Law and Medicine
Assistance Management and other publications of NAMA
Public Contract Law Journal

Recourse to unorthodox sources is strongly recommended, especially for understanding of technical fields in which grants operate and for perspective on how grants will fit into other activities in the field. Some random examples that have been found useful are:

"Blue Sheets" (this is the commonly used nickname for Drug Research Reports)
Government Computer News
Journal of Gerontology
Science
Scientific American
National Institutes of the American Bar Association
Seminars of the Federal Bar Association and National Assistance Management Association
Seminars of National Association of Counties, National Institute of Municipal Law Offices and similar organizations

Material on Appropriations Law and Budget Concepts, especially:

 

GAO, Principles of Federal Appropriations Law (June 1982) (GAO, A glossary of terms used in the Federal Budget Process (March 1981).

Texts on Statutory Drafting generally:

Peacock, Notes on Legislative Drafting (REC Foundation Inc. 1961) *Hirsch, Drafting Federal Law (DHHS, Washington, D.C. 1980) *Bell, Prose of Law: Congress As A Stylist of Statutory English (The Paper Tiger, Elliott City, Maryland, 1981) *Mullins, A Handbook for Legislative Drafters (Arkansas Edition) (Arkansas Legislation Digest, 1986).

B. BIBLIOGRAPHY

The following bibliography includes, in addition to works cited in the Guide, a number of works not cited in the text. It is supplied as a help to reference in this field. The drafting section is drawn very largely from the Minnesota Revisor's Manual (Office of the Revisor of Statutes, St. Paul, Minnesota, 1984), which also includes an extensive listing of State Bill Drafting Manuals, not included here. It also draws on a bibliography prepared by Professor Morell E. Mullins for his book on legislative drafting, prior to its publication. Professor Mullins very generously supplied the listing from his manuscript. Works cited in the Guide by a short title are identified by preceding asterisks. Works on grants and related federal assistance are listed first, then works on statutory drafting and related matters.

1. ACIR and ACUS Studies

ACIR STUDIES. The Advisory Commission on Intergovernmental Relations (ACIR) was created by the Congress in 1959 to monitor the operation of the American federal system and to recommend improvements. P.L. 86-380, 73 Stat. 703, 42 U.S.C. 4271. Its Reports have valuable information and often an illuminating perspective, particularly on the structural respects of grants and their impact on State and local government. ACIR also publishes Intergovernmental Perspective, a quarterly journal. A list of its available publications from 1961 to 1989 can be found in 15 Intergovernmental Perspectives, no. 4 at 34 (fall 1989).

ACUS RECOMMENDATIONS AND SUPPORTING STUDIES AFFECTING GRANTS. The Administrative Conference of the United States (ACUS) was established by statute as an independent agency of the federal government in 1964. Its purpose is to promote improvements in the efficiency, adequacy and fairness of procedures by which federal agencies conduct regulatory programs, administer grants and benefits, and perform related governmental functions.

ACUS RECOMMENDATIONS

| | |
|---|---|
| Rec. 68-5 | Representation of the Poor in Agency Rulemaking of Direct Consequence to Them |
| Rec. 69-3 | Publication of a *Guide to Federal Reporting Requirements* |
| Rec. 69-8 | Elimination of Certain Exemptions from the APA Rule-making Requirements |
| Rec. 71-3 | Articulation of Agency Policies |
| Rec. 71-4 | Uniform Minimum Procedures for Agencies Administering Discretionary Grant Programs |
| Rec. 71-9 | The Enforcement of Federal Standards in Grant-in-Aid Programs: Suggestions for Beneficiary Involvement |
| Rec. 72-5 | Procedures for the Adoption of Rules of General Applicability: The Need for Procedural Innovation in Administrative Rulemaking |
| Rec. 72-6 | Civil Money Penalties as a Sanction |
| Rec. 73-1 | Adverse Agency Publicity |
| Rec. 74-1 | Subpoena Power in Formal Rulemaking and Formal Adjudication |
| Rec. 74-2 | Procedures for Discretionary Distribution of Federal Assistance |
| Rec. 74-4 | Preenforcement Judicial Review of Rules of General Applicability |
| Rec. 75-3 | The Choice of Forum for Judicial Review of Administrative Action |
| Rec. 76-2 | Strengthening the Informational and Notice-Giving Functions of the Federal Register |

 

| | |
|---|---|
| Rec. 76-3 | Procedures in Addition to Notice and the Opportunity for Comment in Informal Rulemaking |
| Rec. 76-5 | Interpretive Rules of General Applicability and Statements of General Policy |
| Rec. 77-1 | Legislative Veto of Administrative Regulat ions |
| Rec. 77-3 | *Ex Parte* Communications in Informal Rulemaking Proceedings |
| Rec. 78-4 | Federal Agency Interaction with Private Standard-Setting Organizations |
| Rec. 79-2 | Disputes Respecting Federal-State Ageements for Administration of the Supplemental Security Income Program |
| Rec. 79-3 | Agency Assessment and Mitigation of Civil Money Penalties |
| Rec. 79-4 | Health and Safety Regulation, use of Cost-Benefit and Similar Analyses in Regulation |
| Rec. 80-3 | Interpretation and Implementation of the Federal Advisory Committee Act |
| Rec. 80-4 | Decisional Officials' Participation in Rulemaking Proceedings |
| Rec. 80-6 | Intragovernmental Communications Informal Rulemaking Proceedings |
| Rec. 82-2 | Resolving Disputes Under Federal Grant Programs |
| Rec. 82-4 | Procedures for Negotiating Proposed Reg ulations |
| Rec. 83-2 | The "Good Cause" Exemption from APA Rulemaking Requirements |
| Rec. 84-5 | Preemption of State Regulation by Federal Agencies |
| Rec. 85-1 | Legislative Preclusion of Cost/Benefit Analysis |
| Rec. 85-2 | Agency Procedures for Performing Regula tory Analysis of Rules |
| Rec. 86-7 | Case Management as a Tool for Improving Agency Adjudication |

 

ACUS REPORTS

ADMINISTRATIVE CONFERENCE OF THE U.S. (OFFICE OF THE CHAIRMAN), FEDERAL ADMINISTRATIVE PROCEDURE SOURCEBOOK: STATUTES AND RELATED MATERIALS, Washington, D.C., U.S. Gov't. Printing office (1985).

ADMINISTRATIVE CONFERENCE OF THE U.S. (OFFICE OF THE CHAIRMAN), A GUIDE TO FEDERAL AGENCY RULEMAKING, Washington, D.C., U.S. Gov't. Printing Office (1983).

Asimow, Michael, *Public Participation in the Adoption of Interpretive Rules and Policy Statements*, 75 MICH. L. REV. 521 (1977); 4 ACUS 615 (1979).

Asimow, Michael, *When the Curtain Falls: Separation of Functions in Federal Administrative Agencies*, 81 COLUM. L. REV. 759 (1981); 1981 ACUS 141.

Bonfield, Arthur E., *Public Participation in Federal Rulemaking Relating to Public Property, Loans, Grants, Benefits, or Contracts*, 118 U. PA. L. REV. 540 (1970); 1 ACUS 306 (1971).

Bonfield, Arthur E., *Representation for the Poor in Federal Rulemaking*, 67 MICH. L. REV. 511 (1969); 1 ACUS 79 (1971).

Bonfield, Arthur E., *Some Tentative Thoughts on Public Participation in the Making of Interpretive Rules and General Statements of Policy under the A.P.A.*, 23 AD. L. REV. 101 (1971).

Bowers, Michael W., *A Review of the Development of Law on Informal Rulemaking Procedure*, unpublished report to the Administrative Conference, 1982.

Boyer, Barry B., *Alternatives to Administrative Trial-Type Hearings for Resolving Complex Scientific, Economic, and Social Issues*, 71 MICH. L. REV. 111 (1972).

Cappalli, Richard B., MODEL FOR CASE MANAGEMENT: THE GRANT APPEALS BOARD, 1986 ACUS 663.

Cardozo, Michael H., *Federal Advisory Committee Act in Operation*, 33 AD. L. REV. 1 (1981); 1980 ACUS 313.

Cass, Ronald A., *Agency Review of Administrative Law Judges' Decisions*, 1983 ACUS 115.

Clagett, Brice McAdoo, *Informal Action-Adjudication-Rule Making: Some Recent Developments in Federal Administrative Law*, 1971 DUKE L.J. 51.

 

Currie, David P. and Goodman, Frank I., *Judicial Review of Federal Administrative Action: Quest for the Optimum Forum*, 75 _COLUM. L. REV. 1 (1975); 4 ACUS 197 (1979).

DeLong, James V., *Informal Rulemaking and the Integration of Law and Policy*, 65 VA. L. REV. 257 (1979).

Diver, Colin S., *The Optimal Precision of Administrative Rules*, 83 YALE L.J. 65 (1983).

Gellhorn, Ernest, *Adverse Publicity by Administrative Agencies*, 86 HARV. L. REV. 1380 (1973); 3 ACUS 67 (1975).

Gellhorn, Ernest and Bruff, Harold H., *Congressional Control of Administrative Regulation: A Study of Legislative Vetoes*, 90 HARV. L. REV. 1369 (1977); 4 ACUS 679 (1979).

Gilhooley, Margaret, *Standards and Procedures for the Discretionary Distribution of Federal Assistance*, 3 ACUS 422 (1975).

Goldschmid, Harvey J., *An Evaluation of the Present and Potential Use of Civil Money Penalties as a Sanction by Federal Administrative Agencies*, 2 ACUS 896 (1973).

Hamilton, Robert W., *Procedures for the Adoption of Rules of General Applicability: The Need for Procedural Innovation in Administrative Rulemaking*, 60 CALIF. L. REV. 1276 (1972); 2 ACUS 834 (1973).

Harter, Philip J., *Negotiating Regulations: A Cure for Malaise*, 1982 ACUS 301 (vol. 1); 71 GEORGETOWN L.J. 1 (1982), 1982 ACUS 301 (Vol. 1).

Jordan, Ellen R., *The Administrative Procedure Act's "Good Cause" Exemption*, 36 AD. L. REV. 113 (1984); 1983 ACUS 49.

Kurzman, Stephen, *Uniform Minimum Procedures for Agencies Administering Grant Programs*, 2 ACUS 181 (1973).

Leifer, Jacqueline C., *Implementation of the Federal Debt Collection Act of 1982*, 1984 ACUS 899.

Martin, Peter W., *Procedures Used in Forming and Carrying Out Federal-State Agreements under the Supplemental Security Income Program*, 1979 ACUS 71.

Mashaw, Jerry L., *The Management Side of Due Process: Some Theoretical and Litigation Notes on the Assurance of Accuracy, Fairness, and Timeliness in the Adjudication of Social Welfare Claims*, 59 CORNELL L. REV. 772 (1974), 3 ACUS 160 (1975).

 

McGarity, Thomas O., *The Role of Regulatory Analysis in Decisionmaking*, 1985 ACUS 107.

Neely, Alfred S., IV, *Statutory Inhibitions to the Application of Principles of Cost/Benefit Analysis in Administrative Decision Making*, 23 DUQ. L. REV. 489 (1985); 1985 ACUS 37.

Pierce, Richard J., *Regulation, Deregulation, Federalism and Administrative Law*, 46 U. PITT. L. REV. 607 (1985), 1984 ACUS 517.

Rosenblum, Victor G., *Handling Citizen Initiated Complaints: An Introductory Study of Federal Agency Procedures and Practices*, 26 AD. L. REV. 1 (1974); 3 ACUS 611 (1975).

Steinberg, Ann, *Federal Grant Dispute Resolution*, published in MEZINES, STEIN, GRUFF, ADMINISTRATIVE LAW, New York, Matthew Bender (1983); 1982 ACUS 137 (vol. 1).

Strauss, Peter L., *Disqualification of Decisional Officials in Rulemaking*, 80 COLUM. L. REV. 990 (1980); 1980 ACUS 375.

Tomlinson, Edward A. and Mashaw, Jerry L., *The Enforcement of Federal Standards in Grant-In-Aid Programs: Suggestions for Beneficiary Involvement*, 58 VA. L. REV. 600 (1972); 2 ACUS 531 (1973).

Verkuil, Paul R., JAWBONING ADMINISTRATIVE AGENCIES: EX PARTE COMMUNICATIONS BY THE WHITE HOUSE, 80 COLUM. L. REV. 943 (1980); 1980 ACUS 513.

Verkuil, Paul R., *Study of Informal Adjudication Procedures*, 43 U. CHI. L. REV. 739 (1976).

Williams, Stephen F., *"Hybrid Rulemaking" under the Administrative Procedure Act: A Legal and Empirical Analysis*, 42 U. CHI. L. REV. 401 (1975); 4 ACUS 499 (1979).

2. Other materials related to grants

• Barnes and Cattell: Barnes, Dennis W. and Cattell, Newton O., *Grants to Educational Institutions*, in FEDERAL GRANT LAW 245 (below in this Bibliography).

BAUMER, DONALD C., AND VAN HORN, CARL E., THE POLITICS OF UNEMPLOYMENT, CQ Press 1985.

BLACKSTONE BICENTENNIAL (AMERICAN/AUSTRALIAN/NEW ZEALAND LAW: PARALLELS AND CONTRASTS, 1980, discussion of grant system at 285-308. Malcolm S. Mason discusses the American system. The Hon. Mr. Justice Else-Mitchell discusses the Australian system.).

 

Boasberg, Tersh, and Hewes, Laurence I., III, *The Washington Beat: Federal Grants and Due Process*, 6 URBAN LAWYER 399 (1974).

Brown, George D., *Beyond the New Federalism - Revenue Sharing in Perspective*, 15 HARV. J. LEGIS. 1 (1977)

- *Federal Funds and National Supremacy: The Role of State Legislatures in Federal Grant Programs*, 28 AM. U.L.R. 279 (1979).

- *Federal Funds and Federal Courts/Community Development Litigation - As A Testing Ground For The New Law Of Standing*, 21 BOSTON COL. L.R. 525 (March 1980).

- *An introduction to the Community Development Litigation and its Impact*, in ACIR, AWAKENING THE SLUMBERING GIANT, M-122, December 1980.

- *The Courts and Grant Reform: A Time For Action*, INTERGOVERNMENTAL PERSPECTIVE, vol. 7, No. 4, Fall 1981, p. 6.

- *Pennhurst as a source of defense for State and Local Governments*, 31 CATH. U.L.R. 499 (1982).

- *Block Grants and Grant Law*, unpublished Report to ACUS (September 1983).

[GEORGE D. BROWN is Professor at Boston College Law School.]

* Budget: The Budget of the United States, and the related Special Analyses, the Budget in Brief, and the Appendix to the Budget are cited by Fiscal Year, thus: BUDGET SPECIAL ANALYSIS H, FY 1987.

* Cappalli: CAPPALLI, RICHARD B., FEDERAL GRANTS AND COOPERATIVE AGREEMENTS, Callaghan & Co., Wilmette, Illinois (1982), with supplements. A sprightly and valuable work. See review of the Treatise in *CURRENT DEVELOPMENTS, vol. 18, No. 4, Summer 1983, p. 15, discussing both some of the strengths and some major points of disagreement. The annual updates seem to be the work of the publisher and are not of the same quality as the Treatise.

CAPPALLI, RICHARD B., RIGHTS AND REMEDIES UNDER FEDERAL GRANTS, Bureau of National Affairs, Washington, D.C., 1979.

- *Federal Grant Disputes: The Lawyer's Next Domain*, 11 THE URBAN LAWYER 377 (1979).

 

- *Federal Grants and the New Statutory Tort: State and Local Officials Beware!*, 12 THE URBAN LAWYER 445 (1980).

[RICHARD B. CAPPALLI is Professor of Law, Temple University.]

* CATALOG OF FEDERAL DOMESTIC ASSISTANCE (OMB and GSA), issued generally annually with interim updates. A valuable guide to grants and listing of individual programs. The information on specific programs is prepared by the agencies administering them and do not reflect a consistent standard, but if you work with grants, you need this book. It is supplied to Congressional offices, and is available in many libraries. It is also available from the Superintendent of Documents.

Conway, *The Federal Grant: An Administrative View*, 30 FED. BAR J. 119 (1971).

* Current Trends: Mason, Malcolm S, *Current Trends in Federal Grant Law*, 35 FED. BAR J. 163 (1976).

* Current Developments: Mason, Malcolm S., Current Developments in Federal Grant Law, a quarterly comment on Federal Grant Law, appearing in ABA Public Contract Newsletter since volume 14, No. 1, October 1978. The title of the column has varied from time to time. It is consistently cited here nevertheless as Current Developments.

* Dembling: Dembling, Paul G. and Ross W., *Significant Legislative Developments*, in FEDERAL GRANT LAW 281.

Dembling, Paul G., *Unsettled Worlds in Federal Grants: Legal Rights and Remedies*, National Briefing Conference on Federal Grants, Arlington, Virginia, April 4, 1975.

- *GAO's Review of Complaints Concerning Contracts and Federal Grants*, The National Graduate University, Washington, D.C., March 25, 1976.

*GAO's Role in Contracting Under Grants*, National Graduate University, Washington, D.C., October 12, 1976.

- *GAO's Review of Complaints Concerning Contracts Under Federal Grants*, Western Briefing Conference, San Francisco, California, October 15, 1976.

 

- *Contracts Under Federal Grants*, National Graduate University Seminar on Administration and Negotiation of Federal Contracts and Grants, Washington, D.C., March 17, 1977.

- *Public Contracts and Grants from Local and Federal Perspectives*, American Bar Association National Institute "Focus 77" Washington, D.C., April 21, 1977.

- *Public Contracts and Grants*: American Bar Association National Institute, Los Angeles, May 17, 1977.

- Remarks before Secretary of Health, Education, and Welfare First Conference on Grants and Procurement, Washington, D.C., October 11, 1977.

- *Grant Auditing and What Needs to be Done*, Seminar on Grant Law, sponsored by the Federal Bar Association, Washington, D.C., February 27, 1978.

- *Issues and Challenges Facing the Federal Grant and Assistance System*, National Assistance Management Association, Washington, D.C., November 1, 1978.

- *Contracts under Grants*, Brigham Young University Conference on Grants and Cooperative Agreements, Salt Lake City, Utah, March 7, 1979.

- *Protesting Contracts under Grants*, ABA National Institute Federal Grants and Construction, Seattle, Washington, May 10-11, 1979.

- *New GAO Procedures Concerning Bid Protests and Contracts Under Federal Grants*, PROCEEDINGS OF FEDERAL BAR ASSOCIATION 16TH ANNUAL WESTERN BRIEFING CONFERENCE ON GOVERNMENT CONTRACTS, 1975.

- *Debarment and Suspension: Government Blacklist of Contractors and Grantees*, THE GOVERNMENT CONTRACTOR BRIEFING PAPER, Federal Publications, Inc., December 1978.

- *Catastrophic Accidents: Indemnification of Contractors Against Third Party Liability*, 10 J. SPACE LAW 1 (1982). The problem discussed and the recommendations apply to federal grants programs such as Disaster Relief and Swine Flu immunization as well as to contracts, ib. 12., cf. p. 1, nn. 1 and 4.

- (with Mason) *Federal Grant Litigation*, 30 THE PRACTICAL LAWYER, No. 7, October 15, 1984, 55.

- (with Mason) Essentials of Federal Grant Practice (expected to be published in 1990 by ALI-ABA)

[PAUL G. DEMBLING, now in private practice, is Previous Past Chairman of the Public Contract Section of the American Bar Association, Past President of the

 

Federal Bar Association, and was formerly General Counsel of NASA and General Counsel of GAO.]

FCR, FEDERAL CONTRACT REPORTS, Bureau of National Affairs, Washington, D.C., weekly. Primarily focused on federal procurement, FCR has abandoned an emphasis it nevertheless gave for several years to grant matters.

* FEDERAL GRANT LAW (M. Mason ed. 1982), published by the Public Contract Section of the American Bar Association.

Federal Grant Law contains the following chapters:

- *Highlights* (Malcolm S. Mason).
- Madden, Thomas J., *The Constitutional and Legal Foundations of Federal Grants.*
- *Grant Rule Making* (Malcolm S. Mason).
- Settle, Norval D. (John), and Yamada, Gerald M., *The Award Process.*
- *Monitoring of Grantee Performance* (Malcolm S. Mason).
- Kirschenmann, Henry G., Jr., *Determination of Rates for Grantee Reimbursements.*
- Wallick, Robert D., and Montalto, William B., *Administrative review and Finality of Grantor Actions.*
- Gavin, Donald G., and Halverson, Steven T., *Contracts under Federal Assistance.*
- Thurman, Bill W., Posner, Paul L., and Sorett, Steven M., *Federal Grants and Intergovernmental Relations.*
- Barnes, Dennis W., and Cattell, Newton O., *Grants to Educational Institutions.*
- Newton, Robert D., *Grant Reform.*
- Dembling, Paul G., and Dembling, Ross W., *Significant Legislative Developments.*
- Lauer, Charles A., and Llewellyn, Thomas S., *Reorganization of LEAA's Grant Programs.*
- Rhodes, Edward T., and Maslyn, Robert T., *HEW Initiatives in Grants Management.*

FEDERAL GRANTS MANAGEMENT HANDBOOK, Grants Management Advisory Service, basic looseleaf handbook with monthly update.

Furman, John Pryor, *Impact of Federal Subsidies on State Functions* (The 1957 Ross Prize Essay), 43 A.B.A.J. 1101 (December 1957).

 

* Gavin and Halverson: Gavin, Donald G. and Halverson, Steven T., *Contracts under Federal Assistance*, in FEDERAL GRANT LAW.

[DONALD G. GAVIN, in private practice, is Chairman of the ABA Public Contract Law Section.]

* Highlights: Mason, Malcolm S., *Highlights*, in FEDERAL GRANT LAW.

HOROWITZ, DONALD L., THE COURTS AND SOCIAL POLICY (The Brookings Institution, Washington, D.C., 1977).

JOHNSON, WALTER LLOYD, DETERMINING GRANTEE COSTS IN FEDERAL GRANT-IN-AID PROGRAMS, (Doctoral Disertation) University of Texas at Austin, January 1974.

Kaden, *Politics, Money and State Sovereignty: The Judicial Role*, 79 COLUM. L.R. 847 (197).

* Kirschenmann: Kirschenmann, Henry G., Jr., *Determination of Rates for Grantee Reimbursement*, in FEDERAL GRANT LAW 99.

* Lauer and Llewellyn: Lauer, Charles A. and Llewellyn, Thomas S., *Reorganization of LEAA's Grant Programs*, in FEDERAL GRANT LAW 309.

- *Federal grant litigation involving Law Enforcement Assistance Administration*, in ACIR, AWAKENING THE SLUMBERING GIANT, M-122, December 1980.

* Madden: Madden, Thomas J., *The Constitutional and Legal Foundations of Federal Grants*, in FEDERAL GRANT LAW 5.

- *When Records of Grantees Are Subject to Public Access Under the Freedom of Information Act*, 4 (NAMA) GRANTS AND ASSISTANCE NEWS, No. 1, p. 8 (June 1980).
- *Supreme Court Affirms Federal Government's Authority to Recover Misspent Grant Funds*, 2 (NAMA) ASSISTANCE MANAGEMENT, No. 1, December 1983, p. 9.
- (with Remes) *The Courts and The Administration: Marching to Different Drummers*, INTERGOVERNMENTAL PERSPECTIVE, vol. 9, No. 2, Spring 1983, p. 23.
- *The Right to Receive Federal Grants and Assistance*, 37 FED. BAR J. No. 4, Fall 1978, p. 17.

 

- *Providing an Adequate Remedy for Disappointed Contractors Under Federal Grants-in-Aid to States and Units of Local Government*, 34 FED. BAR J. 201 (1975).

- *Future Directions for Federal Assistance Programs: Lessons from Block Grants and Revenue Sharing*, 36 FED. BAR J. 107 (1977).

- (with responses by Wallick and Mason), *The Law of Federal Grants*, in AWAKENING THE SLUMBERING GIANT, ACIR, M-122, December 1980.

- *Enforceability of Grant Conditions: Implications of Supreme Court's Decision in Pennhurst State School v. Halderman*, NAMA GRANTS AND ASSISTANCE NEWS, July 1981, 12.

[THOMAS J. MADDEN, now in private practice, was Chairman of the ABA Public Contract Law Section. He was formerly General Counsel of LEAA.]

Mason: listed elsewhere in this Bibliography: Blackstone Bicentennial; *Current Trends; *Current Developments; *Monitoring; *Rulemaking; *Federal Grant Law; (with Dembling) Federal Grant Litigation; (with Dembling) Essentials of Federal Grant Practice.

[MALCOLM S. MASON is a Senior Fellow of ACUS. He was formerly Chairman of the HEW Departmental Grant Appeals Board.]

MICHELMAN, F., & SANDALOW, T., EDS. GOVERNMENT IN URBAN AREAS, 1970.

* Monitoring: Mason, Malcolm S., *Monitoring of Grantee Performance*, in FEDERAL GRANT LAW 79.

Muller & Fix, The Impact of Selected Federal Actions on Municipal Outlays, 1 Study for Joint Economic Comm. 96th Cong. 1st Sess. (1979)

- NATIONAL COUNSEL ON PUBLIC WORKS IMPROVEMENT, FRAGILE FOUNDATIONS: A REPORT ON AMERICA'S PUBLIC WORKS, February 1988.

* Newton: Newton, Robert D., *Grant Reform*, in FEDERAL GRANT LAW 267.

- *Managing Federal Assistance*, 1 ASSISTANCE MANAGEMENT J. 71 (1979).

 

Peterson, Eugene, *Little Old Grantmaker Replies*, 4 (NAMA) GRANTS AND ASSISTANCE NEWS No. 1 (June 1980) ("The Federal Grant and Cooperative Agreement Act was passed over two years ago. How is it working?")

- ("Our organization was just notified that one of our most carefully prepared grant applications has been rejected by the Federal funding agency. Do we have any recourse...")

PUBLIC CONTRACT NEWSLETTER, see *Current Developments, *supra*.

Posner, *From Grants Management to Devolution: GAO's Evolving Intergovernmental Word Program*, 4 (NAMA) ASSISTANCE MANAGEMENT J. No. 1, Spring 1987, p. 13.

Reynolds, Thomas M., *The HEW Grant Appeals Process*, 1979 NIMLO (National Institute of Municipal Law Officers) Mid-Year Seminar, Federal Grant Conditions.

* Rhodes and Maslyn: Rhodes, Edward T. and Maslyn, Robert T., *HEW Initiatives in Grants Management*, in FEDERAL GRANT LAW 333.

* Rulemaking: Mason, Malcolm S., *Grant Rulemaking*, in FEDERAL GRANT LAW 45.

Rosenfield, Harry N., *The Free Enterprise System*, THE ANTIOCH REVIEW, Summer 1985, 352 (discusses subsidies in various forms related to grants).

Sky, Theodore, *Rulemaking in the Office of Education*, 26 AD. L.R. 129 (1974).

- *Rulemaking and the Federal Grant Process in the United States Office of Education*, 62 VA. L.R. 1017 (1976).

* Settle and Yamada: Settle, Norval D. (John) and Yamada, Gerald M., *The Award Process*, in FEDERAL GRANT LAW 59.

- *See also* Yamada, *supra*.

Sorett, Stephen M., *Cleaning the Water When the Well Runs Dry*, 31 FED. BAR NEWS & J. 123 (1984).

 

- (with Feldman, Roger), *Privatization*, in *CURRENT DEVELOPMENTS, vol. 23, No. 4, Summer 1988, p. 8.

* Thurman, Posner and Sorett: Thurman, Bill W., Posner, Paul L., and Sorett, Stephen M., *Federal Grants and Intergovernmental Relations*, in FEDERAL GRANT LAW 211.

* Wallick and Montalto: Wallick, Robert D. and Montalto, William B., *Administrative Review and Finality of Grantor Actions*, in FEDERAL GRANT LAW 117.

- *Symbiosis or Domination: Rights and Remedies Under Grant-Type Assistance Programs*, 46 GEO. WASH. L.R. 159 (1978).

- *How Naked at the Day of Judgment: Improving the Remedies Systems for Grant-Type Assistance*, 10 PUBLIC CONTRACT L.J. No. 2, December 1978, 177.

- *Messenger RNA for Grants: Regulations and Their Niche*, 1 ASSIST. MGT. J. 1 (1979).

Wallick, *DUO on Federal R&D from the University and College Perspectives*, 35 FED. BAR J. 235 (1976).

[ROBERT D. WALLICK, in private practice, was recently Chairman of the Public Contract Law Section of the American Bar Association.]

Whelan, John, and Smith, John M., *Contracts Under Grants-in-Aid, An Aspect of United States Federal-State- Local Relations*, 6 HASTINGS CONST. L. Q. 751 (1979).

Wilcox, Alan, *The Function and Nature of Grants*, 27 AD. L. R. 125 (1970). An important early analysis that argues that grants are trusts.

YAMADA, GERALD H., RULEMAKING REQUIREMENTS RELATED TO FEDERAL FINANCIAL ASSISTANCE PROGRAMS.

- *see also* Settle and Yamada, *supra*.

3. Related to Drafting

AMERICAN BAR ASSOCIATION, LAW STUDENT DIVISION. GUIDE TO LEGISLATIVE RESEARCH AND DRAFTING. Chicago, Law Student Division, American Bar Association, 1979.

 

ANDERSON, ROBERT MILFORD. LEGISLATION. Woodland Hills, Calif. F. Cool Publications, 1950.

AUERBACH, CARL A. AND OTHERS. THE LEGAL PROCESS; AN INTRODUCTION TO DECISION MAKING BY JUDICIAL, LEGISLATIVE, EXECUTIVE AND ADMINISTRATIVE AGENCIES. San Francisco, Chandler Pub. Co., 1961.

*BELL, JOHN A., PROSE OF LAW: CONGRESS AS A STYLIST OF STATUTORY ENGLISH, Ellicott City, MD., The Paper Tiger, 1981.

BISHIN, WILLIAM R. AND STONE, CHRISTOPHER D. LAW, LANGUAGE AND ETHICS; AN INTRODUCTION TO LAW AND LEGAL METHOD. Mineola, N.Y., Foundation Press, 1972.

Bishin, *Law Finders, An Essay in Statutory Interpretation*, 38 CALIF. L. REV. -- (1965).

BISKIND, ELLIOTT L. SIMPLIFY LEGAL WRITING. New York, Arco, 1975.

BLACK, HENRY CAMPBELL. HANDBOOK ON THE CONSTRUCTION AND INTERPRETATION OF THE LAWS. 2d ed. St. Paul, West Pub. Co., 1911.

BLOCK, EFFECTIVE LEGAL WRITING (2d ed., Foundation Press, 1983).

BOWEN, CATHERINE (DRINKER). THE LAWYER AND THE KING'S ENGLISH. Philadelphia, Brandeis Lawyers' Society, 1951.

BRAND, NORMAN AND WHITE, JOHN O. LEGAL WRITING: THE STRATEGY OF PERSUASION. New York, St. Martin, 1976.

BRYANT, MARGARET M. ENGLISH IN THE LAW COURTS; THE PART THAT ARTICLES, PREPOSITIONS AND CONJUNCTIONS PLAY IN LEGAL DECISIONS. New ed. New York, F. Ungar, 1962.

BURTON, WILLIAM C. LEGAL THESAURUS. New York, Macmillan Pub. Co., Inc., 1980.

CHAMBERLAIN, JOSEPH PERKINS. LEGISLATIVE PROCESSES; NATIONAL AND STATE. New York, Appleton-Century, 1936.

 

CITIZENS CONFERENCE ON STATE LEGISLATURE. STATE CONSTITUTIONAL PROVISIONS AFFECTING STATE LEGISLATURES. Kansas City, 1967.

Coffman, *Essay on Statutory Interpretation*, 9 MEMPHIS ST. U. L. REV. 57 (1978).

COHEN, JULIUS. MATERIALS AND PROBLEMS ON LEGISLATION. 2d ed. Indianapolis, Bobbs-Merrill, 1967.

CONANT, ARMAND BROUS. STATUTE MAKING; A TREATISE ON THE MEANS AND METHODS FOR THE ENACTMENT OF STATUTE LAW IN THE UNITED STATES. 2d ed. New York, Commerce Clearing House, 1965.

COOK, ROBERT NEVIN, ED. LEGAL DRAFTING. Rev. ed., Brooklyn, Foundation Press, 1951.

COOLEY, THOMAS M. A TREATISE ON THE CONSTITUTIONAL LIMITATIONS WHICH REST UPON THE LEGISLATIVE POWER OF THE STATES OF THE AMERICAN UNION. 8th ed. Boston, Little, Brown & Co., 1927.

COUNCIL OF STATE GOVERNMENTS. LAWMAKING IN THE WEST: A SUMMARY OF LEGISLATIVE BILL PASSING PROCEDURES IN THIRTEEN STATES. VOL. I - SUMMARY AND ANALYSIS OF PROCEDURES. VOL. II - STATE BY STATE DIGEST OF PROCEDURES. Chicago, 1967.

COUNCIL OF STATE GOVERNMENTS. LEGISLATIVE SERVICE AGENCIES CHARGED WITH STATUTORY REVISION FUNCTIONS. Chicago, 1956.

COUNCIL OF STATE GOVERNMENTS. LEGISLATIVE SERVICE AGENCIES WITH MAJOR RESPONSIBILITY FOR BILL DRAFTING. Chicago, 1958.

COUNCIL OF STATE GOVERNMENTS. STATE BILL DRAFTING MANUALS. Rev., Chicago, 1951.

CRAWFORD, EARL T. THE CONSTRUCTION OF STATUTES. St. Louis, Thomas Law Book Co., 1940.

CULTICE, ROBERT D. A LIST OF SELECTED PUBLICATIONS ON THE DRAFTING OF LEGAL AND LEGISLATIVE INSTRUMENTS. Columbus, College of Law Library, Ohio State University, 1951.

 

DAVIES, LEGISLATIVE LAW AND PROCESS IN A NUTSHELL 110-47 (West 1975).

DICKERSON, FREDERICK REED. THE FUNDAMENTALS OF LEGAL DRAFTING. Boston, Published for the American Bar Foundation by Little, Brown, 1965.

DICKERSON, FREDERICK REED. THE INTERPRETATION AND APPLICATION OF STATUTES. Boston, Little, Brown, 1975.

DICKERSON, FREDERICK REED. LEGISLATIVE DRAFTING. Boston, Little, Brown, 1954 (reprinted by Greenwood Press (1977)).

Dickerson, *Statutory Interpretation: Core Meaning and Marginal Uncertainty*, 29 MO.L.REV. 1 (1964).

Dickerson, *Statutory Interpretation: A Peek into the Mind and Will of a Legislature*, 50 IND. L.J. 206 (1975).

DWARRIS, SIR FORTUNATUS. A GENERAL TREATISE ON STATUTES: THEIR RULES OF CONSTRUCTION AND THE PROPER BOUNDARIES OF LEGISLATION AND OF JUDICIAL INTERPRETATION. Albany, N.Y., W. Gould & Sons, 1871.

Easterbrook, *Statutes' Domains*, 50 U.CHI.L.REV. 533 (1983).

HORACK, FRANK EDWARD. CASES AND MATERIALS ON LEGISLATION. 2d ed. Chicago, Callaghan, 1954.

HOUP, KENNETH AND THOMAS E. PEARSALL. REPORTING TECHNICAL INFORMATION. 4th ed. Encino, California, Glencoe Publishing, 1980.

EBBITT, WILMA R., AND DAVID R. EBBITT. INDEX TO ENGLISH, Seventh edition, Scott, Foresman and Company, 1982.

ENDLICH, GUSTAV A. A COMMENTARY ON THE INTERPRETATION OF STATUTES. Jersey City, N.J., F.D. Linn & Co., 1888.

ETTER, ORVAL. REFERENTIAL PRACTICES IN MUNICIPAL LEGISLATION. Eugene, Bureau of Municipal Research and Service, University of Oregon, 1960.

FELKER, DANIEL B., ET AL. GUIDELINES FOR DOCUMENT DESIGNERS. Washington, D.C., American Institutes for Research, 1981.

 

FLESCH, RUDOLF. HOW TO WRITE PLAIN ENGLISH: A BOOK FOR LAWYERS AND CONSUMERS. New York, Harper Row, 1979. See *supra*, ch. III, Definitions: "Plain Language" can be a trap.

FLESCH, RUDOLF. THE ART OF READABLE WRITING. New York, Collier Books, 1949.

Frankfurter, *Some Reflections on the Reading of Statutes*, 47 COLUM.L.REV. 527 (1947).

FREEMAN, MORTON S. GRAMMATICAL LAWYER. Philadelphia American Law Institute. American Bar Association on Continuing Professional Education, 1979.

FREUND, ERNST. LEGISLATIVE DRAFTING. Indianapolis, Mellett Ptg. Co. Inc., 1916.

Gaylord, *An Appraoch To Statutory Construction*, 5 SW.U.L.REV. 349 (1976).

GOPEN, WRITING FROM A LEGAL PERSPECTIVE (West 1981).

GRAD, FRANK P. THE DRAFTING OF STATE CONSTITUTIONS: WORKING PAPERS FOR A MANUAL. New York, National Municipal League, 1967.

HALEVY, BALFOUR J. A SELECTED BIBLIOGRAPHY ON STATE CONSTITUTIONAL REVISION. New York, National Municipal League, 1967.

HANDBOOK OF THE NATIONAL CONFERENCE OF COMMISSIONERS ON UNIFORM STATE LAWS AND PROCEEDINGS OF THE ANNUAL CONFERENCE MEETING IN ITS EIGHTY-EIGHTH YEAR. Chicago. 1977.

HARVARD UNIVERSITY LAW SCHOOL. AN INSTITUTE ON THE SCIENCE OF DRAFTSMANSHIP. Cambridge, 1951.

* HIRSCH, DONALD, DRAFTING FEDERAL LAW, HHS Office of the General Counsel, Legislative Division, Washington, D.C. 1980. Hirsch's book, an excellent teaching guide, is unfortunately out of print. It may be hoped that interest in the subject will bring this book back, perhaps in a new and enlarged edition. Meanwhile, it is available in Depository Libraries throughout the country. Depository Libraries are libraries officially designated to receive government publications and to make them available to the public. They

 

include major public libraries and some college and law school libraries. *See* 44 U.S.C. 1901, *et seq.*

HORACK, FRANK EDWARD. CASES AND MATERIALS ON LEGISLATION. 2d ed. Chicago, Callaghan, 1954.

HOUP, KENNETH AND THOMAS E. PEARSALL. REPORTING TECHNICAL INFORMATION. 4th ed. Encino, California, Glencoe Publishing, 1980.

HURST, DEALING WITH STATUTES (Columbia, 1982).

ILBERT, SIR COURTENNY PEREGRINE. THE MECHANICS OF LAW MAKING. New York, Columbia University Press, 1914.

INTERNATIONAL SEMINAR AND WORKSHOP ON THE TEACHING OF LEGAL DRAFTING. Bloomington, Indiana University School of Law, 1975.

JONES, CHESTER L. STATUTE LAW MAKING IN THE UNITED STATES. Boston, F.W. Faxon Company, 1923.

KAVANAUGH, KATHLEEN. CONSTITUTIONAL AND STATUTORY PROVISIONS OF THE VARIOUS STATES WITH RESPECT TO SUBJECT MATTER IN THE TITLE OF LEGISLATIVE BILLS. N.Y., New York State Library, 1944.

KENNEDY, DUNCAN LEROY. BILL DRAFTING. St. Paul, 1958.

KOONS, CHARLES VINTON. STATUTORY INTERPRETATION AND CONSTRUCTION; CASES AND MATERIALS. Washington, Lerner Law Book Co., 1959.

LAMMERS, BERNARD. THE TEACHING OF LEGISLATIVE DRAFTING & PROCESS IN U.S. LAW SCHOOLS. Chicago, American Bar Foundation, 1977.

Lehman, *How to Interpret a Difficult Statute*, 1979 WIS. L. REV. 489 (1979).

LENHOFF, ARTHUR. COMMENTS, CASES AND OTHER MATERIALS ON LEGISLATION. Buffalo, N.Y., Dennis & Co., Inc., 1949.

MacCallum, *Legislative Intent*, 75 YALE L.J. 745 (1965).

MACDONALD, DUNCAN A. DRAFTING DOCUMENTS IN PLAIN LANGUAGE. New York, Practicing Law Institute, 1979.

 

McCaffrey, Francis J. Statutory Construction; A Statement and Exposition of the General Rules of Statutory Construction. New York, Central Book Co., Inc., 1953.

McDougal, Lasswell & Miller. The Interpretation of Agreements and World Public Order. New Haven, Yale University Press, 1967.

Mehlman, Maxwell J. and Grossman, Edward G. Yale Legislative Service Handbook of Legislative Drafting. New Haven, Conn., Yale Legislative Services, Yale Law School, 1977.

Mellinkoff, David. The Language of the Law. Boston, Little, Brown, 1963.

Mellinkoff, Legal Writing: Sense and Nonsense. (West 1982).

Minnesota Constitutional Study Commission. *Special Legislation (Local Bills) and Home Rule in Minnesota.* Excerpt from Intergovernmental Relations and Local Government Committee report. Nov., 1972.

Mishkin, Paul J. and Morris, Clarence. On Law in Courts; An Introduction to Judicial Development of Case and Statute Law. Brooklyn, Foundation Press, 1965.

Namasivayam, S. Drafting of Legislation. New York, Panther House, 1971.

Naon, Robert. Title Requirements for Bills. Olympia, Washington State Library, 1975.

N.D. Journal of Legislation. A Handbook on Research and Drafting of Legislation. Notre Dame, Indiana, May 1974.

Newman, Frank C. and Surrey, Stanley S. Legislation: Cases and Materials. Englewood Cliffs, N.J., Prentice Hall, 1955.

Nutting, Charles Bernard and Dickerson, Reed. Cases and Materials on Legislation. 5th ed. St. Paul, West Pub. Co., 1978.

 

PARKINSON, THOMAS I. LEGISLATIVE DRAFTING. New York, The Academny of Political Science, 1912.

PEACOCK, JAMES CRAIG. NOTES ON LEGISLATIVE DRAFTING. n.p., REC Foundation, 1961.

PHILBRICK, FREDERICK ARTHUR. LANGUAGE AND THE LAW: THE SEMANTICS OF FORENSIC ENGLISH. New York, Macmillan, 1949.

Posner, *Economics, Politics, and the Reading of Statutes and the Constitution*, 49 U. CHI. L. REV. 263 (1982).

Posner, Statutory Interpretation - In the Classroom and in the Courtroom, 50 U. CHI. L. REV. 800 (1983).

PROBERT, WALTER. LAW, LANGUAGE AND COMMUNICATION. Springfield, Ill., Thomas, 1972.

QUIRK, RANDOLPH, ET AL. A GRAMMAR OF CONTEMPORARY ENGLISH. London, Longman Group Ltd., 1972.

READ, HORACE EMERSON AND OTHERS. MATERIALS ON LEGISLATION. 3d ex. Mineola, N.Y., Foundation Press, 1973.

Redish, Janice. *How to write regulations (and other legal documents) in clear English*, DRAFTING DOCUMENTS IN PLAIN LANGUAGE 1981. Commercial Law and Practice Course Handbook Series Number 254. New York, Practising Law Institute, 1981.

RUTGERS UNIVERSITY, SCHOOL OF LAW. BILL DRAFTING. New Brunswick, N.J., 1971.

SCIENCE OF LEGAL METHOD; SELECT ESSAYS BY VARIOUS AUTHORS. Translations by Ernest Bruncken and Layton B. Register. New York, A.M. Kelley, 1969.

SQUIRES AND ROMBAUER, LEGAL WRITING (West 1982).

SLOANE, S.B. THE LEGAL SPELLER. Philadelphia, Saunders, 1977.

Sheed, *The Art of Statutory Interpretation*, 62 TEX. L. REV. 665 (1983).

 

STATSKY, WILLIAM P. LEGISLATIVE ANALYSIS: HOW TO USE STATUTES AND REGULATIONS. St. Paul, West Pub. Co., 1975.

STATSKY, LEGISLATIVE ANALYSIS AND DRAFTING (2d. ed. West 1984).

STRUNK, WILLIAM, JR., AND E.B. WHITE. THE ELEMENTS OF STYLE. 2nd ed. New York, Macmillan Publishing Co., Inc., 1972.

SUTHERLAND, JABEZ GRIDLEY. STATUTES AND STATUTORY CONSTRUCTION. 4th ed. by C. Dallas Sands. Chicago, Callaghan & Co., 1981.

Tribe, *Toward a Syntax of the Unsaid: Construing the Sounds of Congressional and Constitutional Silence*, 57 IND. L.J. 515 (1982).

TWINING, WILLIAM & MIERS, DAVID. HOW TO DO THINGS WITH RULES: A PRIMER OF INTERPRETATION. South Hackensack, N.J., Rothman, 1976.

A UNIFORM SYSTEM OF CITATION. Harvard Law Review Association, 1981.

WHITE, JAMES B. THE LEGAL IMAGINATION, STUDIES IN THE NATURE OF LEGAL THOUGHT AND EXPRESSION. Boston, Little, Brown, 1973.

WYDICK, RICHARD C. PLAIN ENGLISH FOR LAWYERS. Durham, N.C., Carolina Academic Press, 1979. (*Also*, same title, 66 CALIF. L. REV. 727 (1978)).

## C. ACRONYMS AND OTHER ABBREVIATIONS

The following common abbreviations are used in the text.

ACIR - Advisory Commission on Intergovernmental Relations. See discussion in Bibliography.

ACUS - Administrative Conference of the United States. See discussion in Bibliography.

APA - Administrative Procedure Act.

CAA - Community Action Agency.

 

CAP - Community Action Program.

CBO - Congressional Budget Office.

CETA - Comprehensive Employment and Training Act.

Catalog - Catalog of Federal Domestic Assistance.

CSA - Community Services Administration.

DGAB - Departmental Grant Appeals Board (of HEW and its successor HHS). *See* 45 CFR 16.

DOL - Department of Labor.

DOT - Department of Transportation.

ED - Department of Education.

EPA - Environmental Protection Agency.

ESEA - Elementary and Secondary Education Act.

FMC - Federal Management Circular, an alternative designation of those OMB Circulars which were at one time transferred to GSA for administration.

FOIA - Freedom of Information Act.

GAO - General Accounting Office.

GRS - General Revenue Sharing.

GSA - General Services Administration.

HEW - Department of Health, Education, and Welfare.

HEW DGAB - Departmental Grant Appeals Board of HEW.

HHS - Department of Health and Human Services.

HHS DGAB - Departmental Grant Appeals Board of HHS. (Name has been changed to Departmental Appeals Board.)

HUD - Department of Housing and Urban Development.

 

LEAA - Law Enforcement Assistance Administration.

NEH - National Endowment for the Humanities.

NEPA - National Environmental Policy Act.

NSF - National Science Foundation.

OEO - Office of Economic Opportunity.

OMB - Office of Management and Budget.

OSHA - Occupational Safety and Health Act.

PHS - Public Health Service (HHS).

UMTA - Urban Mass Transportation Administration.

 

Congressional Research Service

# Tracking Current Federal Legislation and Regulations: A Guide to Resources for Congressional Staff

**Pamela A. Hairston**
Information Research Specialist

March 11, 2010

**Congressional Research Service**
7-5700
www.crs.gov
RL33895

CRS Report for Congress
*Prepared for Members and Committees of Congress*

 

## Summary

This guide is designed to introduce congressional staff to selected official government and non-government sources that are useful in tracking and obtaining background information and specific facts on the status of federal legislation and regulations. It includes government sources such as the Legislative Information System (LIS), THOMAS, the Government Printing Office (GPO) Access/FDsys, and U.S. Senate and House websites. Non-government or commercial sources include resources such as HeinOnline and the Congressional Quarterly (CQ) website.

This report will be updated as new information is available.



 

## Contents



## Tables



## Appendixes



## Contacts





 

# Introduction

Written for congressional staff, this report identifies and provides website addresses and other contact information for official government and non-government sources that are useful in tracking current federal legislation and regulations. It also provides information on the Congressional Research Service (CRS) legislative institutes, which would be useful in learning about this process.

# Tracking Current Federal Legislation

Action on legislation passed or pending in the current Congress, and its status in the legislative process, is reported in the *Congressional Record.* The *Record* is published each day that one or both chambers are in session, except infrequent instances when two or more consecutive issues are printed together. The *Congressional Record* contains the edited transcript of activities on the floor of the House and Senate. It is the primary source for the text of floor debates and the official source of recorded votes. The *Record*'s Daily Digest section summarizes action in each chamber and identifies committee hearings, new public laws, and committee meetings scheduled for the next legislative day. Indexes for the *Congressional Record* are issued twice a month. The subject index section can be used to identify bills by topic, and the History of Bills and Resolutions section tracks action on special bills.

The *Daily Compilation of Presidential Documents* (and its predecessor, the *Weekly Compilation of Presidential Documents*) provides the dates on which the President signed or vetoed legislation. It also contains transcripts of presidential messages to Congress, executive orders, speeches, and other material released by the White House.

## Official Government Sources

**Legislative Information Service**
http://www.congress.gov

The Legislative Information System (LIS) provides Members of Congress and their staff access to legislative information that is accurate, timely, and complete. Accessible only to Members and their staff, this website is a portal to a variety of commercial, academic, and government legislative resources, including specialized LIS databases. These databases, identified by the LIS logo on the search pages, include Bill Summary and Status, Bill Text, the *Congressional Record*, and Committee Reports. Basic information about bills, including the sponsor and cosponsors, committees of referral, official or long title, and bill status, appears in the Bill Summary & Status file the day after the introduction of the measure.

Congressional staff often use the LIS Alert Service, which sends e-mail alerts regarding action on bills and amendments on subjects identified by users. Once established, alerts run automatically and send e-mails Monday through Friday, when there is new information. To subscribe, go to LIS Alerts at http://www.congress.gov/help/about-alert.html.

**Thomas**
http://thomas.loc.gov



 

This Library of Congress (LOC) website makes federal legislation information freely available to the public. Using THOMAS, one can track bills and resolutions, public laws and other activities of Congress, and also access the *Congressional Record.* (See **Appendix** for a comparison of THOMAS and LIS.)

**GPO Access/FDsys**
http://www.gpo.gov/fdsys/search/home.action

The Government Printing Office (GPO) provides free Internet access to a wide variety of legislative, regulatory, and executive materials. Such materials include congressional bills; the *Congressional Record* and the *Congressional Record Index* (which includes the History of Bills and Resolutions section); congressional calendars; public laws; selected congressional reports and documents; the *Daily Compilation of Presidential Documents* and the *Weekly Compilation of Presidential Documents*; the *Federal Register*; and the *Code of Federal Regulations.* Time spans covered vary by title.

"GPO's Federal Digital System (FDsys) is an advanced digital system that will enable GPO to manage government information from all three branches of the U.S. government. FDsys is available as a public beta during migration of information from GPO Access."[1]

**House of Representatives Home Page**
http://www.house.gov

This Web source provides legislative details, including the following:

- recent major House floor and committee actions
  http://www.house.gov/house/floor/thisweek.htm
- legislative schedules
  http://clerk.house.gov/legislative/
- background information on and links to material concerning the legislative process
  http://thomas.loc.gov/home/lawsmade.toc.html
- directories of Representatives by state and by name
  http://clerk.house.gov/member_info/index.html
- the chamber's leadership
  http://www.house.gov/house/orgs_pub_hse_ldr_www.shtml
- House roll-call votes starting with the 101st Congress, second session (1990)
  http://clerk.house.gov/legislative/legvotes.html
- brief descriptions of floor proceedings when the House is in session
  http://www.house.gov/house/floor/thisweek.htm

[1] See the FDsys website at http://www.gpo.gov/fdsys/search/home.action.



 

**House Documents**
http://clerk.house.gov/legislative/housedoc.html

The House documents website provides electronic copies of congressional bills, resolutions, and committee reports via the House Library, LOC's THOMAS, and GPO Access. The House documents room can be reached at (202) 225-7000.

**House Legislative Resource Center**
http://clerk.house.gov/about/offices_Lrc.html

The Legislative Resource Center (LRC) provides centralized access to all published documents originated and produced by the House and its committees, the historical records of the House, and public disclosure documents. Congressional staff can retrieve legislative information and records of the House for congressional offices and the public. For assistance regarding the status of current legislation, call (202) 225-1772.

**Senate Home Page**
http://www.senate.gov

Materials of legislative interest offered at this Internet source include the following:

- Senate calendars
  http://www.gpoaccess.gov/calendars/senate/browse.html
- background information on, and links to materials on the legislative process
  http://www.senate.gov/pagelayout/legislative/d_three_sections_with_teasers/process.htm
- Senate roll-call votes starting with the 101$^{st}$ Congress (1989)
  http://www.senate.gov/legislative/LIS/roll_call_lists/vote_menu_101_1.htm
- the chamber's leadership
  http://www.senate.gov/reference/reference_index_subjects/Leadership_vrd.htm
- descriptions of the Senate committee system and of individual committees
  http://www.senate.gov/pagelayout/committees/d_three_sections_with_teasers/committees_home.htm
- historical information about the Senate
  http://www.senate.gov/artandhistory/history/common/generic/Senate_Historical_Office.htm
- directories of Senators by name, state, class (term expiration date), and party
  http://www.senate.gov/general/contact_information/senators_cfm.cfm
- glossary of common legislative terms
  http://www.senate.gov/pagelayout/reference/b_three_sections_with_teasers/glossary.htm

**Senate Printing and Documents Service**

http://www.senate.gov/legislative/common/generic/Doc_Room.htm



 

The Senate documents room provides free copies of bills, reports, Senate documents, and laws. It offers a maximum of six items per day per individual. Contact information is as follows:

B-04 Hart Senate Building Office
9:00 a.m.-5:30 p.m., Monday-Friday
Phone: (202)224-7701 (availability inquiries only)
Fax: (202)228-2815
E-mail: orders@sec.senate.gov

**Daily Schedule Information**

Both parties in the Senate and the House provide recorded messages about the proceedings on the floor of each chamber every day they are in session. Call the following numbers for cloakroom recordings:

Senate at (202) 224-8541 (Democratic) or (202) 224-8601 (Republican)

House at (202) 225-7400 (Democratic) or (202) 225-7430 (Republican)

**Public Laws Update Service**

Information on new public law numbers assigned to recently enacted laws can be obtained from a recorded message maintained by the National Archives and Records Administration's Office of the Federal Register at (202) 741-6043 or by subscribing to its Public Laws Electronic Notification Service (PENS). To subscribe, send an e-mail to listserv@www.gsa.gov with the text message "SUBSCRIBE PUBLAWS-L."

**White House Executive Clerk's Office**

By way of a recorded message, the Office of the Executive Clerk at the White House provides dates for the following information: presidential signings or vetoes of recent legislation, presidential messages, executive orders, and other official presidential action. If the desired information is not in the taped message, callers can stay on the line to speak with a staffer. The recorded message is available at (202) 456-2226.

## Non-Government Sources

**CQ.com**
http://www.cq.com

This database provides bill texts, summaries, tracking, and analysis. Among its other features are forecasts of major pending bills; versions of bills; links to related bills; roll-call votes; legislative histories; floor and committee schedules; detailed committee coverage; texts of committee reports; transcripts of witnesses' testimony; and publications such as the *CQ Weekly*, *CQ Today* and the *Congressional Record*. Time spans covered vary by the category of information sought. Only CQ.com subscribers can access this system on the Internet. It is available to congressional offices through the LIS portal.

**CQ Today**
http://www.cq.com/displaytoday.do



 

This subscription newsletter, available in print and online, provides daily news on Congress, Monday through Friday, when Congress is in session, with updates throughout the day on the Web. It includes planned floor action for the Senate and the House, bill and amendment descriptions, and notices of bill markup sessions and conference negotiations. Also, daily and selected future committee schedules are given. Significant sections are the "Pulse of Congress," with behind-the-scenes information on Members and committees; "People on the Move," which highlights congressional staff changes; and the "Appropriations" section, which appears during the appropriations cycle. Subscribers also receive an afternoon e-mail newsletter, *CQ Today Extra*, with the day's latest news about Congress and updated information on the next day's congressional schedule.

**CQ Weekly**
http://www.cq.com/displayweekly.do

This weekly summary of congressional action and developments, available in print and online, contains status tables for appropriations bills and other major legislation, roll-call vote charts for both chambers, and topical treatments of committee and floor actions. Most issues have articles that provide current and background information on legislative topics. Occasionally, special reports are printed. Quarterly indexes are issued. The annual *Congressional Quarterly Almanac* is a comprehensive review of the year's legislative session.

**HeinOnline**
http://heinonline.org

HeinOnline is a searchable digital library of current and historical materials, including some congressional documents back to 1789. The database also includes legal journals, texts, cases, statutes, regulations, presidential materials, treaties, as well as international and foreign legal journals, cases, and materials. Many are full text in the original page-image (PDF) format. HeinOnline is fee-based and available only to subscribers.

**LexisNexis Congressional**
http://www.web.lexis-nexis.com/congcomp

This database contains detailed abstracts and links to the full text of many congressional and federal documents, such as the *Congressional Record*, congressional hearing transcripts, committee prints, and legislative histories. Length of coverage varies depending on the category of information sought. It is the enhanced Web-based counterpart of the *CIS/Index to Publications of the United States Congress*. This resource is fee-based and accessible only to subscribers.

**National Journal**
http://www.nationaljournal.com/njonline

The National Journal Group is a source of nonpartisan reporting on the current political environment and emerging policy trends. Its print and online publications and broadcast include *National Journal*, *Congress Daily*, *The Hotline*, NationalJournal.com, *The Capitol Source*, *The Almanac of American Politics*, *Convention Daily*, "National Journal On Air" and "Washington Week with Gwen Ifill," and *National Journal*.



 

# Tracking Current Federal Regulations

Regulations are issued by federal departments and agencies under the authority delegated to them by federal law or presidential executive order and have the force of law. Final regulations are printed in the *Federal Register (FR)* and later codified by subject in the *Code of Federal Regulations (CFR)*.

The *FR* contains the official announcement of regulations and legal notices issued by federal departments and agencies. It includes proposed and final federal regulations having general applicability and legal effect; executive orders and presidential proclamations; documents required to be published by act of Congress; and other federal documents of public interest. It also updates the *CFR*. Daily and monthly indexes, and an accompanying publication, *List of CFR Sections Affected*, aid in its use.

The *FR* also publishes the "Unified Agenda of Federal Regulatory and Deregulatory Actions" twice yearly (usually in April and October). This document provides advance notice of proposed rulemaking by listing all rules and proposed rules that more than 60 federal departments, agencies, and commissions expect to issue during the next six months. Regulations that concern the military or foreign affairs, or that deal only with agency personnel, organization, or management matters, are excluded. The agenda is available online from 1994 through the present.

The *CFR* codifies final regulations having general applicability and legal effect that first appeared in the *FR*. Its 50 titles are arranged by subject. The *CFR* is revised annually (one quarter of the titles at a time) in January, April, July, and October. Because the annual revision incorporates new regulations and drops superseded ones, the *CFR* reflects regulations in effect at the time of printing. Several indexes and tables accompany the set. By using the *FR* and *CFR* sources with their many indexes and tables, it is possible to identify existing regulations in a subject area or pertaining to a specific *United States Code*,[2] identify regulations issued pursuant to a specific public law, and find proposed regulations that are not yet final.

The Electronic Code of Federal Regulations (e-CFR) is a currently updated version of the *CFR*. However, it is not an official legal edition of the *CFR*, but an unofficial editorial compilation of *CFR* material and *FR* amendments produced by the National Archives and Records Administration's Office of the Federal Register (OFR) and GPO. The OFR updates the e-CFR on a daily basis. To access, go to http://ecfr.gpoaccess.gov/cgi/t/text/text-idx?c=ecfr&tpl=%2Findex.tpl.

## Official Government Sources

**GPO Access/FDsys**
http://www.gpo.gov/fdsys/search/home.action

GPO provides Internet access to a wide variety of legislative, regulatory, and executive material, such as congressional bills, the *Congressional Record* and the *Congressional Record Index* (including its "History of Bills and Resolutions" section), congressional calendars, public laws,

[2] For more information, see CRS Report RL30812, *Federal Statutes: What They Are and Where to Find Them*, by Cassandra L. Foley.



 

selected congressional reports and documents, the *Daily Compilation of Presidential Documents* and *Weekly Compilation of Presidential Documents*, the *Federal Register*, and the *Code of Federal Regulations*. Time spans covered vary by title.

GPO's FDsys is an advanced digital system that enables GPO to manage government information from all three branches of the U.S. government. FDsys is a public-beta version during migration of information from GPO Access. The migration is occuring on a collection-to-collection basis thus collections currently available on FDsys are limited. The migration is scheduled to be completed in 2010.

**RegInfo.gov**
http://www.reginfo.gov

The Office of Management and Budget (OMB) and the General Services Administration (GSA) produces this website. RegInfo.gov provides a list of all rules undergoing Office of Information and Regulatory Affairs (OIRA) EO 12866 regulatory review. Updated daily, it also provides a list of all rules on which review has been concluded in the past 30 days; lists and statistics on regulatory reviews dating back to 1981; and letters to agencies regarding regulatory actions.

**Regulations.gov**
http://www.regulations.gov

This website was launched in 2003 to enhance public participation in federal regulatory activities. Users can search and view proposed regulations from more than 160 federal departments and agencies. Also, every entry links to a comment form that readers can complete and submit to the appropriate department or agency. Regulations.gov is updated each business day with proposed new regulations. Among the database's search options are keyword or subject; department or agency name; regulations published today; comments due today; open regulations or comments by publication dates; and *Code of Federal Regulations* citation.

**White House Executive Clerk's Office**

The Office of the Executive Clerk at the White House provides a recorded message with information on the dates that executive orders and presidential proclamations appeared in the *Federal Register*. If the desired information is not included in the taped message, callers can also be connected with a staffer. The recorded message is available at (202) 456-2226.

## Non-Government Sources

**BNA's Daily Report for Executives**
http://www.bna.com/products/corplaw/der.htm

This online report covers a broad spectrum of issues, providing news reports and links to the full text of key documents, such as proposed and final legislation, regulations, testimony, fact sheets summarizing major issues, and more.

***Federal Regulatory Directory***
http://www.cqpress.com/product/Federal-Regulatory-Directory-14th.html



 

The *Federal Regulatory Directory* provides profiles of the mandates and operations of more than 100 federal regulatory agencies and is published every two years. Each profile gives a brief history and description of the agency and its regulatory oversight responsibilities, and lists key staff, information sources, legislation, and regional offices. It also provides an overview of the federal regulatory process. Other aids are the full texts of key regulatory acts and executive orders, a guide to using the *Federal Register* and the *Code of Federal Regulations*, and subject and name indexes.

**HeinOnline**
http://heinonline.org

HeinOnline is a searchable digital library of current and historical materials, including some U.S. congressional documents back to 1789. The *United States Codes*, *Code of Federal Regulations*, and *U.S. Statutues at Large* are accessible through HeinOnline. Users can browse *CFR* indexes, determine if a federal regulation is current, find a presidential proclamation or an executive order. HeinOnline is available only to subscribers.

## Media Sources

Print and Web-based media sources provide useful background information on the status of federal legislation and regulations through "inside" reporting, political analysis, and editorial perspectives.

**C-SPAN.org**
http://www.c-span.org

C-SPAN is a private, non-profit company, created in 1979 by the cable television industry as a public service. Its mission is to provide public access to the political process.

**The Hill**
http://www.hillnews.com

The Hill is a non-partisan weekly newspaper covering Congress and its members.

**CNN.com**
http://www.cnn.com

CNN.com delivers breaking news and information on top stories, weather, business, entertainment, politics, and more.

**The Nation**
http://www.TheNation.com

The Nation is self-described as "America's oldest weekly journal of progressive political and cultural news, opinion and analysis."

**Politico**
http://www.politico.com



 

Politico.com covers political news with a focus on national politics, Congress, Capitol Hill, the presidential race, lobbying, advocacy, and more.

**Roll Call**
http://www.rollcall.com

Roll Call, a daily newspaper, has been covering Capitol Hill news since 1955. Rollcall is free to congressional staff, both online and in print.

# CRS Resources

## Classes at CRS

**Fundamentals of Federal Legal Research: Using Books and the Internet to Locate Laws, Regulations, and Court Decisions**

A six-hour seminar offered 12 times a year by CRS. This seminar outlines the fundamentals of legal research and focuses on sources of federal legal materials: Congress, the executive branch, and the federal courts. It covers print and electronic sources and examines the basic legal documents each branch generates and the types of information contained in them. The documents include the *U.S. Code*, the *Federal Register*, the *Code of Federal Regulations*, the *U.S. Reports*, the *Federal Reporter*, and the *Federal Supplement*. Intended for staff with limited or no experience with federal legal research techniques. To register, go to http://www.crs.gov/events/invite.shtml.

**Advanced Legislative Process Institute**

This Institute builds on the basic procedures and resources provided in Congress: An Introduction to Resources and Procedure. In depth sessions describe processes and procedural strategy that are specific to each chamber. Additional information on this class can be found at http://crs.gov/programs.

## Selected CRS Reports

Additional information on tracking legislation for congressional offices is provided in the following CRS reports:

CRS Report RS20991, *Legislative Planning: Considerations for Congressional Staff*, by Judy Schneider.

CRS Report RS21363, *Legislative Procedure in Congress: Basic Sources for Congressional Staff*, by Jennifer E. Manning.

CRS Report RS20120, *Legislative Support: Useful Telephone Numbers and Internet Addresses*, by Jennifer E. Manning.

CRS Report RL33823, *Congressional Resources in CRS Research Centers and the La Follette Congressional Reading Room*, by Audrey Celeste Crane-Hirsch.



 

# Appendix. A Comparison of LIS and THOMAS

**Table A-1. Comparison of LIS and THOMAS**

| | LIS | THOMAS |
|---|---|---|
| **Address** | http://www.congress.gov<br><br>(automatically goes to THOMAS if user is outside Legislative Branch) | http://thomas.loc.gov |
| **Who Can Use It** | Congress, including state and district offices, and legislative support agencies only. | Available to the public. |
| **Availability** | 24 hours a day, 365 days a year | 24 hours a day, 365 days a year |
| **Best Used For** | Finding the most complete legislative information for Members and congressional staff; obtaining information using databases; and linking to pages that are not available to the public on THOMAS.<br><br>Should not be used for making links from Member or committee home pages (because the public cannot access LIS). | Working with constituents; making links from Member or committee home pages; making printouts that are to be sent to constituents. |
| **Commercial Databases** | Links to databases that have been licensed for use by House and Senate staff, such as National Journal and CQ.com. | No links to commercial databases. |
| **CRS Reports** | Links from Bill Summary & Status display to CRS reports related to a bill. Ability to search all CRS reports via the CRS Home Page; these products can be searched, displayed, and printed. | No CRS reports are available to the public. |
| **Restricted Links** | Links to restricted Capitol Hill websites such as the HouseNet, Senate Webster, and Senate amendment tracking system. | No links to restricted Capitol Hill websites. |
| **Floor & Committee Schedule Information** | Links to Capitol Hill and outside sources of floor and committee schedule information. (Selected to be of most use to congressional staff.) | Minimal links to floor and committee schedule information. |
| **Advanced Search Capabilities** | Special advanced search capabilities in all databases, providing Boolean searching (and, or, not), word proximity searching (quotes to indicate phrases, adj/1, near/1), and other features. | Advanced search capabilities only in Bill Summary & Status database. Basic search capabilities in full-text databases. |
| **Saved Searches and E-mail Alerts** | The ability to save searches and to request daily e-mail alerts of new items added to databases that meet the search criteria. | No ability to save searches or request email alerts. |

**Source:** Compiled by CRS.



 

## Author Contact Information

Pamela A. Hairston
Information Research Specialist
phairston@crs.loc.gov, 7-7838



 

Congressional Research Service

# Legislative Planning: Considerations for Congressional Staff

**Judy Schneider**
Specialist on the Congress

June 5, 2008

**Congressional Research Service**
7-5700
www.crs.gov
RS20991

**CRS Report for Congress**
*Prepared for Members and Committees of Congress*

 

## Summary

The Congressional Research Service frequently receives inquiries about legislative planning. Legislative and office action plans are often used by congressional offices for almost every significant project, from organizing an extensive conference in the district or state to introducing and guiding legislation. A major action plan requires a firm understanding of the project's goal, a research strategy, and a time line for completing the project.

This report presents some of the factors usually considered in preparing an action plan. The information is provided in three sections. The first provides an overview which lays out summary considerations. The second raises questions to consider in preparing an outline for a project. The third details a sample action plan.



 

# Contents



## Contacts





 

## Overview

### Define the Problem and Determine the Solution

Any legislative plan needs a thorough definition of the problem to be addressed and an explanation of what the appropriate solution might be. Solutions may include legislation, regulation, or media attention. A clearly defined issue makes the determination of the themes for developing the message and promoting the solution easier to explain to colleagues, supporters, opponents, constituents, and the press.

Next, a time line for solving the problem should be determined. Is this a one-session, or one-Congress, or longer-term project? Is it one-event or a coordinated series of events? Should the event(s) be held in the Member's district or state, in Washington, or throughout the country?

### Research the Problem

Prior to beginning work on the solution, an in-depth determination of the extent of the problem needs to be undertaken. For example, is the problem limited to one district, state, region, or is it nationwide? Should the solution address the specific issue or the policy in general?

Consultation with local and state officials, community leaders, and constituents is integral at this stage. Discussions in Washington may include committee and subcommittee leaders, the party leadership, think tanks, and interest groups.

### Determine Strategy

One of the most important decisions is whether to conduct an "inside" or "outside" strategy, or possibly a combination of the two. Inside strategy entails work within the legislative process only, i.e., legislation, hearings, committee and floor amendments, floor debate, and conference consideration. Advocates may or may not be involved in any of this activity. An outside strategy calls for advocates to generate mail, press, and office visits, often to force an inside strategy to occur. A combined strategy includes using Dear Colleague letters, coordinated one-minute or special order speeches, Member-to-Member lobbying, and group press conferences.

## Outline for Project

### Goal

- What criteria are used to determine success? Political success? Press attention? Legislative success? Other?
- What is the duration of the project: one event, one session of Congress, two years, or longer?



 

## Description of Project

- Are there other projects on this topic already underway? If so, should the Member conduct an independent project, or join forces? Does the political party or state of other Members involved influence the decision? Should it?
- Has the project ever been tried in the past? If yes, what Members tried it? What was the result? Is the project still needed? Are there lessons to be learned from the earlier attempt?
- What other Members, committees, or party leaders should be involved?
- What advocates should be involved? Which advocates will support, and which will actively oppose, the initiative?

## Legislative Strategy

- Is legislation the appropriate remedy for the problem? Will a free-standing measure be necessary, or is there a vehicle to which an amendment can be offered?
- Should the Member introduce the legislation alone or seek original cosponsors? Should those cosponsors be bipartisan? Should they be of the same "type," e.g., women, philosophy, state and region, or district demographics, serving on the same committee?
- Should a companion measure be introduced in the other chamber?
- Should Dear Colleague letters be sent prior to introduction? Should they be sent periodically throughout the process identifying status?
- When should the legislation be introduced, e.g. opening day, first or second session, a specific time of year?
- What should the legislation be titled? Is there a useful acronym to be found to assist in publicizing the legislation? Should a particular number be reserved, e.g., H.R. or S. 2020 relating to eye care?
- Should a working group be created? Staff only or Members only? What role should the party leadership play? What of committee leadership? What type of coalitions should be created?
- If legislation is being considered on the issue (not necessarily the Member's measure), should the Member testify at hearings? Are there others the Member would recommend as witnesses?
- If a measure is being marked up, should the Member offer an amendment, assuming the Member serves on the committee? If not, should an ally offer an amendment on the Member's behalf?
- Should one-minute speeches or special order speeches be made to keep pressure on the committee or chamber and to maintain press visibility? How often and who should be included?
- Should a Rules Committee (House only) strategy be devised?
- Should opponents strategy be monitored?



 

## Other than Legislative Strategy

- If regulation is the appropriate solution, has the agency or executive branch been consulted?
- What is the appropriate timing?
- Should letters be written to the President? A Cabinet Secretary?

## Outside Groups Strategy

- Which advocates should be contacted? At what stage should they be included?
- What role should the advocates play—research, letters to Members, media appearances, briefings?
- Should a coalition of several groups be created?

## Press and Communications Strategy

### *Inside Communications*

- Dear Colleague letters
- One-minute or special order speeches
- Staff working group
- Member working group
- Speak on floor during consideration of related measure

### *Outside Communications*

- Press conferences
- News releases
- Op-ed pieces
- Syndicated columnists
- Editorial support, local and national
- TV or radio interviews

## Time Line

- Determine time line for target dates for all activities
- Determine periodic dates to review progress and reassess strategy

## Political Opportunity

- Meet with party campaign committees to discuss how project could help candidates



 

- Can state or local officials be given a role in promoting the project

## Sample Action Plan for Legislative Project

Action plans embody the strategies employed to achieve goals. The office's strategic plan should not only identify specific steps, but also the person(s) responsible (including the Member) responsible for each step. It is also useful to include deadlines for completing action on each step. Periodic meetings to review progress on the plan may prove useful in keeping the project on track. Usually each person in the office, whether they have specific responsibility for parts of the plan, should be provided a copy of the plan.

- Identify appropriate executive branch agency(s).
- Meet with agency staff to review present programs and discuss legislative options.
- Meet with advocates to discuss problem and possible solutions.
- Determine if other legislation has already been introduced.
- Work with legislative counsel to draft legislation (or amendments).
- Obtain CBO cost estimate.
- Send out draft for comment to advocates, district and state leaders, constituents, others.
- Send out Dear Colleague letters.
- Determine appropriate Members to cosponsor legislation.
- Work with other chamber for companion legislation.
- Create staff working group after identifying other Members to be involved.
- Meet with committee and party leadership.
- Hold briefings on issue, for staff and Members.
- Develop local and national press strategy.
- Introduce legislation after determining most advantageous time.
- Hold field hearing.
- Hold town hall meeting in district/state.
- Seek opportunities, in committee, on floor, in district/state, in press, to publicize initiative.



 

## Author Contact Information

Judy Schneider
Specialist on the Congress
jschneider@crs.loc.gov, 7-8664



 

# Resources from TheCapitol.Net

## Publications

- *Legislative Drafter's Deskbook*, by Tobias A. Dorsey
  ISBN: 1587330326 <*www.LegislativeDraftersDeskbook.com*>

## Live Training

<*www.CapitolHillTraining.com*>

- How to Research and Compile Legislative Histories:
  Searching for Legislative Intent <*www.LegislativeResearch.com*>
- How to Find, Track, and Monitor Congressional Documents:
  Going Beyond Thomas <*www.TrackingLegislation.com*>
- Drafting Effective Federal Legislation and Amendments
  <*www.DraftingLegislation.com*>
- Capitol Hill Workshop
  <*www.CapitolHillWorkshop.com*>
- Drafting Effective Federal Legislation and Amendments
  <*www.DraftingLegislation.com*>
- Understanding Congressional Budgeting and Appropriations
  <*www.CongressionalBudgeting.com*>
- Advanced Federal Budget Process
  <*www.BudgetProcess.com*>
- Writing for Government and Business: Critical Thinking and Writing
  <*www.WordWorkshop.com*>

## Capitol Learning Audio Courses™

<*www.CapitolLearning.com*>

- Statutory Construction: A Primer on How to Read and Understand Statutory Text,
  ISBN: 1587330784
- Drafting Effective Federal Legislation and Amendments in a Nutshell,
  ISBN: 1587330326
- Authorizations and Appropriations in a Nutshell, ISBN: 1587330296

 

- Researching Federal Legislative Histories: Bills, Resolutions, Committee Hearings, and Committee Reports, ISBN: 1587330822
- Researching Legislative Histories: Finding Legislative Intent in Bills and Committee and Conference Reports, ISBN: 1587330334
- Researching Federal Legislative Histories: Statutory and Code Research, ISBN: 1587330806
- Researching Legislative Histories, ISBN: 1587330334

 

# Other Resources

## Internet Resources

- SCOTUS Blog
  <www.scotusblog.com>
- "Statutory Construction: Not For The Timid," by Jon May,
  The Champion Magazine (NACDL), January/February 2006
  <*www.nacdl.org/public.nsf/698c98dd101a846085256eb400500c01/891b0643641b999c852571240006f9178*>
- "Federal Rules of Statutory Interpretation," by Nicholas Quinn Rosenkranz,
  Harvard Law Review, Vol. 115, p. 2085, 2002
  <*papers.ssrn.com/sol3/papers.cfm?abstract_id=748207*>
- Restatement (First) of Statutory Interpretation, by Gary E. O'Connor,
  forthcoming in the New York University Journal of Legislation & Public Policy
  <*papers.ssrn.com/sol3/papers.cfm?abstract_id=465322*>
- The Shakespeare Canon of Statutory Construction
  <*www.shakespearefellowship.org/virtualclassroom/justicestevens.htm*>
- The Rules Of Statutory Construction
  <*www.virginia1774.org/Statutory.html*>

## Books

- *Legislation and Statutory Interpretation*, 2nd ed., by William N. Eskridge, Jr.,
  Philip P. Frickey, and Elizabeth Garrett, ISBN-10: 1599410788
- *The Theory and Practice of Statutory Interpretation*, by Frank Cross,
  ISBN-10: 080475912X
- *Statutory Default Rules: How to Interpret Unclear Legislation*,
  by Einer Elhauge, ISBN-10: 0674024605
- *Dynamic Statutory Interpretation*, by William N. Eskridge, Jr,
  ISBN-10: 0674218787
- *A Matter of Interpretation: Federal Courts and the Law*,
  by Antonin Scalia, ISBN-10: 0691004005
- *Mastering Statutory Interpretation*, by Linda J. Dellum,
  ISBN-10: 1594603146
- *An Introduction To Statutory Interpretation and the Legislative Process*,
  by Abner J. Mikva and Eric Lane, ISBN-10: 1567066127

 

- *Modern Statutory Interpretation: Problems, Theories, and Lawyering Strategies*, by Linda D. Jellum and David Charles Hricik, ISBN-10: 1594606757
- *Statutory Interpretation: The Search for Legislative Intent*, by Ronald Benton Brown and Sharon Jacobs Brown, ISBN-10: 1556817851
- *A Dictionary of Statutory Interpretation*, by William D. Popkin, ISBN-10: 159460181X
- *Statutes in Court: The History and Theory of Statutory Interpretation*, by William D. Popkin, ISBN-10: 0822323281
- *Using Legislative History in American Statutory Interpretation*, by Christian E. Mammen, ISBN-10: 9041188797

 

# About TheCapitol.Net

We help you understand Washington and Congress.™

*For over 30 years, TheCapitol.Net and its predecessor, Congressional Quarterly Executive Conferences, have been training professionals from government, military, business, and NGOs on the dynamics and operations of the legislative and executive branches and how to work with them.*

*Instruction includes topics on the legislative and budget process, congressional operations, public and foreign policy development, advocacy and media training, business etiquette and writing. All training includes course materials.*

*TheCapitol.Net encompasses a dynamic team of more than 150 faculty members and authors, all of whom are independent subject matter experts and veterans in their fields. Faculty and authors include senior government executives, former Members of Congress, Hill and agency staff, editors and journalists, lobbyists, lawyers, nonprofit executives and scholars.*

*We've worked with hundreds of clients across the country to develop and produce a wide variety of custom, on-site training. All courses, seminars and workshops can be tailored to align with your organization's educational objectives and presented on-site at your location.*

*Our practitioner books and publications are written by leading subject matter experts.*

*TheCapitol.Net has more than 2,000 clients representing congressional offices, federal and state agencies, military branches, corporations, associations, news media and NGOs nationwide.*

*Our blog: Hobnob Blog—hit or miss ... give or take ... this or that ...*

*Our recommended provider of government training in Brazil is PATRI/EDUCARE <www.patri.com>*

T.C. Williams Debate Society

TheCapitol.Net supports the T.C. Williams Debate Society, Scholarship Fund of Alexandria, and Sunlight Foundation

TheCapitol.Net

*Non-partisan training and publications that show how Washington works.*™

PO Box 25706, Alexandria, VA 22313-5706 703-739-3790 www.TheCapitol.Net

CPSIA information can be obtained at www.ICGtesting.com
Printed in the USA
LVOW011042100512

281186LV00001B/223/P